Globalistan

How the Globalized World
Is Dissolving into
Liquid War

D1608344

Pepe Escobar

NIMBLE BOOKS LLC

NIMBLE BOOKS LLC

ISBN: 0-9788138-2-0

Copyright 2006 Pepe Escobar.

Last saved 2006-12-09.

Nimble Books LLC

2006 Medford Suite #127

Ann Arbor, MI 48104-4963

http://www.nimblebooks.com/wordpress/category/globalistan

Contents

TABLE OF FIGURES

To all you nomadic readers out there

NIMBLE BOOKS LLC

INTRODUCTION

If the hoar frost grip thy tent

Thou wilt give thanks when night is spent

—**Ezra Pound**, *Canto LXXXIV*

You are holding a warped travel book. This warped travel book remixes three main themes: globalization, energy wars and the Pentagon's Long War, originally packaged as the "war on terror." Call it a—what else—war travel book. Or a warped geopolitical travel book.

You will be traveling mostly in the arc from Middle East to Central Asia, but also in China, Russia, Western Europe, Western Africa, South America. You're going to revisit the asymmetrical wars in Afghanistan and Iraq. You're going to crisscross the Islamic world. You're going to follow a lot of pipelines. You'll be acquainted with the Iran the next war will probably hit. You'll see how national resistance wars have nothing to do with "terrorism." You'll be confronted over and over again with "strategic competitor" Asia—where the future of the 21st Century is being played out. You're going to revisit how, where and who profits from economic globalization and especially war corporatism. You'll see how more trade does not necessarily mean more peace. You'll see how and where possible New Orders are emerging, and Old Orders disintegrating. And you will finish the pilgrimage back in the middle of a—predictable—global war of the privileged few against the excluded many.

9/11 was the first globalization war. Our warped travel book argues we are now living an intestinal war, an undeclared global civil war. In this early 21st Century context of re-medievalization, where those who control power control weapons, money and The Word, this book also aims to provide a counter-narrative.

You will cross a lot of "stans." The re-medievalized world is being fragmented into "stans," some very exclusive (Pipelineistan, Europeistan, Nuclearistan), some feeding on war (Talibanistan, Americastan in Iraq), some regarded as a supreme threat (Shiiteistan), some spreading like a virus (Slumistan). We still live in a world of nation-states. But you will see that as civilian peace between nations and their populations is being slashed, basically because of economic imperatives, now virtually everyone seems to be threatened by a permanent state of emergence—which is just another way of referring to a global state of siege. This includes of course the plural culture of Islam constantly demonized in a lethal magma as The

Barbarian Other—that silly "clash of civilizations" working out as a self-fulfilling prophecy.

You may ask where I'm coming from. Well, to talk about nomad global wars it helps being a nomad—and a pure product of globalization. As a writer I have lived and worked in North and South America, Western Europe and all across Asia and Islam; since the end of the Cold War I have been tracking the West drunk on its own secular *mission civilisatrice*, eager to globalize Russia, China, Islam/Arabia, Africa. Home is wherever I happen to be. Not accidentally this short introduction comes from one of the great world cities, to the sound of electronic tango. Or as they say in Bangkok and Hong Kong, it comes from "the other side of the world." For me it makes perfect sense being in the Paris of South America dreaming of Asia and selected cities of the heart (and work)– Kabul, Baghdad, Tehran, Peshawar.

You should know that I do not answer to any corporate sponsor; no political party; no intelligence agency; no academic body; no think tank. And I got nothing to spin. The online publication I write for—*Asia Times*, owned by a Sino-Thai visionary businessman and based in Thailand/Hong Kong—allows me total freedom of expression.

This book is another way to tell a story—dissected by towering figures like Immanuel Wallerstein, Zygmunt Bauman, Ulrick Beck or Gabriel Kolko—from the ground level. Bauman's concept of liquid modernity gave me the inspiration for "Liquid War." Only then I found out there was already a videogame called Liquid War. Pop culture rules! The game, whose basic rules are inspired by Japanese *go*, is described as a sort of "psychedelic action" where strategy is crucial. Sounds like a definition of the world out there. Indonesia would say the world out there is like *wayang* theatre—we see the shadows, but we never see the puppeteer.

Beyond strategic and political conflict, Liquid War tends towards the destruction of singular cultures and everything capable of resisting globalization. Its optimum is anthropological genocide. If the future is being configured by Liquid War all actors are positioning themselves for the decisive moment, the catharsis in Greek drama, when Liquid War boils to the point of Hot War. Dear Leader Kim Jong-il is a weak link; his acts are very revealing, denouncing real fears. So are Hugo Chávez's.

Revered Vietnamese monk Thich Nhat Hanh prays that we may all escape the wheel of *samsara*—our addiction to nefarious vicious circles. If only we could accumulate enough compassion—instead of designer weapons: "touched by the Dharma," we would have an instrument to cut through the wheel of *samsara*, we would not legate so much bad karma for future generations, we would escape this demented war logic.

Hope lies in selected humanitarian, social, juridical and ecological NGOs, and the emergence of globally connected civil society. Even Professor Stephen Hawking, with his global-sized brain, does not know "how can the human race sustain another 100 years." He admitted: "I don't know the answer," suggesting improvements in genetic engineering to make humans less addicted to war.

Perhaps Groovemaster General James Brown had come up with the best answer after all: it's time to get funky. But on a less escapist level, maybe what we need is a post-modern Paolo Ucello. We have to come up with a different real time perspective for virtual space, learn how to deal with the telecity, the metacity, telesex, telepolitics, telewar. Paul Virilio warned us that the end of geopolitics is leading us to metropolitics. The enemy is undeclared. The logic is of fear. And widespread urban panic is already drowning for good the political character of the City.

Military/intelligence elites of Globalistan are all immersed in electronic tracking of deterritorialization, monitoring every turbulence caused by globalization—local conflicts, the shrinking of the middle classes, abysmal poverty, incipient civil wars, Salafi-jihadist reaction. Conflicts should be perpetuated, just about anywhere, but without turning into irreparable catastrophe. For these elites, this is just a technical matter. A question of managing chaos.

Robert Musil wrote that parallel universes could be as relevant as reality. Physicists go for a Multiverse that resembles boiling water (where, in Michiko Kaku's words, "the Judeo-Christian genesis takes place within the Buddhist nirvana, all the time"). In philosophical terms, the universe itself may even be a dream. I wonder what Jorge Luis Borges would make of all this. Against our world of nomad wars and Liquid War he would probably counterpunch with a dazzling play on cultures, History and signs. Could it be Kim Jong-il drinking an absinthe at the café La Puerto Rico? Could it be George W. Bush browsing books on Islam at the venerable Libreria del Colegio? Could it be Osama bin Laden dancing a tango with one of his wives at the ultra-atmospheric Bar Sur?

If only Liquid War was no more harmful than a drink. So here's to you, dear reader, a glass of fabulous Malbec. Cheers. Now let's hit the road.

Buenos Aires
September 2006

NIMBLE BOOKS LLC

ACKNOWLEDGMENTS

This book would not exist without my publisher Fred Zimmerman's vision and drive. Then there are those scores of extraordinary, hard-working people I have met on the road, in China, Russia, the "stans" in Central Asia, Afghanistan, Pakistan, Iran, south India, southeast Asia, Dubai, Qatar, Syria, Jordan, Lebanon, Iraq, Palestine, Western Africa, across the US, South America... You know who you are, and my admiration for you knows no bounds.

I owe special gratitude to the critical perspective of Immanuel Wallerstein's world system analysis and to Zygmunt Bauman's concept of liquid modernity, which inspired Liquid War.

Arif Jamal in Islamabad, K. Gajendra Singh in Bucharest, Professor Paulo Alves de Lima and Islamic scholar Rosalie Pereira in Sao Paulo, and Frédéric Maduraud in Brussels have offered precious insight. In the early 2000s Khawar Mehdi and Majeed Babar in Peshawar and Afghanistan have been priceless. A very special thanks to the people in the Red Zone in Baghdad and the Sunni belt, the clerical establishment in Najaf, Mahmoud Daryadel, Emadeddin Baghi and Babak Pirouz in Tehran, Professor Rasul Amin in Peshawar, Mohammad Khan Stanikzai in Kabul, Olga Uzhegova in Almaty, Rustam Muslimov in Tashkent, Yulya Zhukov in Ashgabat, Punyavee Pharktham in Bangkok.

Asia Times publisher Sondhi Limthongkul has always been very generous and tremendously supportive. A heartfelt thanks to the *Asia Times* team in Thailand and Hong Kong, plus Alex, Cher and Joe in Guangzhou (the guys who translate my stories into Mandarin). Over the years, the ice cool copywrong gang in Paris and Brussels has provided good times, caring, hospitality, encouragement and fabulous conversation. And of course my wife Cecilia is always a blast—top of the world in a nutshell.

The soundtrack for this book has been Theme Time Radio Hour, "Themes, Schemes and Dreams... with your host Bob Dylan," courtesy of www.whitemanstew.com. Either talking about Irma Thomas "as a snow leopard ready to pounce" or spinning Sonny Boy Williamson's *Eyesight to the Blind*, Bob's vinyl guerrilla took no prisoners. Thanks, Bob! To wrap things up, this book is dedicated to my son Nicholas, diver extraordinaire, a wise fellow whose brand of Liquid War is of the "scuttling-across-the-floors-of-silent-seas" kind.

~ 1 ~

IT DON'T MEAN A THING IF IT AIN'T GOT THAT EURASIAN SWING

History is a nightmare from which I am trying to awaken.

—**James Joyce**, *Ulysses*

... I saw the Aleph, from all points I saw in the Aleph the earth and in the earth once again the Aleph and in the Aleph the earth, I saw my face and my viscera, I saw your face, and I felt vertigo and I cried, because my eyes had seen this secret and conjectural object, whose name men usurp but which no man has seen: the inconceivable universe.

—**Jorge Luis Borges**, *The Aleph*

GENERAL JACK D. RIPPER: Mandrake, do you recall what Clemenceau once said about war?

GROUP CAPT. LIONEL MANDRAKE: No, I don't think I do, sir, no.

GENERAL JACK D. RIPPER: He said war was too important to be left to the generals. When he said that, 50 years ago, he might have been right. But today, war is too important to be left to politicians. They have neither the time, the training, nor the inclination for strategic thought. I can no longer sit back and allow Communist infiltration, Communist indoctrination, Communist subversion and the international Communist conspiracy to sap and impurify all of our precious bodily fluids.

—**Stanley Kubrick's** *Dr. Strangelove*

In his short story *The Aleph* Jorge Luis Borges—that South American Buddha in a grey suit—leads his narrator to discover "the place where we find, without confusion, all the places in the orb, seen from all of the angles" in the basement of a house in Buenos Aires. For the past few years I have had a feeling that the Aleph might be found in Iran, perhaps in fabled Isfahan, the pearl of Shah Abbas which in the 17th Century reached its full splendor, impressed in the famous rhyme *Esfahan nesf-e jahan* ("Isfahan is half the world").

Figure 1. The world centered on Isfahan.

Perhaps the Aleph would be in the Meidun, the fabulous square built in 1612—the Persian answer to Saint Mark's in Venice. Perhaps inside Sheikh Lotfollah mosque, whose intricately-painted dome tiles progressively change color from cream to strong pink as the days wear out and the light reflection forming the tail of a legendary painted peacock on the dome's roof also, imperceptibly, moves. We may spend hours, days, light-years absorbing this living meditation on the architecture of light. The peacock's tail inside an Isfahani mosque, now that would be a smashing location for the Aleph.

And why not? After all, Isfahan is at the center of Eurasia, roughly equidistant from Paris and Shanghai. And Eurasia is the geopolitical pivot of the world. Would the Aleph be there, it would be nothing but echoing the great 12th Century Persian poet Nezami Ghandjavi, who in the famous *Haft Peykar* ("The Seven Portraits") wrote that "The world is the body and Iran is its heart."

Iran is at the key intersection of the Arab, Turk, Indian and Russian worlds. It's at the key intersection of the Middle East, Central Asia, the Caucasus, the Indian subcontinent and the Persian Gulf. It sits between three seas—the Caspian, the Persian Gulf and the sea of Oman. It's not far from Europe (in fact it will border Europe if and when Turkey accedes to the E.U.). And it's a neighbor to Asia (in fact it is in Southwest Asia). Iran is the ultimate crossroads in the heart of Eurasia.

Now about that oil, gas, Persian Gulf, Arabian Sea and Caspian Sea node. Not for nothing *Khalij-e-Fars*, in Farsi, means exactly "Persian Gulf." So Iran—the largest, most populous and most stable nation of Southwest Asia, strategically straddling most of the world's oil and gas reserves—is at the ideal crossroads for the distribution of oil and gas to South Asia, Europe and East Asia as both China and India emerge as two of the 21st Century superpowers. That is, Iran is the Great Prize *par excellence*. Maybe a larger than life Aleph.

Now suppose you are the world's only superpower with a foreign policy hijacked by neocons of the armchair warrior kind. What you're gonna do? You're gonna declare that you want regime change in Iran—betraying your dream scenario of relieving a puppet in power just like that former tortured soul, the Shah Reza Pahlavi.

Iran is completely surrounded by U.S. military bases in the Gulf, in Pakistan, in Afghanistan, in Turkey, in Central Asia, in Iraq, in Cyprus, and in Turkey, not to mention Israel, a naval base in Oman close to the hyper-strategic Strait of Hormuz (transit point of half the oil sold globally) and another, naval and air base, in the Indian Ocean, in Diego Garcia. Not that Iranian public opinion is particularly freaking out. Osama bin Laden, riding his Flying Carpet One cross legged with a giant F-16 breathing on his neck, side by side with a map of Iran surrounded by Uncle Sam's big guns: that was the cover of a magazine on political studies I found at the University of Tehran only a few months after George W. Bush's first Axis of Evil speech.

U.S. Global Strike planning is able in half a day to smash over 10,000 targets simultaneously in Iran in just one mission using "smart" conventional weapons carried by more than 200 strategic bombers (B-52s, B-1s, B-2s and F-117As). This would mean an even deadlier remix of Shock and Awe over Iraq—destroying the bulk of the political, military, economic and transport infrastructure of Iran. Some "minor" complementary issues should be added on, like mini-nukes redefined as "defensive weapons" thus "safe for civilians" because "the explosion is underground," as well as what Israel would be doing with some 5,000 "smart air launched weapons" it bought from the U.S., including 500 BLU 109 bunker busters.

Who actually wants this mini-Armageddon unleashed over the descendants of Cyrus the Great and Darius I? We find a sort of coalition (of the willing) special interests camouflaged behind national interests, linking Pentagon civilians of the armchair warrior kind, neocons in key government positions, an array of pro-Israeli organizations, Armageddon believers (call them Western Taliban), a great deal of the U.S. mainstream media and a minority of U.S. citizens. Neocons dismiss the International Atomic Energy Agency (IAEA), which is adamant: Iran's civilian nuclear energy program has no military wing. Neocons dismiss the CIA, which has made clear that any possible Iranian WMD would not materialize before 2015. Neocons have even cynically abandoned their "freedom agenda" for the Middle East. No more democracy-inducing Shock and Awe: what's left is just pure Jack D. Ripper logic.

Against mini-Armageddon on Iran we find a majority of retired U.S. military officials, Big Oil (for which, on a cost/benefit basis, this is very bad business), virtually all the Christian and Muslim organizations, the majority of U.S. public opinion and virtually all of the world's public opinion.

These special interests bent on mini-Armageddon derive outstanding business profits from one of the key intersections of Globalistan: globalization and war. In the Middle East the economic interests of the U.S. military-industrial complex happen to merge with the geopolitical interests of *Eretz Israel* (Greater Israel) proponents. During the binary, bipolar Cold War the U.S. rationale was to fight the communist specter. In Globalistan the specter remixed are the barbaric hordes of "Islamo-fascist" terror, Axis of Evil states, "rogue" states and failed states (after all "rogue" states are easier to locate on a map than "terrorists"). As informed Americans are well aware institutional framework and respectability for this agenda is provided by a plethora of militaristic, jingoistic think tanks which work closely with the Pentagon, the industrial-military complex and the powerful Israeli lobby (which could be described as a junior partner in this association).

The neocons profited immensely from 9/11 and the subsequent, nonsensical "war on terror" (which basically—literally?—means war on war). But the mighty profiteer of the neocon drive was actually the U.S. Corporatistan node of the military-industrial complex. Moreover the U.S. ruling class gets paid in tax money by the lower classes; that could not have been a more cunning mechanism of wealth distribution (1% of Americans control 40% of the country's wealth). Of all key neocon players a majority are former executives, consultants or shareholders of major Defense contractors. Think tanks may predominate in the (non) debate of ideas. But those really calling the shots are the military-industrial complex. This is all about business—not ideology. And Long, infinite, permanent war is an extremely profitable business.

The mini-Armageddon over Iran would mean the fulfillment of most dreams outlined in *Rebuilding America's Defenses*, the supremacist roadmap concocted by the warmongering neocon think tank Project for a New American Century (PNAC) in 2000, which could be defined as the Cheney/Wolfowitz roadmap. The "direct imposition of U.S. 'forward bases' throughout Central Asia and the Middle East" has been accomplished—sort of. But preventing the emergence of any potential "rival" or any viable alternative to "free market economy" implies smashing Iran. Further on down the militaristic road there's the "revolution in military affairs" (RMA), which is obsessed with the accumulation of high tech weapons systems for pulverizing infrastructure, but not interested in conquering hearts and minds; the "Strategic Defense Initiative"; and the total militarization of space. "Preemptive war" has already been further enhanced in the March 2005 Pentagon National Defense Strategy, to the benefit of "proactive war." Amid all this frenzy the Council on Foreign Relations was forced to admit, at its 2005 annual conference, that by 2010 the U.S. "will be spending more money than the rest of the world on defense."

By the summer of 2006 all the—ominous—signs were "on the table" (copyright Donald Rumsfeld) for all to see. The Pentagon had its former "war on terror" rebranded as The Long War; Dick Cheney swore that the genuine article will last for decades, a replay of the war between Eastasia and Oceania in Orwell's *1984*. George W. Bush had issued a "wild speculation" non-denial denial that the U.S. was planning strategic nuclear strikes against Iran. A "new Hitler"—but wasn't he Saddam Hussein in 1991 and then Saddam remixed in 2003?—had also been rebranded and his name was Mahmoud Ahmadinejad, the Iranian President, while the previous Hitler was still alive fighting – and then being sentenced to hang – by a kangaroo court in Baghdad.

Ahmadinejad was incessantly depicted by the ideological machine as an angry, totally irrational, Jew-hating, Holocaust-denying, Islamo-fascist who wanted to "wipe Israel off the map." The quote, repeated ad nauseam, came from an October 2005 speech. But what he really said, in Farsi, to an annual anti-Zionist conference in Iran, was that "the regime occupying Jerusalem must vanish from the page of time." He was actually quoting the Ayatollah Khomeini, who had said the same thing in the early 1980s. He was hoping that an unfair regime (towards Palestine) would be replaced by another one more equitable, not threatening to nuke Israel. It didn't matter. Just like in a Monty Python sketch the mob could not stop screaming "Witch! Witch!"

How does the leadership in Tehran analyze all this mess? Tactically, they see neocon Washington going no holds barred for regime change—as much as strategically they see it plunged in a take-no-prisoners war on Islam. The proof was the U.S./Israeli alliance in the summer of 2006 Lebanon war. Whatever the spin for world public opinion, nothing will convince the leadership in Tehran of the contrary. Eventual U.N. sanctions against Iran will never be as hardcore as the neocons would dream. No sanctions will force Iran to deviate from its civilian nuclear program. And then one fine day Iran masters enough technology to produce a nuclear bomb. This could certainly happen before the end of the second Bush administration, in January 2009.

What next? George W. Bush—who Gore Vidal calls "the little emperor"—vowed from the deep recesses of his soul that he would never allow Iran to become a nuclear power. It's another *Blues Brothers*-inspired Mission from God. So the march to mini-Armageddon may be inevitable. The only ones capable of stopping it would be sensible, rational, influential voices inside the U.S. military complex. Threats will proliferate. And then the White House decides that a preemptive nuclear strike—against a non-nuclear power—is a wiser decision than doing nothing. This Persian-American war would finally configure the U.S., for 1.5 billion Muslims, as *Dajjal*, a force of evil bent on destroying Islam. The dark side, no less. And against the dark side, all Islam would have to be united—Sunnis and Shiites. Traditional U.S. allies like Saudi Arabia, Pakistan, Egypt, the Gulf petromonarchies (their governments, not their populations) would not be afforded the luxury to sit on the fence: this would mean certain collapse. The Persian-American war could in fact realign the whole Arab-Muslim world. But not exactly the way mini-Armageddon stakeholders see it.

A Trilateral Commission Report presented in a meeting in Tokyo in the summer of 2006 proposes some sound solutions: direct U.S.-Iran negotiations leading to a Regional Middle East Nuclear Council where every declared (and some undeclared) nuclear powers would be represented: U.S., Russia, China, France, the U.K., India,

Pakistan, Iran, Israel and Japan. The IAEA would be allowed to inspect anything it wanted, with absolutely no restrictions. Israel would get a "security package" and Iran would be reassured of no regime change attempt. The Middle East and the Maghreb would get a sort of Marshall Plan: Palestine, Jordan, Tunisia, Morocco, Egypt and Algeria would join the WTO and get funds from the World Bank. A regional Middle East Water Council—including Turkey, Syria, Lebanon, Iraq, Israel, Palestine and Jordan—would also be implemented, as well as a Middle East Energy Council—including Saudi Arabia, the Emirates, Kuwait, Bahrain, Oman, Yemen, Iraq, and Iran—to take care of regional Pipelineistan, oil security, technology transfers.

Yes, it sounds too smooth to be true. And yes, many of these regimes are not exactly sure they want to be "helped" (or dictated by) the WTO and the Paul Wolfowitz-presided World Bank. This would be a case of the Greater Middle East being achieved not by the barrel of a gun but by "free trade"/market opening for Corporatistan. The marketing ploy would be slightly more sophisticated, and fewer lives would be lost, but the results would be substantially the same.

From the point of view of the Pentagon's Long War, a strategic nuclear attack on Iran has the obvious merit of being spun to oblivion as the crucial next stage of the war on "radical Islam." Buried in the militaristic rubble is the fact that Ayatollah Khomeini, the leader of the Islamic Revolution, had made clear in the 1980s that production, possession and use of nuclear weapons is against Islam. Russia, China, India, key E.U. players like Germany, and the overwhelming majority of the South still take him at his word. For the Iranian government, the nuclear program is a powerful symbol of independence vis-à-vis what is considered Anglo-Saxon colonialism. The view is shared by Iranians of all social classes and all educational backgrounds. Moreover, Iran is pushing for a leading role in the Non-Aligned Movement (NAM), stating that every country has the right to a peaceful nuclear program. What Iran officially wants is a nuclear-free zone in West Asia, and that of course includes Israel, the sixth nuclear power in the world with more than 600 nuclear warheads.

German philosopher Peter Sloterdijk seems to be closer to the mark when he says that "if tomorrow was unveiled a new technology which would end Western civilization's dependence on oil, the clash of civilizations would disappear overnight." We're quite far from it, hence The Long War.

The *Quadrennial Defense Review*—the Pentagon's strategic document which on 34 times, including the title, calls for a "Long War," a "Long, Global War" or a "Long, Irregular War" against terror can be interpreted even by an infant as a call for a war on Islam. The Iranian political elite is more than aware that Washington might release Shock and Awe remixed, including the possibility of unilateral nuclear bombing. The question is when. But everyone—reformists included—downplays the possibility of a street revolution toppling the nationalist theocracy, as the neocons' wishful thinking rules; in the event of a foreign attack virtually the whole population would rally behind the government.

Amid non-stop carpet info-bombing, it's easy for global citizens to forget that oil and gas had, once again, to be at the heart of the matter. Preventing the emergence of any strategic "rival," according to PNAC, means the U.S. exercising a sort of strategic veto over the E.U. and Japan in terms of control of energy. Thus the U.S. by all means needs to control Iran, Iraq, Saudi Arabia and Kuwait in the Middle East. Iraq will be a disaster zone for years, if not decades, and there's no guarantee the U.S. will control its oil reserves. Iran—since 1979—is absolutely off limits, the Big Prize.

From a PNAC/Pentagon point of view, the ultimate nightmare—very plausible in the short to medium term—would be the emergence of a loose alliance of Iran, the Shiite parties in power in Iraq and the Shiites in Hasa in Saudi Arabia controlling a very powerful axis of energy intimately linked to the Asian Energy Security Grid and under the protection of the Shanghai Cooperation Organization (SCO).

An article in the July 2006 issue of *Scientific American* by U.S. scientists affiliated with the U.S. Electric Power Research Institute suggests that a long term (22d Century) solution to global energy issues would be construction of a superconducting (supercold) grid for transmitting electricity around the globe. It's interesting that the article is accompanied by a 1981 map drawn by the polymath visionary Buckminster Fuller that illustrates a global pipeline route that avoids prolonged trips across oceans—and thus tracks very closely with the map of Eurasia. Such a project would require trillions of dollars (or euros!) of investment in highly vulnerable insulated pipeline, and a proportionately large investment in pipeline security—by *someone.*

For now, Iran is the absolutely crucial node of the proposed Asian Energy Security Grid, which includes China, Russia and India. This Grid would do nothing less than bypass Western—especially American—control of energy supplies in the Middle East/Central Asia arc and fuel a real 21st Century industrial revolution all across Asia. It's no wonder that scores of independent analysts in Iran, Pakistan, China, India and Russia view the U.S. war on Iran as essentially a war of the West against Asia. A surefire way to engender a coming conflict with China is to put its energy supply under threat. David Harvey from New York University and author of *The New Imperialism,* goes straight to the point: "Whoever controls the Middle East will control the global oil spigot, and who controls the global oil spigot will control the global economy, at least in the near future."

A war on Iran is a war against China. China created the SCO in June 2001—with Russia and the Central Asians Uzbekistan, Kazakhstan, Kyrgyzstan and Tajikistan as members. At first the SCO was basically a security arrangement to prevent terrorism although officially it was also promoting "cooperation in political affairs, economy and trade, scientific-technical, cultural, and educational spheres as well as in energy, transportation, tourism, and environment protection fields." It slowly evolved to a series of security, economic and infrastructure agreements, coupled with the odd, joint military exercise. By 2006 Iran, India, Pakistan and Mongolia had become participating observers. And Afghanistan, the CIS countries and the ASEAN 10 were visitors. All of them could become full members by 2007 or 2008. Thus the SCO, silent as a kung fu master, had suddenly blossomed as a kind of Asian answer to the E.U. and NATO.

It's very enlightening to contrast the SCO agenda—the wider Asian agenda, in short—with the PNAC/Pentagon worldview. According to its 2006 summit, the SCO:

"has outlined a new norm of international relations aiming at ensuring equal rights for all countries worldwide...a new and non-confrontational model...that calls for discarding the Cold War mentality and transcending ideological differences..."

"opposes interference in other countries' internal affairs, using the excuse of the differences in cultural traditions, political and social systems, values and models of development."

"safeguards each other's sovereignty, security and territorial integrity and in case of emergencies that threaten regional peace, stability and security, we will have immediate consultations and respond effectively to protect our member states."

"in economic cooperation [our goal] is to realize a free flow of goods, services, capital and technology by 2020 amongst members."

"holds that the next Secretary-General of the United Nations should come from Asia."

It's also very enlightening to superimpose the list of SCO members and soon-to-be members on the map of Eurasia. Virtually all the big players—with the exception of the U.S. "protectorates" Japan and South Korea—are represented.

The International Conference on Energy and Security: Asian Vision, held in Tehran in the spring of 2006, could not be a better place to examine how scholars and executives from Iran, China, Pakistan, India, Russia, Egypt, Indonesia, Georgia,

Venezuela and Germany saw the future. The overall message was unmistakable: they see an interdependence of Asia and "Persian Gulf geo-ecopolitics," as an Iranian analyst put it. They want the U.S.-Iran nuclear row solved diplomatically. And they bet on Asian integration with Pipelineistan linking the Persian Gulf, Central Asia, South Asia and China.

This Persian Gulf/Asia interplay is more than enshrined. World demand for natural gas will triple from now to 2020. By 2025, Asia will import 80% of its total oil needs, and 80% of this total will be from the Persian Gulf. Chinese executives like Liu Guochen from the Sinochem Corp., based in Amman, admit that China will keep importing energy from unstable areas, and the Middle Kingdom will remain worried about "U.S. hegemony" over the flow of energy resources. That's why China is frantically diversifying, as Iranian scholar Masoud Akhavan-Kazemi of Razi University puts it, "in its investments, pursuing territorial claims and building up strategic oil reserves." He foresees Asia facing "great imbalances"; potential for conflict in the Persian Gulf, Russia, Central Asia and the Caspian; insecurity suffered by China, India and Japan vis-à-vis the U.S. drive in Asia; and a Chinese sense of vulnerability as China and the U.S. remain de facto strategic rivals.

Akhavan-Kazemi sees the U.S. pursuing three key objectives. The first two may be shared by some in Asia: guaranteeing the energy flows from Asia to international markets; and trying to stop Russian hegemony. But a crucial factor—which the Russians are keen to point out—is that Iran, India and Pakistan are now observers at the SCO. In the mid to short-term, as the organization develops, "the SCO would be able to protect pipelines going in all directions," says a Russian oil executive. As for the third American objective —preventing Iran from exporting its gas— definitely it is not shared by anyone. Akhavan-Kazemi emphasizes that "despite the American military hegemony in the Persian Gulf, its political hegemony is in doubt."

Most Asian oil and gas executives and scholars agree that the way the game is played today in Pipelineistan, everything is politicized. "When Bush tells India you don't need to import gas from Iran, that's totally illogical," says Albert Bininachvili, a Georgian scholar based in Bologna. "The [alleged Iranian] bomb is a pretext," says Manouchehr Takin, a senior petroleum upstream analyst based in London. "The Americans don't want Iran to develop, and that's equally true of China and Venezuela. We need to talk about security through knowledge." To sum it all up, Asia does not want an Iran battered by the West; Iran, after all, is part of West Asia.

It took less than a decade for a full Eurasian swing since former National Security Adviser Zbigniew Brzezinski wrote his landmark 1997 piece "A Geostrategy for Eurasia," published by *Foreign Affairs*. Then, for Brzezinski, it was a question of formatting how to keep America's "global primacy" and "historical legacy" in "the decisive geopolitical chessboard." It was a time when America was still viewed as "the indispensable nation."

Brzezinski may be criticized for being "past his sell-by date," but it's important to follow his thinking through time for two reasons: he's a solid practitioner of *realpolitik*, as much as Henry Kissinger or Brent Scowcroft; and he's dedicated a lot of effort to formulate and publicly explain a U.S. Eurasian policy. A testament to the remarkable continuity of the American hegemonic project—irrespective of who is in power —is that Brzezinski's "swingin' into Eurasia" master plan was enthusiastically incorporated by PNAC, the subsequent Bush-Cheney system and U.S. Corporatistan. It was always clear that the implementation of Brzezinski's agenda would presuppose a Pentagon on a cocktail of steroids and vigilant, non-stop manufacture of internal consent—a state of affairs only arrived at after 9/11.

Brzezinski is a keen Mackinder disciple. Sir Halford John Mackinder (1861-1947) is the celebrated father of geopolitics who in 1902 introduced to the Royal Geographic Society his famous paper The *Geographic Pivot of History*, where he developed the Heartland Theory. According to Mackinder the "world island" was Europe, Asia and Africa, and the "islands" were the Americas, Australia, the British Isles and Japan. The Heartland stretched from the Volga to the YangTze and from the Arctic to the Himalayas. The key for a true global power was to control Eurasia. As the Mackinder formula enunciated, "who rules East Europe commands the Heartland; who rules the Heartland commands the world-island; who rules the world-island controls the world."

Mackinder-drenched Brzezinski correctly stated in his piece that "all the historical pretenders to global power originated in Eurasia" (although, by another historical irony, the last two superpowers, the British Empire and the U.S., were "islands"). As "the world's axial super continent," any power in control of Eurasia "would exercise decisive influence over two of the world's three most economically productive regions, Western Europe and East Asia." This would answer Immanuel Wallerstein's question of which of the members of the Triad dominates the capitalist world system in the next phase.

Brzezinski wanted "the emergence of strategically compatible partners which, prompted by American leadership, might shape a more cooperative trans-Eurasian security system." Yet he could never have predicted the emergence of the SCO as a counter-power.

Brzezinski stated that "America's status as the world's premier power is unlikely to be contested by any single challenger for more than a generation. No state is likely to match the United States in the four key dimensions of power—military, economic, technological, and cultural—that confer global political clout." Yet the U.S. has been challenged in at least two—economic and technological. "Culture" means essentially pop culture—Hollywood, pop rock, TV series, reality shows—but global challenges abound, from world music to Bollywood, from world cinema to Mexican and Brazilian *telenovelas*. Wallerstein and Professor Eric Hobsbawm would argue that the only dimension of power left for the U.S. is the military. Brzezinski's dream of "a benign American hegemony" is gone.

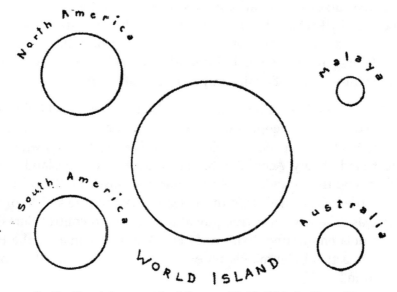

FIG. 12.—These circles represent the relative areas of the World-Island and its satellites.

Figure 2. Mackinder's abstract rendition of the relationship between the World Island and its satellites in Democratic Ideals and Reality *(1919).*

Brzezinski correctly noted "like insular Britain in the case of Europe, Japan is politically irrelevant to the Asian mainland." But he did not believe that China was likely to become a global dominant power for a long time. Brzezinski may have anticipated the Chinese demographic crisis caused by the one-child policy—the U.S., with its younger population and less stress on its "carrying capacity," is in a much better demographic position—but maybe he should review the Chinese economic data.

Brzezinski essentially dreamed of an emasculated E.U. "A larger Europe will expand the range of American influence without simultaneously creating a Europe so politically integrated that it could challenge the United States on matters of geopolitical importance, particularly in the Middle East." He was thinking in terms of a batch of new eastern European members eager to join NATO and benefit from E.U. cash, but not interested in integration. He was not thinking in terms of France and Germany, supported by Spain and Italy, working towards deepening European political integration.

America, for Brzezinski, "should also support Turkish aspirations to have a pipeline from Baku, Azerbaijan, to Ceyhan on its own Mediterranean coast [to] serve as a major outlet for the Caspian sea basin energy reserves." The result was the Baku-Tblisi-Ceyhan (BTC) pipeline, of which Brzezinski himself was a major instigator.

But the crucial point still is what Brzezinski, a *realpolitik* practitioner, had to say about Iran. The solution, for him, definitely was not Shock and Awe. "It is not in America's interest to perpetuate U.S.-Iranian hostility. Any eventual reconciliation should be based on both countries' recognition of their mutual strategic interest in stabilizing Iran's volatile regional environment. A strong, even religiously motivated—but not fanatically anti-Western— Iran is still in the U.S. interest. American long-range interests in Eurasia would be better served by abandoning existing U.S. objections to closer Turkish-Iranian economic cooperation, especially in the construction of new pipelines from Azerbaijan and Turkmenistan. In fact, American financial participation in such projects would be to America's benefit."

Brzezinski dreamed of the U.S. having a "decisive role as Eurasia's arbitrator." Eurasia's stability, in his view, "would be enhanced by the emergence, perhaps early in the next century, of a trans-Eurasian security system. Such a transcontinental security arrangement might involve an expanded NATO, linked by cooperative security agreements with Russia, China, and Japan. But to get there, Americans and Japanese must first set in motion a triangular political-security dialogue that engages China." Forget about an expanded NATO. Forget about Japan engaging China. The future of Eurasia seems to be spelling "SCO" plus Asian Energy Security Grid.

Cue to 9 years later. Nathan Gardels, editor-in-chief of a journal of social and political thought published by Global Services of the Los Angeles Times Syndicate/Tribune, asks Brzezinski whether military superiority leads to eternal enmity or to more security. Brzezinski's answer could not be more *realpolitik*: "The lessons of Iraq speak for themselves. Eventually, if neocon policies continue to be pursued, the United States will be expelled from the region and that will be the beginning of the end for Israel as well."

Brzezinski refined his new worldview—but up to a point—in a September 2006 interview with Germany's *Der Spiegel.* He admitted we were now in a historic stage of "global political awakening" in which "people in China and India, but also in Nepal, in Bolivia or Venezuela will no longer tolerate the enormous disparities in the human condition." But he framed this upheaval not in terms of a global struggle for a more equitable system, but in terms of a collective *danger*, a "challenge to global stability." Irrepressibly the hegemonic, he still viewed "the American leadership role vulnerable, but irreplaceable in the foreseeable future." Well, let's plunge into liquid modernity—or "space-velocity," as French cross-cultural analyst Paul Virilio put it—and see for ourselves.

~ 2 ~

GLOBALISTAN

Visit the market and see the world.

—Western African popular saying

A tawdry cheapness

shall reign throughout our days .

—Ezra Pound

Globalization is like Poe's maelstrom. A black void, rather. No one can escape it. And we don't know how it ends.

What we do know is that it has nothing to do with an "invisible hand." It has to do with maximization of profit; a huge concentration of capital; and the unrestricted power of monopolies. German cross-cultural scholar Horst Kurnitzky tells us globalization has configured "a new world, in which wealth and poverty, with no control by markets or the flux of cash, coexist with no form of social equality." So it's not globalization per se, but greed (that classic Christian sin...) and high concentration of capital that are responsible, in Kurnitzky's formulation, for "the uniformization and cultural and real impoverishment of the world."

Globalization has been with us for quite some time—in business, finance, culture, drugs, music, pornography. What is relatively "new" is the concept. Now let's summon our good ol' friend Baudelaire, and he'll pop up the question: Hypocrite reader, my equal, my brother (sister), are you *sure* that technological, capitalistic globalization is a heavenly invention devised for the greater good of Mankind by Adam Smith and Thomas L. Friedman? Are you *sure* it's inevitable, and that the best that we (and Clyde Prestowitz's *Three Billion New Capitalists*) can do is manage the necessary adjustments to it? Let's take a closer—global—look from a broader, and more questioning, perspective.

The invaluable Immanuel Wallerstein defines our reality (our Plato's cave?), also known as the capitalist world economy, as "a historic system which has combined an axial division of labor integrated by means of a world market less than perfect in its autonomy, combined with an interstate system composed of presumed sovereign States, a geoculture that has legitimized a scientific ethos as the basis of economic transformations and the extraction of profit, and liberal reformism as the way to contain popular discontent with the continuous socioeconomic polarization caused by capitalist development."

This system, as we all know, was born in Western Europe and then took over the whole world. Now fast forward to the mid-2000s. Wallerstein's judgment is like Zeus throwing his lightning bolt: "The capitalist world economy is in crisis as a historic social system." The world we live in, the way this system we take as a natural fact is articulated and produces "reality," is in "a transition phase towards a new historic system whose contours we don't know." What we can do at best is to contribute to conform the new structure: "The world we 'know' (in the sense of *cognoscere*) is the capitalist world economy and it is beset by structural faults it cannot control anymore." Gramsci would have framed it as the Old Order has fallen but the New Order has still not been born.

Inevitably, the stage is set for conflict if not mayhem. Wallerstein identifies for the next decades three geopolitical faults we will have to confront.

1) "The struggle among the Triad—U.S., E.U. and Japan—over which will be the main stage of accumulation of capital in the next decades." The third pole of the Triad– Japan, for Wallerstein—should rather be considered as "East Asia," with an emphasis on China.

2) The struggle between North and South, "or between the central zones and the other zones of the world economy, given the continual polarization—economic, social and demographic—of the world system."

3) Wallerstein defines it as "the struggle between the spirit of Davos and the spirit of Porto Alegre over the type of world system we want to build collectively." That is, the system preaching TINA ("there is no alternative") against anybody believing "another world is possible."

Wallerstein reminds us that the concept of Triad became popular in the 1970s—with its first institutional expression via the Trilateral Commission, which was "a political effort to reduce the emerging tensions between the three members of the Triad" (Chinese gangs happened to become globally popular at the same time). This has happened after what Wallerstein describes as "a phase A of the Kondratiev cycle from 1940-1945 to 1967-1973": euphoria over the fabulous expansion of the world economy, Baby Boom heaven, Elvis, the Beatles, a beautiful house, a beautiful kitchen full of appliances and a red convertible. The next 30 years were "a phase B in the Kondratiev cycle," where speculation became the name of the game, unemployment exploded and there was "an acute acceleration of economic polarization at the global level as well as inside States."

In the early 1920s Nikolai Dmitrievich Kondratiev was the very talented director of the Moscow Institute of Economic Investigations. In 1922 he coined his legendary theory of the "long waves" which not only explains but also previews the sweeping flow of History. Kondratiev ended his days in misery in a Stalinist gulag in Siberia. But his reputation as an economic guru survived him. Nowadays everyone from right to left to all points center invoke Kondratiev to justify the capitalism system forever surfing History in a succession of "long waves."

Trotsky was one who didn't fall for it—as Alan Woods impeccably summarized in a post on www.trotsky.net. Trotsky always mocked robotic Marxists who rhapsodized about "the final crisis of capitalism." But he also could not agree with the Kondratiev assumption that the "unseen hand of the market" would always intervene to restore the equilibrium of capitalism between one wave and the next.

Trotsky accepted there were economic oscillations. But he denied they were cyclical. Trotsky did see History as a series of phases; but all of these phases had different booms and busts, related to different, specific causes. In a famous speech at the Third Congress of the Comintern in 1922, Trotsky stressed how "capitalism establishes [an] equilibrium, disturbs it, then re-establishes it only to break it again, at the same time as it extends the limits of its dominion... Capitalism possesses a dynamic equilibrium which is always in a process of breakdown and recovery."

It's as if Kondratiev had seen capitalism as a pendulum. It's not: capitalism is in fact anarchy, chaos, no "equilibrium" but a succession of crises, revolutions and even wars which no one can reasonably predict (who predicted The Triumph of Capitalism/The Fall of the Berlin Wall double bill?) Woods prefers to quote George Soros—a man "who knows quite a lot about how markets move": for Soros "the market is not like a pendulum striving for a definite point of equilibrium, but more like a smashing ball." Capitalism as we know it is an unpredictable wrecker's ball.

The way Wallerstein himself examines what's been happening inside the Triad seems to privilege Trotsky's intuition over Kondratiev's. Wallerstein's point is that for the members of the Triad, roughly Europe got the better out of the 1970s, Japan out of the 1980s and the U.S. out of the 1990s. "Under the supposition that this long phase B of the Kondratiev cycle will reach its end," Wallerstein wonders which pole of the Triad will jump ahead. That is, which will better survive the current wrecker's ball. The winning player will be the one who sets his priorities in terms of investment in research and development, and thus on innovation; and who best organizes "the ability of the superior strata to control the access to consumable wealth." *Les jeux sont faits*. If this was Vegas, one might suspect that the house was betting on East Asia.

Yet in this chaotic wrecker's ball who's actually fighting whom, with what weapons, and what for? *Trompe l'oeil* is the name of the game. Polish sociologist Zygmunt Bauman has explained how Michel Foucault defined Jeremy Bentham's *Panopticon* as the "arch-metaphor of modern power." Bentham was an English jurist who published his Panopticon at the end of the 18th Century: an exercise on ubiquitous power surveilling society. Foucault examined in detail Bentham's description of a "visibility totally organized around a dominating and vigilant eye" and defined it as the "project of a universal visibility, acting to the benefit of a rigorous and meticulous power." Technically, humankind had finally acceded to the idea of an "omni-contemplative power."

Bauman for his part describes how "the domination of time was the secret of the power of managers—and immobilizing the subordinates in space, preventing their right to movement and routinizing the rhythm to which they should obey was the main strategy in their exercise of power. The pyramid of power was made of speed, access to transportation and the resulting freedom of movement."

There was one problem though: the Panopticon was too expensive. Capitalism needed something more cost-effective. So when power started to move, says Bauman, "with the speed of an electronic signal" it became, in practical terms, "truly extraterritorial, no more limited, or even desaccelerated, by resistance in space." This gave the rulers of the world "an unprecedented opportunity" to get rid of the old-fashioned Panopticon. Bauman tells us that the history of modernity, right now, is in its post-Panopticon stage. In essence: those who operate power now are virtually inaccessible. Welcome to German sociologist Ulrich Beck's society of "the second modernity," or Bauman's "liquid modernity."

The consequences, Bauman tells us, spell no more relation "between capital and labor, leaders and followers, armies at war. The main techniques of power now are flight, cunning, deviation and dodging, the effective rejection of any territorial confinement, with the complicated corollaries of construction and maintenance of order and with the responsibility for the consequences as well as the necessity to pay for the costs." Capital is free—thus the daily, trillion-dollar global Russian roulette of speculation.

"Capital," says Bauman, "travels hopeful, counting on fleeting and profitable adventures," just with "hand luggage—toothpaste, laptop computer and cell phone." It's like the delightfully quirky Richard Quest announcing to his multinational corporate audience on CNN: "Whatever you're up to today, I hope it's profitable." Soft capitalism may be very sexy, but only if you're a player. Bauman adds: "Capital may travel fast and light, and its lightness and mobility become the most important sources of uncertainty for everything else. Today this is the main base of domination and the main factor of social divisions."

We all know how the process is also leading to a control freak horror story. Bauman contraposes the visionary dystopia of Huxley's *Brave New World* to Orwell's *1984*, the "misery, destitution, scarcity and necessity" of Orwell's world to the "land of opulence and debauchery, abundance and fulfillment" of Huxley: "What they shared was the feeling of a world strictly controlled.." Orwell and Huxley essentially saw us going to the same place, but taking different paths, "if we continued to be sufficiently ignorant, obtuse, placid or indolent" to allow it to happen.

Just like "Plato and Aristotle could not imagine a good or bad society without slaves," Bauman tells us, "Huxley and Orwell could not conceive of a society, be it happy or unhappy, without managers, planners and supervisors which in group would write the script that others should follow... they could not imagine a world without towers and control rooms." We're already there—perhaps one step beyond. The post-Panopticon society is actually Sinopticon, where many observe just a few, everyone is disciplined and regimented by spectacle and discipline works by temptation and seduction, not by coercion.

Bauman resorts to Claude Lévi-Strauss, "the greatest social anthropologist of our time," who determined that whenever human history had to deal with the necessity of facing The Other, it came out with only two strategies: "The first consists in 'vomiting', throwing the others out as they're seen as incurably strange and alien: preventing physical contact, dialogue, interaction and all the varieties of *commercium* and *connubium*." Bauman lists as the extreme varieties of this strategy "incarceration, deportation and assassination," and "refined forms" as "spatial separation, urban ghettos and selective access to spaces." That's how the Sinopticon society deals with the vast masses of the urban poor, or with its own Islamophobia.

The second strategy "consists in a *soi-disant* "desalienation"—that means "ingesting, devouring alien bodies and spirit as to make them, by metabolism, identical to the bodies that ingest them, thus indistinguishable." This strategy has included "cannibalism and forced assimilation"—cultural crusades, declared wars against local practices, against calendars, cults, dialects and other prejudice and superstitions." That's how the Sinopticon society also deals with its own Islamophobia.

In between, the faceless multitudes are left with the proliferation of what Bauman refers to as "no places" or "cities of nowhere," places that are ostensibly public but definitely non-communitarian, places of passage like airports, hotel lobbies, highway convenience stores. Already in the mid-1980s French multidisciplinarian Paul Virilio was saying that in the future all prisons, hotels, airports and shopping malls would look exactly the same.

Liquid modernity. Sinopticon society. So many other ways to define the realm of globalization.

Ulrich Beck refers to "the nebulous word 'globalization' as code for 'the struggle of national against international elites', these ones struggling to gain position inside national power spaces." As an alternative he proposes other theories of the State, which would "break the false alternative between deregulation neo-liberal strategies and the interventionist and protectionist neo-nationalist strategies" and also address "what the politics of self-adaptation to neo-liberalism has unforgivingly omitted, that is, those disparities and conflicts (which nevertheless public opinion have sufficiently noticed) that sprang up either from the endemic destruction of Nature and the environment as well as the question...of full employment which, if it exists at all, is precarious."

Beck believes in the possibility of a new pact between economic power and political power and democracy. This could only happen via "a reform of the transnational institutions which coordinate the world economy." That's quite unlikely, to say the least. Beck's proposition of an "active cosmopolitan project" would mean not only grassroots mobilization but major players—from NGOs to top managing officials—trying to change the system from the inside.

Beck compares the irruption of global terrorism to "globalization's Chernobyl: then the benefits of nuclear energy were buried; now neo-liberalism's promises of salvation. The suicide attempts and massive assassinations not only showed the vulnerability of Western civilization but also allowed us to savor in advance to what class of conflicts globalization can lead. In a world of global risk, neo-liberalism's dictum, that is, to substitute the economy for politics and the State, rapidly loses its force of conviction." Beck could be placed in the same company of an array of Islamic scholars who worry about the "globalization of the culture of fear." (As do many commentators in the United States, both liberal and conservative, who worry about the abridgement of fundamental rights or believe that "if we change our behavior, the terrorists win.")

Now compare Beck to Anthony Giddens, former director of the London School of Economics and guru of Tony Blair's Third Way. Giddens could be seen as a globalization insider with a transforming agenda. He never bought the idea that deregulated markets were the most efficient mode of economic production. His emphasis is on civil society. Giddens, in *The Third Way and its Critics*, admits that globalization is not exclusively economic but also social, political and cultural. "In all these levels," it implies a "highly unequal group" of processes which follow up in "a fragmentary and contradictory" manner. He contends that globalization is not Westernization.

Giddens' Third Way, in its ambitious struggle to become a global political philosophy, was supposed to be about integration. He could not but know that "it's a mistake to simply oppose the State and the markets... Without a stable civil society, with norms of trust and social decency, it's not possible neither for markets to flourish nor for democracy to be maintained."

Giddens was convinced that "nation-states remain the most important actors in the international scene" because "they control territory," are able to "legitimaly exercise military force" and are responsible for "sustaining a legal apparatus." He hailed the confluence of global markets and new communication techniques as "a globalizing process that comes 'from underneath'... and is building an infrastructure of global civil society ." But in 2000 Giddens could hardly have imagined that one of the key expressions of this "global civil society" would be on February 15, 2003 when more than 10 million people all over the world marched against an illegal war that had not even started and in which Tony Blair's Third Way government was totally implicated.

French sociologist Alain Touraine has been keen to point out that

> *"Globalization does not define a stage in modernity, a new Industrial Revolution. It intervenes at the level of modes of management of historical change, and corresponds to an extreme capitalist mode of modernization, a category that should not be confused with a type of society, like feudal society or industrial society. And war, hot or cold, belongs to this universe of competition, confrontation, empires and not to the universe of societies and its internal problems, including class struggle."*

What does occupy central stage, according to Touraine, is "the triumph of capitalism." But this does not mean we are facing the end of History, just a "certain mode of administration of historical change, of modernization." In a similar vein Brazilian economist José Fiori describes globalization as little else than a technique for profit optimization in a historically specific world environment—the current situation of a relative abundance of literate workforces outside the Triad.

Unlike Bauman's liquid, fluid, amoral modernity Touraine's concept of modernity is linked to human rights, and modernity is seen as an appeal to the universalism of rights. But he is forced to admit this concept is facing two very powerful enemies. Touraine identifies the first enemy as "Islamic or Asiatic, which refuse any universality to the Western model and affirm that their model, determined by a communitarian conception of social life and the maintenance of traditional family, has revealed to be more efficient than ours, affected by all forms of personal and collective decomposition."

Touraine could be referring to Singapore's resident Confucius and founding father Lee Kuan Yew and the famous 1990s Asian values debate. The two volumes of Lee's political autobiography are nothing but a glossy, extended paean to Asian values. Moreover Lee's masterpiece, Singapore, works wonders, even tough civil society is largely defined by a shop-till-you-drop mentality. Lee's Confucianism is the opposite of the Enlightenment. It's another—extremely effective—model of modernization as the Little Helmsman Deng Xiaoping himself noted on the spot before copying it and launching his own modernization drive in China.

The second enemy of Touraine's concept of human rights-based modernity spans a tradition that stretches from Rousseau to Hobbes, "which defines democracy as the kingdom of the General Will or, in other words, the utmost respect to popular sovereignty." Touraine admits that this idea was attacked "from the right by economic liberalism and from the left by the idea of class struggle" but "it's still predominant, especially in the U.S."

It's inevitable that all those who put globalization at the center of the representation of our world show how it is conformed by American hegemony—since most nodes of the global network are U.S.-owned. It's not that simple.

The world economy's geography is not spatial, but a demented speedball of flux – with globalization as a mechanism configured by trade flux, financial flux, information flux, human flux and the uncontrollable explosion of the key nodes in the grid, the world's megacities. But as much as a "global economy"—Bauman's liquid modernity—a map of those fluxes would also stress a significant black void, a collection of stagnant puddles accounting for the intersection of war and poverty, war and globalization and the "war on terror."

Imbalance and inequality are the names of the game. Trade in goods and services are a virtual monopoly of the Triad—North America, the E.U. and North Asia. This has increased the tension—bordering on open war—between the U.S. and the E.U. on, for instance, civil aerospace, agriculture subsidies or genetically modified organisms. So the Triad does not operate like a unified cartel: there is fierce internal competition. The Triad concentrates no less than 70% of the wealth of the planet.

Africa is on the other end of the spectrum. Africa's exports were 4% of the global total in the early 1980s; they had fallen to 1.5% by 2003. And then there's trade as a weapon; if a country falls foul of the great powers, a commercial embargo—shut up and don't trade!—is the weapon of choice (even though other countries always manage to sneak around them).

The East to West financial market flux—Tokyo, Frankfurt, Paris, London, Wall Street—is a given. As for the human flux as well as the info flux of ideas, they should be increasing in all directions—but the flow still privileges the Triad. "The end of geography" and, in theory, political borders should have led—according to globalization cheerleaders—to a new configuration of the world population and a better division of wealth. Reality proves otherwise.

Flux is not a congregation of random electrons. Flux needs controlling engines—thus the criss-crossing networks and companies articulated with the finance, insurance, innovation, counselling, publicity and security industries. Only megalopolises can function as the ideal providers for all these industries. And this of course increases their seduction appeal. Since 2005 more than 3 billion people—half of the global population—are urban.

So the globalization flow is leading to increased concentration, not dispersion. The real world centers of economic and political power are networked cities monopolizing economic, financial and political flux.

We can identify 3 main nodes—all of them interlinked, of course.

Node 1—New York/Boston/Philadelphia/Washington, linked to "secondary" L.A., Mexico City and Sao Paulo.

Node 2—London/Paris/Frankfurt/Milan, linked to "secondary" Moscow, Dubai, Lagos and Johannesburg.

Node 3—Tokyo/Osaka—linked to "secondary" Shanghai, Hong Kong, Singapore and Sydney.

R&D remains strictly a Triad affair. Less than 1% of patents come from outside the Triad. There is of course the odd foreign hub of technology and research like Bangalore. But as multinational corporations increase the amount of patents they register in the U.S. from overseas branches that gives a false impression of globalization of innovation. Technological innovation in a tectronic-mad world originates from less than 20 countries—accounting for 15% of the global population. Although China and India are mounting challenges to the Triad's R&D supremacy, for now the Triad (including Australia, South Korea, Taiwan, and Israel) still "reigns," in Ezra Pound's words.

The 3 controlling nodes listed above are inserted into the Big Picture of the Great North/South divide—which in itself is also totally fragmented.

Take the North. The former Soviet republics in Central Asia and the Caucasus are not exactly part of the North *en bloc*, some with annual GNPs per capita lower than US$ 2000. Nor are other lower mid-level income countries (GNP per capita less than US$ 10,000 annual)—and these include E.U. member Poland and key global player Russia. Even inside the E.U. Portugal's GNP per capita, for instance, is still two-thirds of Germany's.

Take the South. Australia, New Zealand and South Africa are in fact part of the North. So are the four original Asian tigers—South Korea, Taiwan, Singapore and Hong Kong—plus the United Arab Emirates, Kuwait and Israel. The South is heavily populated by a higher mid-level—Thailand, Malaysia, Indonesia, the Philippines, most of Latin America, central Europe and some scattered players like Botswana and Mauritius. There's China, India and the Andean countries at a lower mid-level. And then we find what we could call the Deep South, the 48 LDCs (least developed countries) which the OECD euphemistically describes as "next emerging countries."

Under the current rules, where future wealth is inevitably tied to the influx of more foreign direct investment (FDI), once again it works in tiers. When sub-Saharan Africa captures only 1.2% of global FDI, Venezuela, Chile, Malaysia, Thailand and Poland capture almost 1% each, Mexico and Brazil almost 2% each, and China a staggering 10% all by itself. In 2004, the whole of Africa captured 4% of global FDI. China captured 22%. Savings usually do not remain in Africa; they migrate to wealthy members of the Triad and assorted fiscal paradises and are not reinvested in Africa.

Wallerstein has been one among many showing how the South remains dis-united politically, pullulating with client regimes of the North in contrast to the few—like the so-called BRIC countries (Brazil, Russia, India, China), plus Indonesia and South Korea—with real or potential geopolitical power.

The bottom line remains polarization "expanding geometrically," as Wallerstein puts it. "The North maintains this structure by means of its monopoly of advanced productive processes, control over the world financial institutions, dominance over knowledge and information media at a global level, and what is most important, by means of military power." Essentially, the North still brandishes an Iron Fist even though sometimes enveloped by a sexy, red velvet glove.

So the mantra that everyone equally profits from globalization is a myth. Further fragmentation flows through internal borders—like between coastal China and the countryside; south India and the rest of the country; Mexico and the southern

Indian states; or southeast Brazil and the rest of the country. Niches prevail—like Silicon Valley, with 2 million people and a GNP bigger than Chile's. The internet may represent the most glaring metaphor of inequality. By 2005, 1 billion people were connected—less than 15% of the world's population, a figure that confronted with 3 billion people barely surviving on less than US$ 2 a day, and 5 out of 6 billion people living on only 20% of global GDP, spells out that the world economy can function just fine serving only 20% of the world's population, that is, virtually the ones who are connected. As for the others, the harsh conclusion is inevitable: they are expendable. Forever.

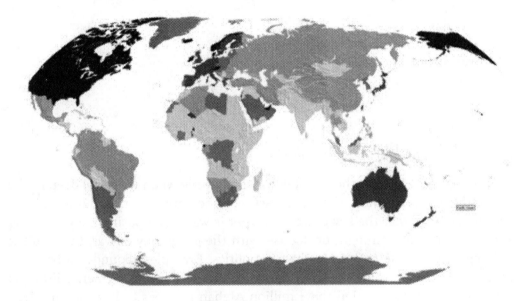

Figure 3. GDP per capita (PPP), Robinson projection.

While 3 billion people barely survive on less than US$ 2 a day; at least 850 million —roughly 1 in every 7—suffer from chronic malnutrition ingesting less than 2300 calories a day (in the wealthy North the average is 3400); hundreds of millions have never made a phone call; and thousands of children die every day from diarrhea due to the absence of clean water, the number of global air passengers, according to IATA, has shot up to over 2 billion since 2005. Hong Kong-Taipei is the busiest air link in the world, followed by New York-London and London-Amsterdam. Once again, all Triad links.

An absolutely key phenomenon for the next few decades will be South-to-North immigration. Wallerstein alerts us to the fact that in the long run "the North is creating an ample strata of resident persons which don't have all the political, economic or social rights" of the citizens of any particular country. There may be differences of gradation, but it's the same picture from the U.S. to France and Spain. This spells endless internal political turbulence.

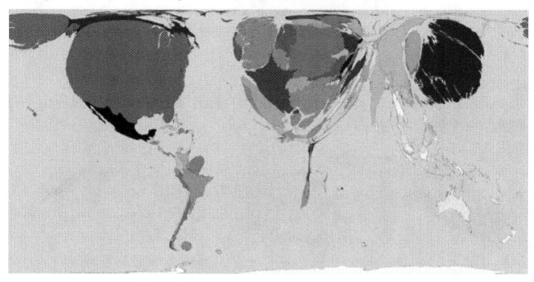

Figure 4. GDP per capita (WorldMapper).

The daily apocalypse of the excluded is what we see when we travel deep in the heart of Africa, China, South Asia, Southeast Asia and Latin America. But what most people don't see is that the key cause of hunger is war. Superposing hunger during the 1990s—because of drought or floods—with the geography of war, the result is that hunger is less due to climate than to politics. Examples abound—in Somalia, Angola, Mozambique, plus the undisguised ethnic cleansing in Liberia, Ethiopia and in Darfur, not to mention the 4 million Afghan refugees to Pakistan and Iran who fled the Taliban during the 1990s. That is hunger as a political weapon.

Wars will still be fought for access to power—like in Afghanistan, Sudan and the Ivory Coast; for territorial control—like in Israel/Palestine; for separation—like in Chechnya, Georgia, Kashmir and Aceh; or for a minority to express their grievances—like in southern Thailand. The privatization of war and its asymmetrical, trans-State mutations will only increase the influence of hunger as a political weapon.

Technically, the world will remain able to feed itself for generations. Demographic growth won't affect it. But how could agriculture win over malnutrition? There are only two possibilities: sustainable development or genetic manipulation..

Two poles of the Triad—the U.S. and the E.U.—produce 40% of the wheat exported globally. 50% of their cereals are exported to developing countries. Both the U.S. and the E.U. practice heavy subsidies to exports. This massive unloading at cut price rates of the rich countries' excess production will continue to lead —in the rest of the world—to massive destruction of rural jobs and irreversible dependence on imported agricultural products. That's trade as lethal weapon.

The Sahel is a fitting example. In the Sahel, traditional cultures such as manioc have receded at a rate of 1% a year for the past 20 years compared to export cultures—like cotton, coffee and cacao—which are the source of precious foreign exchange. Meanwhile imports of wheat have been growing by 8% a year. According to the U.N.'s Food and Agriculture Organization (FAO) at least 50 countries are threatened by this process. In less than 15 years Russia and most of the former Soviet republics became net importers of food.

According to Eric Hobsbawm, for multinational corporations—we call it Corporatistan—"the 'ideal world' is a world without States, or at least with small States." (And perhaps a Super-State to enforce Corporatistan's worldview?) By 2004 there were more than 63,000 multinational corporations. When unreachable by national or international law, ecological preoccupations, social responsibility and all of the above simultaneously, they can become more destructive than hurricanes. According to the Carbon Disclosure Project (CDP), 57% of the Corporatistan Top 500 has absolutely no plans to fight global warming. 140 companies didn't even bother to answer questions by CDP's research team. BAE Systems—a top U.K. weapons producer—happen to be among the worst in environmental protection.

Well, Corporatistan rules. ExxonMobil is bigger than Turkey, Wal-Mart is bigger than Austria, GM is bigger than Indonesia, DaimlerChrysler is bigger than Norway, BP is bigger than Thailand, Toyota is bigger than Venezuela, Citigroup is bigger than Israel and TotalFinalElf is bigger than Iran. Ninety percent of the Corporatistan Top 500 is in the Triad. The Top 1000 accounts for no less than 80% of the world's industrial output.

Figures attest to a demential cornucopia of chaos—capitalism as a wrecker's ball where a happy few profit infinitely more than all the others: no equilibrium here. By 2007 there will be roughly 1.5 billion computers around the world; 38% of business software is already pirated (98% in Vietnam, 95% in China). The motor vehicle industry will remain the world's largest manufacturing business—75% of the world's total output coming from only 6 companies (GM, Ford, Toyota, Daimler-Chrysler, Volkswagen and Honda). 12% of all U.S. manufacturing jobs are concentrated in the chemical industry.

Mammoth construction companies are concentrated between France and Japan. 63% of all wood harvested in the world is consumed as fuel. The four world leaders

in forest and paper products are all based in the U.S. The 5 largest trading companies are all Japanese; of the largest 17, 16 are in Asia (10 in Japan, 2 in South Korea,
one in China). The Japanese *sogo shosha*—the 3 biggest are Mitsui, Mitsubishi and
Itochu—deal with up to 30,000 products per company. Fifty-six percent of the
Fortune 500 is composed by commercial and savings banks. American, German and
Japanese bank payments turn over the equivalent of their country's GDP every few
days. More than US$ 1.5 trillion move around the world every day in foreign ex-
change transactions; the bulk is to profit off of fluctuation between currencies. The
world spends US$ 2 trillion a year in food—10% of all economic activity. 75% of the
world's advertising is purchased in the Triad (as far as Asia is concerned this means
Japan only). Only seven companies dominate the global film market, and only 5
companies dominate the music industry. Major U.S. TV and film studios collect up
to 60% of their revenues overseas, the music business 70%. Corporatistan—or the
consumption of products made by Corporatistan—accounts for 50% of the gases
responsible for global warming, source of much of the world's toxic waste. Two-
thirds of hazardous waste produced in the U.S. comes from chemical corporations.
Corporatistan controls 50% of the world's oil, gas and coal mining and refining.

Since the early 1990s the Clinton and Bush administrations, U.S. big business
and U.S. big media have sold globalization the world over as benign Ameri-
canization. It's really an either/or epic battle.

For apostles of Wild West free trade, Corporatistan stars are engines for
progress, efficency and economic development. They produce an extensive range of
products, find markets and employ people all over the world; this means a globally
connected capitalist marketplace promoting positive competition, innovation and
progress.

For the alterglobalization movement, and a myriad of groups worried about the
social, economic and environmental consequences of globalization, Corporatistan
stars symbolize a system of global capitalism run amok. The enormous size and
unrestricted power of multinationals and their transnationality lead to corporate
profits being the ultimate priority over everything: the welfare of workers, the
environment and the economies—sometimes very fragile—of numerous countries.
Especially when the magic mantra is delocalization. If everyone lived like a citizen
of Triad member France, we would need two planets Earth. If everyone consumed
like an American, we would need five.

In his *Power and Counter-power*, published in Germany in 2002, Ulrich Beck
notes that "the neo-liberal agenda is to institutionalize the benefits of capital,
benefits that are historically fleeting...The perspective of capital, radically taken to
its limits, postulates itself as absolute and autonomous...The result is that what is

good for capital is good for everyone. The promise is that we will be all wealthier and finally even the poor would benefit. Thus the capacity for seduction of this neo-liberal ideology is not in stressing egoisms or maximizing competition but in promoting global justice. The proposition is: the maximization of the power of capital is finally the best way to socialism." That's how the (social) State is rendered superfluous.

That may also explain why former Trotskyites have a penchant to become neo-cons—or in fact bourgeois neo-revolutionaries. It may have to do with the concept of permanent revolution. Permanent revolution would eventually solidify the victory of socialism. Well, real socialism of the USSR kind collapsed—thus demon-strating the superiority of Capital. So why not apply Trotsky to the superior virtues of Capital? Hence we're back to Ulrich Beck—"the maximization of the power of capital is the best way to socialism," and that includes of course capital imposing its will at the barrel of a gun, preemptive or not.

In Western Europe and Latin America societies are extremely alert to the ravag-es of Maximum Capital. Not necessarily the U.S. According to Egyptian economist Samir Amin, director of the Third World Forum in Dakar, Senegal and one of the great transcultural intellectual minds of the developing world, "not benefiting from the tradition by which the social democratic worker's parties and the communists marked the formation of modern European political culture, American society does not have the ideological instruments at its disposal to allow it to resist the dictator-ship of capital. On the contrary, capital shapes every aspect of this society's way of thinking." But we should also remember that the U.S. is the most religious member of the Triad; although capital permeates religion in every way, there is still a healthy undercurrent of resistance that has more spiritual authority than elsewhere in the Triad.

A delightful example of the "capital is good for everyone" syndrome was an Au-gust 2006 *Financial Times* story announcing the demise of the financial journalist. Computers are now so fast that an earnings story is uploaded within 0.3 seconds of a corporation making results public. No financial journalist can possibly compete with that. A Thomson Financial executive, quoted by the FT, summed it all up: "This means we can free up reporters so they have more time to think." Mark Tran of *The Guardian* wisely preferred to connect past and future, alerting readers about "what happened in *[2001: A] Space Odyssey* when HAL took over the spaceship. Or worse still, think of *Terminator 3*, when the Skynet network of computers unleashes nuclear war."

By the mid-2000s the absolute majority of the developing world had noticed that the "globalized" geography of wealth had basically remained the same since the

World Bank-denominated "East Asian miracle" of the late 1980s-early 1990s—and it looked positively calcified as an immutable order. This was compounded with the worldwide suspicion that globalization was a game where Corporatistan—especially from the U.S.—wins and almost everyone else loses.

New York-based investment banker Henry Liu framed some of these "wins" when he wrote in *Asia Times* that "with the U.S. relocating all manufacturing offshore under globalization, high tech and military systems are the main U.S. exports outside of agriculture and financial services."

War and globalization cannot escape each other's seductive embrace. "Borders" and "markets" can be "liberated" as much via the WTO/ IMF/World Bank trio of enforcers as with B-52s and Abrams tanks. As far as Wall Street, Anglo-American and European Big Oil and the interlinked U.S.-U.K. industrial-military complex are concerned, the ends justify the means. The key example of the "war on terror" smashing sovereign, recalcitrant nations into submission to "free markets" has got to be Iraq.

Bauman points to the "new type of war in the era of liquid modernity: not the conquest of new territory, but the destruction of walls which blocked the flux of new and fluid global power" (old-fashioned, physical walls now serve the exclusive purpose of blocking undesirable masses, like Mexicans and Latin Americans confronting the southern U.S. Wall, Palestinians facing the Israeli Wall and Iraqis facing the upcoming—in 2012—Saudi Arabian Wall).

Bauman formulates the new war, paraphrasing Clausewitz, as "the promotion of free trade by other means," stressing that "the power of the global elite resides in its capacity to escape local commitments, and globalization is geared to prevent this necessity so local authorities have to bear the responsibility of being the guardians of law and order (local)." No wonder, adds Bauman, "globalization seems to be more successful in raising the vigor of enmity and inter-communal strife than in promoting the peaceful coexistence of communities." That's globalization dissolving the world into Liquid War.

Investing in war is essential business for key nodes in the U.S.-E.U. poles of the Triad. In the summer of 2006 BAE Systems Plc (the former British Aerospace, privatized in the early 1980s), one of Europe's top weapons corporations, confirmed the sale to Saudi Arabia of 72 Eurofighter Typhoon jets—a deal worth as much as US$ 19 billion, a pittance considering that at the time Saudi Arabia was bagging around US$ 17 billion a month on crude oil sales.

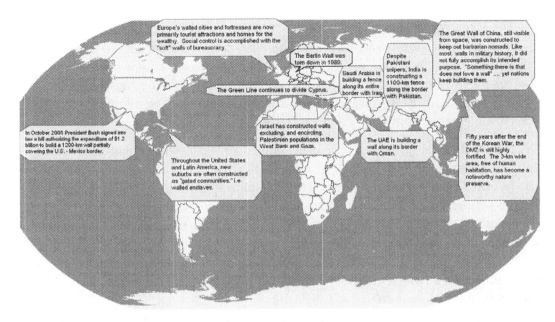

Figure 5. Walls in history and the present day.

Eurofighter is a Munich-based joint venture between BAE, Finmeccanica SpA and European Aeronautic, Defense & Space Co. (EADS). Of course the deal had absolutely nothing to do with a US$ 33.4 million slush fund to finance fun and games to the Saudi royal family, including "sex and bondage with Saudi princes," as Indymedia U.K. had reported in November 2003, based on accusations by a former BAE employee. BAE Systems in North America has long been associated with Boeing and Lockheed Martin and is totally integrated with the Pentagon—as if it was part of U.S. Corporatistan. When BAE Systems bought United Defense Industries in June 2005—the makers of Bradley fighting vehicles, those intimate friends of Iraqi guerrillas—the British became the number 7 Pentagon contractor. Accusations against BAE Systems are of the "business as usual" variety—corruption, pollution of the environment, dirty deals with dictatorships. BAE Systems' CEO Mike Turner of course has dismissed all allegations as "history."

The two Western poles of the Triad are in fierce competition for supplying not only any unsavory regime on hold but every former USSR satellite in Eastern Europe as well. In this dogfight between Lockheed Martin, Boeing, General Dynamics, Raytheon and Northrop Grumman plus BAE Systems on one side, and EADS — a fusion of Deutsch Aerospace (DASA), Aerospatiale Matra and Construcciones Aeronauticas from Spain—on the other, peace is just another word for everything to lose. The Anglo-American industrial-military complex alliance, plus the Wall Street-City of London financial alliance, plus Big Oil alliance, explain why the British pound may never be dropped in favor of the euro.

The U.S.'s top industrial policy is to sell weapons. What kind of globalization is this? Samir Amin points out that "the U.S. only benefits from comparative advantages in the armaments sector, precisely because this sector largely operates outside the rules of the market and benefits from state support." The business of selling weapons is roughly 80% more profitable than shipping Hollywood movies, straight-to-DVD masterpieces and Shakira CDs to the rest of the world.

Hence the marketing strategy of Military Corporatistan has got to be Long—Infinite—War. In the summer of 2006 Frida Berrigan, Senior Research Associate at the World Policy Institute's Arms Trade Resource Center, issued a very detailed report—*Weapons at War 2005: Promoting Freedom or Fueling Conflict*—relayed by *Tomdispatch*, on this discreet business where the stars are Lockheed Martin F-16s, Raytheon Advanced Medium-Range Air-to-Air Missiles or Maverick Air-to-Ground Missiles, a business conducted via "the Pentagon's predilection for less than magnetic Power Point presentations, unbearably unexpressive acronyms, and slightly paunchy, older white men in business suits."

The playground is every dictatorship's dream: as BAE Systems sell their 72 Euro-fighters to Taliban-friendly Saudi Arabia—perhaps to bomb the next Shiite insurrection in Hasa—Lockheed Martin sells 36 F-16s to Taliban-friendly Pakistan—perhaps to be engulfed in the next scramble for Kashmir. For P.R. purposes all this awesome firepower will be channeled towards the "war on terror." Berrigan notes, in quite understated terms, that 20 out of the U.S.' Top 25 weapons clients are "undemocratic regimes and/or governments with records as major human-rights abusers." According to her report, "U.S. arms exports accounted for more than half of total global arms deliveries -- US$ 34,8 billion -- in 2004, and we export more of them ourselves than the next six largest exporters combined."

While the Western poles of the Triad export loads of weapons, the South is busy developing its own version of Corporatistan. A key 2006 report of the Boston Consulting Group (BCG) titled *The New Global Challengers: How 100 Top Companies from Rapidly Developing Economies Are Going Global—and Changing the World* has detailed how the future of Corporatistan is in the so called RDEs: China, India, Brazil, Russia, Malaysia, Thailand and Turkey. The report is convinced the so-called "RDE 100" will "radically transform industries and markets around the world."

Only corporations with a turnover of more than US$ 1 billion in 2004 were taken into account. Economic analyst Kunal Kumar Kundu, writing for *Asia Times* from Bangalore, stressed that "taken together, these companies accounted for US$ 715 billion in revenue" in 2004, and "boasted US$ 145 billion in operating profits, a half-trillion dollars in assets, and a combined US$ 9 billion in R&D spending. Plus, they have grown at an average rate of 24% for the past four years." They may be unknown to many, but then nobody knew Toyota, Honda, Samsung or LG 40 or 30 years ago. Who knows Johnson Electric from China, which is the world's leading manufacturer of small electric motors?

Not surprisingly the Top 100 is dominated in 70% by Asia—China with 43 companies and India with 21. The wave of the future players include Lenovo—which bought IBM's notebook PC business; China National Offshore Oil Corp. (CNOOC); Indian information-technology-services giants Infosys, Tata and Wipro; Embraer from Brazil—the world's biggest producer of regional jets; Brazilian oil giant Petrobras and food processor giants Sadia and Perdigao; and Gazprom and LUKoil from Russia. All these represent fierce competition to the U.S.-E.U. pole of the Triad. As Kumar Kundu notes, they "are in nearly all sectors: industrial goods (auto equipment, basic materials, engineered products); consumer durables (household appliances and consumer electronics); resource extraction; technology and business services."

Samir Amin insists that "faced by European and Japanese competition in high-technology products, and by Chinese, Korean and other Asian and Latin American industrialized countries in competition for manufactured products, as well as by Europe and the southern cone of Latin America in agriculture, the United States probably would not be able to win were it not for the recourse to 'extra-economic' means, violating the principles of liberalism imposed on its competitors." Amin sees the interlocking causes of the decline of U.S. production system as "complex and structural. The poor quality of general education and training in the U.S., the product of a deep-rooted prejudice in favour of the 'private' to the detriment of the public sector, is one of the main reasons." His verdict: "There will never be a 'authentically liberal' globalized economy."

Anyway the rules of the game may be slowly changing. Kumar Kundu details how the RDE 100 are gaining ground. They may use armies of skilled factory workers costing US$ 5 an hour, compared to US$ 25 an hour in the North. Raw materials and equipment are cheaper. They offer excellent value for money products. And crucially, "by 2010 China and India combined will graduate 12 times the number of engineers, mathematicians, scientists and technicians as the U.S." This may be the second phase of globalization. Call it The Revenge of the South.

But what about the Deep South?

Almost everything we need to know about the causes of most of the Arab world's grievances surfaced in the 2002 Arab Report on Human Development in Arab Countries, commissioned by the United Nations Development Program (UNDP) and carefully prepared by Arab college professors and researchers. Not surprisingly the report found deadly connections between poverty and health and education indicators—not to mention a stark contrast between the rulers and the ruled. Wealth concentration is the name of the game in an array of countries comprising 280 million people—5% of the world's population, and much younger than the world average (38% are less than 14 years old).

The Arab states were behind the West and Asia on every possible index—from literacy, job creation and technology to life expectancy, intellectual prowess and human development. Orientalist Bernard Lewis, asking *What Went Wrong?*, answered that institutionalized irrationalism was to blame. Wrong: blame it as much on rapacious, corrupt comprador elites who were more interested in shopping at Harrods and shopping for fighter jets than investing in health, education and productive industry.

Since the early 1980s the rate of income growth per head in the Arab world has been the lowest anywhere—if we except Sub-Saharan Africa. This growth rate was only 0.5% a year by the early 2000s. If persisting, the report said, an Arab citizen "will need 140 years to double his income, against a little less than 10 years in other regions." Median GNP per head by 2002 was half of South Korea, for instance. 40 years earlier, it used to be almost double when compared to the future Asian tigers.

The report also provided numbers to the feeling that Arab culture is closed to interaction with the outside world. The Arab world translates only 300 books a year—five times less than in Greece, for instance. Since Caliph Mamoon in the 7th Century, only 100,000 books were translated. That's what Spain translates in a single year.

And still one person in five keeps living with less than two dollars a day. Labor mobility is practically non-existent—fueling the current number one European nightmare: 51% of Arab teenagers are obsessed about immigrating to the affluent West.

The report points to three main reasons for the overall tragedy in the Arab world: "no freedom of choice, feeble promotion of the rights of women, and a knowledge deficit." At the end of the 1990s the level of freedom—also meaning participation and responsibility—in the 22 member countries of the Arab League was the lowest in the world.

The conclusion was inescapable: Arab governments and human development remain a mutually incompatible proposition.

LDCs are in even worse shape than the Arab world. The E.U., on paper, considers itself to be a policy model for the North—because it actually removed tariff barriers against LDCs. But anybody bothering to read the labyrinth of "annex" rules in Brussels would verify that three absolutely essential items exported by poor countries—rice, sugar and bananas—are liable to be taxed to up to 98%. A theoretically unrestricted opening of rich countries' agricultural, textile and shoe markets to developing countries would mean a staggering US$ 700 billion a year. This is more than 13 times the aid to development budget practiced by the OECD countries by the mid-2000s: this budget is only 0.22% of GNP. The initial target, fixed in 1970, was 0.7% of GNP. This can only mean one thing: a total absence of political will to reduce the glaring North/South imbalance.

As an angry African delegate told me in a 2002 OECD meeting in Paris, the whole system is "a bloated exercise in hypocrisy." No spinning by any government or multilateral organization can disguise the fact that the system is "Europe and the U.S. against the rest of the world"—as recognized by an infuriated U.N. official: "And this is even more incredible when compared to the project of reducing poverty in the world by half until 2015." Development countries' officials ceased to be swayed by the usual mantras— the "virtues of the free market," "good governance," "equality of market access," "the merits of an impartial judge as the WTO." Already by 2002 Professor Jagdish Baghwati from Columbia University saw a risk of "aggressive unilateralism" becoming the new paradigm in international trade relations.

By mid-2006 the collapse of so-called global governance was self-evident. The cash-strapped IMF badly needed its own structural adjustment. The G-8 had turned into an innocuous, security paranoia, anti-alterglobalization media circus. The WTO not only could not negotiate hundreds of custom taxes for 150 countries as it could not reign in U.S. and E.U. subsidies. The consequences for the future are ominous: more protectionism, more law of the jungle, more of Professor Baghwati's "aggressive unilateralism."

A portrait of things to come is the U.S.-controlled Big NAFTA, or NAFTA-Plus, which will evolve into something called SSP—Security and Prosperity Partnership. SSP favors total flux of capital, goods, services, ownership and technology—but definitely not labor, specifically of the poor Mexican worker kind. Thus the 1200 km-long Senate and Congress-approved Wall of Shame that will barricade the U.S. southwest against Mexico and Central America. When SSP goes into overdrive it will simply gobble up Central America and the Caribbean. That's still a long way towards a U.S.-controlled FTAA, uniting Alaska to Patagonia; the dream collapsed with the South American counter-attack of a Mercosur uniting oil-and-gas giant Venezuela to Argentina and Brazil. For the moment the Big Three South American union is a tripod. Mexican oppositionist Lopez Obrador will continue to fight for a progressive government in Mexico, so by the early 2010s Latin America would then become a "chair"—not exactly one Washington would be invited to sit on.

At the World Social Forum in Porto Alegre in January 2003 Samir Amin really let it rip. He emphasized that we, all of us "have all become 'Red Skins', the contemptuous name reserved for the Native Americans in the eyes of the Washington establishment -- that is to say, peoples who have the right to exist only in so far as they do not frustrate the expansion of U.S.-based multinational capital."

Amin was careful to point out that "the U.S. program is not 'imperial' in the sense that Antonio Negri has given the term, since it does not aim to manage the societies of the planet in order better to integrate them into a coherent capitalist system. Instead, it aims only at looting their resources."

In his 2005 lectures sponsored by Harvard's Program in the History of American Civilization, Professor Eric Hobsbawm—whose *Age of Extremes* has been translated into 36 languages—said that from its roots in the Monroe Doctrine, the U.S. has never viewed itself as a part of an international system of rival political powers. It lacks a foundation myth—an Albion or Barbarossa—the basis for most other current nation states. That's the reason for the self-appointed uniqueness—and, according to Hobsbawm, the imperial drive. Hobsbawm—unlike right wing historian proponent Niall Ferguson, as well as civilizational clasher Samuel Huntington—was adamant that the American empire "will almost certainly fail." David Harvey worries that the failure may lead to "a catastrophic rupture of the system...and maybe the return of the Lenin scenario of violent competition between capitalist power blocs."

In the summer of 2006, in one of his invaluable commentaries posted on the Fernand Braudel Center at Binghamton University's website, Wallerstein wondered how the world would look like in 2025. He identified three sets of answers: "The first is that the United States will enjoy one last fling, a revival of power, and will continue to rule the roost in the absence of any serious military contender. The second is that China will displace the United States as the world's superpower. The third is that the world will become an arena of anarchic and relatively unpredictable multi-polar disorder."

Wallerstein doubts the U.S. may remain top dog. The first reason is economic— "the fragility of the U.S. dollar as the sole reserve currency in the world economy. When the dollar falls dramatically, the United States will lose its command on world wealth and its ability to expand the deficit without serious immediate penalty." The second reason is military: "Both Afghanistan and especially Iraq have demonstrated that a nation must also have a very large land force to overcome local resistance. The United States does not have such a force, and will not have one, due to internal political reasons. Hence, it is doomed to lose such wars." And the third reason is political: "Nations throughout the world are drawing the logical conclusion that they can now defy the United States politically"—like in the new impulse of the Shanghai Cooperation Organization (SCO).

China, according to Wallerstein, also faces three problems. The first is internal: "China is not politically stabilized. The one-party structure has the force of economic success and nationalist sentiment in its favor. But it faces the discontent of about half of the population that has been left behind, and the discontent of the other half about the limits on their internal political freedom." The second problem relates to the world economy: "The incredible expansion of consumption in China (along with that of India) will take its toll both on the world's ecology and on the possibilities of capital accumulation." And the third problem has to do with the neighbors: "Were China to accomplish the reintegration of Taiwan, help arrange the reunification of the Koreas, and come to terms (psychologically and politically) with Japan, there might be an East Asian unified geopolitical structure that could assume a hegemonic position." By the same token, there is a distinct possibility that North Korea's nuclear ambitions will lead to China being surrounded by remilitarizing powers, beginning with Japan.

The last of Wallerstein's scenarios is "multi-polar anarchy and wild economic fluctuations. Given the inability of maintaining an old hegemonic power, the difficulty of establishing a new one, and the crisis in worldwide capital accumulation, this third scenario appears the most likely." A key reason for this state of affairs, according to Brazilian economist José Fiori, is that "the U.S. does not have a project, an utopia or an ideology capable of mobilizing world public opinion. The globalization utopia is dead—killed by facts and numbers in the real world. Whatever master plan the U.S. elite currently in power may concoct, adds Fiori, "it cannot be articulated as a project, it cannot mobilize minds and it cannot organize the ideological strategy of American power."

Nevertheless the Bush administration—supported by sectors of the nomad elites of global liquid modernity, as Bauman would put it—will not accept "multi-polar anarchy" without a fight. Thus non-stop Liquid War.

Bauman tells us that "sedentary populations under siege refuse to accept the rules and risks of the new 'nomad' power game, an attitude that the new nomad global elite finds extremely difficult (as well as repulsive and undesirable) to understand... When it's a matter of confrontation, and particularly military confrontation, the nomad elites of the modern liquid world saw the territorially oriented strategy of the sedentary populations as 'barbarian' in comparison with its own 'civilized' military strategy... The tables have been turned—and the old and tested weapon of "chronopolitics" used by the triumphant sedentary populations to expel the nomads to barbaric and wild pre-history is now used by the victorious nomad elites in their fight against what's left of territorial sovereignty and against those that are still dedicated to its defense."

Two scenarios are possible. The "let's-call-it-Aquarius" scenario is provided by Steven Pinker, director of the Center for Cognitive Neurosciences at M.I.T. For neurolinguist Pinker, human nature will not change. Slavery, despotism, Liquid War will vanish, replaced by human rights and the Rule of Law. Science will explain the mysteries of the Universe. Our descendants will not be more intelligent and will not be genetically redesigned (no catalogue-chosen kids). Machines, on the other hand, will understand our language and obey all our commands.

Then there's the let's call it Hobbes-gone-crazy-on-his-way-to-Aquarius scenario. Darwin essentially warned us that we are an accidental mutation condemned to extinction. Marx was more of a humanist: he explained the origins of capitalism, how it would be the dominant force of the world system, and finally how it would succumb to a more sophisticated, egalitarian system—socialism. He was—only partially—wrong: Bakunin had predicted the horror of Soviet bureaucratic socialism. But the idea of a more egalitarian system is not dead. The next world system may well be libertarian socialism—but the act of passage, with capitalism feeding on war, terror and undisguised slavery, and engulfed in a fight to the death for energy resources, will be inscribed in tremendous grief as much as the passage from feudalism to capitalism.

Bauman tells us that power will deploy any strategy to keep flowing: "Any dense network of social links, and in particular one that is territorially rooted, is an obstacle to be eliminated." In *Europe (an Unfinished Adventure)* Bauman analyzes how Capital and the military use the same "hit and run" tactics: "Lands up to now 'virgin' (from the point of view of marketing), or types of commodities that were never included in market circulation...water, genetic stock, intellectual products or even historic traditions and memories... are now transformed into 'mercantilization' targets." After savage privatization raids the expropriated masses are left behind. The main point is to evade the responsibility "for the incalculable lives deprived from their means of subsistence and self-reproduction, and thus virtually incapable of reacting to the exploitation of 'emancipated' manpower under the terms of capital." So for both Capital and the military the weapons employed are the same: the name of the game is "shoot and scoot": to leave the battlefield at full speed, "when the possibility of 'creative destruction' is over."

Bauman's judgment is clear: "The new planetary empire, governed and managed by capital and global trade, launches daily 'preemptive attacks' against any surge of 'thinking under the bases of a social contract' which may appear in the post-colonial world." This logic of Liquid War, if not broken in the short term, fulfills Wallerstein's projection—a world of three furiously competing main blocs, led by the U.S., the E.U. and an Asia led mainly by China, with Russia and/or India on the side, on their way to an Orwellian nightmare. The U.S. may always try to seduce and bully the E.U. towards the formation of a Western Triad bloc bent on controlling the Persian Gulf-Caspian energy Big Prize. In this Triad-at-war world, U.S. "target" Iran will inevitably be associated with Asia via the SCO. Doomsdayers may have a field of dreams gaming the consequences of China or Russia installing military bases to protect their ally in West Asia.

So what if Hobbes loses his map on the way to Aquarius? Welcome to the future. Oil addiction fueling non-stop Liquid War. Law of the jungle. The seas rising five meters in the next decades. A new glacial age. The coming of Icestan—or should it be Waterstan? In the meantime, though, the future will be dominated by Pipelineistan.

~ 3 ~

PIPELINEISTAN

By 2010 we will need on the order of an additional fifty million barrels a day. So where is the oil going to come from? Governments and the national oil companies are obviously controlling about ninety per cent of the assets. Oil remains fundamentally a government business. While many regions of the world offer great oil opportunities, the Middle East with two thirds of the world's oil and the lowest cost, is still where the prize ultimately lies.

—Dick Cheney, speech at the Institute of Petroleum, London, fall of 1999

The Liquid—or Viscous—Wars of 21st Century geopolitics will be predominantly related to oil and gas. The Liquid Wars will be characterized by viscosity—the resistance of a liquid to motion—because while capital is infinitely fungible, the location of petroleum reserves is not. The name of the game is Pipelineistan. From 2003 to 2030 the world's energy security comes with a staggering price tag, according to the International Energy Agency (IEA). The bill runs to at least US$ 16 trillion. It's essentially a matter of investment, which has to grow from currently US$ 150 billion a year to US$ 240 billion a year by 2025. Investment in oil and gas alone will consume US$ 6 trillion—75% of which in exploration and production. At mid-2000s savings rates, 7% of global savings—or 1.6% of global GDP—will be necessary to finance investment on energy alone—to say nothing of the enormous costs of assuring the military security of energy supplies.

Gas, "blue gold" in industry lingo for the color of its flame, is a formidable political and diplomatic weapon in the hands of states like Russia, Iran, Turkmenistan, Venezuela and Bolivia. Gas, unlike oil, complies with the constraints on carbon emissions defined by the Kyoto protocol. It is even more abundant than oil; proven reserves, with existing technology, may last as many as 70 years, compared with 40 for oil. According to the IEA, gas will be consumed in a faster progression (2.3% annually) than oil (1.6%), carbon (1.5%) or nuclear power (0.4%).

As for oil, by 2006 the largest proven oil reserves by country, in billions of barrels, were:

1. Saudi Arabia 264.3

2. Canada 178.8

3. Iran 132.5

4. Iraq 115.0

5. Kuwait 101.5

6. United Arab Emirates (UAE) 97.8

7. Venezuela 79.7

8. Russia 60.0

9. Libya 39.1

10. Nigeria 35.9

As of 2006, 77% of the global oil supply is controlled by governments, not Big Oil. With more than 33% of world oil reserves still closed to Foreign Direct Investment (FDI), and 22% "severely limited," as the Shell 2020 scenario notes, there's not much one can do but pull a Bette Davis: "Fasten your seat belts, it's gonna be a bumpy ride."

History may judge it as one of the capital moves of the 21st Century's New Great Game: in May 2005, high-quality, low-sulfur Caspian light crude oil started flowing through the Caucasus towards the Mediterranean in Turkey. The Baku-Tbilisi-Ceyhan pipeline (BTC)—hyped by Washington as the ultimate Western escape route from dependence on oil from the Persian Gulf—was finally in business.

This was Pipelineistan at its most overwhelming: a supreme law unto itself, untouchable by national sovereignty, serious environmental concerns (expressed both in the Caucasus and in Western Europe), labor legislation and protests against the World Bank; and oblivious to mountains 2,700 meters high and more than 1500 small rivers. BTC took 10 years of hard work and at least US$ 4 billion—US$ 3 billion of which in bank loans. BTC is not merely a pipeline: as we will see below, it enjoys rights in some ways superior to those of a sovereign state.

The BTC state slices Azerbaijan in half from east to west, then slices Georgia in half almost from east to west before taking a dip south, bypassing the secessionist province of Ajaria and slicing Turkish Anatolia diagonally from the northeast towards the south. BTC's founding stone is at British Petroleum (BP)'s gleaming terminal at Sangachal, half-an-hour along the Caspian south of Baku. The BTC state is 44 m wide, snaking along 1767 km across three countries, two of those (Azerbaijan and Georgia) extremely volatile and the other (Turkey) eventually subjected to turmoil by dispossessed Kurds. BTC is an unrivalled celebration of the marriage between Pipelineistan and Liquid War. It straddles no less than six war zones, ongoing or potential: Nagorno-Karabakh (an Armenian enclave in Azerbaijan); Chechnya and Dagestan (both in Russia); South Ossetia and Abkhazia (both in Georgia); and Turkish Kurdistan.

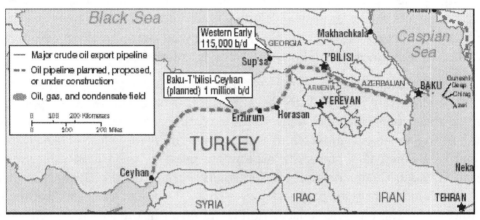

Figure 6. The Baku-Tbilisi-Ceyhan pipeline (Deparment of Energy).

The pipeline itself is only 126 cm wide, a dizzying steel serpent of no less than 150,000 segments made in Japan, finished in Malaysia and delivered by ship to the Georgian port of Batumi, capital of the separatist micro-republic of Ajaria—which is virtually uncontrolled by Tbilisi.

To understand the scope and ambition of BTC we must visit Villa Petrolea, the Baku HQ of BP. BTC's major shareholders are BP (30.1%) and the Azerbaijani state oil company SOCAR (25%), followed by Unocal (U.S., 8.9%), Statoil (Norway, 8.71%), Turkish Petroleum (6.53%), ENI (Italy, 5%), TotalFinaElf (France, 5%), Itochu (Japan, 3.4%), ConocoPhillips (US, 2.5%), Inpex (Japan, 2.5%) and Delta Hess (a joint venture of Saudi Delta Oil with American Amerada, 2.36%). By the mid-2000s BP had invested at least US$ 15 billion in Azerbaijan (exploration, exploitation, pipeline construction). No wonder, according to street wisdom in Baku, the man who really ruled Azerbaijan was David Woodward, BP's chairman, known as "the viceroy," a walking oil atlas with more than three decades working for the company from Scotland to Abu Dhabi and from Alaska to Siberia. Woodward and

BP mercilessly spin that BTC is the cleanest and safest pipeline ever built. Dispossessed Georgian peasants and British NGOs beg to differ.

The British-based BTC campaign stresses that BP extracted no less than an international treaty to back its investment. BTC is subjected to an Inter-Governmental Agreement (IGA) between Azerbaijan, Georgia and Turkey—"but drafted by BP's lawyers," as well as an individual Host Government Agreement (HGA) between each of the three governments and the BP-led consortium. According to BTC Campaign, "these agreements have largely exempted BP and its partners from any laws in the three countries—present or future—which conflict with the company's project plans. The agreements allow BP to demand compensation from the governments should any law (including environmental, social or human rights law) make the pipeline less profitable. The agreements have for these reasons been described by non-governmental organizations as 'colonialist.'"

The BTC campaign also points out that "in the case of Turkey, the country would be effectively divided into three: the area where Turkish law applies; the Kurdish areas under official or de facto military rule; and a strip running the entire length of the country from North to South, where BP is the effective government." Ankara used emergency powers to expropriate peasant land without decent compensation. 3,000 Georgians and 500 foreigners working in the Georgia stretch of BTC complained that their paychecks were sliced. Georgian scientists warned that excavations for the pipeline construction could result in the spread of acute infectious diseases in Georgia. Some Corporatistan assurances were Kafkaesque: among other justifications, BP in Baku said that even in the case of an oil leakage in the Borjomi area there would be no damage to the source of the famous local mineral water— because the pipeline lies 15 km away.

BTC would have been impossible without the usual, strategically positioned U.S.-supported dictator—in this case old, ruthless Caucasus hand Heydar Aliyev, who died in December 2003. A dynastic dictatorship is even better, since his son Ilham became the successor in fraudulent elections in October 2003. It also helped that Ilham, a former playboy and casino owner, happened to be the head of the state oil company, SOCAR. Azerbaijan was never about "liberty and democracy" or color-coded revolutions—failed or otherwise—in the style of Georgia, Ukraine and Kyrgyzstan. Just a few days before BTC's inauguration, Azeri police in Baku beat up and arrested more than 100 opposition protesters demanding "Freedom!" and "Free elections!" This is a regime that according to Transparency International ranks 140th out of 146 in the global perceived corruption index. From Washington's point of view the Aliyev dynasty in Azerbaijan performs the same role as Islam Karimov's in Uzbekistan (at least before Karimov decided to expel the Americans from the Khanabad military base): they are "our" dictators.

Azerbaijan, Georgia and Turkey were all desperate to finish BTC on time. Turkey owed a fortune to the IMF. Georgia survives thanks to American handouts. Azerbaijan at least set up a state Oil Fund to use oil revenues to the benefit of future generations. Very few Azeris believe the Corporatistan myth that BTC will enrich them. Real life in the Caucasus can be found less than one km from downtown Baku: huge families crammed in Soviet-style communal apartments with scarce water and electricity: a case of ethnic populations in the former USSR first excluded by Soviet Liquid War and now capitalist. Azerbaijan could easily be pinned down as a land of rickety Ladas and Volgas crisscrossed by an armada of white BP 4x4s with a satellite dish on top—which allow the HQs either in London or Baku to immediately locate all the troops anywhere in the volatile Caucasus. The only other flourishing industry in the Caucasus, apart from oil, is kidnapping. Not to mention the legendary Kristina, the top belly dancer at the Karavanserai, the favorite restaurant of the oil oligarchy, who is in a class by herself. Hopefully she hasn't retired.

In Georgia the obstacles were more complex than in Azerbaijan. Thus the providential "Rose Revolution" of late 2003 getting rid of Edward Shevardnadze to the benefit of young, photogenic, American-educated and American-aligned Mikhail Saakashvili. The small matter of defending BTC from attacks of alleged al Qaeda-related Chechens holed up in the Georgian mountains remains. But at least protection at the end of BTC in Ceyhan, Turkey is guaranteed: it's not a coincidence that the pipeline ends right next door to the massive American airbase at Incirlik.

As oil geopolitics goes, BTC is a key component in the U.S.'s overall strategy of trying to wrestle the Caucasus and Central Asia away from Russia and bypassing Iranian oil and gas routes. Opportunist Kazakh President Nursultan Nazarbayev, never to skip a beat, has repeatedly announced that Kazakh crude will also flow through BTC before 2010. He even proposed to add Aktau—the Kazakh Caspian oil Mecca—to a new acronym (ABTC?) It's interesting to remember that BP always denied that it needs Kazakh oil to fill its pipeline. The crucial point is how much of its own energy Kazakhstan is willing to export via Baku—and not via Russia. Nazarbayev the opportunist may settle on just enough not to ruffle feathers in Washington.

Everything related to BTC spells tremendous financial and political ambition. It took months to fill the pipeline—and for the supertankers at Ceyhan to be loaded with Caspian crude, thus bypassing the hyper-congested Bosphorus strait. BTC is projected to reach 1 million barrels a day—roughly 1.2% of global production. Compare it with the 500,000 barrels of the Caspian Pipeline Consortium (CPC), which moves crude from Baku to the Russian port of Novorossiysk.

The problem with BTC is that it doesn't make much sense in economic terms. Any serious global oil expert knows the most cost-effective routes from the Caspian are south through Iran or north through Russia. The point has always been power politics. Dick Cheney, already in his previous incarnation as Halliburton CEO, had always been a huge cheerleader for the "strategically significant" BTC.

BTC was only officially inaugurated in July 2006, in a big party in Istanbul. Israel's Energy Ministry was represented; Israel imports 30% of its oil from Azerbaijan. Three months earlier, Turkey and Israel had announced their joint plan to build four underwater pipelines—for oil and gas but also for water from the Tigris and Euphrates and electricity—bypassing both Syria and Lebanon. The overall strategy by then was clear: a U.S./Azerbaijan/Turkey/Israel alliance controlling a key Pipelineistan node of oil and gas to the eastern Mediterranean, now linked to the Caspian, with the intention of exporting at least a substantial amount back to Asia, thus bypassing—once again—Russia and Iran. Officially, BTC would only "channel oil to Western markets." But with Ceyhan soon to be linked to the Trans-Israel Eilat-Ashkelon pipeline, Israel can also become a key player in Pipelineistan, re-exporting Caspian crude from the Red Sea to Asia. This node will be in direct competition with Caspian exports via Russia and Iran.

All over the Islamic world—as well as in most of Western Europe and East Asia—there were few doubts that Osama bin Laden's presence in Afghanistan on 9/11 provided the ultimate excuse for Washington to install a cluster of military bases in Central Asia and the Transcaucasus, a former Soviet sphere. Thus the "war on terror" was never about a "clash of civilizations" between Islam and the West, much less "terrorism." The name of the game, from the beginning, has been Pipelineistan: monster oil Corporatistan profits to be made by controlling Central Asia-Caspian Sea oil and gas, bypassing both Russia and Iran, and exerting extra pressure on China.

"Grand Chessboard" theoretician Zbigniew Brzezinski, in the late 1990s, defined Persian Gulf/Central Asia as the "global zone of percolating violence": he thought it would become "a major battlefield, both for wars among nation-states and, more likely, for protracted ethnic and religious violence." After 9/11 the Pentagon started disseminating the rhetoric of an "arc of instability" running from the Andes in South America through North Africa, the Middle East and into Southeast Asia. Pentagon interference and in some cases intervention is able to make sure this is a self-fulfilling prophecy.

Brzezinski was a BP consultant during the Bill Clinton years. In 1995 he went to Baku himself—on behalf of Clinton—to propel what would become BTC. Brzezinski also sat on the board of the U.S.-Azerbaijan Chamber of Commerce (USACC), whose chairman in Washington was the president of Exxon Mobil Exploration. Other members of the board included the ubiquitous Henry Kissinger and James Baker III, who in 2003 went to Tbilisi to tell Shevardnadze his reign was over. Dick Cheney was also a board member—before he became Vice-President.

The same players are recurrent. The whole U.S. energy strategy is being guided by the notorious Baker report—commissioned by Cheney in 2001. The Baker report stresses "the concentration of resources in the Middle East Gulf region and the vulnerability of the global economy to domestic conditions in the key producer countries." So the big picture, as far as Washington is concerned, is to mould these "domestic conditions" by carrots and by the biggest sticks to be found anywhere. As Larry Everest notes in his book *Oil, Power and Empire*, the Baker report stresses that "more than 90% of the world's proven oil reserves are owned by countries, national oil companies and the Russian oil companies"—an intolerable state of affairs as far as the Pentagon- Corporatistan nexus is concerned.

So it comes as no surprise that the road map for what will happen in the next few years is still Dick Cheney's May 2001 energy report: the strategy is to gain access, leverage, and control of oil and gas from Colombia and Venezuela in South America to Iraq in the Middle East and the Caspian. Thus the American demonization of Hugo Chávez in Venezuela, the fight against FARC in Colombia, the war against Iraq, the push for BTC in the Caspian...

The verdict is open on whether the massive BTC investment will be worth it. Instead of the dreams of a new Kuwait, the Caspian may hold only 32 billion barrels of oil—not much more than the reserves of Qatar, a small Gulf producer.

At an Eurasian Economic Summit in Almaty, Kazakhstan, in 2003, Gian Maria Gros-Pietro, chairman of Italy's ENI, said the Caspian holds 7.8 billion tons of oil. Estimations from different sources run from 13 billion tons to 22 billion tons to even 50 billion tons. For optimistic Kazakh officials they stand at 27.5 billion tons: "If the forecasts are proved, in the nearest future the oil of the Caspian region could make one fifth of the world oil reserves and balance with the reserves of Iraq and Kuwait together."

Kazakhs estimate the Caspian by 2004 was already recovering 4.7 million barrels of oil a day. Saudi Arabia by then recovered 8.1 million barrels a day and Russia 6.3 million. So the Caspian was already positioned in 3rd place, ahead of Iran—4.1 million barrels—and China—2.8 million barrels. Azeri president Ilham Alyev was even more optimistic: he thought that the Caspian could soon be in 2nd place, due to the combined reserves of Azerbaijan, Turkmenistan and Kazakhstan.

Kazakhs are sure the Caspian will become the biggest source of oil not only in the CIS countries but in the whole world. Yet a lot of Pipelineistan is necessary to fulfill the dream. For the moment Caspian oil reaches world markets via only five routes: Baku-Novorossiysk; Tengiz-Novorossiysk; Atyrau-Samara; Neka-Tehran; and finally BTC. The aggregate carrying capacity of these pipelines in 2015 will be 122 million tons—not counting BTC. But production in 2015 will be around 250 to 300 million tons. This means Pipelineistan has to grow exponentially.

Most oil experts agree that the Caspian holds less than 10% of Middle East reserves. In fact, added together, the rest of the world holds only around 53% of the proven reserves of the Middle East. But according to a basket of energy forecasts, by 2050 the Persian Gulf/Caspian Sea will account for more than 80% of world oil and natural gas production. Together, the Persian Gulf and the Caspian may have something like 800 billion barrels of oil and an energy equivalent amount in natural gas. Compare this figure with oil reserves in the Americas and in Europe: less than 160 billion barrels. And they will be exhausted before 2030. No wonder we find everyone and his neighbor haggling at the Pipelineistan bazaar.

Iran insists on an equal division of the Caspian Sea—a formula that would leave each of the five Caspian countries with a 20% share. Azerbaijan, Kazakhstan and Russia favor another mechanism in which Iran would end up with roughly 13%. Nobody knows exactly what Turkmenistan wants, given the total unpredictability of president Saparmurad Niyazov.

Sharing the Caspian territory has been a nightmare. But since May 2003 Azerbaijan, Kazakhstan and Russia have in fact divided the Northern Caspian. Kazakhstan will control 29%, and Azerbaijan and Russia 19% each. Iran and Azerbaijan still haven't reached an agreement: they are wrangling over a yet-to-be developed oilfield known as Alborz in Iran and Alov in Azerbaijan. And both Iran and Turkmenistan are disputing Azerbaijan's possession of three offshore oilfields.

Putin's pipeline chess

The Russian counterpunch to BTC was inevitable. High on the agenda of Russian President Vladimir Putin has always been a constant game of seduction of the E.U. with loads of Caspian oil and Siberian gas—plus nuclear protection—in return for loads of E.U. investment. The Kremlin agenda is to tie up Western Europe—the largest trading bloc in the world—to Russian gas. Once again Western Europe has become the ultimate prize nuclear powers U.S. and Russia are fighting for. From

Washington's point of view, BTC would fit the logic of controlling Western Europe through oil. Not if the Kremlin is able to prevent it. Troubled Yukos was the first Russian company shipping oil directly from Russia to the U.S. The dream was over after the Kremlin intervened; a much better deal would be to sell Russian energy to Western Europe and China.

When Yukos was broken up its jewel of the crown, Yuganskneftegaz, remained a separate state-owned company. The reason was to facilitate Chinese investment. The involvement of China National Petroleum Corporation (CNPC) in what was a de facto re-nationalization of Yukos was unprecedented—considering that the strategic Russian oil industry is extremely protected. CNPC is also involved in several joint ventures with giant Gazprom. And these include a lot of investment in Iran.

Gazprom, with its HQ in Moscow, accounts for no less than 25% of world gas production. It's the world's largest natural gas company. By itself, Gazprom contributes to 8% of Russia's GDP. Along with German companies E.O.N. and BASF, Gazprom is building a US$ 2 billion, 1,200-kilometer pipeline to be finished in 2010, carrying natural gas from Vyborg, near St. Petersburg, under the Baltic Sea to Greifswald in eastern Germany, which will increase the amount of fuel available in Germany by 28%. Former German chancellor Gerhard Schröder was beaming when he signed the agreement alongside Putin, saying that "Germany now secures its energy supply for decades." The pipeline will inevitably be extended to the Netherlands and Britain as well.

Gazprom also wants to build Blue Stream 2, a new pipeline under the Black Sea, to deliver gas not only to Turkey but to Greece and Italy as well; and that would also involve transit countries Bulgaria, Romania, Hungary and Austria. Feasibility studies are already on. The key Pipelineistan node will be a US$ 1 billion, 280-km stretch from the Bulgarian port of Burgas, on the Black Sea, to the Greek Aegean port of Alexandroupolis, to be commissioned by 2009. With this one Russia can export oil to Europe through the Black Sea, totally bypassing BTC.

Turkmenistan holds 20% of the planet's natural gas reserves. But since April 2003, 90% of Turkmen gas exports are in fact under control of—who else— Gazprom. According to a 25-year sweet deal, Gazprom pays US$ 44 for every metric ton, half in cash and half in Russian goods and then re-sells the gas to Turkey for US$ 150 the metric ton, and for Europe for US$ 120. At least that was the situation until a fabulous *coup de theâtre* intervened in 2006, as we will see shortly. Under another contract with Uzbekistan, Gazprom is getting double the volume of Uzbek gas exports in exchange for updating the local gas network. Russia is effectively on its way to creating a "Gas OPEC."

Between China and Japan, the Kremlin chose both—or rather "China first" and then Japan. The construction of the Trans-Siberian oil pipeline started in late 2005 and will finish in 2008. The pipeline will run from Taishet in Siberia to Skovorodino near the Chinese border, and then hit Daqing, in the Chinese province of Heilongjiang. Two-thirds of the oil—of a total of 30 million metric tons a year—will remain in Daqing. The remaining 10 million metric tons will travel by rail to a new port to be built on the Pacific coast near Nakhodka, and then to Japan. According to the Kremlin, the pipeline's final capacity will be 1.2 million barrels a day, more than BTC. From Russia's point of view, this was Christmas in Siberia. Tokyo even offered Moscow to finance the entire construction project, estimated to go over US$ 10 billion. With the added bonus that the whole pipeline—and the control of oil flow—remain with Russia.

The Iranian counterpunch

The black chador-clad secretaries lurking behind rows of flat computer monitors at the Petroleum Ministry building in central Tehran are all smiles. Not to mention their bosses. No wonder. Iran exported at least US$ 60 billion in oil in 2005. With oil hovering around US$ 100 a barrel by 2007, according to a Goldman Sachs report, growth possibilities are endless.

As far as both oil and gas are concerned, Iran has everything going for it: 13% of the world's total fossil fuel reserves (132 billion barrels of crude oil and gas liquids, 27.4 trillion cubic meters of gas), which makes it the second-largest oil-and-gas rich country in the world and second-largest OPEC producer, behind Saudi Arabia.

According to the Petroleum Ministry's own estimates, Iranian oil will last from 70 to a maximum of 86 years while gas may last longer than 200 years. But internal consumption of oil products and gas is growing at a rate of 5.2% a year. The country is already forced to import refined products. That's one of the key reasons, Tehran argues, for its civilian nuclear program.

If the current trends persist, Iran will be forced to suspend its oil exports before 2020. This stunning paradox is caused by a multitude of factors: lack of investment in the maintenance of oil and gas installations; lack of rebuilding of installations destroyed during the 1980s Iran-Iraq war; years of non-relations with foreign companies; terrible management; and crucially, American sanctions.

Iran by the mid-2000s was producing 4.3 million barrels of oil a day. It used to be 6 million barrels a day in 1978, immediately before the Islamic Revolution. According to OPEC's current quota system, Iran will only reach this level again in

2025. The Petroleum Ministry for its part argues that Iran will be producing 7 million barrels a day by 2015.

To increase production and efficiency, estimates by the Office for Planning at the Petroleum Ministry have projected an annual investment of at least US$ 4 billion until 2012. Where will all this money come from? President Ahmadinejad has pledged to favor domestic investors in the oil industry. There are not many, apart from the bureaucracy-infested National Iranian Oil Company (NIOC), the fourth-largest oil major in the world. But every player in the industry at large knows the key for Iran is to be able to attract much-needed foreign investment. The question is how.

As far as the optimistic-sounding Petroleum Ministry is concerned, "the stage has been set for as much exploration as possible for oil and gas in the Persian Gulf and Caspian Sea." This means "introduction of exportable onshore and offshore blocs for the discovery of new oil and gas resources through attraction of foreign capital." Global Big Oil just can't wait to get access to the giant Yadavaran and Azadegan oilfields. Azadegan, with 36 billion barrels of proven reserves, is the largest discovered oilfield in Iran for the past 50 years. Yadavaran, with 17 billion barrels, is capable of producing 300,000 to 400,000 barrels a day.

Just as top officials from Azerbaijan, Georgia and Turkey were opening the much-hyped BTC, Iran started to advertise its counterpunch: an oil pipeline between Iran, Iraq and Syria. True, they are substantially different. BTC will carry Caspian Sea crude to Western Europe, while the Iranian route would initially carry Caspian Sea crude to Asia. But Iran has a tremendous potential to supply Europe as well—as France's TotalFinaElf, Italy's ENI and Anglo-Dutch Royal Dutch Shell know more than anyone. The Iran-Iraq-Syria pipeline arriving at the Syrian port of Ladicia perfectly fits the bill. Iran thus can swap Caspian Sea crude to be refined in the country and then deliver the final product to the Mediterranean. The killer argument: as far as both Asian and European customers are concerned, the cost of using this pipeline route is way lower than using BTC—a fact that even American oil industry insiders recognized long ago.

As much as the Bush administration may have recoiled in horror, regarding this pipeline as an oil version of the axis of evil (or an evil version of the axis of oil), negotiations are ongoing. The pipeline was seriously discussed between Ahmadinejad and Syrian President Bashar al-Assad. Meanwhile Iran and Iraq negotiated for months the construction of a pipeline between Abadan, in southern Iran, and Basra, in southern Iraq, which are practically neighbors. They signed an agreement. The pipeline is a given. Iraq will send crude from Basra to be refined in Abadan, and in exchange will get oil derivatives. Iraq's refineries remain in a disastrous state—and there's no evidence they will be repaired by the Americans anytime soon. Iraq, swimming in oil, by the mid-2000s had to import more than US$ 300 million of oil derivatives every month. Iraq's Shiite-dominated government had no problems agreeing to Iran investing in its petrochemical industry. Tehran insists that despite the appalling Iraqi chaos and the avalanche of pipeline sabotage by Sunni Arab guerrillas, it is fully committed to revitalizing Iraq's petrochemical industry. An oil swap deal between them is inevitable: this way, Iran gets Iraqi crude in Abadan and delivers the same amount to Iraq at its oil terminal on the island of Kharg.

Iran has been swapping oil with Turkmenistan since early 2000—after the Turkmen—against cries of horror from Washington—built a small pipeline to northern Iran. The next inevitable step was to swap with Kazakhstan—negotiations had been going on for years. For this purpose, Iran built a new terminal at the Caspian port of Neka and a new pipeline to Tehran, as well as two new refineries capable of processing 500,000 barrels of Kazakh crude a day.

Alliances may be fleeting in the Caspian. Kazakhstan deals with Iran but at the same time it is Chevron country: the oil giant has invested more than US$ 20 billion in these steppes. As is well known U.S. Secretary of State Condoleezza Rice is a Chevron lady: from 1989 to 1992 she was on the board of directors as the resident Kazakhstan expert.

Kazakhstan's giant Kashagan oil field, the world's largest untapped deposit, was discovered in 2000. It may hold a staggering 38 billion barrels of oil. Kashagan is being developed by a consortium, the North Caspian Production-Sharing Agreement, which includes Royal Dutch Shell, Italy's ENI, France's TotalFinaelf, Exxon Mobil Corp, ConocoPhillips and Japan's Inpex Corp.

The first oil from Kashagan will arrive in 2008. Full production, not before 2010, will reach 1.2 million barrels a day—more than BTC is able to carry. Kazakhstan plans to export 3 million barrels a day of crude by 2015—basically because of Kashagan. This is more than Russia exports today. Kazakhstan would then become one of the world's top exporters. The problem is that for the moment they have only two export routes: Tengiz-Novorossiysk—67 million tons maximum capacity—and Atyrau-Samara—25 million tons maximum capacity after reconstruction, both via Russia.

The 1500 km-long pipeline from Tengiz in the Caspian Sea to the Black Sea port of Novorossyisk is the single largest American investment in the Caspian. The main client is inevitably TengizChevroil, owned by Chevron (50%), ExxonMobil (25%) and Russian and Kazakh partners (25%). Kazakhstan's only outlet to the Russian Transneft system is the Atyrau-Samara pipeline. It's not enough. Kazakhstan desperately needs new pipelines—because crumbling Russian infrastructure restricts Kazakhstan producing and exporting more oil. And Kazakhstan also wants to export its oil to Europe through the Odessa-Brody-Gdansk-Plock pipeline.

Tengiz is being expanded at breakneck pace. Production is doubling already in 2007. Kazakhstan could also export its surplus oil via BTC. That's what Turkey and the U.S. want. Dick Cheney went personally to Astana in May 2006 to perform major lobbying: he wanted the Kazakhs not only to export their oil via BTC but to engage on another proposed Pipelineistan node, this time from Kashagan, across the Caspian to Azerbaijan's Shah Deniz and then to Europe via Georgia—bypassing Russia. Hence the Russian strike to build Blue Stream 2 to deliver to Greece, Bulgaria and beyond. The loser in this equation is another U.S.-backed node, the Albania- Macedonia-Bulgaria pipeline which was already being designed. Russia's pipeline chess inevitably gets the cumulative results it craves: supplying Europe and bypassing BTC.

Kazakhstan is arguably, per capita, the richest country in the whole planet: not only because of oil and gas, but because it inherited more than 60% of all former Soviet mineral resources (at least 80 different types of minerals). In spite of all that, roughly 56% of their 15 million citizens remain poor and invisible to the ballet of Mercedes and Audis of the oil oligarchs in Almaty. Annual GDP per capita is still a meager US$ 3000. The average Kazakh on a salary of US$ 50 a month still has to queue up under the snow waiting for a bus.

Figure 7. Kazakhstan (CIA World Factbook).

Vice Minister of Energy and Mineral Resources Lyazzat Kiinov, speaking at the 11th International Oil and Gas Conference in Almaty, in the fall of 2003, was convinced that "oil production in Kazakhstan will be 2,8 million barrels a day by 2008, and 3.5 million barrels a day by 2015. Kuwait, with its 2 million barrels a day, will be left far behind us." The ambition was, and remains, to more than triple the number of barrels per day Kazakhstan was extracting by the early 2000s.

The myth lingers of Kazakhstan as an immense "new Kuwait" at the heart of the great Eurasian steppes, from the Caspian to western China, from Siberia to the Tian Shan ("Celestial") mountains. President Nursultan Nazarbayev keeps promising an oil boom. Like Mahathir Mohamad in Malaysia with his "Vision 2020," Nazarbayev devised a 2030 economic development strategy. He wants Kazakhstan to be "a Central Asian snow leopard"—a development model for the global South. The transfer of the capital from Almaty to Astana is included in the strategy. Astana is a surrealist off world in the middle of the steppes, sprinkled with architectural wonders like the gleaming Norman Foster-designed pyramid housing the Palace of Peace and Accord. Nazarbayev in the foreseeable future will be on a hunting expedition for at least US$ 70 billion in FDI that Kazakhstan needs to turn its natural riches into palpable wealth—a constant conversation topic among the expat business community in Almaty and Atyrau ("Oil City" and base camp for the monstrous Tengiz oilfield, 350 km south).

Oil matters in Kazakhstan usually follow a Byzantine, long and winding road. Take the case of the Tengiz oil field. The negotiations lasted no less than four years. The joint venture was formalized in 1992. Work on the US$ 2,6 billion pipeline only started in 1997. The pipeline from Tengiz, near the Caspian, to the Russian Black Sea port of Novorossiysk was only ready in December 2001. There are still production capacity delays. Tengiz will reach the mark of 1 million barrels a day only in 2012, according to ChevronTexaco's Eurasian unit.

PetroKazakhstan, which was a Canadian corporation until the Chinese bought it, is very active in the country since 1996 and with very close ties with Nazarbayev. It started cooperating with Russian giant Lukoil to get access to the critical, Russian-dominated Caspian Pipeline Consortium (CPC), whose hub is also in "Oil City" Atyrau, 30 km away from the Caspian shore. The consortium's pipeline also goes west to Novorossiysk. PetroKazakhstan is improving its pipelines from Shimkent, in southern Kazakhstan, to increase its exports to Iran and China. Washington may not like it, but the fact is Nazarbayev wants to explore all possible export routes: east to China, south to Iran, west to Turkey.

Almaty is originally a Silk Road oasis devastated by the Mongols and so "remote" from a Soviet point of view that it was chosen as an exile destination for Trotsky. Appropriately, that's also where the death certificate of the former USSR was signed. At the Kazakhstan Investment Promotion Center (Kazinvest) I learned about the country's many priorities: to explore the Caspian, upgrade refineries, increase oil and gas processing facilities, develop a petrochemical industry, broaden export markets and develop legislation that will attract more investment. Kazinvest of course denies there's too much bureaucracy, too much corruption, and that it takes too long to get anything approved. Business expats think otherwise. They complain of state bureaucratic nightmares and inefficiency—like waiting 20 minutes to cash a check; and they deplore the severe lack of small and medium enterprises and shortage of skilled workers. Kazakhstan still depends on expensive imports. State salaries are a pittance. In Almaty, every car is a potential taxi because there are no jobs.

Decades of demented Soviet practices and avalanches of social cataclysms have cooked up an ethnic mix out of these descendants of Genghis Khan's hordes that is tolerant and frankly globalized: here we find Kazakh vegetarians, Ukrainian Muslims, Russian Buddhists, Uighur Christians, people who have a Kazakh name and look European or look like a Mongol but have a Russian name. They're only two generations away from being nomadic, but visibly, at least in Almaty, are much more stylish, cosmopolitan and cool than any "New Russian." Kazakhs just can't get enough of globalization. Moneychangers in Almaty kiosks will never need to worry: with Tengiz, BTC, Kashagan and the new pipeline to China, rivers of foreign exchange will keep flowing. But the verdict on the snow leopard will be pending—as a model of development or as an authoritarian and corrupt way of wasting the resources of the richest country in the world.

There's no doubt some cities in the Caspian are bound to become world magnets—or at least to recover some of their old glory. Baku's fondest memories are from the golden age when it was "the Kuwait of the Czarist Empire" and "the Paris of the Caspian." The city—with its certified chic CV—now would like nothing more than to celebrate the return of the French branch of the Rothschild family, which had a crucial financial role during the Caspian Belle Époque.

Aktau, cornered between the Caspian and the desert, populated by a drunken pool of Russians, Kazakhs and Caucasians, with its water coming from a nuclear-powered desalinization plant, "attractions" like a huge Lenin statue, a real MiG stuck on a pedestal and literally in the middle of nowhere, looks like a wasteland from an Andrei Tarkovsky movie. Even the monster Tengiz oilfield—operated by the joint venture TengizChevroil—is 200 km northeast. Aktau is not even Kazakhstan's Oil City: that is Atyrau, on the Urals, 350 km north of Tengiz: although Atyrau is not on the Caspian, the Caspian is coming to Atyrau, and the city may be under water by 2050. As for Aktau, it is certain to become a formidable boomtown when Caspian offshore oil exploration starts to pay dividends.

Same for Turkmenbashi, with its clear blue waters (compared to polluted Baku). There are very few Turkmen in this port city: most people are Russian and Azeri. This was a key crossroads when Czarist Russia built the Trans-Caspian railway. Then it was decadence, but now Turkmenbashi is the only port and sea link with Russia and—via the Volga and the sea of Azov—the Black Sea and the Mediterranean. And this is where Turkmenistan's oil and gas reserves are.

In the capital Ashgabat, US$ 1 buys not a bottle of mineral water, but 25 liters of gas. It's the ultimate Corporatistan wet dream. In the markets of Turkmenbashi or Balkanabat, US$ 100 buys one kilo of fresh Beluga caviar straight out of the Caspian. A camel sells for US$ 200, and a tribal wife between US$ 2,000 and US$ 5,000. This desert oasis—sitting on fabulous natural resources—is kept under the strictest surveillance by a wacky Big Brother, Big Father actually: "president for life" Saparmurat Nyazov, the ultimate Asian version of a Sun-King. Thanks to the Sun-King the capital of Turkmenistan—or at least the city center—is modern and as clean as a Dutch hospital. The cool desert climate evokes Arizona or Nevada. Indeed we are in Central Asia's version of Las Vegas—including a strip, Berzengi, with a row of post-anything hotels, actually government guesthouses, all of them empty. At night Ashgabat—"the city of love"—looks like it has sprung up from a Hunter Thompson hallucinogenic fantasy.

Sun-King Nyazov defines himself as Turkmenbashi—"the father of all Turkmen." Genghis Khan and Louis XIV would approve the Turkmenbashi way: there is no opposition, secular or Islamic; no political parties; the media is totally controlled; any group meeting of any kind is forbidden; prison torture is rife; and dissent may be punished by death. In this authoritarian presidentialism—a systemic inheritance from the Soviet Union—coupled with the myth of a strong state, there's no room for ideology. This is radical nationalism embodied by a personality cult which would make any Hollywood—or Washington—spin doctor green with envy. The Turkmenbashi, looking like a chubby Mexican soap opera idol, is ubiquitous in statues, portraits, plaques, outdoors, posters, schoolbooks, always smiling, never threatening like Saddam Hussein or Hafez Assad used to be.

And then there is the *Rukhnama*—subtitled "Reflections on the Spiritual Values of the Turkmen." This is the Turkmenbashi's humble version of the Holy Koran. But it's not a religious book, rather "a systematic worldview, the core of all my political, economic and life targets, with civil content and methods of use in different areas of society," according to the certified English translation by the State Publishing Service. The *Rukhnama* is "the only source that will connect Turkmen's present and its past." And the Turkmenbashi's judgement is final. As he proclaims in the *Rukhnama*, "Turkmen! All my love is for you; all the pain is for me."

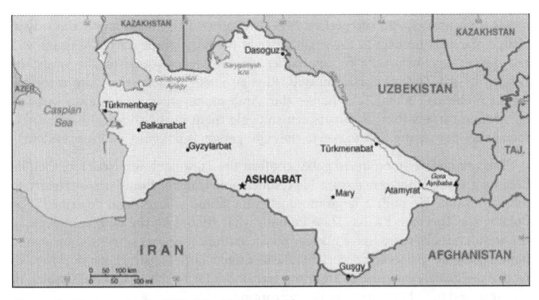

Figure 8. Turkmenistan (CIA World Factbook).

So the *Rukhnama* is now The Word for the 5.500.000 descendants of a formidable race of nomadic horseback warriors who dominated the desert sands for centuries—attacking Silk Road caravans and making incursions to Persia, Afghanistan and Russia to capture slaves. Russian generals who had to fight them during the Great Game described them as the most formidable light cavalry in the world. No wonder: Alexander the Great himself rode a pure bred Akhal Teke horse. Turkmen may belong to 24 tribes, but the political leadership is a monopoly of the two largest, Teke and Yomut.

After independence from the Soviet Union in 1991, the Turkmenbashi vowed this would be "a new Kuwait." Hardly. Although annual GDP per capita is now US$ 5800, roughly 70% of the population lives with around US$ 1 a day. The small wealthy elite, according to a local businessman, consists of "Arabs, the oil and gas people, and high officials." The national currency, the irretrievably unconvertible manat, is a joke. The official exchange rate has always been US$ 1: 5200 manat, because of the hard currency flowing from oil and gas exports. But the real, black market rate is around US$ 1: 22,000 manat.

Tolkuchka—certainly Central Asia's Mother of all Bazaars—is a sprawling Silk Road caravanserai in the outskirts of the city, with containers instead of yurts and Russian techno as the soundtrack. This is where many a foreigner comes in search of the perfect Turkmen carpet. Sometimes the perfect Turkmen carpet can be found in Tolkuchka, sold by lovely Turkmen tribal ladies wearing colorful scarves, loaded with jewelry and carrying those fabulous rug design patterns in their heads and hands for centuries. But the perfect Turkmen carpet will remain home: the lady in charge of export licenses at the small office at the back of the Carpet Museum will not deliver any document to any carpet older than 30 years—or she would be hanged by the Turkmenbashi himself. Russian residents joke there are three big export problems : Akhal Teke horses (but Arab money always finds a way around it); ancient carpets (but diplomats can smuggle them in their luggage); and Turkmen girls ("but paying US$ 50,000 to the right person is possible," quips a resident).

Russian businessmen in Ashgabat confirm the Turkmenbashi "was red, then he became green"—a reference from his chameleonic transfer from Party secretary to pious Muslim. He built a large mosque in his home village—and described it as holding the Turkmen Kaaba. Then he built what should be the biggest mosque in the world: it looks more like a nuclear power station. Russians agree that instead of building marble palaces the Turkmenbashi should rather instruct his ministers to repave the ghastly main roads from the Uzbek border in the east to the Caspian in the west, and to fight rampant police corruption.

The Turkmenbashi knows very well how strategically located Turkmenistan has survived everything—from Alexander the Great to Genghis Khan, from Timur to the bloodthirsty emirs of Bukhara, from the Russian protectorate to Stalinism. A few hours away, on the other side of the Kopet Dag mountains which preside over Ashgabat under the desert sky is Mashhad, the sacred city of Shiite Iran welcoming pilgrims from all over Central Asia visiting the tomb of Imam Reza, the eighth successor of Imam Ali. To the south, the Iran-Afghan border is only 8 hours away by Lada. And 8 hours away to the west is the Caspian sea: with 21 trillion cubic meters of reserves, Turkmenistan is the third- largest producer and the second-largest exporter of natural gas in the world.

The Turkmenbashi is understandably proud of his gas republic. But he also knows that the way out of being landlocked and dependent on Russia is to the south, via Iran. A swap deal has been in place since the early 2000s whereby Iran sells gas extracted from the Persian Gulf in Turkmenistan's name and Ashgabat exports gas to Iran's northeast. Not by accident Turkmen bazaars are filled with Iranian merchandise—from silk stockings to Cola.

But Russia constantly keeps up the pressure: the Gazprom nation insists Turkmen gas has to be exported to other CIS countries and eventually to Europe through the Russian pipeline system—and a price war is always on. Most CIS countries are virtually broke. As they keep not paying their bills Ashgabat is constantly forced to turn off the tap.

The Turkmenbashi has the luxury to diversify by choosing among three main options: a pipeline to Iran, and then to Turkey and Western Europe; the Trans-

Afghan Pipeline (TAP) through Afghanistan to Pakistan and eventually India; and a crucial pipeline to China, which will be on in 2009. In April 2003 the Turkmenbashi and Chinese President Hu Jintao signed a monster deal under which China will buy 30 billion cubic meters of Turkmen gas for 30 years.

The Russian checkmate came in early September 2006. After months of hard-core haggling Gazprom finally accepted the 40% price increase demanded by the Turkmenbashi for his gas. What the Russia/ Gazprom nation got in return for this US$ 16 billion deal was absolutely priceless: control of all of Turkmenistan's gas surplus up to 2009. Plus the Turkmenbashi certifying his preference for Russia to tap the new Yoloten gas fields. Plus the definitive Caspian Beluga washed up with Cristal: the Turkmenbashi saying he was out of any future Trans-Caspian pipeline project (Dick Cheney was killing for this one). In a press conference in Ashgabat, the Turkmenbashi was adamant: "First of all, we will be supplying gas to Russia...Do not think that Turkmenistan wants to go elsewhere with its gas." The marriage between the Gazprom nation and the gas republic was sealed with a kiss.

D.O.A., in fact dead even before arrival, is TAP—the Trans-Afghan Pipeline from Turkmenistan to Pakistan and probably India, the (invisible) star of the show in the ongoing Afghan docudrama of Taliban get to power/Taliban bombed to rubble/Taliban want power again. TAP had been officially approved by Nyazov, Hamid Karzai and Musharraf in late 2001, but everybody knows Karzai is unable "to rule even over his own chair," as they say in Kabul. Washington's plan was to seduce Nyazov to provide Turkmen gas to BTC. Russia checkmated Washington. D.O.A., also by extension, is the U.S. grand strategy of a "Greater Central Asia" centered on Afghanistan and India.

End result of these moves in Russia's pipeline chess: Western Europe ever more dependent on Russia (and Central Asian) gas delivered only by Russian pipelines. And a perfect hand for Russia to negotiate a "strategic partnership" with the E.U.

The Turkmenbashi's foreign policy is infinitely less wacky than we might infer from the main character's antics. The crux is neutrality, symbolized, most appropriately, by the 75 m-high white marble Arch of Neutrality which stands in central Ashgabat, with a golden statue of—who else—the Turkmenbashi on top, saluting with open arms the mountains and his people. The arch rests on a three-legged base—a Turkmenbashi idea to prove the resilience of the traditional Turkmen cooking pot tripod.

The neutrality policy in theory protects Turkmenistan from heavy Russian interference and meddling by other Central Asian neighbors, but progressively isolates the country even more. It has its merits though. When the Taliban were in power in Afghanistan, the Turkmenbashi kept relations with both the Pakistan-backed

Taliban and the Russian-and-Iranian-backed Northern Alliance. With this coup, Turkmen political dissidents and agents of radical Islam could not find exile in Afghanistan. Nowadays there is absolutely no sign of underground radical Islam inside Turkmenistan. And the political opposition is actually exiled in Moscow.

So the Turkmenbashi should not be so paranoid about stability. Moreover, with a population 82% Turkmen and only 3% Russian, this is the most ethnically homogeneous Central Asian republic. Its borders are relatively safe. Which leads us to the free trade problem. The Uzbek border should be the most strategic in the New Silk Road—where merchandise from Turkey and Iran reach most of Central Asia. But that's not exactly the case.

From an administrative and political point of view, the former USSR identified Central Asia to four republics—Uzbekistan, Turkmenistan, Kyrgyzstan and Tajikistan—which corresponded to the Persian Transoxiana, and to the Arab "beyond the river," meaning the two *darya* ("sea," or "river," in Persian), the Amu-Darya (the ancient river Oxus) and the Syr-Darya. Political destiny added Kazakhstan to these four republics. In a broader sense, Central Asia is inserted in the Turco-Persian civilization which was the matrix of cultures and languages from Istanbul to Delhi and from Esfahan to Bukhara. This meant Turkish emirs, Persian administrators and until the Iranian schism in the early 16th Century, Sunni Islam of the Hanafi branch. But from a dialect to another, from dark blue to turquoise ceramic, from a musical mode to a slower variation, there were never absolutely defined borders — until these young nations popped up at the end of the 20th Century. Until 1994, the Uzbek-Turkmen border was nothing more than a table and a chair stuck in the wilderness. Now it's a full-fledged border filled with suspicious officials, endless controls and a 2 km no man's land in between that even local people have to walk through.

Is there life after Turkmenbashi? Nobody even dares to think about it in Ashgabat. Businessmen risk saying that Niyazov's son is unlikely to inherit the playground. Russians with a Turkmen passport fear ultra-nationalism will drive them away. Zoroastrianism may have been born in Khorezm—the Turkmen region that gave algebra to the world. Mazdeism—Zoroaster's religion—was the official religion of the Sassanid empire until the 8th Century Islamic conquests. The Chinese—who came in contact with it traveling on the Silk Road—called it "cult of the celestial God of Fire." The Turkmenbashi may not be the holder of divine fire. But his benevolent reign may not be the worst of destinies for the young gas republic— if only he learned to distribute the fruits of its new wealth. Anyway, if everything goes wrong, one can always find solace by reading the *Rukhnama*.

The Golden Gate of the New Silk Road

Iran already trades its own Persian Gulf crude in return for Caspian oil from Russia and Central Asia. The 300 km-long Neka-Tehran pipeline is crucial in this process. Iran has done everything to position Neka-Tehran as an extremely seductive—and cheap—route compared to BTC. When Kashagan explodes in the market in 2008 Neka-Tehran, as an export channel, will also boom.

Non-biased oil and gas experts agree that Iran beats the competition hands down as the best route to link Central Asia with the global market, as well as the shortest route for any country to reach Central Asia. The railway distance to China is enormous—as well as the costs of building pipelines. Afghanistan is immersed in permanent war. All the existing communication and transportation network—from railways to pipelines—in Central Asia go north via Russia, but the Russian railway system is a crumbling mess.

Pipelineistan's greatest hit in the Caspian, from Iran's point of view, starts in Kazakhstan along the eastern Caspian shore, through Turkmenistan, crossing to eastern Iran, and down to Bandar Abbas. Any official at the Petroleum Ministry or at NIOC in Tehran will recite the same mantra: Iran can get Caspian crude to any market at a fraction of the price of BTC. And there's absolutely nothing Washington can do about it. As Mahmood Khagani, a former Iranian director for Caspian affairs used to say, "the 'golden gate' from the Caspian Sea to the Persian Gulf is now open."

Iran has set its laser eyes on Asia. The overlapping interests with China could not be more evident, as Beijing's ultimate dream is to consolidate a New Silk Road from the Caspian to China allowing the Middle Kingdom full, non-stop access to both the Middle East and the heart of Eurasia.

China imports nearly 50% of its oil, mostly from the Middle East. The Iraq war was a graphic demonstration to the leadership in Beijing that Washington will pull no punches to control and militarize whatever of the world's major oil and gas sources it may land its hands on. So inevitably for China Central Asia and the Caspian became absolutely crucial. According to China's Ministry of Finance, by 2010 China will be importing 120 million tons of oil a year—double what it imported in 2002. By 2045, still it will be importing 45% of the oil it needs.

Thus a pipeline from Kazakhstan to Xinjiang, western China—the US$ 700 million, 1,300-kilometer Atasu-Alashankou pipeline, totally financed by the Chinese—became an absolute priority. By 2011 the pipeline will have a 3,000 km extension to Dushanzi, where the Chinese are building a monster oil refinery to be finished by

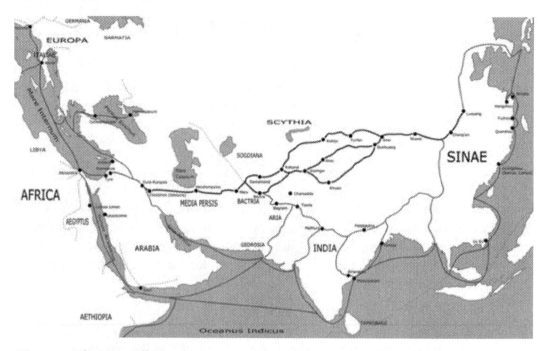

Figure 9. The New Silk Road

2008. Kazakh crude will then be pumped to the highly industrialized Chinese east coast. In 2005 China's CNPC state oil company bought PetroKazakhstan for US$ 4.2 billion. So the Chinese will also be actively involved in developing oil fields in Kazakhstan.

China roared into Pipelineistan with a bang and an even bigger bang—reaching both the Caspian and the Persian Gulf. First it was the US$ 3.5 billion China-Kazakhstan pipeline deal. Then it was the US$ 100 billion, "deal of the century" gas agreement between Beijing and Tehran, which will reach US$ 200 billion when a similar oil agreement is signed. Iran will export 10 million tons of liquefied natural gas (LNG) a year from its Yadavaran field for a 25-year period while China's state oil company Sinopec will invest in exploration, drilling, petrochemical and gas industries, pipelines and services in Iran. And we should not forget that China also made that double deal with Russia for an oil and natural gas pipeline from Siberia to Heilongjiang in Northeast China, to be finished by 2008.

Sooner rather than later Iran will join the Shanghai Cooperation Organization (SCO), which means it will be a de facto member of the Asian Energy Security Grid—which doubles as a geostrategic axis configured as an extremely significant counter power to the U.S. Both Russian and Chinese strategic thinkers view the Islamic Republic of Iran as the absolute key watchtower in the post-Cold War world against real or perceived U.S. hegemonic designs.

Iran is also extremely active in the South Asian front. Bush administration pressure notwithstanding, Iran, India and Pakistan started trilateral negotiations in late 2005 on the mammoth, US$ 7.2 billion Iran-Indian pipeline, dubbed for a while "the peace pipeline." India was considering three proposed pipelines from Iran, Qatar and Turkmenistan, but by Autumn 2005 its deal with Iran was already a certainty, according to India's petroleum minister Mani Shankar Aiyar. This pipeline should run 1115 km in Iran, 705 km in Pakistan and 850 km in India.

Jumpin' South Pars, it's a gas, gas, gas

The pillar of Iran's gas program is the gigantic offshore South Pars field—on the Persian Gulf, 300 km from Bushehr and 580 km from Bandar Abbas—which by itself contains no less than 9% of the world's proven reserves. It's a geological extension of Qatar's North Field. South Pars is Iran's top energy project. Up to 2006 more than US$ 15 billion were invested on it. Natural gas from North Pars, an independent field, will be shipped north of the country via a planned 56-inch, 480-km, US$ 500 million pipeline. But a substantial part of South Pars production will be exported as liquefied natural gas (LNG), which will convert Iran in one of the world's top exporters of LNG. South Pars could earn Iran as much as US$ 11 billion a year over 30 years, according to the Petroleum Ministry. Tehran wants the Pars Special Econo-Energy Zone, established in 1998, to become "one of the most important industrial energy poles of the Middle East."

According to Gholamreza Manouchehrie, CEO of PetroPars Co., not all of its 19 blocks have been negotiated for exploration. Iranian participation stands at 60%. Joint ventures are common; for instance, the LNG operation is shared at 50% each by NIOC, the Iranian state oil company, and TotalFinaElf. But much more foreign investment is needed. "We are 10 years behind Qatar," says Manouchehrie, referring to the neighboring gas emirate. "There is cooperation between our experts, and it's still not enough. But we will catch up with them in production by 2012."

South Pars' enormous strategic importance is that its production will be exported to Asia—after the construction of the "peace pipeline," pumping 150 million cubic meters of gas a day. Manouchehrie recalls that "this pipeline controversy has been going on for 10 years. Now it's a compelling geoeconomic reality. China wants to be a beneficiary. And for Asia, it's the most feasible and the most cost-effective way."

The pipeline should be concluded by the summer of 2011. According to Seyyed Alavi, an Iranian oil executive, "Pakistan needs to build 1000 km of 48-inch pipeline, plus the infrastructure, and India needs to build 600 km." Farshad Tehrani, another

Iranian oil executive based in Norway, is in favor of the project being called Iran Pakistan India Pipeline (IPIL), a joint venture with a cross-section of ownership. Tehrani finds many reasons for India and Pakistan to switch from oil to gas: they reduce their oil imports; they opt for cleaner fuel; and they save foreign currency. For Iran, it's also inevitably about geoeconomic power: "Iran is the only country in the world with more than 15 neighbors. Iran wants to be a true regional power—we are in West Asia after all. Besides, all our neighbors can swap gas with Iran as well."

Rafiullah Azmi from the Institute of Islamic Studies in New Delhi stresses that IPIL will reach way beyond South Asia—offering a vital link between the Persian Gulf, Central Asia, South Asia and China and thus "it goes against the geopolitical game of the U.S. in the Persian Gulf." So basically why is Washington so much against it? "The Americans feel it will help Iran; it will set dangerous precedents for other countries to buy gas from Iran; and it will cement friendly ties between Iran, India and Pakistan." Tehrani says that "it goes back to Bill Clinton, when he said that you're free to buy energy from anywhere, as long as it's not from Iran." Azmi for his part stresses that India is creating "a multitude of options" for its energy needs—from nuclear to gas. Nuclear power in 2010 will attend to no more than 10% of India's requirements. Azmi is convinced "geoeconomics will triumph over geopolitics."

Turkey for the moment is the only importer of Iranian gas, according to the International Affairs bureau at the Petroleum Ministry. But this is about to change—and radically, and not only because of China. Iran's gas exports to Europe—estimated to be 300 billion cubic meters annually—will start most probably in 2009. A gas pipeline to Greece via Turkey is already in construction, but Iran can also use a different route through Bulgaria and Romania. As the need for Iranian gas is more than pressing, the list of Western European buyers is inevitably huge.

Turkey wants to buy gas from Iran and sell it to Europe. But Iran wants to skip the middleman. So the Iranian option is to go through the Ukraine. A cooperation agreement was signed between Tehran and Kiev. Then they started discussing the volume of gas to be exported. Iran, Ukraine, Armenia, Georgia and Russia are involved in the project. According to Iranian Deputy Oil Minister for International Affairs Mohammad-Hadi Nejad-Hosseinian, Ukraine has proposed two pipeline routes to Iran: number one is Iran-Armenia-Georgia-Russia-Ukraine-Europe, and number two Iran-Armenia-Georgia-Black Sea-Ukraine-Europe.

Former Ukraine Prime Minister and billionaire petite blonde Yulia Timoshenko, known in Ukraine as the "gas princess" because of her dodgy operations with former Ukraine Energy Minister Pavlo Lazarenko and Gazprom, will be instrumental in the Ukrainian equation. The Orange revolution is a thing of the past.

What interests Timoshenko is a new oil and gas pipeline from the Caspian across Ukraine into Poland, which would detach Kiev from Moscow. The country gets 80% of its energy from Russia. For this pipeline, Timoshenko negotiates with Chevron, which happens to be Condoleezza Rice's territory. At the same time the state company Naftogaz Ukrainy (NAK) discusses with France's Gaz de France to build the gas pipeline from Iran.

Even before the sealed-with-a kiss-deal between the Gazprom nation and the Turkmenbashi the Trans-Afghan Pipeline (TAP) had disappeared like a mirage, obliterated by the booming comeback of the Taliban, although an agreement between Turkmenistan, Afghanistan and Pakistan was signed in the Spring of 2006, with India as an observer. The US$ 2 billion, 1500-km TAP would link Dauletabad in southwest Turkmenistan to the Pakistani port of Gwadar in the sea of Oman, crossing Afghanistan via Kandahar. Since 2002 Hamid Karzai had hoped that Pipelineistan investment would be his sure fire card to make a quick buck and stabilize unruly Afghan provinces (that is, virtually half of the country). But there's no way Karzai or any amount of NATO troops would be able to guarantee security to contractors and operators against a Taliban guerrilla in incandescence all over the south and southeast. No major investors had entertained the folly of being interested in TAP. And TAP would only be viable if it was extended to India.

As much as the chaos in Afghanistan it was the reliability of the Turkmenbashi that was in question. Turkmenistan had signed multiple contracts—especially with Russia and the Ukraine, but there's no guarantee it will be able to supply all of its customers. Both India and Pakistan may need more than two pipelines for their needs. With TAP discarded that would mean IPIL plus another US$ 2,7 billion project from Qatar via Oman to Pakistan and then India.

Tamine Adeebfar, analyst at the Caspian Energy Politics in Brussels, expects the Middle East to supply energy to East Asia for nearly a century. There's total interdependence, but everything "needs to be anticipated and planned now." This has been dawning on the Iranians.

Iranian oil executives Alavi and Tehrani make two important points—both of them related to the urgency of foreign and local direct investment in its gas industry. Iran still cannot compete with Russia in exporting gas to Europe—one of its priorities for the 21st Century. And incredible as it may seem, Iran still imports gas from Turkmenistan—even though it holds the second-largest gas reserves in the world.

The E.U. would love nothing better than to free itself from the Russian bear hug and also buy gas from Iran. With Central Asian gas out of the picture, the only other serious way out would be Qatar. But Pipelineistan from Qatar to Western Europe means crossing Saudi Arabia and Iraq—an absolute impossibility. Iran, though concentrating on Asia, wants by all means to massively export to the E.U. Pipelineistan in this case is more sensible—via Turkey and the southern Caucasus.

The strategic implications of the Gazprom nation sort of "taking over" Central Asian gas are immense, and obviously reverberate in the ultra-sensitive Iran nuclear dossier. Iran and Russia are in fact two competing suitors for the E.U. bombshell bride. The bride is about to marry Russia but she always had a crush on Iran. There's some fatality about the marriage that makes the bride weep in despair. But there's not much anyone can do about it, much less the bride's distant cousin, the U.S. This spills out to how each of these players regard the Iranian nuclear "problem." Russia wants a peaceful settlement, but above all wants to keep the marriage intact. Iran wants a peaceful settlement as a preamble for, who knows, she may be able one day to spoil the marriage.

Who will profit from Iraq's oil?

The future of Iraqi oil revolves around one acronym: PSA.

Production share agreements (PSAs), such as in Kazakhstan, essentially mean that a government may own its oil and gas, at least technically, but who's really raking the bucks is Big Oil Corporatistan. PSAs apply mostly to countries where extracting oil costs a lot of money (not the case in Iraq, where the production cost of a barrel is a mere US$ 1) or with small reserves (again, not the case in Iraq). PSA is a very sweet deal: applied to Iraq, that is the most delicious chocolate mousse on the planet. Not that Iraqis will have a taste.

Iraq, with its oil industry nationalized by Saddam Hussein in 1972, holds the world's second-largest known oil reserves (at least 115 billion barrels). Unexplored oil fields account for roughly 60% of Iraq's known reserves. Only the al-Majnoon megafield holds an estimated 20 billion barrels by itself. If Exxon Mobil, for instance, "got" al-Majnoon its global reserves would instantly double. Imagine the profits with a barrel at US$ 100. Thus the Holy Grail in Iraq is not "democracy" or "defeating the insurgency": it's PSAs for Big Oil Corporatistan. The US$ 1 trillion question is which Iraqis would be willing to hand over their oil this way. One is already guaranteed: corrupt, double-dealing President and former Kurdish warlord Jalal Talabani, who will do whatever Washington—and its Green Zone fortress— say. Iran may advise the Shiites not to commit this folly—and that's one of the key reasons for Washington's demonization of Tehran. But ultimately this is an Iraqi decision. Or is it?

Iraq's oil union—the General Union of Oil Employees (GUOE)—is firmly against the sellout. *Crude Designs* is a crucial report available on the www.carbonweb.org website by the U.K.-based NGO Platform. The report stresses that at least 64% of Iraq's reserves may be gobbled up by Big Oil Corporatistan; it also conservatively estimates, assuming oil at US$ 40 a barrel, that during the 25-to-40-year span of secret and unalterable PSAs Iraq may lose from US$ 74 billion to US$ 194 billion ("between two and seven times the current Iraqi state budget"). And about all those profits: the report makes the crucial point that rates of return for Big Oil may reach from 42% to 162%.

In pure Liquid War fashion Iraq was starved and decimated by 12 years of U.N. sanctions. It was Shocked and Awed into oblivion. Then one of its provisional "governments" on the road to "democracy" asked the IMF—i.e., an arm of the U.S. Treasury Dept.—for a US$ 685 million loan to rebuild what the U.S. shocked and awed. The IMF—true to form—inevitably forced Iraq to scrap oil subsidies and privatize the economy. With unemployment at around 70% the only way millions of Iraqis were surviving was thanks to food and fuel subsidies. The IMF's "structural adjustment" also means, on a much serious scale, the dismantling of essential social services in Iraq where under Saddam oil money paid for some of the best hospitals and universities in the Middle East. For instance, my translator during the 2003 U.S. invasion was a bright young Jordanian whose father had sent him to study civil engineering in Baghdad.

Now, on top of all that grief, Iraqis have to hand over their oil. Meanwhile a lot of the US$ 16 billion in Iraqi money destined for "reconstruction" simply evaporated—like those US$ 8.8 billion when viceroy Paul Bremer was still the head of the rapacious Coalition Provisional Authority (CPA), not to mention the free-for-all distributed to private "security" mercenaries. Iraq is in deep debt. Greg Muttitt from Platform is correct when he argues that "Iraq's debt will [likely] be used to force the government to sign PSAs" with Big Oil Corporatistan.

From Big Oil Corporatistan's point of view, the road to the Babylon Holy Oil Grail will be fraught with disasters. Arabs, Turkmen, Assyrians, Bedouins and Chammars will fight to the death in case there's some form of ethnic cleansing in Kirkuk. The proposed pipeline from Kirkuk to Haifa (the new Rotterdam) in Israel, in view of the Sunni Arab guerrilla's attacking record, will be virtually unprotectable.

Syria closed the pipeline Kirkuk-Baynas in 1982 when it was supporting Iran in the war against Iraq. That's why Israel wants regime change in Damascus: to build one of two pipelines—either a Mosul-Haifa pipeline or a section linking Haifa to a reopened Kirkuk-Baynas. A U.S.-aligned Iraq Kurdistan implies ethnic cleansing clearing the way for full exploitation of Kirkuk oil and gas. There will be a crucial referendum on Kirkuk in December 2007. If the Kurds try to expel the Turkmen, Turkey will go ballistic. Turkish nationalists may not like it one bit, but a sure fire secret passage for Turkey to enter the E.U. with minimum hassle would be to accede to one of Washington's whims: a semi-autonomous Turkish Kurdistan with a smooth link to independent Iraqi Kurdistan. This would mean an oil-rich, pro-Washington, free Kurdistan with a population of 25 to 35 million people—larger than today's Iraq—and converted into the 6th largest oil power in the world.

Borders may change in the Middle East when oil is at stake. Ever since the dream of a unified Arab nation was betrayed by the Sykes-Picot agreement, every-thing that happened was connected to oil: the fake borders drawn by colonial powers Britain and France; the parade of puppet/client "governments"; the birth of OPEC; the rise of political Islam; the U.S. mad rush to control Cheney's "big prize." For Big Oil Corporatistan—like Exxon Mobil or Chevron—what really matters is reserves as part of their assets. There could not be anything juicier at this stage than to own reserves in Iraq.

In an April 26, 2006 report *The Economist* argued that the "global oil industry is on the verge of a dramatic transformation from a risky exploration business into a technology-intensive manufacturing business." These were actually the words of Big Oil itself, via Chevron P.R. "The product that big oil companies will soon be manu-facturing," *The Economist* added, is "greener fossil fuels." Shell, for instance, is already blending diesel with a clean new hybrid of diesel and natural gas (gas-to-liquids, or GTL). Others will be blending diesel with ethanol and biodiesel.

That's inevitable. Big Oil needs to find other ways to make money. Astronomic profits for Big Oil only apply when Big Oil controls oil fields—and new oil fields are getting scarcer by the day, from super giant fields like Ghawar in Saudi Arabia (5 million barrels a day) and Kashagan in Kazakhstan to their smaller cousins. It's by owning oil fields that Exxon Mobil's 2005 profit can reach US$ 32 billion, the largest single profit in the history of Corporatistan—the U.S. branch.

Contrary to renowned Irish geologist Dr. Colin Campbell's predictions, *The Economist* report argues that Peak Oil is not happening. Dr. Campbell, arguably the world's top oil depletion expert, since the late 1990s has been predicting that world oil production would peak in the early 21st Century. Not so fast, cried *The Econo-mist*: production might actually "increase by as much as 15 million barrels a day between 2005 and 2010—equivalent to almost 18% of today's output and the biggest surge in history over the next few years," according to data by the Cambridge Energy Research Associates (CERA), an energy consultancy. For the United States

Geological Survey (USGS) the world must hold some 3 trillion barrels of recoverable oil. For the USGS the Peak will happen beyond 2025. The IEA places it after 2030.

Big Oil also says there won't be Peak Oil anytime soon, or "in decades to come," according to Exxon Mobil P.R. Peak Oil students won't be easily convinced, stressing that the world is already consuming two to three barrels of oil for every barrel of new oil that is found. Some analysts contend that by 2015 the gap between demand and existing production will be so huge that the world economy may collapse. Dr. Campbell is the founder of the Association for the Study of Peak Oil & Gas, whose illuminating website www.peakoil.com discusses in intricate detail the facts involved in the approaching end of Pipelineistan as we know it.

The absolutely crucial point for the moment is that essentially Big Oil is barred from owning oil fields in Russia and most OPEC countries—occupied Iraq included. Non-OPEC oil production may peak as early as 2010. To make matters worse energy investment banker Matthew Simmons argues in his book *Twilight in the Desert* that the Saudis are overproducing their fields; this causes a rupture in the continuity of the oil-bearing strata, with the result that part of the reserves are permanently unrecoverable. Simmons essentially argues that the Saudi oil fields will collapse— that is, a permanent loss, globally, of 9.5 million barrels of oil a day. That's not how the Saudis see it. Saudi Arabia's oil minister, Ali Naimi, has repeatedly promoted an unexplored area on the Iraqi-Saudi border the size of California that could yield at least an extra 200 billion barrels.

But Peak or no Peak, one thing is certain: if China is to become as industrialized as the U.S. (that's the Beijing collective leadership dream anyway), there won't be enough oil for everybody. At least for the near future the West may count on being supplied by plenty of Caspian oil and gas. Hopefully the Caspian seal will not be extinct by then, and the seven kinds of Caspian sturgeon—victims of indiscriminate poaching, illegal production and export of caviar, pollution and the rising level of the Caspian—will be finally protected by the Convention on International Trade of Endangered Species.

Wishful thinking would see harmony between Russia, Iran, the U.S. and China all engaged in a sensible exploitation of Central Asia's natural wealth. This would lead to economic development everywhere and eventually more political freedom. It doesn't look like it's going to be this way. The perception in Islam, in the Chinese universe and in the Russian sphere is that the U.S. used and continues to use the Long War to exclusively advance its own strategic oil and gas interests. This is a recipe for disaster. The China-Russia-Iran-India Asian Energy Security Grid is a decisive counterpunch to Washington's global ambitions.

Geopolitically, as a key energy supplier to China as well as India's major supplier, Iran will be in a more than enviable position. Its political relations with both China and India are excellent. Its trans-Caspian alliance with Russia is strong, as both countries are set, in diplomatic language, not to allow "another great foreign power" to penetrate the Caspian. And even if that brings friction with Russia, Tehran will do all it takes to position itself, long-term, as a key supplier to Western Europe as well. This scenario implies a peaceful, non-confrontational solution to the Iranian nuclear issue is in the interest of all players involved. But not necessarily in the interest of neocon armchair warriors.

~ 4 ~

CORPORATISTAN: THE DUBAI POST-OIL DREAM

The ultimate sociopolitical model for the 21st Century is a *Blade Runner*-esque melting pot of neo-liberalism and "subterranean" economy, Sunni Arab Islam and low taxes, souks and artificial islands—a giant warehouse *cum* tourist paradise where life on the fast lane gleefully coexists with post-modern slavery. The model spells out an apolitical, consumer-mad, citizenship-free society, ideal for the nomad elites of global liquid modernity. In sum: a Corporatistan dream (No taxes! Free repatriation of profits!)

Dubai, pop. 700,000 by the mid-2000s, a true Warehouse of Babel, is a self-described "door to a market of more than 1 billion consumers." Its megalomaniac desire is to fashion itself not only as the first post-oil economy in the Persian Gulf but as one of the Top 5 postmodern world cities. Dubai represents the essence of Globalistan at work: globalization as the ineluctable triumph of Western *laissez faire*; world trade as the definition of democracy; and the economy always trumping all things political.

In 1971 Bedouin Sheikh Zayed bin Sultan al-Nahyan founded the Persian Gulf nation United Arab Emirates (UAE)—a confederation of hereditary monarchies composed of seven city-states roughly the size of Portugal. When he died in early November 2004 he was a multibillionaire owner of banks, industries and villas on Spain's Costa del Sol and Switzerland's Lake Geneva. But he still preferred falcon hunting and camel racing to being an Arab version of the Rothschilds. Most of all he had every reason to be proud of his family's intuition and business acumen—as already in the 1940s they had decided to drain Dubai's port while competitors were still counting dates. And he was certainly proud of the way Dubai had evolved, a Hong Kong-by-the-desert with loads of glitz, the second-highest water consumption level in the world just behind the U.S., no "war on terror" and, of course, no free elections. Sheikh Zayed was promised as he lay dying that Dubai would continue to flourish—even without gambling casinos, although few schemes could be more enticing for casino sharks than an Arab Vegas in Arabia.

During the Middle Ages, Gulf port cities were the essential node in the Arabic peninsula's monopoly on trade between Europe and Southeast Asia. Today, Dubai as a city-state/world port city by the "Arabian Sea" (locals wouldn't be caught dead referring to the "Persian Gulf") is positioning itself as the essential trade crossroads between Europe, Africa, the Middle East and the Indian subcontinent. The richest of the seven city-states in the UAE may be the capital, Abu Dhabi, floating on a sea of oil; as late as 1962, when oil started to be pumped, there was no electricity of telephones. But 63% of the country's income by the mid-2000s already derived from commerce and tourism, and the bulk transits through Dubai.

In this turbo mish-mash of Vuitton-carrying Arab women covered in silk black chadors, Indian families in saris, young poseurs with Iranian pop T-shirts, armies of men in *dishdashas* and fake gold Rolexes, phalanxes of Japanese minibuses and South Korean vans, and the frenzy of trading simultaneously in English, Arabic, Bengali, Urdu, Turkish, Farsi, Russian, German, Tagalog, Thai, Gujarati, Afrikaans, Swahili and 50 other languages, the lingua franca is inexorably English, not Arabic. As much gold as is extracted all over the world transits every year through Dubai, legally or through smuggling.

Only 25% of the multicultural 2.4 million people living in the UAE are citizens—or "nationals," as they are known in local lingo. In Dubai they represent only 15%. Dubai may be run like a Corporatistan dream. But unlike a Triad multinational, which perpetually delocalizes to profit from cheap labor, Dubai imports cheap labor in droves. The result is immigration without citizenship—a model that absolutely fascinates apostles of neo-liberalism, with the added bonus that unlike Mexicans and Central Americans in the U.S., immigrants to Dubai totally renounce their political rights in the altar of economic Big Time. Neo-liberalism always refers to Dubai as proof that Islam is not incompatible with globalization.

It's fair to argue what distinguishes a citizen from a non-citizen in a state where simply there's no democracy at all. The absolute ruler, Crown Prince Sheik Mohammed bin-Rashid al-Maktoum's power could be defined as Genghis-Khan-like. Only a dozen tribes control power in the whole Emirates. But when you're an over-ambitious immigrant coming from Iran's theocratic nationalism, India's bureaucratic nightmare or the dictatorship in Musharrafstan, the last thing you'll want is an interventionist state. So Deng Xiaoping's dictum—"to get rich is glorious"—ultimately prevails. Lee Kuan Yew applied it in Singapore—and it worked marvels. Dubai, of course, is meta- Singapore.

Racism in Dubai—as in the U.S. south—is pervasive, but off-limits to discussion, even as the fragile social pact between citizens and foreign residents, which essentially means "shut up and do your job," is faltering. A 15% minority could not possibly impose either its language nor its religion on a cosmopolitan majority—especially when religion is usually the Wahhabi interpretation of Islam. Hence (Western and Arab) men can get drunk in licensed bars, pubs and restaurants and (Western only) women can wear a bikini on the beach.

Every night an army of multicultural girls—from Southeast Asia to the former Iron Curtain—officially staying in Dubai as "kindergarten teachers" or "domestic help," descend in mini-skirts, halter tops and high heels on selected nightclubs and behave as if they were in Bangkok's girlie bars. At the same time some internet sites are blocked "due to incompatibility with the religious, cultural and moral values of the United Arab Emirates." A famous Dubai joke has a real estate agent telling a client to "buy a house in Jumeirah Beach. It's very safe! That's where the bin Ladens live." Whatever its compromises, Dubai's globalization kicks always seem to veer towards an optimum: a society of apolitical consumers.

Unelected male elders of a single ruling family—with a taste for expensive whisky, cognac, yellow Ferraris and fast blonde women—may control it with no opposition, South Asians may be treated as no more than slaves, and the country may remain essentially a protectorate—a status not substantially different from the tribal sheikdom dominated by the British until 1971. It's a wonder; but the Emirates' medieval feudalism somehow has managed to impress global perception as the most "progressive" state in the Middle East. Certainly that's not the perception of vast swathes of the Arab and Muslim street—which view the Gulf states *en bloc* as decadent, corrupt, anti-Islamic and sold to hegemonic Anglo-American, and not Arab and Muslim, economic and strategic priorities.

From the point of view of Pentagon hawks, this promontory advancing into the Strait of Hormuz—through which transits every day virtually half of the traded oil in the world—could not but represent one of the key strategic nodes of Liquid War. "Axis of Evil" permanent member Iran is just around the corner, 55 km away from the Musandam peninsula, in Oman, on the other side of the Persian Gulf. Any military scenario of an attack on Iran includes a crucial American beachhead positioned in Dubai and "protecting" the Gulf.

For Salafi-jihadists Dubai may be worse than Sodom and Gomorrah put together (or maybe not: from as far away as Baluchistan I have always been bombarded with juicy stories of henna-bearded clerics getting down to the funky beat whenever they hit the Emirates). An al Qaeda attack in Dubai would instantly demolish the overbuilding capitalist frenzy into ship-me-to-China rubble. So why does it not happen? First and foremost because al Qaeda and assorted Salafi- jihadists funds still transit through Dubai.

Money laundering in the financial Mecca of the Persian Gulf has been virtually uncontrollable. The U.S. government's case against Zacharias Moussaoui documented how 9/11 money was laundered through the UAE. During the mid-to-late 1990s the air path from the UAE to Kandahar was crammed with private jets taking Arab notables to falcon hunting in Taliban-controlled Afghanistan. Frequent fliers may have included former Saudi intelligence minister Prince Turki and UAE Crown Prince Sheik al-Maktoum. Return flights laundered exhausted Taliban and al Qaeda operatives.

During the 2003 invasion and occupation of Iraq, Dubai was neutral. Thus no al Qaeda attacks. But in March 2005 al Qaeda finally struck—but in Doha, in neighboring Qatar, home of a massive U.S. air base, a CIA base and an array of U.S. Special Forces crammed in secluded compounds. Bahrain houses the U.S. fleet. U.S. warships are constantly docked in Dubai. A 2005 audio message by Saleh al-Aoofi, an al Qaeda leader in the Gulf, had been explicit: "To the brothers of Qatar, Bahrain, Oman, the Emirates and to all the lions of jihad in the countries neighboring Iraq, every one of us has to attack what is available in his country of soldiers, vehicles and air bases of the crusaders and the oil allocated for them." Nevertheless an al Qaeda attack on Dubai remains unlikely.

The relationship between the Emirates and Iran is even more nuanced.

During the 1980-1988 Iran-Iraq war the UAE supported Saddam Hussein. Later on, when Rafsanjani and then Khatami were in power in Iran, there was a certain détente. Now the UAE—awash in billions of dollars of expatriate Iranian cash—somehow fear messianic Ahmadinejad. Arab countries including the UAE have regarded with alarm Iran's nuclear program, which includes the Bushehr nuclear plant right on the other side of the Persian Gulf. Rashid Abdullah, the UAE's Foreign Minister, points out that Dubai is closer to Bushehr than Tehran—and would not be spared the ghastly consequences of a nuclear disaster (or a preemptive American nuclear strike). The Gulf Cooperation Council (GCC) countries—Saudi Arabia, Bahrain, Kuwait, Oman, Qatar and the Emirates—appealed in late 2005 for a "denuclearized" Middle East, including both Iran and Israel. Not surprisingly, neither have committed to the idea.

The combination of the post-9/11 "war on terror" world plus oil at US$ 70-plus a barrel has translated into an unmitigated business bonanza for Dubai. According to data by HSBC, from 2002 to early 2006 Gulf states were deluged with over US$ 300 billion in excess cash. HSBC said that the so-called "Gulf liquidity" fueled, among others, booms in the Egyptian and Turkish stock markets, the Lebanese property market and supported Western equity markets and the U.S. national debt. Unlike the 1970s, when petrodollars ended up in Anglo-American banks, this new wall of cash translated into foreign direct investment (FDI). If only Dubai realized that US$ 300 billion would buy the entire outstanding debt of the developing world. Now *that's* what Brave New World would be all about.

The Emirates are the world's sixth top oil exporter, behind Saudi Arabia, Russia, Norway, Iran and Venezuela, with an average export of 2.4 million barrels a day, At least in Dubai, it's easy to spot where the money is going (apart from the overbuilding frenzy); for instance, to building up an aerospace industry, relieving its dependence on the U.S.; and to targeting more foreign contracts for its airport management business. And there are plenty more options for "Gulf liquidity" to choose from in case problems arise with the U.S. German Corporatistan wants to build a high-speed train network parallel to the Gulf coast, and arms dealers want to sell new communication systems, missile defense systems and brand new submarines.

Crucial questions always come back to the fore. How come descendants of Bedouins and pearl divers have become high-tech über-capitalists—the Asian tigers of the Persian Gulf—while the bulk of the Arab world has stagnated politically and economically? Could this economic boom be replicated in Northern Africa or in an Arab world—Syria, Egypt, Saudi Arabia—hostage to petrified social structures and isolated, disconnected political leaders? And what if the Pentagon had not messed up so ignominiously and Iraq, with the help of qualified Iraqis (no need to import cheap labor) could be able to fashion a country, swimming in oil revenues, even more dynamic (and certainly more democratic) than the UAE?

Now let's meet the CEO. Crown Prince Sheikh Mohammed bin Rashid al-Maktoum is the de facto CEO of Dubai. Rumor has it that he's not exactly fluent in reading and writing his native Arabic because he did not finish school. He only acceded to power in January 2006 after the death of his elder brother, Sheikh Maktoum bin Rashid al-Maktoum. But he is widely credited by every "national" as the man with the vision to build, in the words of a businessman munching lobster at the 7-star Burj Dubai, "the first modern Arab metropolis in history."

As far as the Arab world is concerned General al-Maktoum (he's also the UAE's Minister of Defense) has certainly been wise enough to warn his neighbors to clean up their act. He was not referring to George W. Bush's "Greater Middle East," but to urgent economic and social liberalization.

The UAE obviously had a crucial asset that escapes, for instance, both Syria and Egypt: oil. But the key point in the overall strategy was to liberate the Emirates from oil dependency and diversify the economy (a lesson for Saudi Arabia). Oil production in the UAE fell by more than 30% since 1998; but at the same time revenues from oil and gas exports are now only 37% of the budget. Dubai will run out of oil by 2025; the UAE as a whole only by the end of the Century. The "diversification" may have been one-sided so far—it revolves around tourism and a real estate and commercial boom. But it works.

To see the flesh and bones of Globalistan exposed, it just takes a drive towards the western border of Dubai, site of the largest man-made harbor in the world, a monstrous, 7 million containers a year, 24/7 operation even when in summer the average temperature is an unbearable 50 degrees Celsius, humidity is 90% and seawater almost boils at 38 Celsius. Just on the other side of the harbor are the American carrier battle groups which usually stop by, the vigilantes of the Persian Gulf. The whole port system belongs to—who else—the ruling al-Maktoum family, who devised the master plan to make Dubai a worthy rival of both Singapore and Hong Kong. Dubai Ports now operates harbors in China, Hong Kong, Australia, South Korea, India, Yemen, Djibouti, Saudi Arabia, Romania, Germany, in Latin America, and is itching to take over the harbors of southern Iraq.

Dubai is not really a city-state: it's Corporatistan as family business (only five families control the whole UAE). Call it Singapore Plus—a fact confirmed after a visit by Singapore's resident Confucius and founding father Lee Kuan Yew. Behind CEO Sheikh al-Maktoum are three technocrats responsible for what is called Project Dubai. The trio has their offices at the sleek Emirates Towers—constantly voted best business hotel in the Middle East.

Mohammed Al-Abbar is the head of Emaar —an enormous real estate corporation with business interests throughout the Arab world. Al-Abbar was a keen student of the Singaporean model. He's the man who translated Singapore to the Gulf.

Sultan Ahmed Bin Sulayem manages the Nakheel construction conglomerate. Nakheel develops humongous, wow factor-targeted projects like the artificial Palm Islands and the artificial archipelago known as "The World"—the epitome of the global gated condo craze.

Mohammed Al-Gergawi is the political mind of the al-Maktoum family. He is the man in charge of strategic long-term projects—such as the positioning of Dubai as a major global banking and service center, media hub and leading center for medicine.

The way things get done in Dubai could be interpreted in the absolute majority of the bureaucratic-afflicted South as nothing short of a miracle. Usually there's an invitation. Then the next day a cluster of businessmen gets together—say, at the

Emirates Towers. A sleek presentation then details the next megaproject—be it the new, expanded mega airport, the world's tallest skyscraper, the largest artificial island, a new mega mall. Dubai gets down to it, and sooner than anyone can count how many cranes are working at the site the project is completed. One wonders what Osama bin Laden and Ayman al-Zawahiri could learn from these business meetings at the Armani-Arabic lettering Emirates Towers.

Spectacular, head-spinning announcements, spiced by hyperbolic rhetoric ("History rising," "A legend in the making") are Dubai's stock in trade—only natural when one in every five cranes in the world is busy working 24/7 in the city-state. It's a positively Shanghainese overbuilding frenzy. When we fly in from Tehran or, with a detour in Amman, from Iraq, the contrast is absolutely breathtaking. Along a Persian Gulf strip of less than 40 km, there is at least US$ 100 billion invested in projects already ongoing or planned for short-term; that was, by the mid-2000s, almost twice the FDI in China.

In May 2006, for instance, Dubai World Central was unveiled: the biggest airport in the world (equal to the combined capacity of Chicago's O'Hare and London's Heathrow), surrounded by an entirely new city for 750,000 people, in an area of 140 square km, at a cost of US$ 33 billion, financed by the government, and located in the free trade zone of Jebel Ali.

And this came on top of the expansion of Dubai International Airport, "the largest airport development project underway in the world," scheduled for completion in 2007, with as many as 18,000 people working on site, and including five gates to exclusively handle the new, mega Airbus A380. Dubai International will be linked to World Central by an express train.

Then there's the announcement of a US$ 27 billion tourist complex including the biggest hotel in the world (wasn't it supposed to be The Venetian in Las Vegas? Not anymore). The US$ 1 billion Burj Dubai (Dubai Tower) is going up at a dizzying pace and should be completed by the end of 2008. The height is officially secret, but it should be something like 700 meters, including the word's first rooftop spa. The tallest commercial tower in the world, designed by Japanese and Singaporean architects, will then knock out Taipei's Tower 101. Apartments and offices are sold out—although that does not mean much in Dubai because speculation is endemic. Around Burj Dubai is mushrooming the inevitable, work-in-progress, multi-skyscraper mega-development called Business Bay.

The artificial islands shaped like palm trees off the Dubai coast have become a pop icon from Beirut to Bangkok. Four major islands are springing up, with Palm Island Jumeirah already advanced, along with Palm Island Jebel Ali, Palm Island Deira and the overambitious, US$ 3 billion The World—no less than 250 artificial islands made of 200 million cubic meters of sand dredged from the sea floor and designed to look like, what else, the world map. This dream world—call it Gulag De Luxe—is of course protected from the real world by an ultra-high tech Wall. Builders Nakheel assure that most of the islands are sold to "local money," and the rest to Americans and Brits. By 2015, the company says, there will be 250,000 people living in The World, which will then look "like Venice."

As for the original Palm at Jumeirah, it was conceived by none other than Crown Prince Sheik al-Maktoum; according to Nakheel, "he wanted to put Dubai on the map with something really sensational."

A hotel developer is building a fake lost city of Atlantis. Fake scuba diving sites—the Maldives, the Barrier Reef, the Caymans, the Red Sea—are also part of the package. 7,000 South Asians work on one of the Palms: instead of causing what would be a perennial traffic jam, every day they are ferried from further along the coast. In another one of the Palms there will be houses on stilts which seen from above will spell out a poem written by—who else—the Crown Prince: "Heed the wisdom of the wise: It takes a man of vision to write on water. Not everyone who rides a horse is a jockey. Great men rise to great challenges."

In the early 2000s Dubai's Internet City was literally desert sand. Five years later it housed the Middle East HQ of every major, global IT company. For the multinational shop-till-you-drop brigades, the Mall of the Emirates bills itself as the largest outside the U.S., and the third largest in the world—and that includes the only artificial ski resort in the whole Middle East (it looks like a freak, twisted steel tube standing out in the Dubai skyline). At the monster Souk Madinat Jumeirah everything is fake—it's a fake souk inside a fake medina with its own five-star hotels and apartments crisscrossed by fake water channels. Ibn Battuta—the legendary Muslim navigator—died and was reborn as a mall, complete with fake Ibn Battuta medieval sailing ship and "Chinese," "Indian," "Persian" or "Moroccan" halls. The Giorgio Armani Hotel and the Palazzo Versace are coming. And so is a US$ 500 million underwater hotel, a Chess City (32 tower blocks of 64 floors, each in the form of a chess piece), an apartment tower shaped like the Big Ben, an Aviation City with its Cargo Village, an Aid City-cum-Humanitarian Free Zone, an Exhibition City, a Festival City, a Healthcare City, a Flower City...

There's also Dubailand—the US$ 4.5 billion Arab Disneyland, which will be bigger than Monaco, providing jobs for at least 300,000 people. There's the new urban railway with 37 stops. The US$ 1,7 billion Silicon Oasis for the IT giants (Internet City is now passé...) And the US$ 6 billion Dubai Waterfront/Arabian Canal, bigger than Barbados. Meanwhile, what has been built for the people of Baghdad? U.S. military bases and the largest U.S. embassy/fortress in the world.

No wonder the ultimate psychedelic night drive in Dubai is to glide along the ghosts of giant buildings buried in the desert sand, all surrounded by a myriad of scaffolding and overhung by giant, tower cranes; it's like watching a glowing, larger than-life, steel-and-glass equivalent of the buried terracotta army of Emperor Qin in Xian.

Now let's meet the slaves. The social pyramid in Dubai is unforgiving. At the base is your average construction worker, inevitably South Asian, either Pakistani or Indian. He is, of course, invisible. But he and his fellow workers now comprise an astonishing 80% of the UAE's population. Human Rights Watch has repeatedly denounced that this archetypal construction worker is never treated like a real human being. For Corporatistan UAE this is irrelevant.

Your average worker toils for a minimum of 12 hours a day in up to 50 degrees Celsius, with a half-an-hour break, 6 days a week, and earns no more than US$ 150 a month. He lives in a camp, four and sometimes as many as twelve to a 15 square meter room lost in the dreary al Quoz industrial suburb. In his day off, exhausted, he watches Bollywood DVDs and catches up with news from home in the crowded Deira souk. One night at the Emirates Towers (in a standard room) would consume five months of his salary. He can only come back home to see his family—who gets an average of 50% of his monthly salary—once every two years. If he's really lucky— or an elderly expat, a former skilled worker—he may eke out a comfortable living as a taxi driver.

He has no rights. Trades unions are banned. If he speaks up, he's instantly de-ported. Or, in desperation, he may follow the path of thousands who escaped to massive slums crammed with illegal immigrants in neighboring Sharjah. If she's a woman and works as a maid or in a hotel, she can be sexually harassed—and there will be no consequences.

Dozens of construction workers died in 2005. Most of these Spidermen of the Gulf simply fell from the huge new towers as slings and ropes are not exactly high tech. A worker died of suffocation in Palm Jumeirah, when the local press discov-ered that many were being fed half a lemon a day at 45 degrees Celsius. An array of dodgy companies is addicted to delaying payment of salaries—or not paying at all, as well as confiscating passports.

Slightly better off than the South Asians are the Filipinos, some other Southeast Asians and some Eastern Europeans serving—or playing—in bars, restaurants, hotels, the whole tourist, fun-in-the-sun industry. Well-paid (and white) Western-ers—more than 100,000—live lavishly as engineers, surveyors, managers, analysts, teachers. The overwhelming majority are Anglos—British, Irish, South Africans,

Australians. Every major Western and Japanese information technology and audi-ovideo giant, as well as every major financial services company is based in Dubai.

There are many constraints even for the well off. If you are a non-UAE national you can only buy land in designated "free zones." Foreign companies can only operate by paying a UAE *kafeel* (sponsor, guarantor) to be their local representative (it is a *kafeel* who also monopolizes the "import" of foreign workers). Only UAE nationals can work for the government. And education and healthcare are free only for UAE nationals—certainly not for the South Asians.

Finally, at the top of the pyramid is the al-Maktoum family and its associates, controlling and investing the wall of cash derived from oil, exercising total political and social control and building the futuristic version of Arabia based on trade and finance.

Enron was a Corporatistan dream. It collapsed. Everyone knows the property market bubble will explode and the stock market is bound to fall—the only question is when. The Dubai dream model of gated condo/megamall/golf course/designer food, preferably in an artificial island, may not be exactly Arabian Nights material, or bound to be replicated in other parts of Africa, Latin America and Asia. Strikes like in March 2006—by 2500 workers at, of all places, Burj Dubai, the tallest tower in the world—will be replicated. The petrodollar dream remains attached to the absence of rights to most people building the dream. Without these "invisibles," the dream would disappear like a mirage—as if all the oil wells turned dry.

Sheik Zayed's and Sheik al-Maktoum's dream of modern Arabia will nonetheless continue to entice (quagmire Iraq is not exactly an alternative), conforming the image of an apolitical, consumer-mad, citizenship-free society: Corporatistan at its apex. It's as if Dubai's ruling family had kept to heart the words of the late, great Indonesian writer Pramoedya Ananta Toer: "Just as politics cannot be separated from life, life cannot be separated from politics. People who consider themselves to be non-political are no different; they've already been assimilated by the dominant political culture—they just don't feel it anymore."

Figure 10. The United Arab Emirates from space (NASA). The Corporatistan playground of Dubai is surrounded by sand.

~ 5 ~

JIHADISTAN

Verily, never will Allah change the condition of a people until they change it themselves.

—**The Holy Koran**, *XIII:11*

The chickens of "jihadis" once sponsored by imperialism and the state have been coming home to roost. Afghanistan threatens to become a metaphor for the future.

—**Eqbal Ahmad**, *Jihad International, Inc., 1988*

Diana Christensen: "I'm interested in doing a weekly dramatic series based on the Ecumenical Liberation Army. The way I see the series is: Each week we open with an authentic act of political terrorism taken on the spot, in the actual moment. Then we go to the drama behind the opening film footage. That's your job, Ms. Hobbs. You've got to get the Ecumenicals to bring in that film footage for us. The network can't deal with them directly; they are, after all, wanted criminals."

—**Paddy Chayefsky**, *Network*

If Muslims close ranks and unite, no one in the world would dare to attack them and insult their religion and the Prophet. Those who accuse Islam of intolerance and violence are either ignorant or full of enmity."

—**Sheikh Salah al-Din Nassar**, Imam of Al-Azhar in Cairo, September 2006

A prologue

It was written by an obviously learned Saudi anonymously and published in the summer of 2006 in the Arab website *Shafaf*. The plot might have come straight from Saturday Night Live. Here's a short version.

Osama bin Laden has finally reached Paradise. He's not exactly at ease. There are too many weird people around and on top of it he has to work. Osama is assigned to a vineyard, whose nectar delights the Almighty. Osama's boss is one Sarah Michowsky. His palace—yes, he gets a palace—is in the Garden of Rujz (an inferior paradise imagined by the 10th Century Arab skeptic poet Abu Al-Ala' al-Maarri, hated by Salafi-jihadists). Osama is saluted by a Christian and a Sudanese mystic. One day, when Osama is admitted on a visit to paradise First Class, he meets Nelson Mandela and All-Hallaj, an Islamic mystic martyr tortured and decapitated in 922 A.D. Osama starts to lose it. He wants to meet some of his old friends. An angel tells him that if they lounge in superior Paradise, he needs to apply in writing for a permission to visit. Abu Qatada and Abu Hafs—both al Qaeda operatives—are not on the angel's list. Nor Bush, Cheney and Rumsfeld. Yet Marx is on the list—but to see him Osama needs permission. Osama goes nuts. Paradise is full of Christians, Jews, Sufis, Shiites, secular people, atheists. So Osama starts looking for a door to escape Paradise. Just then he feels a hand touching his shoulder. It's his old friend Ayman al-Zawahiri.

"Hey pal, wake up! Go back to your cave."

By the way: Osama bin Laden's Thuraya sat phone number is 00873-682505331. Anybody can try it. But nobody has picked up on the other side since September 2001.

Once upon a time in the 1960s the Stones sang about a "sleepy London town" where "there's just no place for the street fighting men." Four decades later it seemed like über-post-swingin' London—facing its summers with increased trepidation—had all but been taken over not by street fighting but sky-flying and tube-riding suicide bombers.

In 2005 it was London 7/7—a deadly subway strike. In 2006 it was the alleged, joint made–in- U.K.-Pakistan plot to blow up U.K.-U.S. airliners in waves mid-flight over the Atlantic in classic al Qaeda method-is-the madness fashion.

The British and the wider world were sold a carefully constructed official narrative—non-stop spinning of anonymous "security sources" included—of an al Qaeda

British cell within 48 hours of perpetrating something worse than 9/11. The perpe-trators were alienation victims aged between 17 and 35—a taxi driver, a pizza delivery guy, a used car salesman, all suburban, most with pregnant wives or young kids, all football and cricket fans but crucially "British-born Muslims"(as draped by the BBC in an elegant cloak of racism lite). They would have been able to mix Gatorade with a peroxide-based paste to make an "explosive cocktail" that could be triggered by an iPod or a Motorola mobile, the whole package smuggled through airport security checks in hand luggage. But there was a slight hitch. They had not bought their plane tickets—in the height of the summer season—and some didn't even have passports.

This was really the stuff of Jerry Bruckheimer's dreams—the outcome of more than a year of surveillance and investigation by MI5 and British police targeting a group of about 1,000 terror suspects, the largest counter-terror operation in Brit-ain's history, MI6 frantically in contact with counter-intel in the U.S., Pakistan, Germany and the Maghreb in an orgy of phone tapping and high tech bugging. And the whole package sprinkled with characters straight from central casting: a mix of youngsters radicalized in Britain and influenced by traveling to Pakistan, all al Qaeda supporters in global jihad mode. But something was missing: the evil al Qaeda mastermind.

If this was *C.S.I.* Grissom would have been the first to discover that these guys were mere copy cats. The original liquid explosive gambit was the 1995 Bojinka plot, developed by evil al Qaeda genius Khalid Shaykh Muhammad to blow up a dozen U.S. commercial jets over the Pacific. For this purpose Ramzi Yousef—who master-minded the World Trade Center 1993 bombing—had developed liquid nitroglycerin which could be disguised in contact-lens solution bottles. Yousef also customized a digital watch with a timer and used two batteries hidden in his shoes to power light-bulb filaments and spark an explosion.

In December 1994 a Philippines Airlines 747 was the object of a dry run directed by Yousef himself. He positioned the explosives under one of the seats and timed them to detonate after he left for a connecting flight. The explosion killed only an unsuspecting Japanese businessman who Fate (Allah?) placed directly above the bomb.

So the 2006 version was supposed to be a dry run for the replay of an operation that had originally failed. The supposed explosive device this time was TATP (Tri Acetone Tri Peroxide). Officially the lethal cocktails would have been mixed on board—even though every serious researcher in England debunked the myth that high, powerful explosives could be mixed in a plane toilet at room temperature. Anyway, the incredibly exploding iPod plot was pure Liquid War.

With waves of disinformation clashing about, sectors of the Arab-language press and incorrigible Western cynics started to express suspicions of official motives—from wag the dog tactics provoking media hysteria to concocting a false flag smoking gun. Or maybe they were overdosing on episodes of *Sleeper Cell*. The plot was uncovered just when world public opinion was sympathizing with Lebanon's plight over the summer of 2006 Israeli bombing. British MI5 tipped off Pakistan's CIA—the redoubtable Inter-Services Intelligence, ISI—on one Rashid Rauf as the crucial link. Rauf is a member of the Kashmir-active, ISI-financed, clandestine outfit Jaish-I-Mohammad, which is not only funded but operates under ISI guidelines. So the liquid bomb plot mastermind was in fact an ISI agent—as much as alleged 9/11 mastermind Khalid Shaykh Muhammad was repeatedly protected by the ISI.

A clear indication that this was all nonsense and that the actual dimensions of the threat did not present materially significant new risks to the interest of global capital was provided by Wall Street and the City of London. Markets did not crash. Oil prices actually fell. Both George W. Bush and Tony Blair remained on vacation. And 80% of Britons told polls the "war on terror" was being lost. Political schemer and former Jemima Goldsmith husband Imran Khan has already tried to seize power in Pakistan with the help of the Army; now he's trying with the help of Islamic clerics. He understands that the future in Pakistan is in the hands of the clerics. So it was enlightening to see Khan stressing that the plot was met "with complete skepticism in Pakistan, since the intelligence had been provided by the Musharraf government. The biggest winner from the war on terror has been Musharraf, who has aligned himself with the U.S. as a frontline state, and been rewarded by gaining legitimacy in Washington's eyes for his military dictatorship." The Pakistani daily *The News* corroborated the collaboration "in unison" of Pakistani, U.S. and U.K. intelligence: "The operation was coordinated at the highest level by all the three agencies," supervised by Lt-Gen. Ashfaq Pervez Kiyani, the director-general of ISI.

Whoever was on top, in the end it was the powerful, sensationalist Springer group in Germany who outshone everyone else in this terror thriller, spinning the story of a Mossad secret unit in Lebanon discovering hard drives with intel on more than 20 terrorist cells in Britain. Subsequently ISI intel from Rawalpindi—actually straight from the tribal areas—relays that al Qaeda had ordered its agents in Britain to be ready for action. Mossad finally adds it all up to the benefit of MI6. The message: it was an Israeli effort that prevented a bloodbath in Europe in the ever-evolving war of the "free world" against "fanatical Islam."

The Canada-based Center for Research on Globalization has been remarkably consistent in arguing that the "war on terror" is a fabrication and that al Qaeda, a creation of the U.S. intelligence apparatus in the 1980s, remains an "intelligence asset." The summer of 2006 incredibly exploding iPod plot seemed once again to legitimize the hypothesis. With no substantive evidence, the ISI-coordinated intel effort could not come up with anything more credible than fuzzy, shadowy al Qaeda meetings in the Pak-Afghan tribal areas plotting multiple bombings linked with fuzzy Pakistani-British youngsters' terror connections. The pattern is bound to be replicated to oblivion: a sophisticated propaganda overdrive spreading cluster disinformation bombs into the news cycle, with spin sold off as intelligence.

Anyone familiar with al Qaeda's worldview knew it would never have chosen to strike in Europe while Hezbollah was resisting Israel's bombing of Lebanon to rubble. Some conclusions, anyway, were inevitable. If the deadly iPod plot was true, it was stopped by good, old law enforcement on the ground—not by axis of evil rhetoric or Shock and Awe over Afghanistan, Pakistan, Lebanon, Syria or Iran. Whether it was true or fake, a message was imprinted that Londonistan was not dead but alive and kicking, with a large pool of young "British-born Muslims," five years after 9/11, fully integrated to global jihad. This state of affairs could only benefit clash of civilizations stenographers and apostles of the "free world" fighting "fanatical Islam."

So after so much sound and fury, signifying literally nothing, Europe was left in the end with the sound of mass hysteria. Fear internalized. The shape of things to come. Liquid War.

Immanuel Wallerstein reminds us of the overall logic of Islamic movements: if you want to defeat oppression from the outside and fire up a renovation from the inside, the first thing is to get rid of Arab modernist regimes—from the Wahhabis in Saudi Arabia to Mubarak in Egypt. "Of course," adds Wallerstein, "this is the same thing that Ayatollah Khomeini said about the Shah in Iran and what the Taliban said about the pseudo communist regime in Afghanistan."

Wallerstein also stresses how Islamic movements dedicate a lot of effort to social care, and highlights their capacity to attract young scientists and engineers. This should be reason enough to prove that "the Islamists are not romantics nostalgic for a long-gone agricultural society." Rather they are "the providers of an alternate form of modernity, open to technological advance but which refutes secularism and its values."

So what's happening in the Islamic world at large, the rise of Islamism as a social and political force "is just a variation of what's been happening in all the parts of the peripheral zones of the world system." People want an alternative to the current world system.

University of Chicago Political Science professor Robert Pape, in his much-quoted August 2003 study *The Strategic Logic of Suicide Terrorism* (188 attacks analyzed from 1980 to 2001), later expanded to a book—*Dying to Win: Why Suicide Terrorists Do It*—analyzing 462 suicide bombings around the globe, concluded that terrorism has very little to do with religious extremism. It's all about politics. When Pape studied Hezbollah suicide bombings from 1982 to 1986 against U.S., French and Israeli targets, he discovered that only 8 people held a fundamentalist worldview; 27 were leftists, from the Lebanese Communist Party to the Arab Socialist Union; and 3 were Christians, including a female secondary-school teacher with a college degree. What moved them all was resistance to foreign occupation—a geopolitical issue if ever there was one. Pape thoroughly debunked the myth that Islamo-fascists are at the root of terrorism. What virtually every suicide bombing campaign has in common is a strategic objective: to get rid of an illegal occupying power. Terrorism—or resistance—always grows in the soil of revolt. And revolt is always fed by the perception of injustice.

Wallerstein also stresses the complex relation between the West and the demonization of Islam. This is "a family quarrel" between three monotheistic religions; it is conformed by the geoeconomic reality of lots of oil; and is a consequence of the end of "possible alternative demons in the neocolonized zones of the world." This has led Wallerstein to conclude that the West cannot possibly function without a demon—especially as the West "faces a massive crisis, not only economic, but fundamentally political and social. So when you're consumed by doubt and self-belief, nothing is easier than blaming it on en 'evil' outside enemy."

This analysis necessarily leads us to the concept of Islamo-fascism. Islam is a universal, monotheistic religion that defends peace. Fascism is an exclusionist, racist European-born ideology that abhors universalism. It's not surprising that the crude amalgam Islamo-fascism was shaped by a congregation of U.S. neocons, Zionists, Christian fundamentalists and Christian Zionists to legitimize the "war on terror," equating "terror" with "Islam." The concept—an absolute nonsense—vilifies Islam while allowing the flourish of the extreme Salafi-jihadist view. Before 9/11 practically 70% of suicide bombings all over the world were the work of the so-called "black tiger" warriors of the Hindu Tamil Tigers in Sri Lanka. Nobody at the time described them as "Hinduist" suicide bombers. It's positively silly to believe that Muslims or converted Muslims yearn to become suicide bombers *en masse.*

In fact the whole concept of suicide bombing is not Islamic: it's Japanese. Kamikaze pilots in World War II inspired both the *Nihon Sekigun* (the Japanese Red

Army) and the *Zengaturen* (the Committee of Radical Students). These two movements infiltrated and seduced the Popular Front for the Liberation of Palestine. The key conceptual leader was a woman, Fusako Shigenobu, a.k.a. The Red Queen, who hijacked a Japan Airlines jet in 1969, subsequently went to the Middle East and, in Paul Virilio's term, "inseminated" the Palestinians with the notion of a terrorist attack. The Red Queen is still in prison in Japan. What's also extraordinary is her birth date: September 9, 1945, only one month after a U.S. plane dropped a nuclear bomb on Nagasaki.

Víctor Pallejà de Bustinza, a specialist in Islamic thinking and History of Religions, a professor at the International University of Catalonia and visiting professor in Istanbul, Cairo and in Morocco, characterizes the current configuration as a political war. While the E.U., in the early 21st Century, has blurred virtually all borders between States, this was something that Islam had already enjoyed for centuries under the Ottoman Empire. Islam until the 17th Century was one of the world's great powers—as much as China was also superior to the West. But in the early 1920s—after the betrayal of the Arab nation via the Sykes-Picot agreement whereby Britain and France carved up the Middle East for themselves—the heart of the Islamic world lost its unity, carved up by the West into small States. Up to the early 20th Century the Caliphate in Istanbul would issue a passport to anyone declaring himself a Muslim.

Borders—Western-defined—are at the center of the drama currently played out, notes Bustinza, alongside the economic disaster of the Arab world and the insoluble Israel/Palestine problem. Bustinza interlinks the lack of legitimacy of Arab regimes, the lack of political alternation, the mounting collective popular pressure and an atmosphere of permanent angst. This is the atmosphere we find in every teahouse or café from Rabat to Amman, from Algiers to Damascus, from Baghdad to Ramallah, as if people were perennially asking "what have we done to deserve this."

European silence is much to blame. European public intellectuals, for decades, have been absolutely incapable to think about Islam—and that was compounded with European political incompetence, even abjection, when confronted with the Bosnia carnage in the early 1990s. (America, with its history of explicit religiosity, may actually be better equipped to think about Islam. Harvard, that factory for Corporatistan, announced in the fall of 2006 that it is adding a course on "reason and faith" to its required undergraduate curriculum, and a course on international law to its first year Law School program.)

Bustinza, like Wallerstein, insists Islam's problems are not religious. "These are social problems—the widespread struggle for more social justice and a better distribution of wealth." It is in this sense that he believes Islam may soon be following the Chinese model *en masse*—mixing State control with private economy.

Meanwhile moderate Islam has to deal with terror tactics involving its name. High tech terrorism is essentially a hardcore media war. Each attack is a thermonuclear media bomb. Whatever its actual magnitude it has to register as an attack on the whole info-hungry world. Without propaganda, now in real time, terrorism would be totally irrelevant. Bombs may kill innocents, but their true lethal effect is in the frantic info-sphere of accelerated media particles. Al Qaeda and all the other nodes of the Salafi-jihadist (or Islamist) front have known this better than most.

By the mid-2000s, even before London 7/7, al Qaeda and the Salafi-jihadist were on the verge of scoring a major double blow. Unlike 9/11, their fight not only was becoming recognized by top Islamic scholars as legitimate, but they had managed to capitalize on major blunders in the "war on terror" to broaden what was in effect an anti-U.S. hegemony drive among global, moderate Muslims. How could that possibly happen?

At the time of 9/11, Osama bin Laden and Ayman al-Zawahiri made two crucial mistakes. First mistake: Because of their (not so splendid) isolation, they didn't notice that most Afghans, in fact Pashtun, had had enough of the ultra-reactionary Taliban. The Pashtun had never supported the Taliban because they would be the vanguard of a worldwide jihad against the U.S. (this never crossed the Taliban's minds) but over more mundane topics such as maintaining law and order and perpetuating Pashtun supremacy. For them, the whole point was to advance the eventual reunion of their ancestral land, Pashtunistan.

Second mistake: Osama and al-Zawahiri overestimated the reaction of the Arab street. They didn't understand that the average Arab living in the Middle East—and especially in Western Europe—may detest U.S. foreign policy, but this has never translated into solid, political mobilization. If it ever existed, the political drive would be sparked by the carnages in Palestine and Iraq: these were specifically Arab and not wider Islamic problems.

So al Qaeda may have behaved like Russian revolutionaries in the late 19th Century: call them Islamo-anarchists. Osama and al-Zawahiri believed that sensationally plunging Boeings-turned-into-missiles into the heart of the American power elite they would show the Promised Land to the alienated masses. It didn't work.

For its part the "war on terror"—the American response to al Qaeda—was a silly, meaningless metaphor in the first place: al Qaeda essentially poses a security problem. It is not a strategic threat to the U.S. and it still isn't—even after a series of overlapping mutations, after Guantanamo, the invasion of Iraq, the Abu Ghraib scandal, the leveling of Fallujah.

For all al Qaeda's strategic mistakes it was manna from Heaven to count on such a golden ally as the Bush administration. Already at 11:00 A.M. on 9/11 al Qaeda was officially designated as the evil perpetrator—with no time whatsoever for evidence to be collected at the crime scene, or an investigation to be launched. At 11:00 P.M. on 9/11 the nonsensical "war on terror" was officially launched, with absolutely no one in U.S. mainstream media reminding the public that Washington had fabricated jihadis *en masse*—along with Saudi Arabia and Pakistan—during the 1980s and enthusiastically supported the Taliban when they took power in 1996.

After 9/11 Washington, among other feats, restored the credibility of the Taliban, went on a rampage against Islam (that's how the Arab and Muslim street predominantly saw it), invaded and occupied the eastern flank of the Arab nation (Iraq), helped to fashion al Qaeda as a global brand, demonized Iran and gave green light for Israel to kill Shiites in Lebanon. With "enemies" like these who needs friends?

The new geopolitical configuration spelled victory for al Qaeda and the Islamist camp from the beginning. Especially because al Qaeda and Islamists are not Salafis. Salafism was conceived by the visionary Jamaluddin al-Afghani, a Shiite born near Hamadan in Iran, in the late 19th Century as a reform movement capable of equipping Islam to fight Western colonialism. But to put it bluntly, Jamaluddin al-Afghani had very little to do with mullah Omar, the dashing one-eyed Taliban emir who escaped American fury in the fall of 2001 in the back seat of a Honda 50 cc; Jamaluddin al-Afghani was a political activist, not a theologian like Mullah Omar.

The Salafis were the embryo of the Muslim Brotherhood and the contemporary Islamists, al Qaeda among them. Jamaluddin Al-Afghani is considered a "founding father"—the first to forge Islam into a political ideology capable of uniting Muslims against Western domination.

But if Salafism was originally a project based on a fight against Western domination, it soon ceased to be a global political project to modernize the Muslim world. Salafism today is an ultra-conservative program to purify Islam from "pernicious" cultural influences—Muslim as well as Western. That's where Salafis intersect with the ultra-conservative Wahhabis in Saudi Arabia. Well, it can be confusing. Technically, there is no difference between Salafis and Wahhabis. As Arif Jamal, arguably Pakistan's leading expert on jihad explains, "the Taliban are not Salafis. They are Hanafis in an Islamic context or Deobandi in an Afghan context. The Hizb-ut Tharir also are not Salafis. Jaysh-i-Mohammad and Sipha-e-Sahaba in Pakistan are also Hanafis in an Islamic context or Deobandi in a local context." As for al Qaeda, or the Algerian GIA, for example, they go one step further: they are Salafi-jihadist, considering violent jihad to be a personal, religious duty of every Muslim.

Jihad, in Arabic, literally means "to struggle." There are two forms of jihad. The "lesser jihad" (*al-jihad al-asghar*) is linked to the defense of Islam, and doctrinally allows the use of violence, but only if Islam is under attack by non-Muslims. In this case, every Muslim must adhere. A jihad can also be launched for the expansion of Islam; in this case every Muslim must also adhere but as an individual can contribute with goods, services and cash, and not necessarily become a warrior.

The "Greater Jihad" (*al-jihad al-akbar*) takes place inside each Muslim's soul. That's the jihad that really matters. These two jihads—against the enemy and against the ego—have always coexisted in Islam. Salafi-jihadists emphasize that as the fight against a heretical adversary is an imperative, self-sacrifice is also a must. But in mystical Islam the fight against the enemy is just an illusion—not far away from the Buddhist fight against the kingdom of Mara ("illusion"): what matters is inner purification on the way to mystical spirituality. Essentially, it's also what Lao Tzu formulated as "To know others is wisdom. To know oneself is superior wisdom." Islam has always been convulsed by the tension between these two jihads. Sufis have been banned because of their mystical approach. But sometimes a theological master like the Ayatollah Khomeini promotes a fusion: for him, the unbounded love of Allah makes the martyr want to dissolve himself into Him.

The interpretations of jihad in the Holy Koran change all the time, according to the socio-historic context. But if we study the history of Islam—something the cheerleaders of "Islamo-fascism" never do—we realize that since the 16th Century there has been no violent jihadi movement anywhere, not to mention a pan-Islamic jihad. There were only national liberation struggles.

Jihad Inc. is an American invention, along with associate executive directors Saudi Arabia, Egypt and Pakistan. It was U.S. strategy in USSR-invaded Afghanistan in the 1980s (let's launch 1 billion Muslims against the Evil empire!) that catapulted jihad to the forefront of political Islam. Zia ul-Haq, the Pakistani dictator, supported by billions of dollars, could not pass up the opportunity to launch a true, pan-Islamic jihad against Russian infidels. Wahhabi Saudi Arabia also jumped at the golden opportunity to spread its rigid interpretation of Islam. In 1985 Ronald Reagan described Afghan jihadis visiting him at the White House as the "moral equivalent of America's founding fathers." Even at the time Whitney Houston fan Osama bin Laden would frown if landed in the same corner of lower Paradise in the company of Thomas Jefferson. The *Looney Tunes* element of it all is delirious funny—if it was not tragic. First the U.S. pitted political Islam against communism.

Then communism died. Now it's the U.S. against political Islam. A historical "what if" perfectly allow us to think that were the Cold War still on, everyone would still be watching the same movie.

What's important is to bear in mind where Salafi-jihadists are coming from. Wherever Islam is a minority, they consider that the faithful must follow *Dar al-Sulh* ("momentary peace, or truce"). Parts of Europe, for the moment, are considered to be in a momentary truce; but not the U.K., for instance. Wherever Islam is stronger, the faithful must follow *Dar al-Harb* ("war zone"), where all infidels are enemies: this applies to the Middle East and of course the U.S. Non-Muslims are considered *harbiyyûn* and should submit to Islamic jurisdiction either by *harb* ("war") or conversion. And then there's *Dar al-Islam* ("the kingdom of Islam"), where other monotheists are tolerated as *dhimmis* ("protected"). It's never enough to stress how this worldview relates to an extreme minority among the 1.5 billion *umma*.

Talking to Salafis is always very instructive. They tell us that for them there's essentially nothing to be learned from the West (just as American evangelical Christians tell us there is nothing to be learned from Islam). "Moderate" Salafis at least concede that non-belligerent infidels—i.e. most of us —should be treated kindly. The main difference between Salafis and the Salafi-jihadist is that Salafis totally reject the concept of Islamic ideology, as well as any Western conceptual category (political parties, representative democracy, social justice, even Revolution; for them Che Guevara is a nutcase). This means that Salafis don't accept political struggle as a means to establishing an Islamic state. They are in Greater Jihad mode: the soul of each individual Muslim takes precedence over politics, and this is a consequence of the fact that infidel domination only exists because of the loss of true Islamic faith. Salafi-jihadists are much more politicized—even though their political agenda can be as muddy as the waters of the Kabul river.

Sayyid Qutb—the Egyptian intellectual mentor of Ayman al-Zawahiri, hanged by the Nasser government in 1966—almost managed to bridge the gap between Salafis and the Salafi-jihadist. As British filmmaker Adam Curtis masterfully demonstrated in his 3-part BBC documentary *The Power of Nightmares*, Qutb is to al Qaeda what Leo Strauss is to the American neocons. Qutb encouraged political action but at the same time had a profound, almost Schopenhauerian pessimistic view of the modern world, combined with venomous contempt of all things Western—the reason for his appeal among Salafis.

The Shakespearean "jihad or not jihad" dilemma is, and will continue to be, a political decision. It's impossible to accuse Salafis—like the strident Islamo-fascism neocon rhetoric does—of defending a theology of violence per se. When an Islamic religious leader favors jihad, it's fundamentally a political decision, even though it's always framed as religious dictum. In 2001, both the highly-respected Sheikh Yousef al-Qardawi—who is a kind of Islamic David Letterman on alJazeera—and the new grand mufti of Saudi Arabia, Abdulaziz ibn Muhammad al-Sheikh issued *fatwas* condemning 9/11 as un-Islamic, clearly at odds with al Qaeda's interpretation of jihad. On the other hand it's possible to find many mainstream Salafis who are opposed to Qutb—for religious reasons—but favor jihad and al Qaeda (as a legitimate means of defending Islam against the West).

This being the society of spectacle, sooner or later the "jihad or not jihad" dilemma would end up being cannibalized by the life-as-a-reality show syndrome. That may have signaled the end of any serious political discussion; the feeling was that the revolution would, in fact, be televised.

We thought we had seen it all. As spectators we were jaded over gangsters in ski masks and greasy combat boots hovering over a hapless victim to read their jihadist manifesto. As journalists we have been summoned to press conferences in the burning desert or in mosquito-infested jungles of thugs brandishing Kalashnikovs and RPG-7s under crackling fluorescent lighting with a tattered red banner advertising their group's name and slogan in the background. But this was before the media division of the Jaish Ansar al-Sunna—JAS, at the time number 2 in the charts after al Qaeda in Iraq—came up in 2004 with a talk show, recorded on a real studio, with professional lighting and three camera angles where a host interviewed guests and showed the inevitable JAS compilation video of guerrillas blowing up Humvees, firing-off missiles and laying IED hell all over the Sunni triangle. Guests would gloat that JAS had infiltrated spies in every single U.S. military base in Iraq.

Not to be outdone jack-of-all-trades and then-most-wanted-man-in-the-world Abu Musab al Zarqawi, who was still alive, came up with his own reality TV show, with Zarqawi's Omar Brigades showing off the capture and commenting on the execution of members of the Shiite Badr Brigades. The audience for this extreme-sports-lethal-reality show was of course the amorphous, angry, impoverished, radicalized Middle Eastern masses.

What next? *Queer Eye for the Jihadi Guy? Jihadi Idol? Desperate Jihadi Wives?*

Reality TV, propaganda, infotainment—it's all in the same demented flux. Al Qaeda profited handsomely from the remix with the spectacular timing, much more effective than a thousand bombs, of Osama's address right before the 2004 U.S. Presidential elections. The al Qaeda remixed video dispensed with the Islamic phraseology window-dressing: this was the Sheikh as statesman, way above the terrorist fray, assuming the persona of a benevolent Abraham-like prophet in a

Emmy-worthy performance trying to patiently open the eyes of the 1.5 billion worldwide Islamic *umma* and almost 300 million Americans.

It may or may have not been true—because at the time Osama was deeply involved in the anti-Soviet Afghan jihad. But to credit the Israeli bombing of Lebanon in 1982 as the source of his anger against the imperialist West played extremely well all over the Middle East, and drew a steely link between al Qaeda and the Palestine liberation struggle. Al Qaeda had stated since 1996 how it is formally at war with the Crusader and Zionist West because Islam has been humiliated for centuries: the latest manifestation was Israel's crushing of Palestine. Now, in late 2004, Osama was finally saying this is not a religious war: it is political.

So no more talk of a Caliphate: from now on the theme would be political freedom from Western-imposed or Western-sanctioned dictatorships or puppet governments. Intellectual jihadis like Osama and al-Zawahiri decided to go one step further in appealing as much to the young Salafi-jihadists—for whom jihad is a state of mind—as to moderate Muslims. So nothing more sensible than toning down the fiery rhetoric of cosmic struggle between good and evil, believers and infidels, to the benefit of a broader theme—legitimizing the fight against injustice, everywhere.

Yet simultaneously the Osama-as-statesman address was fishy in many ways. It could almost be a psy-op. The speech was carefully scripted as an "Osama address to the American people." For the first time it was awash in references to 9/11, including American-style catch phrases like "striking the towers" and "another Manhattan." Another al Qaeda first, sources in Peshawar confirmed at the time that the video was delivered to alJazeera complete with an English-language translation and a transcript (by 2006 al Qaeda was firmly delivering video specials with English subtitles). In late 2004 for the first time ever Osama admitted on the record that he personally ordered 9/11. The man hastily tried in absentia was entering a guilty plea. The windfall included the very handy theme of increased fear, as the tape remembered Americans of the preeminent human face of terror—The Other, the Dangerous Outsider *par excellence*.

The al Qaeda remix video, of course, was instrumental for George W. Bush's reelection. So inevitably Osama had to be resuscitated prior to the mid-term 2006 U.S. elections. Osama remixed (this time by the White House) was rebranded to sell the "war on terror" all over again (forget The Long War, nobody knows what it means) as a cross between historic icon and foreign dignitary, supported by the usual charismatic iconography. Al Qaeda was so delighted that its multimedia arm as-Sahab delivered to *alJazeera* a super-pro 90-minute special in two parts with English subtitles to "celebrate" the 5 years of 9/11 (if CNN can do it why not us?) Of course the message was not exactly corporate America: al Qaeda once again was detailing how the "Zionist-Crusaders," led by America, are trying to (re)colonize the Middle East.

Here we had the "war on terror" in all its glory reduced into the non-revolution being televised.

The Jihadistan virus had always mutated non-stop. By the summer of 2005, it was all about self-service jihad. In the free territory of Brussels—the European apex of trafficking—danger suddenly could lurk behind that little corner shop selling beer after hours or that kiosk offering cut-rate fees for calls to Morocco or Egypt: they could all be al Qaeda sleeper cells, only a five-minute walk from Brussels' Gare du Midi—the central train station. E.U. and Moroccan Jihadistan experts were certain that al Qaeda's operational HQ in Europe was now located in Belgium and the Netherlands.

They were swearing that Moroccans had become top executives in al Qaeda cells operating in Europe, Saudi Arabia and Iraq, logistical and financial support transiting among the 300,000-strong Moroccan diaspora in Brussels and Amsterdam. Recruitment was on the rise—among the pious as well as among born-again Islamists, among the delinquent as well as among young immigrants who see jihad as the way to redeem themselves from their sins. At the same time, the exodus to jihad lands was also on the rise. It was not only destination Iraq; more and more so-called "white Moors"—white Muslims carrying E.U. passports—were leaving for jihad training in Chechnya. Bauman defines these mobile jihadis as "faithful replicas of the new globetrotter elite and the extraterritorial capital that this elite represents."

Both German and French secret services were now concentrating on young, E.U. Muslims who leave for jihad training in Iraq and come back to Europe to join or start sleeper cells. The British for their part were concentrating on individual jihad—extremely autonomous groups who either manage to contact or be contacted by an al Qaeda operative so they can discuss targets and logistical support: theoretically the modus operandi of London 7/7 and the exploding iPod plot one year later.

Moroccan expert Abdallah Rami stressed there was one thing more important than the rush towards the Iraqi training ground and its wealth of information in urban warfare, clandestine networks and the privatization of means of mass destruction: it was the appeal of "individual jihad." According to Rami, thanks to the internet (more than 4000 websites, mostly in Arabic), "an individual may become radical, acquire a terrorist education and prepare and execute an attack all by himself, without ever being in contact with al Qaeda." This is what self-service jihad is all about. This is certainly the future of Jihadistan.

But by the summer of 2005 the avant-garde brigades were still the stars of the show. The members of al Qaeda's new elite were either born in Western Europe—many hold a legitimate E.U. passport—or came to the West while still very young and then became radicalized. As George W. Bush is a born-again Christian, they are sort of born-again Islamists. The most important fact is that this "return of the repressed" (Islam) is above all a political radicalization. The new breed's brand of political Islam is much more "political" than "Islam." Jihad Inc. could not but profit from it.

Very few of these new brigades come directly from Islamic countries. And their exile is one-way: they never come back to where their families came from. For the previous generation the classic itinerary was to sharpen the knives at a peripheral jihad—Afghanistan, Kashmir, Chechnya—to become widely respected mujahedeen, and then go back to Western Europe. They never went to fight in the Maghreb or in the Middle East. The war in Iraq started to change this pattern.

In 1997, Osama obtained from his goat milk drinking pal Mullah Omar monopoly control over the Arab-Afghan training camps in Afghanistan. Meanwhile, the Pakistanis and the Uzbeks maintained their own, separate training camps. This means that every single jihadi who was not Pakistani or from Central Asia who went to Afghanistan between 1997 and 2001 was trained at an al Qaeda camp.

Unlike the faithful, none of the new breed of Arab-Afghans was close to Osama. But they inherited a legendary al Qaeda *esprit de corps*. The best and the brightest were trained to come back to Western Europe, wait and then raise hell. They form the current backbone of al Qaeda— some of the operatives who may have masterminded global attacks since 2004. They remain a very tight bunch, although now thoroughly globalized; treason—and squealing—is out of the question; and most astonishingly, there's nothing to it of a secret society. They work as a band of brothers, sharing everything—apartments, bank accounts—sometimes even in the open. Al-Qaeda's joint chiefs, the command and control structure, the base cells and the complex networks, everything works like some family enterprise in northern Italy, based on personal relationships. But then a complex process of deterritorialization sets in, and the virus spreads.

For al Qaeda, this posed a tremendous problem. It was easy for Western intelligence (or for Musharraf's intelligence apparatchiks, when they're up to it) to grab a bunch of operatives after identifying a single one of them. And with no al Qaeda training camps in Afghanistan anymore, there were no places left to meet: Chechnya is part of Planet Gaza, the tribal areas in the Pakistan-Afghan border were teeming with FBI and Special Forces, and the Shawal region that straddles Pakistan and Afghanistan is too remote and under constant satellite surveillance.

In *Les Nouveaux Martyrs d'Allah* Farhad Khosrokhavar, a director at the respected French School of High Studies on Social Sciences conceptualizes the new specimens of the "warrior neo-*umma*," "the annex product of a plural modernity which has no center of cultural gravity." These are the new martyrs of the Islamic diaspora, and we may include in this category future self-service jihadis. They may be multicultural, but at the same time they frontally reject the West. As Khosrokhavar describes it, "Islam crystallizes the rejection of the West. Islam fits as a religion of the dominated, of those smothered by Western arrogance." As their alienation leads them to consider that "the whole earth is a land of exile" the only refuge left is the virtual *umma*, wherever they may tread (usually in the womb of global cities like London, Paris, Madrid, but it can be the Gaza strip, Cairo or the *casbah* in Algiers).

They see the West as ignoring, despising or violently rejecting Islam. So they react with Islamism remixed, blending "Westernization, hate of the West, the mythification of the original Muslim community, the utopian will to restore Islam to its past splendor and the promotion of death as a martyr in a jihad against a frightened West where people, unlike them, are incapable of dying." Why a suicide bomber is so powerful? Because he represents a "challenge to Western technical, economic and military superiority." The martyr may claim ritualized sacred death as his victory.

Once again we see that jihad is in the mind. It is already implanted, and flourishing, in the heart of the West. It cannot possibly be smothered by the mere technicalities of a Long War. This is not even a clash of civilizations. As Khosrokhavar interprets it, this new jihadi concept of Islam is like the shadowy face of our global civilization conformed by the hegemonic West. It's like the face of Lee Marvin after suicide blonde Gloria Grahame throws a pot of boiling coffee at him in the classic noir *The Big Heat*. Call it the dark side of the Globalistan moon.

As self-service jihadis started seeing the light (or revealing their dark side) al Qaeda kept mutating still further. To survive and prosper, it needed more converts, and it needed to strike an array of strategic alliances. An additional problem was that al Qaeda was never a political movement: it is basically an attack machine. Jihad yes, always. But the local objectives involved could not be more disparate— from Chechens fighting Russian occupation to Iraqis fighting U.S. occupation. Franchising, anyway, worked wonders. As more people in more countries started blaming al Qaeda for each and every attack, the desired cumulative effect was the same: al Qaeda is everywhere. Brand recognition is the name of the game.

Local al Qaeda loose alliances now include everybody and his neighbor: Jemaah Islamiya in Indonesia (the Bali bombing) and Southeast Asia; warlord Gulbuddin Hekmatyar's jihadis in southeastern Afghanistan; the Islamic Movement of Uzbekistan, IMU (responsible for repeated attacks in Tashkent); and even, for a while, the shadowy, thuggish, one-legged jack-of-all-trades Abu Musab al-Zarqawi, configured by the Bush administration as the new Osama in the Sunni triangle and then killed when he was of no use for the spinning machine anymore.

"Al Qaeda," the global brand, lives. Like Coke or Nike, "al Qaeda" suits everybody. For Putin in Russia, the truculent Islam Karimov in Uzbekistan, even Gloria Macapagal-Arroyo in the Philippines, "al Qaeda" could always be the ideal excuse for any repressive or inept regime presenting its credentials as a full-fledged member of the "war on terror." For al Qaeda's purposes, Osama's status as supreme evil is an invaluable propaganda coup. And for al Qaeda franchises—free to pursue their own initiatives—using the brand means guaranteed media impact.

From the mid-2000s "al Qaeda" the brand embarked on an inexorable logic of expansion. Al Qaeda will keep deepening its alliances with ethnic and nationalist movements—with the heirs of Chamil Basayev, the emir of the mujahedeen in Chechnya and trainer of the Black Widow squadrons of female suicide bombers, killed by the Russians in July 2006, or with sectors of the Iraqi resistance in the Sunni triangle. "Global" al Qaeda in all these cases works and will continue to work as a sort of "Foreign Legion," as French scholar Olivier Roy puts it, a hard-as-nails military vanguard that is useful for a local agenda for a determined period of time.

"Global" al Qaeda may also even profit if some national liberation movements, in desperation, decide to go on an all-out offensive, improving their alliances of circumstance with al Qaeda. The al Qaeda brand might also become attractive to fringe sectors of the extreme left because more than appealing to radical Islam, al Qaeda was succeeding in branding its image as the revolutionary vanguard in the fight against American imperialism—at least until Hezbollah stole its thunder by the way it resisted the Israeli Shock and Awe on Lebanon in the summer of 2006.

There is no evidence the moderate Sunni Arab world will find any answers anytime soon to counterpunch the spread of self-service jihad. Even major Arab-language media like *al-Hayat* and *Asharq al-Awsat* started debating "Islamo-fascism." But the debate would be more profitable if it concentrated on al Qaeda's foreign policy. Just like Washington neocons, al Qaeda seems to be engaged in regime change—fighting to place rulers, especially in the Arab world, who do not clash with its political ambitions, even if such leaders don't subscribe to al Qaeda's worldview.

Al Qaeda will continue to make a killing among alienated Pakistanis in the U.K. It's certainly not surprising that Ayman al-Zawahiri broadcasted the final tape of Shehzad Tanweer, one of the alleged perpetrators of London 7/7, where Tanweer, facing the camera, and with a thick Yorkshire accent, says that "what you have witnessed now is only the beginning of a string of attacks that will continue and become stronger...until you pull your forces out of Afghanistan and Iraq."

To fight this threat, the E.U. will never adopt a U.S.-style Patriot Act. Moreover, E.U.-based humanitarian or charity organizations are not as controlled as they are in the U.S. What E.U. analysts are seriously considering is what in intelligence circles is regarded as al Qaeda's master plan, a document called *al Qaeda strategy up to the year 2020*, probably written by Egyptian war strategist Muhammad Mekkawi. Mekkawi talks about the establishment of a jihadi battleground ranging from Afghanistan to Syria and Lebanon. Iraq of course is crucial in the overall strategy. Al Qaeda wants nothing less than control of Baghdad.

As Michael Scheuer, the former head of the CIA's Bin Laden unit, anonymously warned in a prescient book *Through Our Enemies' Eyes*, the West has simply refused to listen carefully to Osama and al-Zawahiri. They've always repeated the same themes: if you bomb our cities, we will bomb yours; if you leave our lands, stop planting corrupt leaders and stop plundering our resources, we will stop.

The main challenge for the Salafi-jihadist, though, still remain: how to "convert" *en masse* modernized, well-educated Muslims—from the wealthy Kuwaiti, Saudi, Jordanian middle classes to the dilapidated suburbs of London and Marseilles—to what is essentially a political struggle. The Salafi-jihadist violent methods will always repulse the overwhelming moderate majority of the 1.5 billion *umma*. Prof. Bustinza from Catalonia paints a broad picture of jihad-adverse Islam: "Islam will rebound. The new wave of Islam is more introspective. If the mosques were empty during the 1960s and then full by the 1980s, now people are praying inside their homes. This is a personalized Islam. The majority of the new youth in Islam is saying that they will not engage in sacrifices anymore—not for homeland and not for the *umma*. Now it's time for individualism." He places great faith in the "dynamic Islam of Asia—in Malaysia, Indonesia and India."

Once again it's important to re-examine the role of Abdullah Azzam, the Muslim Brotherhood Palestinian carrying a Jordanian passport who founded the *Maktab al-Khidamat* (the Office of Services) in Peshawar in the early 1980s—the embryo of what one day would be known as "al Qaeda." Crucially, Azzam was neither a Salafi nor a Wahhabi. He thought at the time that the only winning jihad strategy was to fight for the liberation of the entire Islamic *umma*. The anti-Soviet Afghan jihad was at hand and it would be the perfect model. Afghanistan for Azzam was essentially a training ground for the revolutionary vanguard that would lead the *umma* in a war of resistance against the West. Azzam was never interested in creating an Islamic state in Afghanistan. Also crucially: he never targeted civilians, and never even thought of conducting a terrorist bombing. al Qaeda's harsher and more lethal tactics had nothing to do with Azzam: the transformation was operated by Osama and al-Zawahiri—blessed by their powerful Saudi and Pakistani sponsors/protectors.

After al Qaeda lost its Afghan sanctuary, it adapted extremely fast. It's fair to say that now in many ways it is reverting to some of Azzam's conceptualization. It tried to stop behaving as a sect (true, it never had a political branch; but it tried to kickstart a "press office," via the notorious, sporadic Osama or al-Zawahiri audios and videos). It abandoned any pretence of finding a new training ground: but now the actual "Talibanistan" in the Pakistani Northwest Frontier Province might be the ideal candidate—since it's not infested with Musharraf's troops or the FBI anymore.

Ever since the late 1990s there has been a heated, serious discussion all over Islam over al Qaeda's strategy—if there ever was any. Should *dawah* (propaganda, political proselitism) be privileged instead of jihad?

But then, around mid-2004, Islamic scholars from Morocco to Malaysia started to finally legitimize al Qaeda as a *muqadamaul Jaish*—in fact a revolutionary vanguard. This totally Western concept was absolutely unheard of in Islam—well, at least until the symbolically charged spring of 2003 when Baghdad was "liberated" by George W. Bush's Christian armies.

The concept of revolutionary vanguard simply does not exist in Islam. Before Hezbollah surged to the fore in the summer of 2006, al Qaeda's internationalism might conceive of merging with some radical strands of the only other global protest movement: the alter-globalization, anti-imperialism brigade. But even then al Qaeda and the Islamist front still faced a daunting task: if they wanted more Western allies, they would have to abdicate from their strict Islamic platform. And if they wanted more allies in the Muslim world, they would have to be much less radical. Even though al Qaeda is in fact configured as a throwback to the extreme left and pro-Third World radical movements of the 1970s, al Qaeda's latest successes have undoubtedly been in the Muslim world.

As much as al Qaeda's only strategic goal is trapping the U.S., Washington helped al Qaeda by trapping itself in Iraq and in still another, dangerous form of hubris, George W. Bush's Greater Middle East. Al Qaeda's dream of mobilizing the *umma* by way of jihad may have been derailed. But if al Qaeda somehow keeps winning Muslim hearts and minds, the Bush/Cheney system has only itself to blame. Considering all the "clash of civilizations" rhetoric, all the barely repressed

Islamophobia and a "war on terror" turned The Long War bound to last indefinitely, as Dick Cheney himself said on the record, it may have been the system's original intent anyway.

Amidst all this drama, intervened a most spectacular plot twist. Al Qaeda didn't see it coming—and will take a long time to react: suddenly, al Qaeda had become a minor player in the Salafi-jihadist constellation and an even minor player among the 1.5 billion *umma* in terms of how to fight back against the hegemony of the West.

Hezbollah—the most sophisticated guerrilla movement in the world—showed the way, in reality show time, during the summer of 2006 Israel-Hezbollah asymmetric war. The contrast of a Shiite resistance movement enjoying broad popular support with the cultish, isolated bunch of Salafi-jihadists could not be starker. In the Top 5 of the most popular leaders of the Arab world al Qaeda was already losing ground to the Muslim Brotherhood and Hamas in Palestine. Now it was positively blown out of the court by the Iranian leadership and especially Hezbollah's Sheikh Nasrallah—the "new Nasser." Hezbollah imprinted its mark as fierce defender of Palestinian rights. The organization of Sunni Hamas is now modeled on Hezbollah.

In the complex battle for hearts and minds of the Arab and wider Islamic worlds, moderates had assured a strategic victory with long-ranging repercussions. In Egypt and in Jordan the Sunni Muslim Brotherhood—the oldest, largest modern Islamist movement in the world—supported Hezbollah unconditionally. That meant it was supporting Hezbollah's patron the Islamic Republic of Iran as well—this Sunni-Shiite convergence illustrating an overwhelming Shiite prestige revival much to the chagrin of Salafi-jihadists and the House of Saud. Plenty of Sunnis may still dream of the (improbable) return of the Caliphate but at the same time they simply can't get enough of Shiite discipline and organization. In the summer of 2006 Muslim Brotherhood scholars, almost in awe, stressed that Hezbollah could be finally offering the model for an Islamic state. Sheikh Yousef al- Qardawi publicly regretted there was no Hezbollah in Egypt, Jordan and the wider Arab world.

But this ain't no honeymoon: Shiites won't easily forget the thuggish Zarqawi cipher calling for their extermination in Iraq. Salafi-jihadists do regard Shiites as apostates. But there are conditionalities. The "original" al Qaeda never attacked Shiites per se. "al Qaeda in the Land of the Two Rivers," the thug Zarqawi's outfit, was a different story: a tactical alliance . It's not that Osama or al-Zawahiri themselves were endorsing the killing of Iraqi Shiites. But the danger is clear: al Qaeda's undisputed strategic defeat vis-à-vis Hezbollah may embolden Salafi-jihadists to go ballistic.

Nothing will shake off the Tehran leadership's certainty that al Qaeda was and remains a prized CIA asset. From the point of view of Iran the 1980s anti-USSR jihad was won purely by Afghan mujahedeen—including a substantial contingent of Shiite Hazaras. Iran was not directly part of the Afghan jihad because it was fighting the armies of Saddam Hussein in the unbelievably bloody 1980-1988 Iran-Iraq war. Iran totally ignores the Arab-Afghan legend—widely propagated by Osama himself and assorted Salafi-jihadists—that the jihad was not only won by Arab-Afghans but symbolized the death knell of the Soviet empire, thus enabling the rise of the U.S. as sole superpower.

The theological—and ideological—abyss between Salafis and Salafi-jihadists on one side and Shiites on the other is unbridgeable. Not to mention the accumulation of historical horrors. In 1801, for instance, 12,000 Wahhabis, led by Ibn Saud in person, who founded the first Saudi state with crucial support by Sheikh Abd al-Wahhab, invaded Karbala, killed more than 2000 people and violated and demolished the tomb of revered Imam Hussein, the son of the revered Ali and Fatima. Not by accident Ibn Saud was later assassinated by a Shiite. For any Iranian Salafism is identified with the hegemonic and sectarian Islam of the Ummayad dynasty. In contrast Iran practices—as codified by Ayatollah Khomeini—*Islam-e-Nab-e-Mohammadi* ("the pure Islam of Prophet Muhammad"). The 1978/1979 Islamic Revolution was not even a jihad: it was *Enghelab* ("Revolution," in Persian). "Jihad" only came up briefly in the first years of the Revolution as *Jihad-e-Sazindazi* ("jihad for reconstruction").

Al Qaeda's ideology as transfigured by al-Zawahiri rules that the priority is to get rid of the "far away" enemy—the U.S. After the U.S. abandons occupied Islamic lands then the myriad problems inside Islam will be tackled. Essentially this might be considered as the same agenda of the theocratic nationalist leadership in Tehran. The difference is the method. Iranians always argue—successfully—that al Qaeda's methods simply do not work because as you attack the U.S. the only political dividend you reap is even more American hegemony. It should not be forgotten that Osama himself over the years has deployed a full seduction strategy vis-à-vis the leadership in Tehran—to no avail. Supreme Leader Ayatollah Khamenei and the top ayatollahs in Qom regard the 1979 Islamic Revolution as the undisputed vanguard of Islam. Obviously al Qaeda simply cannot match it. Especially with all those dodgy CIA connections.

Whatever al Qaeda's and Salafi-jihadists next moves, and whatever Jihadistan's new tactics, the ultimate choice for the Middle East is not between secular dictatorship and secular democracy; it's between U.S.-backed secular dictatorship (of the Mubarak kind) and Islamic democracy (such as Hamas winning elections in Palestine, Hezbollah participating in Lebanon's government). What the people of the Middle East want and what Washington insists they want will always amount to a clash of different galaxies. It will remain so until the U.S.—and Triad member E.U. as well—allow the Middle Eastern masses to choose what they really want to do with their future. This is not gonna happen at least for the next generations—because of all that oil. Thus we're all left, once again, suffering the appalling consequences of Liquid (and Viscous) War.

~ 6 ~

OSAMASTAN

"We have never seen anything that was convincing to us at all that Osama bin Laden was present at any stage of Tora Bora -- before, during or after."

—**Rear Admiral Bruce Quigley,** spokesman for General Tommy Franks, quoted April 17, 2002, in *The Washington Post*

Meteoric mediocrities of our celebrity/popularity-contest "culture" may snarl that the totalitarian nihilists of Salafi-jihadism attack our Western model of secular, liberal democracy, our Enlightenment heritage, and globalization. But it's much more complex than a mere "they envy our mall freedom" mechanism. It's not the success of the Western liberal democracy model that engenders attacks against it; it's the double standards, the hypocrisy, the betrayals, the crude violence—from the betrayal of the Arab nation in the 1920s and the support to repressive Egypt and Saudi Arabia to the invasion and plunder of Islamic lands, Abu Ghraib, Guantanamo, Israel crushing Palestine, the neglect of Afghanistan, the U.S. green light (twice) for the destruction of Lebanon.

It would be very foolish for the West to take the grievances that Osama represent lightly. Just like the Great Helmsman Mao for legions of Chinese taxi drivers, I have seen Osama the pop hero in T-shirts, videos and cassettes (and now, in Peshawar, on DVD) make his mark over bazaars, mosques and madrassas from Palestine to eastern Java, from southern Philippines to Peshawar and the neighboring, medieval Pakistani tribal areas, and even in Bangkok's smoggy streets. The Bush administration may have demonized him as the Prince of Darkness in a 24/7 planetary soap. But for millions of urban, radicalized, dirt-poor seething in anger in an immense Islamic slum nebula, Osama is comparable to El Comandante Fidel in 1959 Cuba—a true mass hero. Destitute Arab brothers knew there are no more heroes rising from the desert like Muhamad in the 7th Century, so for them Osama became the remixed version of the Holy Prophet—the media-savvy Warrior Prophet. A 2005 pan-Islamic poll revealed that Osama is supported, among others, by 51% of Pakistanis, 60% of Jordanians and 35% of Indonesians.

After 5 years and billions of dollars—including an Osama Central at the barbed-wired-to-death U.S. Consulate in Peshawar dripping with ultra high tech decryption and eavesdropping gear—his head still had not been brought to the White House on dry ice. Who's to blame? It's actually a whole chain (of fools? Somebody please bring Aretha Franklin). Americans blame Pakistanis who blame Afghans who blame the Taliban who blame Pakistanis who blame Americans.

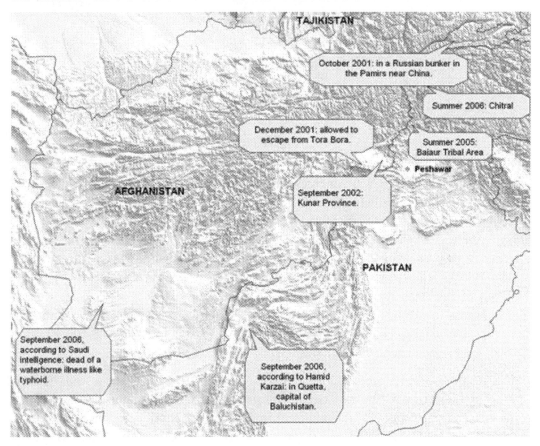

Figure 11. Rumored locations of Osama bin Laden, 2001-2006.

Every major player in Peshawar and the tribal areas knows selected ISI big guns protect Osama. I was part of this circus/parallel universe of tribals, spies, soldiers, sherpas, operatives, hacks and "counterinsurgency experts" for quite some time, spending a great deal of 2001 and 2002 tracking Osama. Before the U.S. started bombing the Taliban in October 2001 I had "surefire" Peshawar info that Osama was in a Russian bunker in the Pamirs, near the Chinese border. When I got to Tora

Bora in early December, he had left only a few days before. In September 2002 I was tracking him in Kunar province, in Afghanistan (Gulbuddin Hekmatyar's background), just to be told he "might" have been there only a few days before in an al Qaeda/Taliban/Islamist front jihadi love fest.

In the summer of 2003 Osama was for the first time "surely" in south Waziristan. In the summer of 2005 he might be further north, in Bajaur. In the summer of 2006 he might be even further north, in Chitral, very close to the Hindu Kush and with perfect access, once again, to Kunar. It would be no problem for Osama's party to cross from ultra-conservative Chitral to deserted Kunar and back: my photographer Jason Florio and myself, we did it half-way in August 2001 enveloped in a pair of light-blue burkas, until our contact on the other side royally messed up. We were on our way to Nuristan, formerly Kafiristan which much a propos means "land of the infidels": another postcard-perfect Osama location. As of the fall of 2006 Musharraf said Osama was in Kunar (his ISI should know). Hamid Karzai said Osama was in Quetta, Baluchistan's capital (not absurd, because of the tight Baluchistan-Hadramut connection). Saudi intelligence said Osama was dead (diversionist tactic). Inside word in Peshawar was that Osama was "certainly" around the magnificent, 7700-meter-high Tirich Mir, in the Hindu Kush, way north of Chitral, almost in Afghanistan, where he could easily stay in cross-border mode with Kunar. His health was excellent. Maybe Google Earth would find him taking a short, slow walk in the Hindu Kush.

He may not be Sheikh Guevara. But he did read Chairman Mao. His Long March took place when he had to leave Sudan and set up camp in Afghanistan (just like the communists had to set up theirs in a Chinese back of beyond). And he organized a "base": the term "Qaeda" is a literal translation of "base" as theorized by Mao in the 1930s. And just like the communists, the base spread out to conquer a countryside ripe for Revolution: from Afghanistan to the Indus valley and then to Central Asia, the Middle East and beyond.

He is idolized in large swathes of the Arab world because he knows the Holy Koran and the *hadith*—the traditional teachings. He knows how to tweak the financial markets. And of course he knows everything about Globalistan. No wonder. People from the bin Laden clan are bedouin fishermen from the Hadramut region. They have been "global" since time immemorial. Their ships have been everywhere since the Middle Ages. They always knew eastern Africa very well: that's why Osama was based in Khartoum, in Sudan. As with the Chinese *guanxi*, the whole thing about al Qaeda boils down to connections. And Osama's connections are also very well introduced to Southeast Asia. With Suharto, the Yemenite clan was in power for more than three decades; a few million Indonesians of Arab descent still have close contact with the people from the Hadramut.

In al Qaeda's global jihad, the most important prizes remain Saudi Arabia, Egypt and Pakistan. The key to all of Osama and al Qaeda's business is the intersection of the Persian world, the Indian world and the Arab world: this means the vast deserts of Baluchistan (which is half-Iranian and half-Pakistani), and legendary Peshawar. Baluchis—redoubtable fighters—comprise one-third of the army of their neighbors, the sultanate of Oman; and in Baluchistan ports the men who lay down the law are Arabs from Oman and the Hadramut.

To understand Osama's long-term view, it's essential to consider his Four Pillars of Jihad: 1) the Arab peninsula, with all its oil wealth and Islam's two most sacred sites, Mecca and Medina. 2) the Indus valley, which means basically Pakistan—a technology-savvy nuclear state with an Islamic Army permeated by fervent Salafis and Salafi-jihadist. 3) Egypt, the heart and soul of the Muslim world, and the base for al-Zawahiri, al Qaeda's brain. 4) This is the trickiest pillar: his dream of a worldwide Sunni Revolution.

Of course Osama's bête noire is the House of Saud—which was born from a bedouin revolt and was supposed to reestablish the "purity of Islam" through the ultra-conservative Wahhabi faith. But for Osama the Saudi royal family boils down to a bunch of corrupt cowards and traitors. It's important to remember there is no hereditary monarchy in Islam. The only family widely respected is the Hashemite family —who are the legitimate descendants of Prophet Muhammad.

Pakistan is vital to Osama's design. It was never a secret in select circles in Pakistan that Musharraf controls what the ISI—a state within a state—is up to: he may want public opinion to believe otherwise. Musharraf is a master of deception. (And quite a good book promoter, as evidenced by his appearance on Jon Stewart's *The Daily Show* in the fall of 2006: not many American politicians would have been able to pull that off as smoothly, even with the advantage of operating in their own culture.)

Osama immensely profited from the fact that during the 1980s he had two key Pashtun allies. General Hamid Gul may have come very late to handle the Afghan anti-Soviet jihad, but he definitely took the credit for it—alongside the "money-man," Prince Turki of Saudi Arabia. General Nasirullah Babar—today living a cosy life in Peshawar—was no one else than the man who invented the Taliban. These two generals from prominent Pashtun families were the real masters of Afghanistan. When evidence collected by Western intelligence showed that al Qaeda, prior to 9/11, was directed by a sort of Central Committee, it was clear that the committee also included high-ranking Pakistani generals, some from the ISI and some of them Pashtun. If Musharraf somehow "disappears" the ISI Islamist hardcore will have nearly direct access to the Pakistani nuclear bomb.

The most plausible definition of victory for Osama, even long-term, means three things: the end of Saudi Arabia as we know it—where Islam's holiest sites are not guarded by "traitors" and where immense oil reserves would not revert to the West's benefit; a nuclear Pakistan; and the death knell to any Muslim regime defined as moderate or allied with the U.S. This is what Osama bin Laden really wants.

Osama's most hardcore supporters were not in Afghanistan. They are in Yemen—a federation of tribes where Shiites and Sunnis are equally represented. Yemeni secret services remain in al Qaeda's pocket. They control as many as 50,000 fighters in north Yemen, all of them Salafi-jihadist.

Osama wants to reign not only over Riyadh, but most of all over Mecca and Medina. He may be terribly wrong about a multitude of factors: his belief that Muslims won't go to war against other Muslims; the strength of Salafi-jihadists in different latitudes; the anti-Salafi-jihadist stance of the moderate majority of Pakistanis; the force of will of his two mortal enemies, Pakistani President Musharraf and Saudi King Abdullah. He may be spectacularly wrong. But he (and the descendants of the global al Qaeda brand) will keep on trying to detonate his own Islamic Revolution, his Allah-blessed self-appointed mission—the stuff of dreams emanating from the bowels of the Thousand and One Nights Hindu Kush cave where he is hiding right now.

The key face-off is between Osama and Saudi Arabia's King Abdullah. The plot has all the elements of a Hollywood blockbuster. It may be convoluted, but essentially not very hard to follow. Psychoanalysis—Freudian, Lacanian or even the Paris sidewalk café variety—would have a field day comparing notes on these two main characters. It all starts with Mom. Both Osama and Abdullah are the only sons of their respective mothers. And both mothers happen to be from Syria. Osama's mother is reportedly 100% Syrian, and Abdullah's is part Syrian. Osama as well as Abdullah are also in conflict with their half-brothers—more conservative, more "Saudi" and more pro-American in both cases.

King Abdullah, according to diplomatic sources, is also a man who tolerates different expressions of Islam. He is almost a hedonist, for Islamic parameters. There are plenty of Iraqi, Syrian and Lebanese intellectuals in his entourage. Osama, on the other hand, is austere and ascetic, almost a hermit (but I always wondered if his caves come with dry cleaning, room service and satellite TV): his brand of violent jihad is his means of self-expression.

King Abdullah's dream is to turn the Arab peninsula into an open house for the whole Arab world—including Iraqis, Syrians, Yemenis, Palestinians, Egyptians, Sudanese, and, the ultimate prize, even Shiite Iranians (who are Persians, not

Arabs). In terms of disparity between the rulers and the ruled, it's hard to find a match for Saudi Arabia (a Saudi bank, based on a Merrill Lynch study, estimated in 2002 that the kingdom had at least US$ 750 billion outside its borders, 4 to 5 times its GNP, 60% invested in the U.S. and 30% in Europe). Most of the national wealth is concentrated in the hands of the 6000 to 7000 Saudi princes. E.U. intelligence sources are sure that Osama controls at least one Saudi Prince—if not at least half of the ruling circle of power. Osama's Prince could be Prince Turki. They went to school together, and it was Prince Turki who sent Osama to Afghanistan. Connections have also been made between members of the Saudi family and shady Saudi Wahhabi charities which are major al Qaeda fundraisers. In Saudi Arabia there's no separation between what belongs to the state and what belongs to the crown. There's no public accountability. Osama's business operations have been supported by many Islamist banks directly or indirectly controlled by the Saudis.

Abdullah dreams that one day all Arabs will forge a common front to face the Americans—and Israel—but without having to go to war. The U.S. already handed him a "gift"—closing down U.S. bases in the Kingdom after the invasion of Iraq. This was also one of Osama's most pressing demands. What is still unclear is what Washington got in return. E.U. diplomats, requesting anonymity, swear it is a prominent Saudi role as the guardian of a comprehensive peace treaty with Israel.

The Abdullah dream scenario would mean a certain triumph of Arab nationalism packaged in an embryonic form of democracy. E.U. diplomats believe this semi-democratic Arab world certainly would not be allied to the U.S.—it would rather strike a closer relationship with Japan, Korea and with the E.U. itself.

But a Saudi oil crisis may derail all these plans, as Mathew Simmons has argued in *Twilight in the Desert: the Coming Saudi Oil Shock and the World Economy*. Simmons stresses that "as far as I know, there is not a single contingency plan in place or currently being written by any of the think tanks of the world that sets out a model illustrating how the world can continue to function smoothly once it is clear that Saudi Arabian oil has peaked."

On the opposite end of King Abdullah's large and ambitious spectrum, what really matters in Osama's grand design is those connections he was able to build during the 1990s: al Qaeda's priceless connections inside the Pakistani Army and the ISI; al-Qaeda's influence over the Yemeni intelligence service; and the privileged connections with key *ulemas* in Saudi Arabia and with the Muslim Brotherhood in Egypt.

Inside Saudi Arabia, Osama plays on two key fronts. The Nejd region is in the center of Saudi Arabia, around Riyadh: this is where the founder of the regime, Ibn Saud, comes from. The rest of the kingdom is deeply anti-Nejd. The consensual attitude used to be secular and anti-Wahhabi,, but Osama's operatives are trying their best to turn it into hardcore Islamist. And Osama's pious Islamic credentials remain a major hit with the *ulemas*: a substantial majority is pro-Osama and regards the pro-American stance of the Saudi family as the plague.

In the—for the moment unlikely—event of healthy Saudi-Iranian cooperation, and with the U.S. military out of Saudi Arabia, there would be a lot less tension inside the Kingdom. Abdullah definitely does not want a new Caliphate. On the contrary: revolution is the last thing in his mind. He wants to reinforce secular states like Syria. He is regarded by E.U. intelligence circles as an Arab patriot. He wants a winning Arab world. He is sick of so many failures, like the abominable failure of both Ba'ath parties in Syria and Iraq and the failure of the Israeli-Palestinian peace process.

Emirates businessmen pointed me to a crucial fact: even Saudis who hate Osama were against handing him over to the Americans. Virtually nobody wanted him to fall. Otherwise he would have fallen a long time ago. Although Abdullah and the House of Saud dwell in a rarified world off limits to foreigners (especially infidels, unless they are George Bush senior or James Baker), it's fair to assume they are mulling the only two options left. Osama's revolutionary folly may lead al Qaeda to a spectacular debacle. Or this may be the beginning of the end for the House of Saud. Osama has raised a lot of Hell right at the heart of the Saudi court. The Saudi opposition is totally pro-Osama. And a revolution in neighboring Yemen can happen anytime – with an overspill effect on Saudi Arabia.

To compound the distress the Saudi royal family began to suspect that the U.S. may engineer for them the same fate to be met by Saddam Hussein's Iraq; that is, a partition. Saudi Arabia would be split in three:

- The Hashemite family once again controlling holy Mecca and Medina;
- Emboldened, autonomous Saudi Shiites controlling all that oil in the Eastern Province of Hasa;
- And the Wahhabis left for dead, baking in the inclement sands of the Nejd desert.

That's enough to ensure many a cognac-drenched sleepless night in Riyadh.

~ 7 ~

AMERICASTAN IN BABYLON

KILGORE: I love the smell of napalm in the morning. You know, one time we had a hill bombed, for 12 hours. When it was all over, I walked up. We didn't find one of 'em, not one stinkin' dink body. The smell, you know that gasoline smell, the whole hill. Smelled like... victory. Someday this war's gonna end...

—**Francis F. Coppola's** *Apocalypse Now*

POGUE COLONEL: Marine, what is that button on your body armor?

PRIVATE JOKER: A peace symbol, sir.

POGUE COLONEL: Where'd you get it?

PRIVATE JOKER: I don't remember, sir.

POGUE COLONEL: What is that you've got written on your helmet?

PRIVATE JOKER: "Born to Kill," sir.

POGUE COLONEL: You write "Born to Kill" on your helmet and you wear a peace button. What's that supposed to be, some kind of sick joke?

PRIVATE JOKER: No, sir.

POGUE COLONEL: You'd better get your head and your ass wired together, or I will take a giant shit on you.

PRIVATE JOKER: Yes, sir.

POGUE COLONEL: Now answer my question or you'll be standing tall before the man.

PRIVATE JOKER: I think I was trying to suggest something about the duality of man, sir.

POGUE COLONEL: The what?

PRIVATE JOKER: The duality of man. The Jungian thing, sir.

POGUE COLONEL: Whose side are you on, son?

PRIVATE JOKER: Our side, sir.

POGUE COLONEL: Don't you love your country?

PRIVATE JOKER: Yes, sir.

POGUE COLONEL: Then how about getting with the program? Why don't you jump on the team and come on in for the big win?

PRIVATE JOKER: Yes, sir.

POGUE COLONEL: Son, all I've ever asked of my marines is that they obey my orders as they would the word of God. We are here to help the Vietnamese, because inside every gook there is an American trying to get out. It's a hard-ball world, son. We've gotta keep our heads until this peace craze blows over.

PRIVATE JOKER: Aye-aye, sir.

—**Stanley Kubrick's** *Full Metal Jacket*

The occupation is the first and last cause of the problem, it has overthrown the [former] regime without a plan, it has suppressed the state with no reason, it has led to the resistance and it has infiltrated it, it has brought al Qaeda to Iraq... Iraq today is Americastan.

—**Dr. Mahmoud Al-Mash'hadani**, Speaker, Iraqi Parliament, summer of 2006

I like to tell people when the final history is written on Iran—Iraq—*it'll look like just a comma. Uh, because, um, there is--my point is there is a strong will for democracy...*

—**George W. Bush**, CNN interview, September 24, 2006

I had to hear it from one of them. Straight from the heart. Well, he was one of them. And his father had been one of Ho Chi Minh's comrades at the *maquis*. We used to meet every early evening by the Hoam Kien Lake. It was the summer of 2003 and I was working for a few weeks in Cambodia and Vietnam, taking a break from Iraq, although "Highway to Hell" on the way to Fallujah kept eating up my neurons non-stop. One night we were having a *pho* at a roadside stall when he told me—in perfect French: "A specter haunts the White House. No, not Osama bin

Laden. Not Saddam Hussein. The name is Vietnam." This was barely three months after George W. Bush, remixing Tom Cruise in *Top Gun* aboard an'aircraft carrier off San Diego harbor, had proclaimed that the war against Iraq was "over." It ain't over till the fat (guerrilla) lady sings.

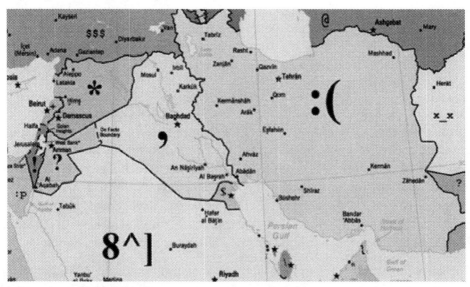

Figure 12. Commaland (Ken Layne/Wonkette.com).

Just as it had taken a few years to lose the hearts and minds of the South Vietnamese, it took the U.S. only a few days to lose the hearts and minds of the majority of Iraqis—which ultimately means losing the war, whatever the strategic final result. Topographic denials—this is the Mesopotamian desert, not the Indochinese jungle—wouldn't cut it, nor would denials by stenographer historians saying Iraqis are not as politicized as were the Vietnamese by the Communist Party. As well as in Vietnam, what was happening in Iraq already in the summer of 2003 had everything to do with patriotism and nationalism.

Tarik Aziz, wily Christian and Saddam's Grand Vizir, used to crow, before the U.S. invasion: "Let our cities be our swamps and our buildings our jungles." Mohammed Saeed Al Sahaf, a.k.a. Comical Ali, the inimitable former Minister of Information, used to say Iraq would be "another Indochina." The guerrilla war strategy against what was considered an inevitable American invasion had been perfected in Iraq for years. And the master strategist was no Assyrian or Mesopotamian general, but the legendary Vo Nguyen Giap, the former historian turned Vietnamese general who was ordered by Uncle Ho to build a popular army from scratch and later smashed both French colonialism and "American imperialism."

Iraqi strategists—from Army officials to Ba'ath Party officials—had always been thorough students of the Vietnam War, or "American War," as it is referred to in Vietnam. Iraqis were also not gullible to the point of believing the occupying power's propaganda of "nation building"—as they had not seen any building whatsoever since the "fall" of Baghdad on April 9, 2003. From the beginning—the first huge popular demonstration departing from Abu Hanifa mosque in Baghdad on April 18—the "liberation" of the Iraqi people by America had been viewed inside Iraq as a national liberation war, a "popular war" in the Giap sense against an imperialist aggressor.

The whole package could be found in the *Writings of General Giap,* a collection spanning the years 1969-1991 and published by The Gioi Editions in Hanoi: the strategy and tactics of a war of national liberation and how a "popular war against the American aggression" was organized. Initially the Ba'ath Party and the Republican Guards had not implemented what they learned—as the top Army commanders, after a campaign of preventive intimidation, were finally bought out by Pentagon cash and safe refuge. But basically the same strategy was now being implemented by the array of groups forming the Iraqi national resistance.

The objective was always to harass, bog down and demoralize a hugely superior army. Veterans of the American war in Hanoi would tell me that it was all about national consciousness, patriotism and local traditions: according to General Giap, "patriotism associated with the democratic spirit and love of socialism." In Iraq, the impetus was the same—with "love of Islam" substituting for "love of socialism." Iraqi patriotism and anti-imperialist sentiment was as strong as it was in Vietnam.

Giap wrote that "conditions should be created to attack the enemy by all means appropriated," and urban revolutionary forces should be coordinated with the countryside: in Mesopotamia in 2003 this meant attacks both in Baghdad and in the Sunni belt, already spreading towards the Shiite south. The next step of the Iraqi resistance would be, according to Giap, "to combine armed forces with political forces, armed insurrection with revolutionary war." This would mean a concerted strategy of the Sunni belt alongside Shiite groups, which so far had already switched from a "wait-and-see" attitude towards barely-disguised hostility with the American pro-consular regime.

Giap is adamant: "The strategy of popular war is of a protracted war." The Iraqi resistance was following it to the hilt. Giap wrote that the Americans and the puppet South Vietnamese government were supported by "a brutal repression and coercion machine, applying against our compatriots a fascist policy of barbarity." This is exactly how the resistance—and increasingly the whole Iraqi population— was seeing robotized, scared, misguided American soldiers shooting to kill innocent women, children and even the odd Reuters cameraman. Against the "repression machine," Giap advises "guerrilla and self-defense militias" in strategic zones— exactly the way the Iraqi resistance had been acting.

Iraq in the summer of 2003 was already like Vietnam after the 1968 Tet offensive (George W. Bush would finally have his "Tet moment", but only in the fall of 2006). The U.S. could have left Vietnam anytime—but this would mean to lose face, in an Asian sense, and to admit defeat: ultimately, this is what happened when that last helicopter abandoned the American embassy in Saigon on April 1975. The U.S. would not leave Iraq. But by remaining in Iraq for "years"—as the Pentagon would have it—there was only one question: how many body bags would it take for U.S. public opinion to demand a withdrawal?

I had learned of countless former high-ranking Iraqi Army officials—now un-employed—who had been called to join the resistance: they answered they would, sooner or later, "if the Americans continue to humiliate us." Others were financing small guerrilla groups to the tune of thousands of dollars. The reward for someone launching a rocket against a Bradley fighting vehicle was around US$ 350—enough for many to buy what was now the rage in Baghdad's free market: a new color TV with satellite dish.

In Vietnam the resistance was organized by the Party. In Iraq, it was organized by the tribes. Tribal chiefs were about to reach the deadline of the "grace period" they conceded to the Americans. The resistance could count either on former Ba'ath Party and army officials as well as on a mass of angry, unemployed youngsters following the call of Sunni Arab clerics, their own tribal chiefs and, more broadly, Arab patriotism. The "popular war" was getting bolder—surface-to-air missiles launched against military transport planes, sabotage of the Kirkuk-Ceyhan oil pipeline. These were the "soft" days when U.S. Central Command would reluc-tantly admit there were some 25 attacks a day.

These Sunni Arab mujahedeen—the counterparts of the Sunni Afghan mujahe-deen fighting the anti-American jihad in Afghanistan—could count on the active complicity of the local population, just like in Vietnam. It was a "popular war" in the sense that people in any given neighborhood would know who organized an attack and obviously would not tell the invaders about it.

In 1995, on the 20th anniversary of the end of the American War, former De-fense Secretary Robert McNamara met the legendary Giap in Hanoi. The old warrior told him that the U.S. had entered a war without knowing anything about Viet-nam's complex history, culture and fighting spirit against wave after wave of foreign invasions. McNamara was forced to agree. America emerged from Vietnam with nothing to show but wounded pride. In Iraq, Corporatistan at least expected to get away with the oil. And this was basically what young American soldiers were dying for: Executive Order number 13303, signed by George W. Bush in late May 2003.

Executive order 13303 stated with respect to "all Iraqi petroleum and petroleum products, and interests therein," that "any attachment, judgment, decree, lien, execution, garnishment, or other judicial process is prohibited, and shall be deemed null and void." Commenting on it, Jim Vallette of the Institute of Policy Studies in Washington said that "Bush has in effect unilaterally declared Iraqi oil to be the unassailable province of U.S. oil corporations."

Giap wrote that the resistance in Vietnam should "smash the Macchiavellian design" of "making Vietnamese fight Vietnamese, of nourishing war by war." The U.S. was making the same mistake in Iraq. The U.S. went into Vietnam, among other factors, to flex its symbolic credibility and to show off its military technology: in Iraq, the theatrical demonstration was certainly awesome, but early on it was already possible to preview the symbolic credibility collapsing. In Vietnam, the U.S. wanted to write the textbook on how to smash a nationalist Revolution in the still dismissively denominated Third World. It failed. In Iraq, the U.S. wanted to show off how to "correct" former client regimes that deviated from the righteous path. It was also failing—as the conditions became ripe for a popular war ultimately leading to perhaps a revolutionary but certainly nationalist regime.

In Iraq—just as in Vietnam—the U.S. had de facto installed a military system. This military system would be controlling—or euphemistically "overseeing"—the political structure, and more crucially the new American-subsidized economic order. By all means, Iraq in Paul Wolfowitz's original project was supposed to become an American colony.

By the summer of 2003 it was already clear that what French historian Emmanuel Todd had defined as "theatrical micro-militarism"—"to demonstrate America's necessity in the world by slowly smashing insignificant enemies"—was the *ordre du jour*. But Shock and Awe was one thing: post-Shock and Awe was the real thing— facing the consequences of daily preemptive attacks against the social contract in a developing country. *Realpolitik* practitioner Colin Powell had been sufficiently wily to send the message: "If you break it, you own it."

Shock and Awe had been conceptualized by Harlan Ullman, a retired U.S. navy pilot. Before being upgraded to the Centre for Strategic and International Studies Ullman taught at the National War College, where his Shock and Awe was regarded as a smooth demonstration of preemptive power—forcing your enemy to give up any hope even before the battle started (Genghis Khan did the same thing, but moved by horsepower). Slightly before the war on Iraq Ullman told *The Guardian* that the one, successful historical example of Shock and Awe were the nuclear bombs unleashed over Hiroshima and Nagasaki. Iraqis didn't have to be reminded. Post-Shock and Awe Hiroshima-style wasteland was actually worse than those March 2003 sonic boom days in Baghdad.

Figure 13. Giap is adamant: "The strategy of popular war is of a protracted war." (CIA World Factbook).

Fast-forward to November 2004—the second siege and invasion of Fallujah by U.S. Marines. No one will ever know the extent of the horror: we're not talking about the embedded Hollywoodish version. Of a population of roughly 350,000, less than 8,000 people—eating roots and sometimes burying the dead in their gardens, as confirmed by the Red Cross—remained when the Americans entered the city, which was 80% reduced to rubble. There was no medicine in the hospitals to help anybody. The wounded were left to die in the streets—their remains to be consumed by packs of stray dogs. As www.iraqresistance.net, a Europe-wide collective put it, "world governments, international organizations, nobody raised a finger to stop the killing." Dozens of limbless children were taken to Baghdad's Naaman hospital. Refugees swarming towards Baghdad told horror stories of the U.S. using cluster bombs and spraying white phosphorus, a banned chemical weapon. The "surgical" operation to smash the *muqawama* (the guerrilla resistance) may have cost as much as US$ 5 billion.

Fallujah was Planet Gaza in action. Alain Joxe, sociologist, strategist and president of the French think tank Cirpes, wrote one of the most devastating indictments of the neocon worldview (*L'Empire du Chaos*, published in France in 2002). Joxe goes to the heart of the matter when he analyses the reason why Israel is so important to Washington: "Israel maintains itself as a model of delocalized border demarcation that technically interests the American military: the creation of a prototype of suburban war, with no hope of peace, but placing the prototypes of the perimeters of fortified security which will be very useful if the Empire of Chaos of George W. Bush keeps its progression."

So the key point in the whole exercise is the "military interest for a technical prototype." Joxe notes that nowhere else the prototype of suburban war is so precise and high tech as in Palestine. He then analyses how the Israeli model has been applied to the control of Baghdad. A natural development had to be the application of the Gaza model—invasion, leveling of whole neighborhoods, loads of "collateral damage"—to Fallujah.

As much as Planet Gaza in action Fallujah was also counterinsurgency run amok; or the practical failure of "Iraqification"—the Mesopotamian counterpart of Vietnamization.

In Fallujah, roughly 3,000 urban guerrillas with mortars, Kalashnikovs and rocket-propelled grenades resisted more than 12,000 marines supported by F-16s, AC-130 gunships, Cobra and Apache helicopters, an array of missiles, 500-pound and 2,000-pound bombs, Abrams tanks and Bradleys. After 19 months of occupation, the Pentagon still had not been able to put an Iraqi army in place. The backup plan had been to give U.S. troops a 182-page counterinsurgency field manual.

During the Vietnam War, counterinsurgency was conducted by Special Forces (not by GIs and marines, as in Iraq). Even then, in Vietnam, American generals simply did not understand that the force of the resistance was its complex clandestine infrastructure. By killing indiscriminately in massive covert operations like Operation Phoenix, Americans totally alienated the average Vietnamese.

In *Multitude: War and Democracy in the Age of Empire,* Tony Negri and Michael Hardt, discussing counterinsurgencies, point out how "guerrilla forces cannot survive without the support of the population and a superior knowledge of the social and physical terrain." They could be describing the guerrillas in the Sunni triangle: "Guerrillas force the dominant military power to live in a state of perpetual paranoia." In asymmetrical wars like Vietnam and Iraq, U.S. counterinsurgency tactics must not only lead to a military victory but to control of the enemy with "social, political, ideological and psychological weapons." There was ample evidence these tactics were failing in Iraq 20 months after Shock and Awe.

Negri and Hardt argue that in counterinsurgency "success does not require attacking the enemy directly but destroying the environment, physical and social, that supports it. Take away the water and the fish will die. This strategy of destroying the support environment led, for example, to indiscriminate bombings in Vietnam, Laos and Cambodia, to widespread killing, torture and harassment of peasants in Central and South America." This—"take away the water and the fish will die"—is exactly what happened in Fallujah. And it didn't work, because "the many noncombatants who suffer cannot be called collateral damage because they are in fact the direct targets, even if their destruction is really a means to attack the primary enemy." Fallujah's population had been the direct target this time—the "water" that was essential to the resistance "fish."

But the "fish" are always able to turn the tables "as the rebellious groups develop more complex, distributed network structures. As the enemy becomes increasingly dispersed, unlocalizable and unknowable, the support environment becomes increasingly large and indiscriminate."

Iraqification mimicked Vietnamization in at least one aspect: the logic of collective punishment (once again "take away the water and the fish will die"). The Pentagon maintained there were no civilians in Fallujah.

In yet another echo of Vietnam, for the Pentagon any dead Iraqi in Fallujah was a dead guerrilla fighter—and just like in Vietnam this figure included "noncombatants," women and children. In Fallujah the Pentagon declared, after fully encircling the city, that women, children and the elderly might leave, but not men and boys from ages 15 to 55. Most of the 50,000 to 100,000 civilians initially trapped in the city were these men and boys—many with no taste for war—along with the unlucky elderly, women and children who were too poor to leave. But under Pentagon logic the problem was solved: everyone inside the city was a fighter.

After Fallujah, the guerrilla strategy changed. No more occupying a territory that could be organized as a safe haven (the city of Fallujah, for instance). The guerrillas were now network-centered. Negri and Hardt: "The network tends to transform every boundary into a threshold. Networks are in this sense essentially elusive, ephemeral, perpetually in flight ... And, even more frighteningly, the network can appear anywhere at any time." The new Iraqi resistance morphed into small, mobile armies striking in Baqubah, Samarra and Mosul, running away and melting into the local population, which fully supported them. This was, once again, pure Vietcong tactics.

The U.S. in Iraq, totally unprepared, was now confronting a network enemy. Negri and Hardt say that "confronting a network enemy can certainly throw an old form of power into a state of universal paranoia." Hence the fiction of "invisible" civilians in Fallujah. Hence the "capture" of Fallujah general hospital. Hence destroying Fallujah in order to "save it." Hence the marine executing a wounded man, live, on camera, inside a mosque. Hence the Vietnam nightmare all over again.

No wonder military historian Martin van Creveld, a professor at the Hebrew University in Jerusalem and the only non-American author on the Pentagon's list of required reading, called for George W. Bush to be impeached and put on trial "for misleading the American people, and launching the most foolish war since Emperor Augustus in 9 B.C. sent his legions into Germany and lost them."

But all was not lost. The myth of "civil war" could always be resurrected.

Month after month, the bodies kept piling up at Baghdad's morgue—handcuffed, blindfolded, hanged, garroted, shot with a single bullet, blown up to pieces. Virtually 80% of Americans started to believe that Iraq was on the brink of civil war. American ambassador and former White House pet Afghan Zalmay Khalilzad—the most powerful man in Iraq—was finally forced to recognize "we have opened the Pandora's box." Peter Pace, the Pentagon's top general, believed Iraq was not on the brink of civil war. Retired Major Generals said there was already low intensity civil war. Donald Rumsfeld blamed—who else?—Iran.

The tragedy of Iraq is that a simmering civil war had always been a fact on the ground—at least since the summer of 2003. The structural causes of Iraq's appalling disintegration are not "barbarian" Arabs at each other's throats, but the invasion and brutal occupation itself. These causes—or a serious, informed debate about them—were permanently absent from the official, Orientalist American narrative.

As for critical media the *Washington Post*, for instance, for all its glorious tradition of investigative journalism, had always blindly supported the war.

The new mantra of "civil war," Iraqis against Iraqis, assumed the invasion and occupation came from an alien planet. It was the same narrative of the Pentagon referring to Sunni Arab guerrilla resistance as "foreign fighters," as if marines and GIs blossomed from Mesopotamian soil. But the Orientalist narrative of Muslim fighting Muslim did serve a purpose. From the Pentagon to the Green Zone every-one stayed—and remains—on message, trying to save the "barbarians" from them-selves. Meanwhile, those crucial, sprawling, permanent military fortresses are erected as facts on the ground. The "snake"—as young, fiery Shiite nationalist cleric Muqtada al-Sadr described it—won't leave Iraq. The snake will not disappear into a hole on the ground. The snake will redeploy.

80% of the Iraqi population is Arab. The other 20% are Kurds, Turkmen, Assy-rians and Kildans. 95% are Muslims; 5% are a mix of Christians, Yazedis, Sabe'ah and a dwindling Jewish community. Muslims are either Sunni or Shiite. There are Arab, Kurd and Turkmen Shiites, as well as Sunnis. The historical identity of Iraq has never been sectarian; Iraqis have always considered themselves Muslims first, as well as the proud defenders of the eastern flank of the Arab nation. So Iraq's pro-found identity has never been hostage to religious and sectarian division. There's never been a civil war in Iraq. This is still fundamentally a tribal society.

The key difference between Sunnis and Shiites is in the way they socially organ-ize. At the top of the Shiite pyramid is Grand Ayatollah Sistani, a *marja*—source of imitation. Sunnis for their part don't have an undisputed leader. Their frame of reference is above all Iraq, and then the Arab world at large. Shiites, because they are contiguous to an Islamic Republic which happens to be a Shiite state, are also close to Iran—but that does not mean they pledge allegiance to the Iranian state. Shiite political organizations are overwhelmingly religious, like the Da'wa party and the Supreme Council for the Islamic Revolution in Iraq (SCIRI). But there are only two major Sunni religious organizations—the Association of Muslim Scholars (AMS) and the Islamic Party. Shiites always talk about themselves in terms of Shiism. Sunnis prefer to state they are Muslims.

Ever since Shock and Awe the pattern has not changed—and it won't. While Baghdad burns outside political games go on inside the massive concrete barriers of the Green Zone perpetually surrounded by American tanks, conducted by a familiar cast of characters—from Khalilzad to Talabani—that could have sprung from a Chinese opera. They all wear masks. They never venture into the mean streets of Baghdad, they never see how real Iraqis cope with their mind-blowing hardships, they never see a suicide bomber explode right in their faces. The Iraqi population never plays dangerous political games—they are too busy just trying to survive, barely. But inside the Green Zone the games are a mini civil war in itself.

Iran does not need to plunge Iraq into civil war. In fact the official consensus in Tehran has always been that the occupiers are trying to ignite sectarian and ethnic hell in order to break up Iraq into mini-states. The Iraqi occupation, costing by the fall of 2006 between US$ 10 billion to US$ 20 billion a month, resulted in SCIRI and Da'wa, both very close to Iran, taking over power. Tehran is showering Baghdad with economic investment and humanitarian action, not to mention hordes of flush pilgrims and tourists. Tehran also perfectly understands the sensitive mechanics of Iraqi Shiite class struggle, pitting Najaf clerics, shopkeepers and the urban middle classes against Muqtada al Sadr's revolutionary masses. Dialogue channels are open to all. And instead of civil war, great numbers of Sunnis and Shiites prefer to get their act together. Muqtada, ever more influential, made two crucial trips to Saudi Arabia and Jordan to garner support among Sunnis. Muqtada's master plan is to "cut the head of the snake"—and there could not be a more popular platform in Iraq. The historical precedent exists. Shiites and Sunnis united in the 1920s in a guerrilla war against the British empire. The British were expelled. It may happen again—against the Americans.

And then there's the hardly negligible matter of vengeance. After Shock and Awe and while the resistance was growing a cross-section of Baghdad never failed to invoke this modern rape and pillaging of the fabled seat of the Caliphate, the Land between the Rivers, a fate worse than under the Mongol Hulagu in the 13th Century. This is a casus belli strong enough to fuel hatred of the infidel for, well, centuries.

Ordinary Iraqis, ever since the resistance started on April 19, 2003, never framed the disintegration of the country in terms of civil war. So who wants civil war? Shady factions, Sunni or Shiite, do. Nobody really knows who or what factions have perpetrated the steady, gory stream of bombings and suicide bombings. Kidnappers for their part wear "police uniforms" or "Army uniforms" or "Interior Ministry commando uniforms." They can be in disguise but they can actually be real police, real Army or real members of death squads. They could have been trained by Iran's Revolutionary Guards, if they are Badr Brigades. But they could have been trained by the CIA as well. Nobody really knows. Nothing is as it seems in Baghdad— because no one knows what machinations go on inside that cement Shangri-La riddle, the Green Zone.

Hence the most logical hypothesis circulating from Baghdad to Najaf, from Basra to Samarra: it comes back to engineered chaos creating the need for the occupying troops to "maintain security"—a "security" they have never provided in the first place. A simmering civil war is the perfect lethal weapon against the very realistic possibility of a unified Iraqi national movement getting stronger and stronger and pouncing to end the occupation once and for all. It does not make any sense for any indigenous Iraqi movement—Sunni or Shiite—dedicated to fight the occupation to try to plunge the country in a civil war.

On the other hand, the whole strategy of the American project was based on a single factor: sectarianism. Even before the invasion and occupation, already in 2002, every single reference to Iraq was broken down into Sunni, Shiite or Kurd divisions. Sectarianism was King. Not surprising when it is well known how the break up of Iraq—classic Divide and Rule—was enshrined in numerous Pentagon analysis.

For instance www.stratfor.com, the American geopolitical intelligence report, was telling in October 2002 of a plan to carve up Iraq into three separate statelets: the Sunnis would somehow be bundled up into Jordan, the Shiites would be linked with Kuwait, and the Kurds would finally get their free Kurdistan. Iraq would "cease to exist," and Baghdad would be the capital of a non-entity. According to Stratfor, the authors of this madcap "Hashemite" plan were none other than Dick Cheney— who today blames everything on Iran—and former Pentagon number two Paul Wolfowitz—the architect of the war who was rewarded with a golden parachute at the World Bank.

Later in 2004 the Rand Corporation, in a study titled *U.S. Strategy in the Muslim World* suggested to exploit each and every fault line between Sunni and Shiite and Arab and non-Arab to advance American interests. Even before the invasion and occupation of Iraq, the objectives seemed to be clear: the country should "cease to exist," puppet or pliable governments should be put in place, and—last but not least—let's grab all that oil.

Even during the ghastly Iran-Iraq war in the 1980s Baghdad was one of the world's cleanest cities. Today it is a repellent, fetid archipelago of rubble and garbage. A great deal of its infrastructure—buildings, bridges, sewage system, telephone networks—is in tatters (and not rebuilt). As of the summer of 2006 five Baghdad neighborhoods were controlled by the resistance—and more were on the way (people in Baghdad tend to refer to the "resistance" as a whole, not distinguishing among the myriad groups). The Tigris may not be the Seine, but now it boasts a Shiite Rive Gauche (Al-Rousafa) and a Sunni Rive Droite (Al-Karkh), both sides with their own, crucial enclaves, Shiite Khadimiya and Sunni Adhamiya. The takeover of the majority of the city is a work in progress. This means in practice swarms of hooded characters loaded with Kalashnikovs, hand grenades and rocket launchers telling people to stay out of trouble—i.e., holed up at home. In a variation of American black ghetto folklore—where the "Man" controls the day, we control the night—the resistance in these areas controls both day and night. And there's nothing any government holed up in the Green Zone can do about it.

Militia hell rules day and night. Some militias—such as the Badr Organization, the armed wing of SCIRI—are part of the government. Bewildered, desperate citizens are repeatedly caught in the crossfire because yes, everybody—militias, police, the new Iraqi Army, overlapping strands of the resistance—is wearing that same uniform which anyone can buy in the bazaar. The Salafi-jihadists target "apostate" Shiites indiscriminately—except those who are not collaborating with the occupation. Their car bombings and suicide bombings, be it in Hilla, Balad or Baghdad, killing scores of poor women and children, are usually blamed by the locals on Saudis, Jordanians and Palestinians, never on Iraqis. The Salafi-jihadists are financed by Sheikhs in Saudi Arabia and the Gulf, and most of their suicide bombers are Saudis.

The different strands of the nationalist, Sunni Arab resistance—disguised as police—attack above all the government, which means basically Shiite officials, Shiite police officers, Shiite members or aspiring members of the Iraqi Defense Forces. On the other side of the fence, as secular Sunnis see it, the Badr Organization terrorizes secular, urban Shiites, while its death squads—formed by individuals who claim to be working for the Interior Ministry—exterminate secular, Iraqi nationalist Sunnis. No one has a monopoly on death, but these "Interior Ministry" types seem to be responsible for a considerable amount of mayhem.

But this is nothing compared to attacks against the occupation. The embedded lie rules that killings are overwhelmingly sectarian. It is indeed a lie. For instance, 70% of the 1,666 bombings conducted by the resistance in July 2006, an extremely violent month, were against the U.S. occupation. 20% were against the police—viewed as collaborators. Civilian "collateral damage" was only 10%. Translation: this was still predominantly a nationalist war against foreign occupation and the resistance—as in Vietnam—was winning.

The advance of militia hell logic was inbuilt in the occupation. Already in June 2003 proconsul Paul Bremer's coalition hands were hiring Saddam's Mukhabarat pals for "special ops" against the Sunni Arab resistance while Torture Central Abu Ghraib was again operating in full force under American management. In the Shiite south, the Badr as well as Muqtada al Sadr's Mahdi Army were gaining ground. The Badr, later renamed Badr Organization, were then formally incorporated into the Interior Ministry, where Sunni units had also been carving up their own turf (under the protection of then interim Prime Minister, "Saddam without a moustache" Iyad Allawi). Former Ba'athist Sunnis—and later the Shiites—benefited from the invaluable knowledge of American "counter-insurgency" experts who organized death squads in Colombia and El Salvador, as well as retired American Special Forces soldiers. Commandos operating in the "Salvador option" manner have been very much in the cards from the beginning, responding to a sophisticated, state-of-the-art command, control and communications center even while the absolute majority of the Iraqi population had no electricity, no fuel, no medicine and very little water.

The pattern will remain the same: people "disappearing" after they are accosted by groups of men armed to their teeth in police commando uniforms, with high-tech radios and driving Toyota Land Cruisers with police license plates. Needless to say, the resulting mass murders are almost never investigated. The objectives also remain the same: to keep the Pentagon and its military bases inside an Iraq mired in sectarian bloodshed and with a weak central government. As for the "follow the money" trail it leads to an array of profitable privatizations and the sale of Iraq's fabulous oil reserves to a few, select U.S. Corporatistan investors. On December 22, 2004 Abdel Mahdi of SCIRI, just a few weeks before he was appointed as one of Iraq's deputy Presidents, laid down the script, announcing in Washington a new oil law: "This is very promising to the American investors and to American enterprise, certainly to oil companies."

So the visible legacy of the occupation is the former capital of the Caliphate and Oriental legend, the former proud metropolis of the eastern flank of the Arab nation turned into an uninhabitable, lawless pit—militia hell at the heart of a social breakdown leading to failed state status. Does this matter to the people who brought us the war on Iraq? Not really.

In his book *The End of Iraq: How American Incompetence Created A War Without End,* former Ambassador Peter Galbraith—the son of the great, late economist John Kenneth Galbraith—stresses that Washington knew next to nothing about Iraqi culture and society and how the post-Saddam era would develop. That's exactly what General Giap told Robert McNamara 20 years after the end of the Vietnam War.

Al Qaeda simply did not exist in Iraq before 2003. It was brought to Iraq by Shock and Awe and its sequel. But it's not al Qaeda who's winning big in Iraq. The long-term winning recipe in Iraq lies with those who have mixed Islam, nationalism and a true fighting spirit against the occupation. The best representing icon of the trend may be fierce Shiite nationalist Muqtada al-Sadr, who wants to "cut the head of the snake."

Iraq anyway will remain scissored by two overlapping wars: the multifaceted resistance fighting the occupation, complemented by the hardcore tactics of al Qaeda in Iraq, and a bunch of shady Sunni factions fighting against a bunch of shady Shiite factions. By the summer of 2006 attacks had skyrocketed to at least 800 a week—the majority against the occupation—and no less than 3000 people were being killed every month.

Iraq is already de facto broken up. Kurdistan has its own government, its own Peshmerga army and its own flag. The South is governed by the Shiite religious parties. The Sunni Arab center is at war—Sunni Arab guerrilla factions vs. the U.S. allied with the Shiite Iraqi Army and police. Baghdad will continue to be split in two, the Tigris dividing the city roughly into a Shiite east (that's where the monstrous Sadr City slum, pop. 2.5 million, is, controlled by Muqtadas's Mahdi Army) and a Sunni west (controlled by the Sunni Arab resistance, former Ba'athists, al Qaeda affiliates or copycats, or all of the above).

This hellish scenario translates, by any definition, into the U.S. losing this war. Not to mention losing a staggering US$ 1 trillion by the time George W. Bush leaves office in early 2009. The temptation is irresistible to evoke Greek historian Diodorus of Sicily, the author of the 40-book *Library of the World History* who in the 1st Century B.C. wrote "neither the King of the Persians, nor the Macedonians, in spite of their power, ever managed to subjugate the Arab nation."

As far as the modern Arab nation is concerned, the Kurds are in overdrive Free Kurdistan mode: Baghdad for them might as well not exist anymore. The Shiite religious parties will never relinquish their grip on power in the South. On the contrary: they want a Shiiteistan. SCIRI's leader, Abdul Aziz al-Hakim, wants a 9-province Shiiteistan as independent as Kurdistan, with his Badr Organization surveilling the borders with a mini-Sunnistan (as if Sunnis would accept being confined to a statelet with lots of desert and no oil). Shiite militias—more than 100,000 and counting—simply cannot be disarmed. The Sunni Arab guerrilla will be even more relentless. This fragmentation was actually enshrined by an Iraqi constitution largely devised by the Americans themselves inside the Green Zone fortress.

So what's left for the U.S.? Actually a (very valuable) lot: the Kurdistan protectorate and client state (which entails the control of Kirkuk's oil); the Green Zone fortress (controlling the rest of Baghdad is a mirage); and the most important asset—the military bases.

To get these prized crumbs the U.S. must face minefield hell, i.e., keep an army of "barbarian" infra-nomads outside the Walls, à la Roman Empire. The Pentagon must deploy (and expose to guerrilla action) dozens of thousands of U.S. troops in Baghdad. By the fall of 2006 Baghdad was already under siege – Sunni Arab tribes controlling all access to the capital while the Mahdi Army had taken control of several neighborhoods and the American-trained Army and police had control of nothing: after all, they are trusted by no one.

The Pentagon must protect by all means necessary a puppet government in Baghdad and its constantly-under-attack collaborationist Army. The Pentagon must go after the Mahdi Army: everyone is breathlessly waiting for the inescapable Battle of Sadr City—which will make Fallujah look like Disneyworld. The Pentagon must prevent by all means necessary the growth of an already incipient Shiite mass revolt bent on throwing out all vestiges of American occupation. The Pentagon must fight "the terrorists," i.e. emboldened al Qaeda in Iraq, now a crucial part of the Mujahedeen Shura Council and under new management: the new Abu Musa al-Zarqawi is Abu Hamza al-Mujahir. Finally the Pentagon, after falling in their deadly trap, must not allow the multilevel Sunni Arab resistance—al Qaeda in Iraq included—to get totally out of control.

It's all an impossible dream, considering the Pentagon has already lost the "countryside"—in this case the sprawling Anbar province —as in Vietnam. The foremost political force in Anbar is now none other than al Qaeda in Iraq, even without the leadership of thug/cipher/former scarecrow Zarqawi. Osama must be having a ball before schedule with either 72 or 72,000 wide-eyed *houris*: not bad to be presented with a sprawling desert Emirate bordering Saudi Arabia, Jordan and Syria to conduct a jihad in the heart of the Middle East.

So when "the center cannot hold" (Yeats), what's the only tactic available for the U.S. to at least project an illusion? It's good ol' civil war, instigated via a series of black ops and frantic participation of U.S.-trained death squads. That's when the accumulated experience in Latin America in the 1980s comes in handy. Repression-in-Central-America specialist John Negroponte's stint in Baghdad must have had a purpose.

There's more. The real power broker of the new Iraq, Muqtada "cut the head of the snake" al-Sadr, may pull a Nasrallah remix. All the conditions are in place. The ascetic, incorruptible Muqtada is almost as popular in Iraq as Hezbollah's Sheikh Nasrallah is popular in Lebanon. His family credentials are impeccable—the Sadr clerical Shiites were on the frontlines of resistance to Saddam Hussein. Muqtada is a committed Arab nationalist—like Nasrallah—whose fight is against U.S. and Israel's hegemony and interference. Muqtada is still young, in his early 30s, controlling 32 seats in the Iraqi Parliament and 5 ministers in the Nuri al-Maliki government, not to mention his own militia, the Mahdi Army, which solves even personal problems of his supporters. What Muqtada does not have is Nasrallah's immense charisma and Iran's financial and military support. But he's learning fast how to turn into a wily politician. And Iran may like what it sees.

In the summer of 2006 Muqtada clinched a stunning strategic victory, with Grand Ayatollah Sistani, the foremost Shiite religious authority in Iraq officially abstaining from politics in disgust. His aides in holy Najaf—where he lives in virtual seclusion—were saying that Sistani had asked the politicians in the Green Zone to demand a full withdrawal timetable from the Americans, but nothing happened.

Even Saddam feared Sistani—because of the Sistani-supported, 1991 post-Gulf War Shiite rebellion. Saddam knew he could not kill Sistani because that would detonate a real civil war. In 2004 Sistani single-handedly prevented the U.S. from implementing the Iraq-as-a-post-modern-colony agenda, a masterful Gandhian approach from one of the most eminent and influential religious leaders in the whole of Islam. Sistani saved Muqtada's neck when Muqtada literally challenged the Americans to war in April and then in August 2004. But in the next two years things changed dramatically. U.S. blunders were so immense that the Shiites masses have no more patience for Sistani's brand of appeasement and cooperation with the occupiers. The masses may be ripe for a more aggressive Hezbollah model.

Once again it's a class thing. Sistani is intimately connected to the Shiite upper middle class and the urban elite—as well as in Iran, where he was born, in Sistan-Baluchistan province (he speaks Arabic with a soft Persian accent, and does not carry an Iraqi passport). Muqtada, even hailing from the clerical aristocracy, is like a gangsta rap "brother," the king of the slums of Baghdad and the dispossessed in the South. Sistani is wisdom. Muqtada is protection. Who you're gonna call in a war of all against all?

They may all want a theocratic nationalist regime, not unlike Iran. But there are substantial differences in method. Sistani wants a unified Iraq under heavy Iranian influence. Muqtada wants a united Iraq but as a proudly independent Arab nation. Abdul Aziz al-Hakim, a Sistani ally, is very well connected in Iran and wants an independent Shiiteistan in the South. The al-Hakim family historically rivals the Sadr family for the role of preeminent Shiite family. This ongoing family war may still generate earth-shattering implications, but their differences are bound to dissolve when it comes to preventing civil war. Because then it would be a case of Saudis backing Sunni Arabs against Iran and Hezbollah backing Shiites. The only winning party in this scenario would be the U.S.

U.S. strategic thinking anyway would more than welcome accelerated "creative destruction." In June 2006 Nafeez Mosaddeq Ahmed from the University of Sussex, Brighton, author of *The War on Truth: 9/11, Disinformation and the Anatomy of Terrorism* called attention to a radical article by retired Major Ralph Peters—a former "future warfare" planner—in the Armed Forces Journal which in fact proposed ethnic cleansing all over the Middle East to "correct" past Western mistakes.

Peters' remixed Middle East is something that in Brazil would be mocked as a *samba do crioulo doido* ("crazy nigger samba"). But for military planners it may look as enticing as an army of lap dancing G-string divas. Not surprisingly Peters dreams of "a Free Kurdistan, stretching from Diyarbakir through Tabriz," which would be "the most pro-Western state between Bulgaria and Japan." Iraq of course would be broken up, the "three Sunni-majority provinces as a truncated state that might eventually choose to unify with a Syria that loses its littoral to a Mediterranean-oriented Greater Lebanon: Phoenicia reborn."

As for the Shiite south, it "would form the basis of an Arab Shiite State rimming much of the Persian Gulf." The "unnatural" state of Saudi Arabia, as well as Pakistan, would be amputated. Iran would "lose a great deal of territory to Unified Azerbaijan, Free Kurdistan, the Arab Shiite State and Free Baluchistan, but would gain the provinces around Herat in today's Afghanistan."

For the geopolitical remixer in all of us, the winners in Peters' world are Afghanistan, the Arab Shiite State, Armenia, Azerbaijan, Free Baluchistan, Free Kurdistan, Iran, the Islamic Sacred State (including holy Mecca and Medina), Jordan, Lebanon and Yemen. The losers are Afghanistan, Iran, Iraq, Israel, Kuwait, Pakistan, Qatar, Saudi Arabia, Syria, Turkey, United Arab Emirates and the West Bank.

The whole project is justified with the usual "democratization" and "fighting terror" house of mirrors, but Peters also highlights the "cat is in the bag, bag is in the river" factor: access to oil (for U.S. Corporatistan, that is). The refreshing side of Peters is his un-CNN frankness: "The de facto role of the U.S. armed forces will be to keep the world safe for our economy and open to our cultural assault. To those ends, we will do a fair amount of killing."

Yes, it's a *Faster Pussycat! Kill! Kill!* Russ Meyer Liquid War world. But forget about the disintegration of Iraq. As much as the Vietnam War was won by Hollywood, Iraq will eventually be cloned by Disney as a theme park—complete with a Mainstream Green Zone, the Sunni Triangle megamall, Adventureland jihad rides, spot-the-IED fun and games, fake kalashnikov target practice in Frontierland, a multi-season *Survivor* pitting Sunnis against Shiites, a multi-season *Jihadi Bachelor*, a multi-season *Desperate Ba'athist Wives* and a monster kebab food court. As German cross-cultural scholar Horst Kurnitzky observed even before Shock and Awe, "the true theme parks present historical events, technical visions and heroic deeds in the manner of Hollywood productions. What they offer is 'visitable History'…virtual authenticity." History as a souvenir postcard. Or the perfect Iraq the Bush administration could not concoct: an idyllic park peopled with human beings exclusively subjected to private economic interests. A trip to this Iraqi Freedom Village beats any trip to (real) Fallujah. And you don't end up dead.

All that sound and fury and blood and destruction in "liberated" Iraq anyway was just a minor inconvenience towards...a mere bunch of PSAs, as we have seen in the Pipelineistan chapter. And to ensure these PSAs rule, nothing beats the US$ 787 million, 21-building, 3500-staffed, fully self-sufficient, Starbucks-equipped, in fact full amenities-equipped top piece of real estate in Mesopotamia: the new U.S. Embassy. Actually Disney is late: the Iraqi Freedom Village already exists. Call it the heart of Americastan in Babylon.

This all started, as we all remember, on January 2001 when George W. Bush created the National Energy Policy Development Group (NEPDG), directed by Dick Cheney. When the group published the so-called Cheney Report, one thing became clear: the absolute priority was U.S. dependence on energy sources. The Cheney Report was not strategic analysis. But it was published during the Enron scandal— with Enron executives working as NEPDG members. So what were they really up to?

In July 2003 the Department of Commerce was forced by the U.S. Supreme Court to unveil the documents used by the Cheney Energy Task Force. There were plenty of maps of oil fields in Iraq, the Emirates and Saudi Arabia as well as charts detailing which foreign companies closed deals with Saddam for exploring oil in Iraq. Among other things, these documents also proved that long before 9/11 regime change in Iraq was the order of the day.

Bill Richardson, Energy Secretary for the last two years of the Clinton administration, had a starring role in all these proceedings. In February 2000, Richardson went on a VIP tour of OPEC (except Iraq, Iran and Libya). He discovered that none of the countries he visited had excess production capacity. Conclusion: an energy crisis, sooner or later, would be inevitable. Matt Simmons, a consultant for the Council on Foreign Relations, learned about this and later became a consultant to the Bush administration.

The eighth chapter of the Cheney Report, titled "Strengthening Global Alliances," says it's imperative for the U.S. to get rid of strategic, political and economic "obstacles" in its quest to assure the extra 7.5 million barrels of oil a day it will need by 2020 (this was the equivalent of the total consumption of India and China by 2004 put together). Hence secure supplies to the U.S. imply the presence of U.S. troops in many of these "obstacles," i.e. nations. The Cheney Report stresses the growing dependence of the Triad on Middle East oil. And as the solution for the energy problem, the report calls the Pentagon. This was the meaning of Gen. Tommy Franks saying on the record that "we will be in Afghanistan for years," and the meaning of the sprawling American military bases built in Iraq.

At the time, the Cheney Energy Task Force also had to refer to the U.N. sanctions imposed on Iraq. Lifting the sanctions on Iraq would mean the go-ahead for contracts frozen by the sanctions—most with Russian and E.U., not U.S. Corporatistan as Saddam was definitely not in business with the U.S. So war was the only option for Cheney to get his Big Prize.

It was possible to extract a major conclusion from the Cheney Report. The White House had always maintained that "the terrorists" want to destroy the American way of life. But what if the whole thing was upside down? To preserve an American way of life that wastes tremendous amounts of energy, Washington was forced to go ballistic under the pretext of the "war on terra." And the process, on top of it, is a snake eating its own tail as the largest world consumer of energy is the U.S. Army.

By the summer of 2005 Anglo-American Big Oil—from BP, Shell and Exxon Mobil to Halliburton—met in secrecy in London to have a go at Cheney's Big Prize: Iraq's oil reserves, the second largest in the world, which may be worth more than US$ 6 trillion. Greg Muttitt, a researcher with independent environmental think thank Platform, stressed at the time that "the decisions on how to carve up Iraq are being made behind closed doors in Washington, London and Baghdad." No one paid much attention.

One year later U.S. Energy Secretary Samuel Bodman duly landed in Baghdad, insisting that Iraqis must "pass a hydrocarbon law under which foreign companies can invest." Iraqi Oil Minister Husayn al-Shahristani seemed to be convinced: the law would be passed by the end of 2006—before this book went to press—as promised to the "structurally adjust or bust" IMF. No wonder: the Green Zone U.S. embassy colossus made sure that the U.S. controls—via well-paid Iraqi servants— the Petroleum Ministry as well as all key management posts in key Iraqi ministries. As revealed by the Platform website, the draft hydrocarbon law was reviewed by the IMF, reviewed by Bodman, reviewed by Big Oil executives. But it was not and it will not be reviewed by Iraqi civil society: that was left to the Iraqi Parliament—which can be largely bought for a fistful of dinars.

The plunder of Iraq's oil wealth may not be a subject fit to public debate—but it will be a subject fit to fuel overlapping guerrilla wars of apocalyptic proportions. Which begs the *Full Metal Jacket* question: what will it take for the U.S. plutocracy to learn that inside every "gook"—and "towel head"—there is not an American trying to get out? While body bags pile up we're left staring at the most astonishing deconstruction and dissolution of a sovereign nation ever perpetrated by relentless Liquid War.

~ 8 ~

ERETZ ISRAEL MEETS ARABISTAN

And what rough beast, its hour come round at last,

Slouches towards Bethlehem to be born?

—**Yeats**, *The Second Coming*

KURTZ: Are my methods unsound?

WILLARD: I don't see any "method" at all, sir.

—**Francis F. Coppola's** *Apocalypse Now*

BRIAN: Excuse me. Are you the Judean People's Front?

REG: Fuck off! We're the People's Front of Judea.

—**Monty Python's** *Life of Brian*

There are no Palestinians.

—**Golda Meir**, *Israeli prime minister, 1970*

August 14, 2006. A flimsy, delayed U.N.-brokered ceasefire between Israel and Hezbollah starts to apply in Lebanon. Future historians may well remember it as the day the intractable Arab-Israeli conflict was turned upside down.

Strategically, Israel had just allowed the emergence of a formidable Dome of the Rock of an enemy: Arab self-belief and pride—something no Arab army had been able to deliver thus far. The psychological blow for Israel was cataclysmic. Sheikh Nasrallah, Hezbollah's leader, proclaimed a "strategic, historic victory." Clausewitz, from his perch in geopolitical heaven, would certainly define it as a tactical, operational and strategic victory—although the price paid was horrific: one million homeless Lebanese, thousands killed or maimed, a relentless, savage destruction of Lebanon's infrastructure.

Sheikh Nasrallah—transcending the perpetual Sunni-Shiite divide—instantly became even more of a hero and mobilizing force than Nasser ever was. Hezbollah suddenly became the most appealing movement in the whole Middle East—with its strategic victory possibly being the catalyst, in the medium term, for regime change all over the Arab world, not exactly according to the neocon catechism. In the first days of the war U.S.-aligned Sunni Arab regimes like Egypt, Saudi Arabia, Jordan and Bahrain—fearful of the "Shiite crescent" construct—all condemned Hezbollah. Subsequently, with the Arab street rallying behind the Lebanese resistance Mubarak, King Abdullah and co. were forced to perform an abject about face.

The rise and rise of political Islam in the Middle East was now more than re-established. And all according to the rules of the game—via elections: Hezbollah in Lebanon, Hamas (*Harakat al-Muqawama al-Islamiyya*, the Islamic Resistance Movement) in Palestine, the Shiite religious parties in Iraq, the Muslim Brotherhood in Egypt. But in what sense Nasrallah could be regarded as the new Nasser?

The Muslim Brotherhood was born in Egypt in 1928. Nasser, who regarded himself as a hero of Arab socialism, lost the 1967 war to Israel. But what Israel managed to do at the time transcended a mere military victory: it smashed secular Arab nationalism to pieces. Where else to turn for solace? Egyptians—and most of the Arab street—turned to Islam. That's when the Muslim Brotherhood—though still outlawed—started to rise again, brandishing its famous slogan "Islam is the solution."

Four decades later, both Arab socialism and neo-liberalism had thunderously failed to elevate the standard of living of the Arab street. Now Nasrallah was showing there is a Third Way: it is political Islam, yes, playing by representative democracy rules, not tainted by corruption, and profoundly implicated in social work. And all this humus spiced with an indigenous Arab resistance movement winning a war against the supposedly invincible Israeli military machine.

Yet even more crucially, Hezbollah's strategic victory signaled the defeat, in the wider Arab and Islamic world, of al Qaeda and the Salafi-jihadist logic. No wonder al Qaeda panicked, and right in the middle of war Ayman al-Zawahiri was forced to go live in breaking news mode, proposing a Sunni-Shiite alliance against the "common enemy," the Jews and the Crusaders. In the 1980s an alliance between the Reagan administration, the Saudis and the Pakistanis had created the conditions for the emergence of an extreme, anarchist sect such as al Qaeda. Hezbollah's strategic victory smashed this logic. Now a counter-power was emerging—aligning Hezbollah, Syria and Iran (or, with Hamas added, the new "Quartet of Evil," according to the neocons). The theocratic nationalist leadership in Tehran could be confident that by 2015 at the most Shiites would inevitably form the political majority in

Lebanon—and that could provide Iran with an extra, key trade/commercial node in the Eastern Mediterranean. Resurgent political Islam more or less agrees that the rule of the State must be superseded by the *umma*. But the long and winding road to get there is much more difficult to negotiate than Sunnis dreaming of a reconstituted Caliphate and Shiites dreaming of an enlarged Shiitesistan (Iran, Iraq, Lebanon, Bahrain and beyond)—as misinformed clash-of-civilizationists see it.

What is already clear is that a Nasrallah-infused neo pan-Arabism and even pan-Islamism has all the potential to metastasize into a new jihad against Arab U.S. client states. Nasrallah is even entitled to be bold, remix loads of ideological baggage and go one step further—proposing the allegiance of Islamic liberation theology to a broad, global, anti-imperialist secular front. Many in the Left—in the Arab world as well as in the West—still are not ready to accept what would be a logical consequence of Hezbollah's strategy. For many in the Right this unholy alliance of a Quartet of Evil of "rogue" states plus alter-globalizers would have to be "neutralized" by all means necessary.

Nasrallah is sufficiently well informed to establish a clear nexus between the struggles in the Arab world and Latin America. From the Cold War to globalization, democracy has become a conceptual victim of geopolitics. U.S. propaganda demonized every Third World nationalist hero from Mao and Ho Chi Minh to Fidel, Nasser and Kim Il-sung. The propaganda may have convinced only American public opinion. All over the South nationalist heroes are back with a vengeance—from Nasrallah to Chávez. The heart of the matter for this generation of leaders should be how to strengthen a broad, multi polar, definitely non-ideological anti-hegemonic front—as the White House and the Pentagon will continue to see Nasrallah as (yet another) anti-Christ, and apocalyptic neocon/Christian fundamentalism will obviously keep demonizing the Quartet of Evil and their "interference" on Iraq as paving the way for the Iranian nuclear bomb.

As'ad AbuKhalil, a Lebanese-American born in Tyre, professor of political science at California State University, Stanislaus, visiting professor at U.C. Berkeley and host of the Angry Arab website, noted that the war "foiled Saudi/U.S./Israeli plans to foment Sunni-Shiite discord... as Nasrallah is now more popular in the entire Arab world than any other Sunni Arab figure." He was expressing a virtual consensus all over the Arab street while stressing that "a century of Zionist violence has not killed the Palestinian national impulse: it certainly has made it grow and expand. The Zionist project is doomed."

A more nuanced perspective was enounced by the Shiite mufti of Tyre, Ali al-Amin, who stressed that Hezbollah's "unprecedented victory" might have been meaningless, and the war's pain and suffering might have been prevented. For al-Amin what was catastrophic was the war itself.

Impasse will remain a fact on the ground—with no evidence in the near future that Hezbollah would agree to "disarm" under U.N. Security Council resolutions 1559 and 1701 as much as Israel would not respect U.N. Security Council resolution 242 which determines it should return all the Arab lands occupied in 1967.

Israel created both Hamas and Hezbollah. Hamas developed in Palestine as a counter-power to the hegemonic and corrupt PLO. Hezbollah developed to fight Israel's 1982 invasion and occupation of southern Lebanon. Both Hamas and Hezbollah are indigenous, seriously organized and disciplined resistance movements enjoying widespread local popular appeal because of their dedicated social work and because they are not tainted by corruption.

It's hard to believe that in the 2006 Lebanon war Israel failed in all its objectives—from killing Nasrallah, preventing missiles being fired on its territory and totally destroying Hezbollah's military power to occupying the region south of the Litani river, showing off its military might to remind all Arabs that resistance is impossible, and intimidating both Syria and Iran.

The British Mines Advisory Group (MAG), a Manchester-based charity, accused Israel of "extreme" carpet bombing, showering southern Lebanese villages with cluster bombs—a carpet in fact thicker than the one deployed in the U.S. invasion of Iraq. This forced the indefatigable Jan Egeland, the U.N.'s humanitarian chief, to stress that "what's shocking—and I would say to me completely immoral—is that 90% of the cluster bomb strikes occurred in the last 72 hours of the conflict, when we knew there would be a resolution." At least 100,000 unexploded cluster bombs will keep maiming, wounding and killing (mostly poor) southern Lebanese Shiites for years to come.

For 27 days the Israeli Armed Forces (IDF) launched 5,000 missiles, 5-ton bunker-buster bombs, cluster bombs and anti-personnel phosphorus bombs each day into Lebanon. That's a total of over 135,000 missiles, bombs and artillery shells. During the last 7 days it increased to 6,000 bombs and shells a day. The grand total approaches a staggering 177,000 hits. On the receiving end there were all those hundreds of thousands of (poor) Shiites. In contrast to Israel, Hezbollah launched 4,000 Katyusha rockets during 34 days—a rough average of 118 per day. So the Israeli/Hezbollah ratio was 44 to 1—and that does not take into account the sophistication of Israeli made in USA weapons and the 100,000 unexploded cluster bombs. Ninety-two percent of the Lebanese dead were civilians. Over 47 Lebanese civilians were killed for each Jewish Israeli civilian. If Hezbollah was guilty of war crimes, as human rights organizations sustained, should Israel's war crimes guilt be multiplied by a factor of 47?

With no heavy Merkava tanks, no F-16s, no U.S. high-tonnage bombs, no "smart" bombs and no U.S. anti-missile batteries, out-numbered, out-gunned, out-tanked and out-bombed, Hezbollah deployed the whole textbook of 21st Century asymmetric war: nomad war—a network of bunkers plus a stockpile of Katyusha missiles sprinkled with a choice of Chinese-designed guided missiles, light anti-tank weapons (Russian RPG-29s, used by the Russian army since 1989, and the Iranian Ra'd-T and Tufan), all tempered by disciplined training, secrecy and an iron will forged with the hammer of Shiite martyr ethos.

Israel's logic in southern Lebanon replicated in frightening detail the Pentagon logic applied in late 2004 in Fallujah: let's destroy it in order to "save it." As in Fallujah the scorched-earth tactics amounted to ethnic cleansing of (poor) Sunni Arabs, in southern Lebanon scorched-earth tactics amounted to ethnic cleansing of (poor) Shiites. In both cases humanitarian help was not allowed and civilians were expendable "collateral damage." Call it the preferred modus operandi of Liquid War.

There was stupor in some circles over why the Bush administration itself bombed the "Cedar Revolution" it fought so hard for, and why it allowed the incineration of any remaining U.S. credibility in the Islamic world. It took the *New Yorker*'s investigative icon Seymour Hersh once again to conclusively prove that Israel's Kosovo-style offensive had been planned—and presented in Washington—more than a year before the fact as a sort of dry run for a Bush administration war on Iran. Dick Cheney's point, as a former senior intelligence official told Hersh, was "what if the Israelis execute their part of this first, and it's really successful? It'd be great. We can learn what to do in Iran by watching what the Israelis do in Lebanon." It all went, once again, spectacularly wrong. Iran's Revolutionary Guards were sufficiently alert to grasp the implications.

The logic sequence runs like this: Afghanistan as a dry run—augmented with Shock and Awe—for Iraq. Gaza as a dry run for Fallujah. Shock and Awe plus Fallujah as a dry run for Lebanon. Lebanon as a dry run for Iran. If the Pentagon were a result-oriented corporation, by now its controllers would have established that the Shock and Awe video-gaming model simply does not defeat nationalist-fueled asymmetric war.

This war was studied in Iran by the millimeter. Reza Amir Khani, in the website *Baztab*, offered an enlightening overview of the Iranian approach—juxtaposing the concepts of *Ghale'ie* (fortress) and *Meydani* (field) warfare. He argued that Western military planning had learned what happened in Troy and thus decided to abandon the fortress for the open fields, as a strategy to cut their losses. But Iran, for Kahni, was one step ahead: instead of waiting for an U.S. attack, it was already fighting U.S. proxy Israel in Lebanon and in Palestine.

So in the end what was this? The 6th Arab-Israeli war? The 3rd Palestinian Intifada? The good ol' "war on terror"? The first salvo of the Long War? What the 2006 Lebanon war did was to calcify the geopolitical "birth pangs" of not a Greater Middle East, but a Greater West Asia, which was always there in the first place as all the turmoil in Afghanistan, Pakistan, Iran, Iraq, Lebanon and Israel/Palestine has always been interconnected. The Afghan "model"—bombing + puppet government + no nation building = widespread chaos—was replicated in Iraq. The Pakistani ISI has always supported Salafi-jihadists in Pakistan/Afghanistan and is closely connected to the jihad in the Middle East. Neo pan-Arabism and pan-Islamism are the new burning ideals across West Asia—from the Levant via the Persian Gulf to South Asia.

Overall prevails the configuration of Liquid War—a seamless matrix of deranged flux pitting "rogue," unstable or regional hegemonic states against each other, non-state radical Islam against the West, nuclear powers against aspiring nuclear powers, long-lasting social and political grievances against autocratic repression, a minority of insiders against the vast masses of the excluded, and all those hidden agendas swirling like mad in the grand bazaar of Pipelineistan.

Immanuel Wallerstein once again put it all in perspective: "What the Israeli governments do not realize is that neither Hamas nor Hezbollah need Israel. It is Israel that needs them, and needs them desperately. If Israel wants not to become a Crusader state that is in the end extinguished, it is only Hamas and Hezbollah that can guarantee the survival of Israel. It is only when Israel is able to come to terms with them, as the deeply rooted spokespersons of Palestinian and Arab nationalism, that Israel can live in peace."

The 2006 Lebanon war also showed, among other things, that Lebanon will never be part of *Eretz Israel*—and the waters of the Litani river will not irrigate Israeli colonies. Control of the Litani river would be essential to solve Israel's tremendous water problem. Of its three major sources of water, two are in the occupied Golan Heights and West Bank, and the other is on a West Bank border. The only source of water in Israel proper is the coastal aquifer. But that translates only into less than 50% of Israel's need—and the water is getting saltier by the day. Up to 40% of Israel's water comes from the Golan Heights via the main tributaries running into the Sea of Galilee (which by the way is getting drier all the time). This fact in itself explains why Israel will do anything not to return the Golan Heights to Syria. The rest of Israel's water comes from the so-called West Bank mountain aquifer. The absolute majority of the best points to draw water from the aquifer are, not by accident, in the Israeli side of the Wall separating it from the West Bank.

Ari Shavit, writing on *Ha'aretz*, believed that Israel must create "a positive anomaly to answer the negative anomaly at the heart of its identity," which is to be condemned to live in a very hostile environment. "Israel wanted to be Athens." But in this day and age "there's no future for an Athens which would refuse to also be Sparta."

That's not the point: the point is that if Israel eventually decided to abandon its configuration as a neo-Sparta guided by exclusive military logic, all the elements—intellectual expertise, business savvy, global connections—would be there for it to dazzle and shine as the neo-Athens of the Middle East. Israel could be infinitely more successful than Dubai if it shelved what amounts to a land-grabbing war ethos. Gaza and the West Bank would be integrated in a two-tiered service sector. There would be a perpetual Summer Rain over the West Bank not of bullets but foreign aid and investment. But this won't happen as long as the IDF remains the most powerful institution by far in Israeli society.

For virtually anyone from Western Europe, Latin America or Asia the degree of militarization of Israeli society is simply astonishing. The IDF sit in an ivory tower: criticism, even mild, is absolute taboo. The IDF dominates the economy. Generals are very close pals of the U.S. industrial-military complex. When they retire they are reconverted into multimillionaire business executives. Israel's high tech industry follows the same pattern. The army, academic establishment and high tech business interlink is fueled by a military logic. No wonder: every one above 18 must follow military service. The whole official narrative defining the country's identity is military. Israel is virtually an offshore U.S. military base and high-tech business node. There's virtually no dissent about it—even from the left intelligentsia. Ergo, Arabs on the other end are totally, completely dehumanized—and demonized. Lévi-Strauss tells us how it works. The Other is reduced to an animalistic, barbaric, perpetual menace that has to be destroyed.

On the same morning of Ariel Sharon's stroke in January 2006 *Ha'aretz* published an insightful analysis—titled *Eating Palestine for Breakfast*—of Sharon's plan for the future of Palestine: the major Israeli colonies in the West Bank would be annexed (East Jerusalem has already been annexed), bringing in 90% of a total of 425,000 Israelis living in confiscated land; and the Wall would conform the official, permanent borders of the State of Israel. Palestinians would be left with 60% at the most of the West Bank, plus Gaza. That amounts to 12% at the most of the original, historic Palestine—which of course would be totally encircled and/or trespassed by Israeli territory, and configured as an amorphous collection of Bantustans. That would represent the death knell of an independent Palestinian state. And that remains the future envisaged for Palestine by the Israeli political/military elite.

Nowhere else in the world has the adoration of the same God spilled so much blood. Nowhere else in the world the line dividing theology from politics is more blurred. Jerusalem incarnates three essentially similar visions of a city at the center of a theocracy—where there's no place for infidels. Exceptions amidst all this fury can be surrealist. Like the pragmatic Israeli tourism body picking up the Dome of the Rock—the third-holiest place in Islam—to sell Jerusalem to multinational camera-clicking hordes predominantly Jewish and Christian.

Urushalim was already inscribed in Egyptian statuettes in 2500 B.C. But in its last 2000 years of History it was never the "eternal and indivisible capital" of Israel—the official mantra since 1967. The history of Jerusalem is above all a history of foreign domination. After Saladin Jerusalem was Muslim for more than 9 centuries. Then, after 1967, when Jerusalem represented only 6% of the West Bank, it was expanded to represent a third. That's the result obtained by a formidable annexation machine. Arab and Western analysts qualify it as ethnic cleansing.

The Wailing Wall, this—white—blackboard filled with messages to God is technically Muslim property, glued to the Haram al-Sharif, the "Noble Sanctuary" which congregates almost a fifth of the Old City and works as a pedestal for the splendid Dome of the Rock. Jerusalem—with its hills drenched in dreams, prayers and blood—persists as the divided House of three religions and two fierce nationalisms. When in the summer of 2006 the Vatican envoy to the Holy Land, Latin Patriarch Michel Sabbah, a Palestinian, plus bishops from the Episcopal, Evangelical Lutheran and Syrian Orthodox churches issued a Jerusalem Declaration on Christian Zionism —a strong element of the U.S. pro-Israel lobby—all rhetorical hell broke loose. The bishops were rejecting a Christian Zionist agenda that "provides a world view where the Gospel is identified with the ideology of empire, colonialism and militarism" and thus sabotage any hope for Middle East peace. Christian Zionists believe Christianity's Jewish roots warrant Israel's occupation of the West Bank—not to mention the matter of the return of Jews to the Holy Land detonating the end of the world and the Second Coming of Jesus.

In this incandescent atmosphere it's hard to envisage a solution for Jerusalem. Moreover Israel never respected the U.N.—which does not recognize the annexation of East Jerusalem. Israel never respected The Hague—which prohibits an occupying power from imposing its laws on, or expropriating land from, a subdued population. Israel never respected the Geneva Convention—which prohibits the colonization of an occupied territory. And this all took place under the absolute indifference of the "international community."

The U.S. and Israel demanded that Hamas accept the 2002 Saudi-inspired Arab Peace Initiative adopted in a summit in Beirut for full, normal Israel/Palestine relations after an Israeli withdrawal. The peace proposal is unmistakable. It "requests Israel to reconsider its policies and declare that a just peace is its strategic option as well." It asks for "full Israeli withdrawal from all the territories occupied since 1967, including the Syrian Golan Heights, to the June 4, 1967 lines as well as the remaining occupied Lebanese territories in the south of Lebanon." It calls for "a just solution to the Palestinian refugee problem to be agreed upon in accordance with U.N. General Assembly Resolution 194." And it calls Israel to accept "the establishment of a sovereign independent Palestinian state on the Palestinian territories occupied since June 4, 1967 in the West Bank and Gaza Strip, with East Jerusalem as its capital."

As a result, "the Arab countries affirm the following:

I - Consider the Arab-Israeli conflict ended, and enter into a peace agreement with Israel, and provide security for all the states of the region.

II - Establish normal relations with Israel in the context of this comprehensive peace."

This is what reason dictates—a comprehensive solution for the Arab-Israeli conflict. The PLO accepted it. Iranian Supreme Leader Ayatollah Khamenei accepted it. Sheikh Nasrallah accepted it (if and when the Palestinians did). Hamas itself said it would accept it. But the U.S. and Israel in fact don't accept what they had demanded in the first place.

How to extricate U.S. national interests from Israel's? Jean Bricmont, author of *Humanitarian Imperialism* and a member of the Brussells Tribunal—a think tank against the logic of permanent war trying to act as a bridge between the Arab world and the Western peace movement—proposes a radical cure: a de-Zionization of the American mind via sabotage of the overwhelming power of the pro-Israel lobby over Washington policy making, Congress and the media: "It is enough to open any mainstream U.S. newspaper or TV and read or hear opinions expressed by Zionists calling for more war. War needs war propaganda and a supporting ideology, and the Zionists provide it, while none of this is offered by Big Business in general or the oil industry in particular."

Addressing 15,000 Muslims in Chicago in early September 2006 former Iranian President Muhammad Khatami—an eminent Islamic scholar-philosopher who when in power proposed a "dialogue of civilizations" instead of Huntington's nonsensical "clash"—also clearly distinguished the interests of the U.S. and the lobby's: "We are unfortunately witnessing the emergence of policies that seek to confiscate public opinion in order to exploit all the grandeur of the nation and country of the United States ... policies that are the outcome of a point of view, that despite having no status in the U.S. public arena as far as numbers are concerned, uses decisive lobby groups and influential centers to utilize the entirety of America's power and wealth to promote its own interest and to implant policies outside U.S. borders that have no resemblance to the spirit of Anglo-American civilization and the aspirations of its Founding Fathers or its constitution, causing crisis after crisis in our world."

Bricmont argues that the notion of Israel as a U.S. strategic ally makes no sense: "In the Middle East, the main charge against the United States is that it is pro-Israel, because it lets itself be 'manipulated by the Jews.' Can anyone doubt that...a change of policy would facilitate U.S. access to oil fields and help it gain strategic allies (if any were still needed) throughout the Muslim world?"

The Bricmont proposal, as he is the first to admit, would only be feasible if the majority of American public opinion really started empathizing with The Other—the peoples of the Middle East—as well as ceasing to stigmatize Islam through the myopic lens of Islamo-fascism. This would imply a massive educational campaign that would have to be conducted by U.S. corporate media. Don't count on it.

We can only understand The Other when we put ourselves in his/her position. I tried: call it a Palestinian psychological apprenticeship. So imagine you are a Palestinian and you own a piece of land in your ancestral home. Let's see how you cope living in Planet Gaza—a non-citizen in the ultimate reality TV show. Only it's real. And the shocking numbers are real too—courtesy of the Palestinian Central Bureau of Statistics (PCBS).

You have to organize your whole life around checkpoints (877 established by 2005). You can be arrested. You can be injured. You can be gunned down by armed settlers. You can be killed by made in USA missiles—even if you are a kid (451 did, from the beginning of the Intifada to the summer of 2006). Your olive, citrus and almond trees can be bulldozed. Your land can be razed (2115 *dunums*—1 *dunum* equaling 1000 square meters—were razed in 2005, plus 29,713 confiscated for the building of the Wall). If you're lucky you get a warning from the Israeli Army on your mobile: "You have the right to remain in your house for another half an hour before we reduce it to rubble." The judgement is—always—final. If they raze your land and expel you from your house it's a "controversial" policy—not blatantly illegal. After your land is stolen it's designated as "Israel proper." You can scream and shout to no avail—even if all this violates the Geneva Conventions and constitutes in effect a war crime according to the Rome Statute of the International Criminal Court. "Israel proper" is whatever Israel says; what it says, goes. Later on it's not "reasonable" to expect the Israeli settlers who colonized your land to pack up and leave.

You have to buy most of your water from Israeli water companies while Israelis keep pumping more water from the West Bank aquifer, which is (was) your property. Kiss goodbye to 83% of your water resources. Your natural gas off Gaza is managed by an Israeli company: you don't get a cent. Your problems are invisible in the Israeli and world mainstream media. Thoughtful World Bank reports sanitize your life saying that you face "a year of unprecedented economic recession" or some other platitude. The relentless construction of the separation Wall is invisible. It's not even a Wall: it's a "barrier," a "fence," or a "security barrier."

Then you suddenly discover that Israel has found a "solution" to your problems—and it's called "disengagement," guaranteed by the U.S., a "honest broker." There used to be a "road map" to solve your problems. But it died because Israel scrapped it, engaging instead in unilateral "disengagement." Israel may announce that you have "sovereignty"—even though you don't know where your borders are, you control none of your natural resources, you have to supply full details of, or snitch on, every person in your land so they can keep extensive police tabs on anyone, and you have to ask please can I go from A to B.

You are forbidden, perpetually, to use the racially segregated roads connecting Israeli colonies and the colonies to "Israel proper." And yet this is the transportation network basis of your new "viable state." The 1948 ethnic cleansing of your people never happened. When the PLO was in power the only task it was allowed was to provide "internal security"—that is to repress you and your ilk. When Hamas rose to power they all were and remain "terrorists," supported by yourself and your ilk, thus you are also a terrorist. Even then, if you still want to go from A to B, if you want to go from Gaza to the West Bank, if you want to travel, you may have the chance to negotiate. You may even get what you need, but you need to offer "concessions," especially "security" concessions; security for Israeli settlers, of course.

If you are in Gaza you live in an 8 km wide and 23 km long strip of extremely arid land by the Mediterranean crammed with other 1.5 million people, at least half of them refugees —the highest population density on Earth. There's a 33% chance you live in a refugee camp—like sprawling Jabaliya. There's a 50% chance that you are not yet a 15-year-old. But you have a 30% chance of being unemployed; a 50% chance of living below the poverty line; and a 40% chance of having no sewage system. You're likely to have access to only a few drops of water a day, at the most: Israeli missiles destroyed a lot of your pipelines and pumping stations. 70% of your orange groves were also destroyed, replaced by "security zones." Carnations and strawberries—two of your main exports—were left to rot. But Israel makes a lot of money with your vegetables, cultivated in your own land: 60% of all exported vegetables actually end up in U.K. supermarkets. Your electric power station was bombed, so now you have less electricity than Baghdad (which is also part of Planet Gaza anyway). Your food is imported from Israel: any imposition of collective punishment to harm "terrorists" means that you starve. Your per capita annual income, if you're lucky, is US$ 700 at best; in Israel it's US$ 20,000 and up. In a nutshell you live on the Ground Zero of humanitarian crisis: an open air, fetid concentration camp ethnic-cleansed in slo mo.

Yet if you—or anybody else—had enough of this and decided to engage in suicide bombing in utter desperation, there will be a "response." The response will always be collective punishment: everyone has to pay because everyone is a terrorist. Your land will be invaded—over and over again. You may be killed by Israeli snipers. And if you—or anyone anywhere on Earth for that matter—even mildly criticize any piece of this hellish machine you're guilty of "anti-Semitism," and dismissed as a lunatic.

By any definition this is Conrad's "the horror...the horror" right here, right now. But let us dream. "The horror" might disappear overnight if only Israel returned the Golan to Syria, the Sheba Farms to Lebanon, and Gaza, the West Bank and East Jerusalem to Palestine. Systematic raping and pillaging of the enslaved West Bank plus bombing enslaved Gaza to the Neolithic will only breed unimaginable hatred—and inevitably engender blowback after blowback. Let us dream of the day the U.S. managing elite finds out that return of occupied Arab lands is the obvious solution for virtually all of the U.S.'s problems in the Arab and Islamic world, for neutralizing the terrorism sequential bomb and for igniting the beginning of a Golden Age for the Middle East. Let us... Stop. Wake up, you fool: there's a Long—Infinite, Liquid—War goin' on.

Figure 14. A photomap of the crowded Gaza strip (CIA).

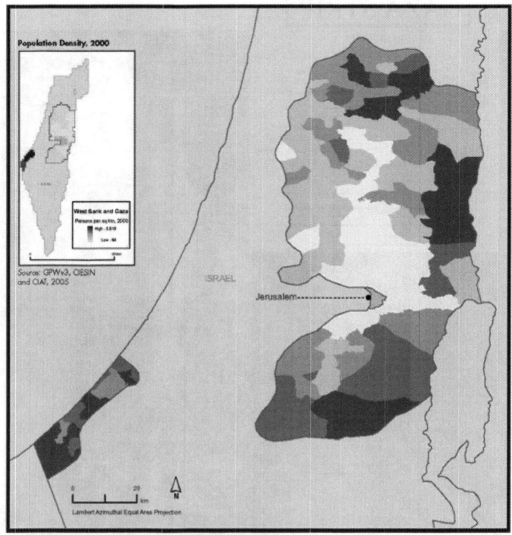

Figure 15. Poverty in Gaza and the West Bank. In the darkest areas, more than 40% of the population is below the poverty line (CIESIN).

~ 9 ~

TALIBANISTAN

These may be the pages of History,

telling stories of the haloed Bamiyan.

It may be the dust that flies,

taking tribute from the skies.

—Pashtun mystic poet **Benawa**, *The Kohistan Twilight*

The tigers of wrath are wiser

than the horses of instruction

—**William Blake**, *Proverbs of Hell*

It's the same donkey, but with a new saddle

—Kabul Persian proverb

The new Anti-Christ, or crypto-Osama bin Laden has been christened—if not by the counterinsurgency lobby at least by shady circles of Pakistan's intelligence/military apparatus. His (pre-household) name is Matiur Rehman—an al Qaeda bomb guru, trained in the 1990s in Afghan camps, and allegedly connected to multiple mayhem from assassination plots against Pakistan's President Musharraf to the summer of 2006 London exploding iPods plot.

Rehman, a former operative for the Pakistani, Kashmir-active, ISI-fueled radical groups Harakat-ul-Jihad-ul-Islami and Lashkar-e-Jhangvi, used to be closely associated with his boss Amjad Farooqi—a Harakat-ul-Ansar operative killed in Pakistan in September 2004. Both held what is known in the counterinsurgency underworld, from Islamabad to Washington, as "the Jihad rolodex"—the full, detailed list of virtually everyone, more than 20,000 holy warriors, who were trained by al Qaeda in Afghanistan from 1996 to 2001.

ISI officials swear that the Farooqi-Rehman double trouble was responsible not only for the complex infrastructure web that has allowed Osama bin Laden, Ayman al-Zawahiri and other al Qaeda commanders to roam the tribal areas as ghosts, but they also planned complex operations. Nevertheless their expertise did not prevent some Salafi-jihadist big fish like Abu Zubaydah, Ramzi Binalshibh and Khalid Shaykh Mohammed—all allegedly part of the planning committee of 9/11—from being arrested inside Pakistan.

After Farooqi was killed Rehman shot up to the top of the most wanted list in Pakistan—widely considered to be the new head of al Qaeda's military committee, or al Qaeda's "planning director" as the previous commander, Saif al-Adel, continues to be under house arrest in Iran, kept as an ultra-valuable bargaining chip. Rehman's extremely shadowy moves concentrate between tribal south Waziristan, Karachi and his ancestral home in the south of Punjab.

The fall of the Taliban in November 2001 definitely did not register in Talibanistan—whose center is in the Pakistani tribal agencies of north and south Waziristan. Other places like Dera Ismail Khan, Khyber and Peshawar may have been drifting towards Talibanistan as well; but especially in south Waziristan it's as if we were still in Afghanistan in the late 1990s, that is, a Mad Max version, also in spirit, of the 7th Century. And there's still a network of command and control centers to be dealt with—from Bajaur to Quetta, the capital of Baluchistan, which is only three hours away from Kandahar and houses the new pad of one-eyed Taliban legend Mullah Omar (at least if we believe Afghan President Hamid Karzai).

So Pakistani counterinsurgency wants us to believe that the new Prince of Darkness in these dusty realms is none other than Matiur Rehman; that is, the brains for the next 9/11 which will inevitably happen either in the U.S. or the U.K.

But wasn't this all supposed to have been dealt with by 2001 or 2002?

The day the "war on terror" was lost

"Omar Omar." Silence. "Omar Omar." Radio cackle barely interferes with the bang of another set of cluster bombs showered from a B-52 over the mountains of Tora Bora, in the Spin (White) Mountains in eastern Afghanistan. The message is merciless: "Kandahar has fallen"—repeats commander Ali Shah, enveloped in his light-gray blanket. This is the way the Taliban ends: not with a bang, but a whimper. This is the way the last frontier in the New Afghan War got hold of it all.

The mujahedeen don't even smile under their *pakools*. They bob their heads—a way of commenting on this weird pact between new Afghan interim government leader Hamid Karzai, a Pashtun moderate very close to former King Zahir Shah's family, and mullah Naqibullah, a pro-Taliban Pashtun mujahedeen. They recharge their tanks, anti-aircraft guns and kalashnikovs, and continue to wait for new orders from commander Ali Shah. A mujaheed, contemplating the mountains, volunteers: "Maybe Osama is there after all, because Kandahar is being conquered." Osama had been seen a few days ago on horseback commanding his troops—or maybe that was a mujahedeen's imagination fired up by ass-kickin' hashish.

Osama knows the area extremely well: he fought some of his first 1980s muja- hedeen battles in this terrain. Tora Bora has also been a center of operations for mujahedeen stalwarts Gulbuddin Hekmatyar and Younous Khalis. People in Jalala- bad confirm this has been the most well-organized area of jihad operations for the past 25 years. But in characteristically evasive Afghan fashion, nobody from Jalala- bad to Tora Bora is able to confirm the whereabouts of Osama. The mujahedeen, though, keep insisting they have cut al Qaeda's main supply route from Pakistan— which originate in the tribal village of Parachinar, in north Waziristan.

Mini-earthquakes shake the freezing cold night in Bamo Khel plateau. Massive B-52s continue to bomb Tora Bora at regular 1-hour intervals, after slowly circling overhead in the crisp black sky. In a former Taliban prison—a cement box beside a depot filled with grenades, rocket launchers, ammunition, the works—14 mujahe- deen under commander Shah and 2 journalists, Jason Burke of the London *Observer* and myself, pile up amid the wool blankets. "Omar Omar." Silence. "Omar Omar." The silence is pierced only by radio cackle and wood fire burning—our only source of heat and light. We sleep in a cell literally filled with smoke. Everybody rises at 4 A.M. It's time for Ramadan breakfast: stale pieces of *nan* and the remains of a chicken stew from the previous night. During the whole day of war, nothing in the stomach until Iftar, the breaking of the fast at 5 P.M.

War starts at 6:30 A.M.: the mujahedeen go to work elbowing each other in the trunks of Toyota pickups, smiling like the kids they mentally are. One of them plays with a hand grenade, oblivious to the possibility of sending us all to Paradise. The B-52s resume their deadly circular ballet. Flashes of light emerge from the moun- tains. The mind boggles when we think that less than 4 miles away a lethal concen- tration, according to the mujahedeen, of 3000 Arabs, Chechens and Uzbeks bent on fighting to the last man is being bombed to oblivion.

These mujahedeen—harder than Tora Bora rock—are the commandos of Ha- zrat Ali, currently "chief of Law and Order" in the eastern Afghan city of Jalalabad. They may be members of the loosely configured Eastern Alliance. But above all they are Pachis—a Pashtun sub-tribe with its own language and fierce code of war. Many of them spent years living in Peshawar during the Taliban holocaust. They have arrived to the frontline only a few days ago. They number a maximum of 2000—operating an almost medieval hardware, inherited from the anti-Soviet jihad. They swear that on the other side there is no Afghan Taliban. So the last frontline in the New Afghan War is an affair between Arabs and Afghans.

The Arab commander is feared Abdul Kuduz—known by the mujahedeen because they always intercept al Qaeda's radio traffic. But none of them speaks Arabic—just like none of the Arabs understand the Pachi dialect. The mujahedeen say the Arabs have only 2 tanks—both in shambles. All the time we spend in the frontline the Arabs produce only scattered mortar fire.

The theater of war can be contemplated in a 180-degree arc from a natural stage: the desert plateau of Bamo Khel. The mujahedeen have positioned three T-55 tanks on the plateau. Downhill, there is a valley around a dry riverbed, close to the village of Melawa. On the road skirting around Melawa, and across the surrounding hills, the mujahedeen have positioned another 10 tanks. Beyond the valley are three superimposed layers of mountains. Al Qaeda positions are on top of the second range of mountains. This is the area known as Tora Bora—under which there is a complex network of caves, some natural, some man-made. The rock face is now subjected to massive B-52 bombing. Beyond the highest layer of mountains—which include some 4000-meter-plus eastern Afghan versions of Mont Blanc in the Alps— are the tribal areas of Pakistan: locals say they can be reached only after a 80 km circuit around the mountains.

The war between Arabs and Afghans evolves in extremely slow motion. A few dozen mujahedeen are surrounded by the Arabs: only 2 are captured. A mujaheed arrives at our cell extremely depressed: one of the captured is his friend. He displays some of the Arab's belongings: passport photos (one of them with a bullet hole), letters, an ammunition belt, a ghostly photo of a black woman in Nigerian dress with a note in Arabic. The feared Arab fighters are revealed to be beardless young men looking like well-behaved graduate students.

Zarin Jan, 40, mujahedeen since 79 ("I have no other career") knows the Tora Bora caves by heart: "There are enormous holes. You can go inside with a big car. The caves are at the base of the mountain. When the Arabs want to fight they come to the top." Drawing on his experience, he says "the Russians had many heavy weapons and a complete Army. War was very difficult. These people disappear inside the mountains." Jan says the Arabs "have everything inside: schools, hospitals, even parking." It's hard to believe they don't have kalashnikovs: according to the mujahedeen, only "heavy weapons," which for them means rocket launchers.

The most absurd aspect in this surreal asymmetrical war is the lack of coordination between the devastating B-52 and F-16 attacks and the slow offensive of the

2000 mujahedeen. The mujahedeen take 3 B-52 attacks just to position a Zu—a double-barreled anti-aircraft gun from Soviet pre-history. But their knowledge of the terrain is matchless: not the commanders, but the soldiers, always smiling, say the Americans should be bombing the base of the mountain, not the top (later we would learn that by then all top al Qaeda commanders on site had already escaped unharmed). The only sat-phone in sight—a Thuraya belonging to commander Hazrat Ali, bought in Dubai—remains absolutely mute.

Suddenly, we are contemplated with evidence of the "invisible war" constantly evoked by Donald Rumsfeld: 2 pickups with tinted windows with 6 men inside and their high-tech kits. "We believe you wouldn't like to speak to us," we say. Startled, one of them reacts with an "Er...Good morning." Security tries to push us away. These gentlemen are a mixed commando of American Special Forces and British SAS. They don't seem very pleased to see the media. They go to the top of a hill and study the war map. The result comes less than an hour later: a tank and an APC are repositioned. The offensive will restart from zero.

On November 17, 2001, as the Taliban regime was self-disintegrating, Osama bin Laden, his family and a convoy of 25 Toyota Land Cruisers left Jalalabad towards the mountains of Tora Bora. In late November, surrounded by his fiercest and most loyal Yemeni mujahedeen, in a cold and damp Tora Bora cave, Osama delivered a stirring speech. One of his fighters, Abu Bakar, later captured by Afghan mujahedeen, said Osama was exhorting them to "hold your positions firm and be ready for martyrdom. I'll be visiting you again, very soon."

A few days later, in what would have been November 30, Osama along with four Yemeni mujahedeen left Tora Bora towards the village of Parachinar, in the Pakistani tribal areas. They walked undisturbed all the way—and then disappeared forever.

On December 1, as the merciless B-52 bombing raids were about to start, Osama had already left Tora Bora—as a number of mujahedeen told us. They had seen Osama on the other side of the frontline in late November. Hazrat Ali was outsourced by the Pentagon to go after Osama and al Qaeda in Tora Bora. He bagged a handful of Samsonites full of cash. He put up a show for the cameras. And he was barely in touch with the few Special Forces on the ground. One of his commanders, Hashimi, complained bitterly over the lack of coordination between B-52 bombing and his tanks firing.

The crucial point is that while Osama was already safe in tribal Pakistan, General Tommy Franks at Centcom HQ in Tampa, Florida, was being directed by Donald Rumsfeld to concentrate on toppling Saddam Hussein. Bob Woodward's *Plan of Attack* registers how on "December 1, a Saturday, Rumsfeld sent through the chairman of the Joint Chiefs of Staff a Top Secret planning order to Franks asking him to come up with the commander's estimate to build the base of a new Iraq war plan. In two pages the order said Rumsfeld wanted to know how Franks would conduct military operations to remove Saddam from power, eliminate the threat of any possible weapons of mass destruction, and choke off his suspected support of terrorism."

In early December, I would also see Pir Baksh Bardiwal, the man responsible for intelligence operations in eastern Afghanistan, absolutely puzzled: why didn't the Pentagon block all the obvious exit trails from Tora Bora, when any of Hazrat Ali's mujahedeen, paid by the U.S., knew them by heart? Only a few Arab al Qaeda fighters were captured in Tora Bora—after Osama had left: later they were sent to the ninth circle of Dante's hell in Gitmo, along with dozens of Afghan bystanders. Most al Qaeda fighters that remained in Tora Bora died in battle, as "martyrs," buried under the rubble caused by bunker-buster bombs. As far as the American military were concerned, Pir Baksh was adamant: "al Qaeda escaped right out from under their feet."

So it was a major Pentagon blunder. It was a major Donald Rumsfeld -Tommy Franks blunder. It was a major White House blunder. And there were two reasons for it. First, the Pentagon outsourced the war in eastern Afghanistan to the wrong warlords, who were collecting suitcases full of cash with one hand and spreading disinformation with the other. Second, the White House and the Pentagon's attention were already directed towards toppling Saddam.

By early December 2001 we also already knew that the Taliban were not dead. On the contrary. Most of the men who matter had already comfortably parked their turbans in Peshawar—global capital of the Afghan diaspora, including 6 former Taliban ministers and diplomats who now wanted... a voice in the new Afghan government. Mullah Omar may have —or may have not—left Kandahar, depending on which Kandahari faction you listened to. Mullah Omar may have been offered— and may have already used—protection to go quietly underground. Of the 3 Durrani sub tribes in control of the border city of Spinbaldak—essentially a canyon of containers full of smuggled goods in the middle of the desert—two said they would protect fellow Pashtun Omar, and one said they would prefer to capture him.

Back in Tora Bora, the mujahedeen knew that this war could last weeks, even months, or even years. Muhamad Issa Mishin, a hardcore Pachi from Dar-I-Noor, also fought in Tora Bora during the jihad in the 1980s: "The Russians came here many times, but they never managed to advance." This had happened 18 years ago. The Russians were attacking the mujahedeen exactly from the same position where Hazrat Ali's Pachis were attacking the Arabs. Mishin remembers: "We had enough to light a fire every night. We spent the whole winter here. The Russians bombed the mountains many times. Nothing happened."

Mishin could have been describing Talibanistan, Pashtunistan, Pakafghanistan, or whichever way we choose to portray it, years after the fact. "Nothing happened." Osama and al-Zawahiri were already moving in shadows B-52s and F-16s were not able to penetrate. Nobody—not least the Pentagon and the West—knew what was happening then, nor knows what is happening right now.

On August 2001, a few weeks before 9/11, I was once again in the heart of Afghanistan. After an extremely tortuous journey in northern Pakistan and Tajikistan I had finally managed to take that green MI-17 Russian helicopter in Dushanbe and hit the Panjshir Valley to track the Afghan resistance fighting against the Taliban and al Qaeda.

Then one fine morning we were finally able to talk. For millions all over the post-everything digital world desperate for a bit of Romance, he was as iconic as Che Guevara: the romantic ideal of the Intellectual Warrior. But he looked in fact like a beat generation poet—with his trademark felt Chitral hat always cocked to the side and a Sartrean existential twinkle in his eyes. He had wanted to be an architect when, as a youth, he was studying at the French Lycée in Kabul. Instead, he was to spend half his life as Afghanistan's Guerrilla Master. He started waging war with just 20 men, 10 kalashnikovs, 2 rocket launchers and a single machine-gun. The intellectual arsenal was certainly deadlier: Mao, Che, Ho Chi Minh, revolutionary tactics adapted to the Afghan mind to wake up rural peasants petrified by stony Islamic clerics. In more than 2 decades, he had defeated an Afghan dictator (Muhamad Daoud) and then the mighty Red Army. For someone who escaped countless total encirclement situations by ultra- hardcore Soviet generals, fighting the black hordes of the Monty Pythonish Taliban should be a cakewalk.

Ahmad Shah Masoud was as modern as a legendary crossroads of Empires like Afghanistan could be. His Islam was as soft as a Panjshir peach—bearing not even a remote comparison with the demented, Deobandi-influenced Taliban version. According to Afghan astrologers, Masoud would live another 40 years—he was 48 in 2001: this should be enough for him to liberate Afghanistan, put the house in order, and die in peace. It was a mythology as uplifting as the Shangri-La landscape of the Panjshir.

He always slept less than 4 hours a day. Officially, he was the vice-president of the Islamic State of Afghanistan—a government that in spite of controlling only 10% of the country's territory, was recognized by the U.N. (the Taliban controlled the non-recognized Islamic Emirate of Afghanistan). Through a bunch of satellite phones and walkie-talkies, Masoud was coordinating a resistance war financed basically through revenue from emerald and lapis lazuli mines. Whenever he was not commuting by his military helicopter number 570 between the Panjshir, the various frontlines and the Tajik capital Dushanbe, he took some time off to swim in his pool with his five children, or to read in his fabulous library of 3,000 volumes—including some that are centuries old. Madame Masoud—also a Panjshiri—was proud to open her closet to reveal she did not wear a *chadri*, the Afghan dress that completely veils a woman's body.

All over the Panjshir, Masoud was revered as a feudal lord—or even a King. He now seemed to have learned a lot from his major setback, between 1992 and 1996, when he controlled Kabul after the Soviet withdrawal but could not operate the transition from strategist to Statesman. That's exactly what he was trying to attempt by August 2001. War was not his only strategy: he was actually creating a State from scratch—with ministries of Foreign Affairs, Defense and Education. But everything was still subordinated to the war effort. He had only 10 military helicopters, and no jets—compared to the Taliban who might have no more than 3 jets from a previous total of 10 old MIGs and Sukhois. He wanted to establish a regular State Army—trained by experienced mujahedeen—and stationed in his base in Khwaja Bahaoud-din, a desert wasteland near excavations of Greek ruins, the Amu Darya river and the Tajik border. This Army would have between 10,000 and 14,000 fighters. The Taliban militia was supposed to have around 45,000—but most with minimal training.

Masoud's military mantra in 2001 was "active defence": opening many fronts simultaneously, a strategy that was driving the Taliban crazy. One of the most brilliant among his young commanders had been capable not only of resisting the Taliban but was about to unleash an offensive to recapture the key city of Talo-qan—in the northern province of Takhar. Masoud smiled when asked about the possibility of legendary commander Ismail Khan reconquering the Persianized Herat, in western Afghanistan—a key source of revenue for the Taliban by way of taxes: "I'm not saying we're going to take it back today or tomorrow, but he's going further step by step."

Masoud was closely monitoring the arrest and trial in Kabul of foreign NGO workers from Shelter Now International, accused of Christianizing Afghans. He explained the big picture: "The Taliban have a special program to expel foreigners. They need excuses for it, and to fill their places with Arabs and Pakistanis. There is an organization named Al Rashid which has promised the Taliban to accomplish this task. In the next weeks and months there will be more and more episodes like this. And behind all this there is a tribal problem. Most of the people with economic problems living in Afghanistan are non-Pashtun, especially in Kabul. The Taliban are trying to intensify these problems so these people leave Afghanistan for Pakistan. Half of the financial budget of Osama bin Laden's organization is spent on buying the houses of people who are not Pashtun."

Masoud did not believe there would be a drastic American action to capture Osama inside Afghanistan—according to rumors that were circulating wildly in Pakistan: "There were no steps taken by the American government to solve the incidents concerning the ship exploded in Yemen by Arabs living in Afghanistan, or the bombing of the embassies in Kenya and Tanzania. There will be negotiations between the Taliban and the American government, but no actions."

He emphasized "there is no military solution" to the Afghan crisis: "But to make the Taliban ready for negotiation—because they are not ready right now—there are two points to be considered: the resistance inside Afghanistan, and the international pressure against Pakistan. The resistance inside Afghanistan is getting stronger day by day, especially this year. And if the government of Pakistan stops interfering in the Afghan issue, I'm sure there will be no Taliban in 5 or 6 months." He acknowledged nonetheless that the Taliban were an ultra-hard nut to crack.

Tribalism is Afghanistan's way of life, but Masoud refused the notion that all the troubles in Afghanistan were tribal-related: "For example, (exiled King) Zahir Shah is Pashtun, and he cannot live under the Taliban. In the same breath, we have some Tajiks who cannot live with us. The tribal problems that exist now are intensified by Pakistan." So inevitably Masoud did not trust President Musharraf, who was trying hard to project a moderate image: "He is following the same line of his military, from General Zia to now."

His obsessive dream was really more democracy for Afghanistan. In the unlikely event of a referendum in the near future, he said "depending on the time of the election, most of the population of Afghanistan would vote for a political national party who could have the power to reconstruct the country." For him, "the future has to be solved through only one way: democracy."

This could only happen, of course, if he was capable of reconquering Afghanistan: "I'm not waging war against the Taliban. I'm at war with Pakistan." Masoud was certain that "40% of people in the frontlines are not Afghans: they are foreigners—mostly Pakistani military, Taliban educated in Pakistani madrassas, and Saudis faithful to Osama bin Laden. These can come from all over—since Osama issued an worldwide appeal for 'good Muslims' to come to Afghanistan to engage in a jihad." So, along with Russians, Americans, Chinese and everybody else, Masoud was also clearly worried about the possible Talibanization of Central Asia.

Masoud had spent most of his life in the frontlines. By the summer of 2001 he was regarded all over the world as the only credible savior of Afghanistan. But he knew he was no solitary Messiah: "It's not only me resisting against the Taliban. This involves people from all over Afghanistan. As you can see in the IDP camps and with other refugees in the Panjshir, they don't have enough food and clothes. But even with these problems, they do not want to live under the Taliban, they prefer to stay here (in the Panjshir valley). I'm completely sure our resistance will be successful one day, Inch'Allah. This country will go towards peace." And when it did, his vision for the future couldn't be more straightforward: "To be honest, I would spend the rest of my life reconstructing my country." This way, and only this way, the Warrior turned Statesman could die in peace—as the Afghan seers had read it in the stars.

The stars dictated otherwise. A few days after we met, on 9/9—two days before 9/11—Masoud's heart was pierced by two pieces of shrapnel, victim of a bombing perpetrated by two al Qaeda operatives disguised as TV journalists. The plot to kill him was carried out by a Brussels-based Tunisian terrorist cell. Masoud was assassinated by two killers in their 30s posing as journalists and carrying fake Moroccan passports. The "reporter" called himself Karim Touzani—affable and relaxed. The surly, burly "cameraman"—who carried explosives in his battery pack—called himself Kacem Bakkali. Their letters of introduction presented them as television journalists from a certain Islamic Observation Center, based in London and concerned with "human rights issues for Muslims all over the world."

The key element in the Masoud plot is the way the fake Moroccan journalists managed to get into the Panjshir. This happened through an introduction by one Dr. Hani, an Egyptian friend dating back from the 1980s anti-USSR jihad of notorious "Professor" Abdul Rasul Sayyaf—renamed by his Arab patrons Abd al-Rabb al-Rasul Sayyaf. Dr. Hani called Sayyaf from Bosnia. Sayyaf agreed to endorse the "journalists" and request permission for them to follow the usual tour of the frontlines.

One year after 9/9 and 9/11, again in Afghanistan, all my attempts to reach Sayyaf via Afghan sources proved unfruitful. Some people said he was incognito in Kabul. Some people said he had been to a secret meeting in Kunar province alongside fierce Pashtun warlord Gulbuddin Hekmatyar, at the time promoted by the Pentagon to the status of America's number one "wanted dead or dead" villain in Afghanistan. Some people said Sayyaf would never agree to talk to foreigners about his controversial role in the Masoud plot. But a source in Kabul told me that during the Loya Jirga in June 2002 Sayyaf admitted the two fake journalists had spent two weeks with him and his people—in Taliban-controlled territory—before crossing to the Northern Alliance areas.

Sayyaf, a Kharruti Pashtun from Paghman, in Kabul province, is the leader of the Ittihad-e-Islami (The Islamic Union for the Freedom of Afghanistan), a party that during the anti-USSR jihad was basically a vehicle for himself to get loads of funds and weapons from wealthy Arab donors. Sayyaf is still a big supporter of Wahhabism and thanks to his solid Arab connections remains the most well known mujahedeen leader in Saudi Arabia. Unlike Masoud, he was fiercely opposed to nationalism, and supported a pan-Islamic ideal. By 2002 he was plotting alongside Hekmatyar to undermine the fragile Hamid Karzai government in Kabul.

Sayyaf's relationship with Masoud was extremely complex. Masoud had tremendous problems dealing with fundamentalists like Sayyaf and Osama bin Laden himself. During the chaotic mujahedeen "governments" of 1992-1996, Masoud was Defense Minister to President Barhanuddin Rabbani, and Sayyaf was a presidential adviser. These "governments" were governments in name only: warlords at the time wreaked havoc in Afghanistan and created the conditions for the emergence of the Taliban.

One week after talking to Masoud in the Panjshir I left northern Afghanistan on an U.N. flight and went back once again to Peshawar, the Islamic Rome. The Osama bin Laden T-shirt (boasting, among other inscriptions, "World Hero" and "The Great Mujahid of Jihad") was the number one hit in Peshawar's Saddar bazaar, selling for less than US$ 2 a pop, along with Osama rappin' (not in all formats, cassette only), Osama mug shots with psychedelic overtones and an Osama video—where the number 1 in the FBI's Most Wanted list was preaching in a mosque and talking to faithful jihadis on the field.

Peshawar, the Islamic Rome, was by then the HQ of Jihad Inc.: a kalashnikov-infested version on steroids of the Middle East captured by Martin Scorsese in *The Last Temptation of Christ*. For 2000 years this had been one of the busiest kaleidoscopes of Asian peoples. Then it became the capital of the Northwest Frontier Province (NWFP)—a 19th Century British imperial concoction to contain Russian expansion in Central Asia. The province is spread out along 700 km of the porous border with Afghanistan, including the legendary Khyber Pass—traversed by everybody from Alexander the Great and Genghis Khan to British imperialists—and other historic doors to India, Persia and Central Asia.

Here Buddhism was refined and catapulted to Asia through the snowy Karakoram peaks. Peshawar literally means "city of flowers." From here the Pakistani government maintains a fragile control over the Pashtun (or Pathan), the largest tribal society on Earth. By August 2001 Peshawar was flooded with 2.5 million Afghans, most in unbelievably squalid refugee camps. Everything moving west of Peshawar was going to the tribal areas, the Pashtunistan on both sides of the absurdly artificial, British-designed Durand line. In this Mecca of Afghan exile, most of what I learned about Pashtunistan, Talibanistan and Pakaghanistan had to be tracked to an infinite succession of ceremonies—everyone seating cross legged on tribal carpets after a communal meal of kebab with Kabuli rice, amidst endless cups of green tea, all those solemn bearded gentlemen lying over cheap made-in-China velvet cushions, Sheherazades in *shalwar kameez* weaving a toxic, hypnotic, lethal, high-and-low tech version of the Thousand and One Nights.

It was in Peshawar that I was briefed by trusted friends on President Musharraf losing his sleep over the full force of the Bush administration requesting his OK for an imminent, high-tech "Get Osama" operation.

An American commando would infiltrate Afghanistan supported by formidable airpower to snatch Osama. Officially, Musharraf had rejected this Hollywood stunt and was frantically trying to convince the Americans any brutal action against Osama or his "terrorist sanctuaries" would fuel radical Islam in Pakistan, Afghanistan and Central Asia to "burn, baby, burn" proportions. But Musharraf badly needed a lot of cash from the IMF and the World Bank to keep the economy afloat. If he said yes to the Americans, all hell would break loose in Talibanistan, but he would certainly bag a crucial US$ 3.5 billion Poverty Reduction Growth Fund from the IMF. He didn't have to lose a lot of sleep on it. 9/9 and 9/11 showed him the way. Actually Musharraf saw the light thanks to a push by the Bush administration threatening to bomb Pakistan "back to the Stone Age," as Musharraf himself revealed in September 2006.

A few days after 9/9 and 9/11, another green MI-17 Russian helicopter landed in the Panjshir Valley. On board there was a CIA party. Masoud had been trying—unsuccessfully—since 1996 to convince the U.S. to go after the Taliban first and then get to Osama and al Qaeda. Now, after 5 years, and only after 9/9 and 9/11, the Bush administration had been forced to admit this was the only way to go. All these years Masoud and his small army had been fighting the Taliban single-handedly he had begged for weapons, cash and logistical help from both the U.S. and the E.U. It took his death—and the death of 3000 people on 9/11—for him to get the weapons, the cash and the logistical help.

Five days after Masoud was killed the Northern Alliance issued an official communiqué, identifying "a triangle between Osama bin Laden, ISI, which is the intelligence section of the Pakistani army, and the Taliban" as responsible for the plot. The affable Dr. Abdullah Abdullah, the Northern Alliance's foreign affairs spokesman, confirmed to Agence France Presse that "this was a premeditated plan. They have tried it several times in the past as well but all of them have been thwarted."

It got worse. The ISI might have been not only involved in Masoud's 9/9 killing but in 9/11 itself. On October 9 the *Times of India* revealed that US$ 100,000 in 9/11 money was "wired to WTC hijacker Mohammed Atta from Pakistan, by Ahmad Umar Sheikh, at the instance of General Mahmoud [Ahmad]." Gen. Mahmoud Ahmad was none other than the ISI Director-general (he was quietly "retired" in October 2001). Ahmad Umar Sheikh later would be the mastermind of the kidnapping and killing in Karachi of *Wall Street Journal* writer Daniel Pearl. As the Canada-based Center for Research on Globalization has extensively demonstrated, Gen. Mahmoud was on a red carpet visit to Washington during 9/9 and 9/11. On the morning of 9/11 Gen. Mahmoud was having a power breakfast on Capitol Hill with Senator Bob Graham and Rep. Porter Goss—later promoted to CIA director.

The whole point, once again, has to do with the confluence of nationalism and Pipelineistan. Masoud was an Afghan nationalist. He would naturally become Afghanistan's leader after the demise of the Taliban—and not pliable former Unocal employee Hamid Karzai. Masoud would pursue his—not Washington's—agenda for rebuilding Afghanistan, enjoying close relations with both Russia and Iran. It's no wonder that Washington, under Clinton, had supported both the Taliban (when they came to power in 1996) and Hekmatyar (before he was turned into a public enemy) against Masoud.

Masoud had told me only a few days before his death that his dream was to see peace in Afghanistan, and then work to maintain peace until he died an old man. He died relatively young—at 48; and Afghanistan is still not in peace. Afghans still contemplate what they describe as an ominous future. They wonder if the sacrifice of a quintessential Afghan hero was still not enough to placate the Gods.

The Taliban must have had a ball in Houston when they visited the control tower of Planet Oil in 1997 to negotiate the Trans-Afghan Pipeline (TAP). They also visited Unocal in Sugarland, Texas. We can imagine mullah Omar's finest, in full black-turbaned regalia, at the Houston Galleria—amid all those blonde, dermatologically sublime trophy wives credit-carding their way to the Valhalla of conspicuous consumption at Saks, Macy's, Nordstrom and Neiman Marcus. Not to mention the red meat feast in all those steakhouses and the sexy groan of all those SUVs—from Kandahar-friendly Toyota Land Cruisers to Durangos, Silverados, Discoveries, Cayennas and even BMWs.

Of course this was ages before the cluster bombing of the Taliban back to *Jurassic Park* became the secret *casus belli* for the "war on terror" after 9/11.

Between the Taliban taking over Kabul on September 1996 and the G-8 summit in the summer of 2001, both the Clinton and Bush administrations never designated Afghanistan as a terrorist or even a rogue state: the Taliban were wined and dined as long as they played the Pipelineistan game. Unocal—which had put the CentGas Pipeline Consortium in place—hired Henry Kissinger as a consultant. Unocal also hired two very well-connected Afghans: Zalmay Khalilzad, a Pashtun with a PhD from the University of Chicago and former Paul Wolfowitz aide; and Hamid Karzai, a Pashtun from Kandahar. In 1996 both Khalilzad and Karzai were ultra pro-Taliban. Even the *Wall Street Journal* loved the Taliban. Not to mention the *New York Times:* on May 26, 1997 the paper of record, in full Pipelineistan mode, printed that "the Clinton administration has taken the view that a Taliban victory would act as counterweight in Iran...and would offer the possibility of new trade routes that could weaken Russian and Iranian influence in the region."

As everyone knows Karzai later became Afghanistan's puppet ruler. And Khalilzad also made splendid career moves: Bush-appointed National Security Council member (working under Condoleezza Rice), "special envoy" to Afghanistan (only 9 days after the Karzai government was sworn in), U.S. Ambassador in Afghanistan and U.S. Ambassador in Iraq.

The whole problem is that the Taliban didn't want to play ball: what they wanted was more money and more investments for the roads and the infrastructure of ravaged Afghanistan. This went on until an exasperated Washington decided to finish them off. The details were discussed in Geneva in May 2001, at the G-8 summit in Genoa in July 2001 and finally at a secret meeting in a Berlin hotel also in July and involving American, Russian, German and Pakistani officials. I would later learn in Islamabad that the American plan was to strike against the Taliban from bases in Uzbekistan and Tajikistan before October 2001. This was a complement to the "Get Osama" plot that provoked Musharraf's insomnia. But then came 9/11, providing Washington the perfect excuse to go it alone.

There's still no Pipelineistan in Afghanistan—and there won't be for years to come; the Taliban will fight to their death not to let it happen. If it happens it has to be under their terms. Underestimating the Pashtun is always a *big* cultural mistake. Their very long memory spans centuries. In the *Pashtunwali* tribal code there are two supreme values: utmost loyalty and implacable revenge. Betrayal is simply unforgivable. As the Taliban are essentially Pashtun (although not every Pashtun is a Taliban), Washington's actions have engendered implacable enemies for generations. "Bring it on," claimed George W. Bush. Oh, they will bring it. On. Non-stop. Forever.

Iiiiiiiiiiiit's back! The Islamic Emirates of Afghanistan

It's unlikely dashing, black-turbaned Pashtun with kohl-rimmed eyes will be parking their brand new SUVs at the Houston Galleria anytime soon. But everyone caught in the hypnotic grip of Afghanistan's tortuous history saw this one coming: the Taliban proclaiming the Islamic Emirates of Afghanistan remixed, this time in the southwest (the huge, desert provinces of Zabol, Kandahar, Uruzgan, Helmand and Nimruz).

The U.S. had certainly promoted the "liberation" of private enterprise in post-Taliban Afghanistan. The liberation was also parallel to an orgy of lawlessness. Smelling a goldmine, Afghan farmers had to come up with the great idea of sowing poppy all over the country—again. Arif Jamal, arguably the top Pakistani expert on jihad, went to eastern Afghanistan in the summer of 2002 as a reporter and met nothing other than the rebirth of Narcoland. He found "the country's second-biggest opium market ... in the sleepy village of Ghani Khel, 16 km south of the highway connecting Kabul and Peshawar. Every shopkeeper in the Ghani Khel market 'can provide several tons of opium/heroin at the blink of an eye.' Mastan Khan says that the buyers include, among others, Americans, Pakistanis, British, Iranians, and Turks."

By the mid-2000s, with the absolute majority of Afghans fervently opposing the de facto occupation of the country by "foreign powers"—the U.S. and NATO—the pressing question was how to forge any semblance of national unity with war-and-narcolords dictating the script. Once again the Taliban occupied the power vacuum. Not accidentally a great deal of Afghanistan's opium—92% of the world's production, 35% of the country's GDP—is cultivated in the Taliban-dominated south. Opium peasants are Taliban-protected.

Latif Pedram is a poet, a former director of the Baghlan library (destroyed by the Taliban) and a secular candidate to the 2004 Afghan Presidential elections (he arrived an honorable fourth, without any corrupt or narco sponsors). By mid-2005 Pedram had had enough of U.S. and U.K. promises of eradicating drug cultivation after confirming that "everyone—including Hamid Karzai's younger brother—was directly involved in trafficking." The Taliban were—literally—back in town, from Wakil Muttawakil (the former Foreign Minister) to the dreaded Mullah Khaksar (a former head of Taliban intelligence), all running for Parliament. Pedram was as horrified by the return of the "good" Taliban as by the regrouping of the "bad" Taliban in the east and southeast—while "the frustration of the people is more and more palpable" in a Kabul eerily reminiscent of Baghdad, "without electricity or water." Hail Globalistan: half of Kabul still looks like Dresden but now an expat with an expense account can choose among more than 80 brothels.

And although the Great International NGO Ball was alive and kicking—more than 2400 participants, foreign and Afghan, congesting Kabul's pizzerias—there was not much serious reconstruction going on. What was definitely on, said Pedram, was the U.S. military bases ballet. "A base already exists on Shendan, near Herat, 40 km away from Iran, and two others in Kandahar and Bagram. And there are other secret installations, in the Pamir, near the Chinese border and in Bamiyan, where a zone is totally forbidden to Afghans." Pedram added that "after a quarter of a century of war," himself and the peoples of Afghanistan "refused to see their country turned into a theater of operations for future tensions in the region."

By mid-2006 the whole scenario spelled "irredeemable failed state"—shorthand for "corrupted narco-state infiltrated by Taliban." The impotent Hamid Karzai—known in Kabul as "the assistant to the American ambassador"—turned into a sartorially impeccable de facto petty dictator, "ruling" by exploiting tribal and ethnic frictions, ignoring Parliament and threatening to repress the media. Tony Blair promised a US$ 10.5 billion development program—but US$ 5 billion had already been promised in late 2001, with the bulk disappearing in a black void or never sent to Afghanistan at all (according to the NGO Action Aid 86 cents of every dollar of U.S. aid is "phantom aid").

The U.S. unloaded "peacekeeping" to NATO—in fact pitting NATO against the Taliban in a merciless de facto war. The Taliban—flush with a new batch of Arab-Afghans and deploying PhD guerrilla tactics learned in Iraq, including suicide bombing —were only 40 km away from retaking Kabul, burning schools virtually every day as far away as the Iranian border. All over the south—in Kandahar, Helmand, Zabol and Uruzgan provinces—one-legged Taliban commander Mullah Dadullah led no less than 13,000 heavily armed mujahedeen, squads of suicide bombers included, against roughly 20,000 NATO troops, with an extra 12,000 U.S. troops deployed in Bagram base and the east searching for al Qaeda. Mullah Dadullah, from Helmand, a Mullah Omar protégé, had used his considerable diplomatic talents to concoct a formidable anti-Karzai alliance linking the Taliban, Hekmatyar's Hezb-e-Islami and the forces of ultra-hardcore Younous Khalis.

As Hamid Karzai is just a helpless pawn in the Long War agenda, ordinary Afghans since late 2001 were left with absolutely nothing: no peace, no security, and no reconstruction—except for the 389 km-long Kabul-Kandahar highway. But then Afghan journalist Mirwais Harooni discovered that the U.S. Louis Berg Group got the job for a whopping US$ 700,000 per km (other companies were offering US$ 250,000), used Indian and Turkish subcontractors, and delivered a shoddy masterpiece, a narrow, two lane highway that is already disintegrating. Even the Taliban were better road builders. And the rape is two-fold: drivers have to buy a US$ 20 permit, valid for one month only, to use the highway. This in a country where US$ 20 is close to the average monthly salary.

The "international community" visibly does not give a damn to Afghanistan. 25 times more money was invested, and 50 times more troops per person deployed in Kosovo, compared to Afghanistan. The Senlis Council is an international policy think tank with offices in Kabul, London, Paris and Brussels, and field offices in key Afghan cities like Kandahar and Herat. 5 years after the "end" of the Taliban, the Council's conclusions were unmistakable: failure of the U.S./U.K. counter-narcotic strategy; a Taliban frontline cutting the country in half; and a monster humanitarian crisis. In short: Afghanistan as a war zone. Just as it was before the Taliban rose to power. Just as it was during the 1980s jihad.

Cui bono? Pakistan, of course. Pakistan had lost its much prized "strategic depth" after Musharraf traded the Taliban for Washington, but Islamabad had not given up. For their part what do the Pashtun really want? A de facto Pashtunistan, both sides of the Durand line finally united. They are on their way. In the Pakistani side of Talibanistan, the Taliban now totally control North and parts of South Waziristan. That's the strategic base of the Taliban fighting the West in eastern Afghanistan. But there's also another base, as we will see shortly.

By another fascinating twist of History the U.S. was in fact undoing what the British did—with their obsession in conducting search and destroy missions across Talibanistan. The U.S. was implicitly recognizing this is the one and same land—even tough only for counterinsurgency purposes. But Musharraf simply could not afford to accept this: the Pashtun tribals would retaliate by fiercely fighting his own government *en masse*.

So a new arrangement for the Waziristans had to be found. Mullah Omar was instrumental in pulling it off, because after all it has him who reminded everyone of the whole purpose of fighting: this was a jihad against the American infidels and their collaborators, not against the Pakistani Army. The new arrangement runs like this. Pashtun tribal elders—the traditional leaders—provide the front. Hardcore fighters—former mujahedeen or Taliban—remain discreet. Arabs, Chechens, Uzbeks and every other "foreign" brigade dissolve in the background. And the Pakistani Army will probably fence the Durand line. What Musharraf and the ISI essentially did was to legitimize Taliban—and al Qaeda's—rule in a key node of Talibanistan. It makes sense considering that the ISI itself invented the Taliban and may have been an essential part of both 9/9 and 9/11.

Osama and al-Zawahiri must have celebrated with a torrent of goat's milk. 5 years after 9/11 a redeployed al Qaeda was ready to invest in a series of small cross border bases in Khost-North Waziristan, South Waziristan, Kunar-Chitral and Kunar-Bajaur. Al Qaeda commander Ghulam Mustafa, a key Osama ally and expert in al Qaeda-Pakistan military connections, was back in business. And the Islamic Emirate of Waziristan was in effect—anticipating the comeback of the Islamic Emirates of Afghanistan. The Taliban won't stop—and will go after the Khyber agency, Peshawar and Dera Ismail Khan. According to jihad expert Arif Jamal, "I feel they are already trickling down to Southern Pakistan. The Taliban from southern Pakistan (Karachi etc.) are trickling up. Both will reach the centre in Lahore (where I am) very soon." There's virtually nothing U.S. Special Forces and squadrons of F-16s can do about it, even though the Pentagon has been itching to bomb Quetta or—here we go again—send a commando to capture Osama, this time inside Musharrafstan.

Musharraf himself was forced to admit in the summer of 2006 that although Waziristan remains Pakistani territory, it is untouchable: "On our side of the border there will be a total uprising if a foreigner enters that area...We will never allow any foreigners into that area. It's against the culture of the people there." Pashtun tribals control the borders. On both sides they are all Pashtun "cousins." So in fact there is no border to speak of.

In their "Don't stop till we get enough" mode, the Taliban's crucial move could not but be a back-to-the-8os revival: the launch of an Afghan Intifada, actually an "Islamic Afghan Intifada," as it's known across Talibanistan. As blowbacks go, this one was a given: as the U.S. fabricated Jihad Inc. in the 1980s in Afghanistan, Jihad Inc. resurrects two decades later to fight the U.S. Call it a post-mod remix of Michael Jackson's *Thriller*. And yes, it's a global affair, pan-Islamic, not restricted to the Kandahar plains and the Hindu Kush.

The Quincy Jones of this new collection of jihadi hits could not but be Ayman al-Zawahiri himself. In the early fall of 2006 Syed Saleem Shazhad from *Asia Times* met with al-Zawahiri's Afghan Intifada head Mullah Allah Haq Yar. Guerrilla expert Haq Yar is a multilingual (he speaks fluent English, Arabic, Urdu and Pashtu) Mullah Omar faithful. Since 2004 he's been patiently doing exactly what al Qaeda did in the 1980s—assembling all foreign jihadis in Pakistan and transferring them to the action in Afghanistan.

Haq Yar told Shahzad that "the whole Islamic world is waiting for the revival of the Islamic Emirates of Afghanistan, but it will take some time." He revealed what by the fall of 2006 had become obvious: "We have now established a network under which we are allied with many big and small mujahedeen organizations." This explained how the Taliban could deploy their firepower simultaneously in the south and also in the east, under the command of seemingly eternal mujahedeen Maulana Jalaluddin Haqqani. As well as a vast array of Pashtun tribal chiefs, both Hekmatyar's and Khalis' groups were also part of the alliance.

It's interesting that Haq Yar defines al Qaeda as "partners" with a "significant role," not the mastermind of this Afghan and global jihad remixed: "Wherever mujahedeen are resisting the forces of evil, Arab mujahedeen, al Qaeda and leaders Osama bin Laden and Dr. al-Zawahiri have a key role." So for the Pashtun Taliban the whole point is exactly similar to the 1980s: a jihad to expel a foreign invader, then the USSR, now the U.S. (and NATO). Will the West *ever* learn?

In this complex tribal masquerade by the summer of 2006 a troubled Musharraf by all means had to deliver some goods for the Long War. After all he had delivered next to nothing in the home front. Pakistan is still a feudal mess of rapacious landowning elites in cahoots with the Army. There's next to none productive investment. Corruption is abysmal. Across the whole Pakistani madrassa matrix, math, science and social sciences remain gloriously absent.

With Waziristan virtually off limits to Pakistan, converted into Talibanistan, the solution for the Army was to head south. The name of the game now was the vast, empty, oil-rich deserts of Baluchistan (40% of Pakistan's area, housing half as many people, only 6 million, as Karachi). Baluchistan has always been intimately linked with the Hadramut bin Laden clan and was now bordering all the Afghan provinces de facto controlled by the Taliban. But the murder of Baluch independentist leader Nawab Akbar Bugti in August 2006 by Musharraf's forces was a terrible blunder. Once again: *Cui bono?* In this case the U.S., not Pakistan.

There are three extremely secluded U.S. military bases in Baluchistan—officially on "war on terror" mode. But there are actually two, neighboring Baluchistans—the Pakistani and the Iranian. Moreover China is financing Pipelineistan in the form of a natural gas pipeline to China from the port of Gwadar—very close to the Iranian border and not so far from the ultra-strategic Strait of Hormuz that would be inevitably blocked in case of a Pentagon attack on Iran, In fact everyone in the area—the Pakistani government in Islamabad, the Baluchis and the leadership in Tehran—is convinced that the Pentagon wants to use Baluchistan as a base to attack Iran. When I was in Iran in the spring of 2006 the talk of the town was U.S. Special Forces hit and run incursions across Baluchistan's borders. And who does the Pentagon rely on for local, strategic intel? The CIA-twin ISI, of course.

It is a truly *Monty Python*ish situation. For example, the ISI—pullulating with Taliban connections—told the Americans that the 2006 Taliban summer offensive would be an Eastern Afghan affair, starting from Khost, Paktia, Paktika and Kunar, which are close to the Waziristans. Wrong. The offensive came from the opposite side—the southwest—from Zabol, Kandahar, Uruzgan and Helmand provinces. Anyone really familiar with the region and the culture would know that the real strategic rearguard for the Taliban is the desert vastness of Baluchistan, not the mountainous tribal areas. This tragicomedy of errors will be in Now Playing mode for years to come.

It's like one of those circular tales spun by the Scheherazade in Peshawar: in the end we had to come back, once again, to the Turkmenistan-Afghanistan-Pakistan (TAP) pipeline. That is: Pipelineistan.

The only reason why Afghanistan matters in the Long War worldview remains the same one when the Taliban rose to power: as a transit corridor for TAP from Turkmenistan to Baluchistan, and eventually India. The Asian Development Bank may even approve TAP (2000 km long, at an estimated cost of US$ 3 billion but possibly reaching US$ 7 billion, to be completed by 2010). But the only way for TAP to be profitable is with India as a final destination—and Delhi knows its best bet for natural gas is from Iran, and the second best from Qatar. Hamid Karzai wants TAP by all means—not TAP in itself but the badly needed US$ 300 million a year he could collect in transit fees. In Pakistan, the independentist Baluchistan Liberation Army (BLA) would certainly raise some hell to get a piece of the action.

The Taliban also have TAP on their sights—but for more ballistic motives: if there ever was a TAP it would be very easy for the Taliban to smash it to pieces every week, Sunni Arab guerrilla-in-Iraq-style, either in southwest Afghanistan or in Baluchistan. Russia in fact all but killed TAP, as we've seen in the Pipelineistan chapter. With no TAP the regional winner, once again, is Iranian Pipelineistan, totally incorporated to the Asian Energy Security Grid with China and India. The U.S. could always deploy NATO forever in Afghanistan to assure a hypothetical TAP's security. The Taliban would forever relish the prospect as much as their daily banquet of kebab chicken rice.

~ 10 ~

SHIITEISTAN

With one stroke, a world which billowed with

fertility was laid desolate, and the regions thereof

became a desert, and the greater part of the living

dead, and their skin and bones crumbling dust;

and the mighty were humbled and immersed

in the calamities of perdition.

—Persian historian **Juvaini***, on the Mongol invasion of Khorasan*

A *ziyarah*—a pilgrimage to Mashhad—is a key event in the life of a Shiite. As a pilgrim to Mecca receives the honorific title of *Haji*, a pilgrim to Mashhad receives the title of *Mashti*. For some Shiite scholars the pilgrimage could even assure a place in Paradise. As gateways to Paradise go the Astan-e Qods-e Razavi—housing the holy shrine of imam Reza—is one of the most dazzling religious complexes in the world. We are totally immersed in a celebration caravan featuring elaborate minarets, blue domes, an unequaled Golden Dome, a Timurid mosque, a kaleidoscope of calligraphic and floral motifs, museums, breathtaking *iwans* (two of them entirely coated with gold), madrassas, courtyards, libraries, stalactite stucco decorated with multicolored glass and marvels like the 30-million-knot Carpet of the Seven Beloved Cities. On sunset—lost in the multitude of black chadors and white turbans occupying every square inch of this huge walled island—the power of the Shiite faith strikes us like lightning, as powerful as Buddhism when we circumambulate the Jokhang in Tibet. The shrine complex was built by Shah Abbas at the beginning of the 17th Century—and enlarged ever since. Imam Reza's shrine itself— where pilgrims from all over the Shiite world touch and kiss and weep and cling to a silver cage—is absolutely off-limits to non-Muslims.

The public relations officers that care for foreign pilgrims tell us that "your holy host is in fact imam Reza," the 8th Shiite imam, born in Medina in 765 A.D. and martyred by the Abbasid caliph Mamoon in 818. Mashhad means literally "the burial place of a martyr." It also means big business. The foundation that manages the complex is now an enormous conglomerate including almost 60 companies. Most of the funds come from donations, bequests and the selling of gravesites beneath the shrine: being buried next to imam Reza is an invaluable honor. The foundation is heavily involved in charity, runs pharmacies and hospitals, provides housing, builds mosques and develops poor areas in the Iranian province of Khorasan.

A specter haunts the Middle East—at least in the minds of selected Sunni Arabs, especially Wahhabis, as well as a collection of right wing American think tanks: a Shiite crescent, spreading from Mount Lebanon to Khorasan, across Mesopotamia, the Persian Gulf and the Iranian plateau. Yet facts on the ground are much more complex than this simplistic formula whereby, according to Riyadh, Amman and Kuwait City, Tehran controls its allies Baghdad, Damascus and southern Beirut.

Seventy-five percent of the world's oil reserves are in the Persian Gulf . 70% of the Gulf's population is Shiite. As an eschatological—and revolutionary—religion, fueled by a mix of romanticism and despair, Shiism had to instill fear, especially in hegemonic Sunni Islam.

For more than a thousand years Shiite Islam has been in fact a galaxy of Shiisms. It's as if it was a Fourth World, always cursed with political exclusion, a dramatic vision of history and social and economic marginalization.

The background for all this is no less than extraordinary. The armies of Cyrus— the founder of the Persian Empire, 2500 years ago—and Darius I extended their will from the Indus to Egypt. Out of the belly of this empire blossomed Zoroastrianism—politicized and socially engaged. Zoroaster imprinted the concept of a just and beneficial God and influenced the art, architecture, customs and traditions that make up Persian culture. We could say that Zoroaster gave a soul to Cyrus' worldly domain and Cyrus gave a body to Zoroaster thought. We still can hardly fathom the impact: in less than a century, from Cyrus' ascension to the death of Xerxes, the Persians replaced a religion that eschewed idols and rituals with a God and a moral system. They created a government for a diversity of nations living in peace. They created a philosophy concerned with ethics, tolerance and justice. And they created art celebrating an extremely sophisticated civilization.

The problem is that in the 7th Century Persia dissolved under the Arab peninsula armies which were conquering the world for Islam. A superior culture was subdued by a bunch of illiterate nomads with a psyche formed by survival in the desert. From a Persian point of view the Arabs only brought Muhammad's religion. But in the end the Persians civilized the Arabs. Islam's golden age reached its pinnacle in the 7th to 8th centuries—until Persia broke Islam's religious kernel to embrace and refine Shiism.

The great Islamic schism happened in 680. But Shiism only took over Iran in 1501 when—brandishing the word and the sword—the great cleric Ishmail and Shah Abbas weaved the population's ethnic and linguistic diversity by means of a state religion. Iran started being defined by Shiite theology and Persian culture—a dynamic already in place by half a millenium, which had even prevailed over the overwhelming national trauma: the devastating Mongol invasions by Genghis Khan and his grandson Hulagu. Only in the mid-20th Century modern Iran's population reached the same number before the first Mongol invasion in the 13th Century. The total population of Khorasan, Iraq and Azerbaijan may have dropped ten fold at the time due to the Mongol war machine plus widespread famine.

From the point of view of an eagle flying over History, all conflicts in 20th Century Iran, the Revolution and its own future, can be regarded as a cultural conflict between Islamic identity and Persian identity. The Islamic Revolution, in a spectacular way, polarized it into two icons: the Shah versus the Ayatollah. We may forget today that Khomeini was fascinated by Plato and Aristotle. He seized on a Greek model and applied it to an Islamic Republic, where a Shiite theologian—not the Philosopher-King—would be the sovereign. In an Iran of profound literary tradition, Khomeini imposed himself as a master of the word (on cassette tapes), transforming a silent revolt into an articulate voice of protest sanctioned by Allah Himself. We may also forget today how much the American "Great Satan"—with its rationalism, Western quantitative thinking, mass production logic and linear vision of History—totally clashed with Iranian culture. It was a clash of technology against mysticism, wealth against poverty; once again, North against South. It was the barrel of a gun against the power of the word. The word won.

Historically the Christian West has always trembled when faced with the passion of Islam. But since the Crusades there has never been a challenge like this: Islam not only denouncing the West's arrogant economic and cultural imperialism, but also condemning its lifestyle. The problem is that the new, post-1979 Iranian model essentially did not deliver. So in a sense the true Islamic Revolution is only beginning.

Shiites finally won political power in Iraq. They have conquered it in Lebanon, and are actively claiming it in Bahrain. They are the majority in each of these countries. Shiism is the cement of their communal cohesion, and essential in fueling their political action to change their historically inferior socioeconomic status. That's demography fueling political power. But that does not mean that all

Shiite political roads lead to Tehran; it does not mean that Beirut or Damascus are clones of Tehran.

Ayatollah Mohammad Hussein Fadlallah, the top Lebanese Shiite cleric, is extremely independent from Iran. Hezbollah, being a movement founded in a multi-religious country, could never impose Khomeini's concept of *velayat-e-faqih*—the ruling of the jurisprudent—to the whole country. Hezbollah's Sheikh Nasrallah—who studied in Iran as well as in Iraq—juggles the cloaks of religious leader and pragmatic political leader.

With the Islamic revolution for the first time in history the Shiite clergy was able to take over the state—and to govern a Shiite-majority society. No wonder this is the most important event in the history of Shiism. It's a totally different story in Saudi Arabia, where Shiites are a minority of 11%, repressed as heretics and deprived of their rights and fundamental freedoms by intolerant Wahhabis. Not for much longer. The Shiites are concentrated in the eastern province of Hasa, Oil City *par excellence*; as the majority of the skilled workforce they are itching to control their oil wealth as much as their Iraqi brothers may have finally managed to. These are Arab Shiites who constantly go on pilgrimage to Iran's holy sites in Tehran, Qom and Mashhad.

The tension between Tehran and Qom is at the heart of Iran's future.

Whenever I go to Qom I'm reminded that as far as major ayatollahs are concerned, their supreme mission is to convert the rest of Islam to the original purity and revolutionary power of Shiism, always critical of the established social and political order. But as a nation-state at the intersection of the Arab, Turk, Russian and Indian worlds, as the key transit point of the Middle East, the Persian Gulf, Central Asia, the Caucasus and the Indian subcontinent, between three seas (the Caspian, the Persian Gulf and the sea of Oman), close to Europe and at the gates of Asia, Tehran on a more pragmatic level simply cannot go preaching: it must conduct an extremely complex foreign policy.

Olivier Roy, expert on Islam and a director of the CNRS think tank in Paris, characterizes Tehran thinking as "pan-Islamist," always emphasizing anti-imperialism, Arab nationalism and anti-Zionism. Diplomats in Tehran never admit it explicitly, but what it boils down to in *realpolitik* terms is a counter-encirclement foreign policy. And not only because of the post-9/11 American military bases which today encircle Iran almost completely. Iran rivals Turkey for influence in Central Asia and rivals Saudi Arabia for hegemony in the Persian Gulf—with the added complexity of this being a bitter Sunni-Shiite rivalry as well. Rivalry with Pakistan—again for influence in Central Asia—subsided after the Taliban were chased out of power in Afghanistan. But basically Tehran regards Pakistan as a pro-American Sunni regional power, thus not exactly prone to be attentive to Shiites. This goes a long way to explain the Iran-India alliance.

There's a fierce competition goin', with different civilizations like Turks, Persians and Russians placing all bets on future trade routes in Central Asia. In the early 21st Century Iran is positioning itself as a bazaar-State with its mind set on becoming the unavoidable player in an oil-and-gas-fueled New Silk Road and thus recovering the preeminence it enjoyed in the era of Darius, the King of Kings.

But how to get there? Way beyond spin, "diplomacy" and manufacture of consent, the heart of the matter is that the President of the United States ("all options are on the table") is seriously considering a nuclear first strike against Iran before he leaves power in early 2009.

Due to the opacity of Iran's theocratic nationalism, outsiders may be tempted to assume that the official Iranian position is the one expressed by Defense Minister Mostafa Mohammad Najar in the spring of 2006: "The United States has been threatening Iran for 27 years and this is not new for us. Therefore we are never afraid of U.S. threats."

Javad Zarif, the Iranian ambassador to the U.N., has also endlessly relayed the official position. Iran's nuclear program is peaceful; there is no proof by the IAEA of a military development; the religious leadership opposes atomic weapons; and Iran has not invaded or attacked any nation for the past 250 years. The power spheres in Iran seem to bet that even in the event of a Shock and Awe of B-2s, guided missiles and bunker busters, that simply is not enough to snuff out accumulated Iranian nuclear know how.

A key question is which Iranian leadership will have its final say. There are at least four main factions in the complex Iranian game of power politics.

The first faction is a sort of extreme right, closely aligned from the beginning to the Egyptian Muslim Brotherhood and involved with a rapprochement with Sunni Arabs in general, while opposing even a tactical rapprochement with the U.S. The faction includes the dreaded *hojjatieh* fanatics and may even include the Hezbollah, who support of course both the Lebanese Hezbollah and the Arab nationalism of Muqtada al-Sadr in Iraq (the difference between Iranian and Lebanese Hezbollah is that in Beirut and southern Lebanon Hezbollah is comparatively much more active, pushing to be at the heart of political life and improving people's living conditions). Former Defense Minister Chamkhani, from Khuzestan (where Iranian oil lies) is very close to this faction. They are very conservative religiously and socialist economically.

The role of Ahmadinejad—a former Pasdaran middle rank official—in molding this first faction has been crucial. In 2005 Supreme Leader Ayatollah Khamenei had the support of former President and Macchiavellian master of ambiguity Hashemi Rafsanjani at the highest levels of power—the Expediency Council. But as a balancing act the Supreme Leader also decided to boost the profile of Ahmadinejad, who happened to be totally opposed to the pragmatist Rafsanjani. To add more arabesques to this Persian miniature, Khamenei's favorite candidate in the 2005 presidential elections was actually Qalibaf, a former chief of police—basically a conservative but in favor of a controlled opening of political life, the Supreme Leader's own policy. What this all ultimately means is that Ahmadinejad—even winning against Rafsanjani and Qalibaf—and as the new leader of the extreme right, is not really in charge of the government. An anti-Ahmadinejad coalition runs from Qalibaf supporters to—believe it or not—pro-secular intellectuals close to former President Khatami like Soroush and journalist Akbar Ganji, released from prison in the spring of 2006.

The Supreme Leader knew that Ahmadinejad would revive the regime with his populist rhetoric, very appealing to the downtrodden masses. But the ruling ayatollahs may have miscalculated that since they control everything—the Supreme National Security Council, the Council of Guardians, the foundations, the army, the media—they could also control the "street cleaner of the people." That was not the case, so plan B—restraining the President, and the powerful Pasdaran—went into effect.

The second key power faction in Iran is composed of provincial clerics, whose master is none other than the Supreme Leader himself. These are pure conservatives, attached to the purity of the Islamic Revolution, and even more patriotic than the first faction. They are not that interested in more integration with Sunni Arabs. Faithful to the Supreme Leader, they want to keep both progressives and extremists in the same house, *Ahl al Bait*, with the *velayat-e-faqih*—the role of the jurisprudent—as the supreme law of the land. Ever since the 2004 parliamentary elections—largely boycotted by the Iranian population—an association of clerics totally dominates the *Majlis* (Parliament).

But there are huge problems behind this appearance of unity. Iranian money from the *bonyads*—foundations—badly wants a reconciliation with the West. They know that the relentless flight of both capital and brains—which is being actively encouraged by the Rafsanjani faction—is against the national interest. But they also know this can hurt Ahmadinejad's power. Some Western-connected Iranians even started comparing the Ahmadinejad era to the Gang of Four in China a little while before the death of Mao in 1976.

The Pasdaran for their part want to keep their fight against Zionism and go all the way with the nuclear program. This entails the extraordinary possibility of an American attack against Iranian nuclear sites counting on the complicity of a great deal of the mullahcracy—which does not hide its desire to get rid of Ahmadinejad and his Pasdaran gang.

The third power faction is the left—initially former partisans of the son of Ayatollah Khomeini, Ahmad Khomeini, who died in mysterious circumstances in the 1990s. After that they operated a spectacular mutation from Soviet-style socialism into some sort of religious democracy, which found its icon in former President Khatami of "dialogue of civilizations" fame. They became the so-called progressives—and even if they lost the 2004 and 2005 elections they are still a force, although already debilitated by the slow awakening of a younger, more secular and more radical opposition.

The fourth and most unpredictable power faction is Rafsanjani's. The consummate Machiavellian masterfully retained his own power during the late 1990s and the early 21st Century, juggling between Supreme Leader Khamenei and President Khatami. He may be the ultimate centrist, but Rafsanjani is and will always remain a supporter of the Supreme Leader. What he dearly wants is to restore Iran's national might and regional power, and reconcile the country with the West, essentially because of one reason: he knows an anti-Islamic tempest is already brewing among the new generations in Iran's big cities, who dream of integrating with the nomad elites of global liquid modernity. As head of the Expediency Council, fully supported by the Supreme Leader, and in his quest to "save" the Islamic Revolution, Rafsanjani retains the best possible positioning.

Meanwhile, Ahmadinejad holds as much power as his predecessor—the urbane, enlightened and sartorially impeccable Khatami: that is, not much. What Ahmadinejad's over the top performances did was to solidify the support the Rafsanjani faction gets from the intelligentsia as well as the urban youth, not to mention the "enlightened police" faction of Qalibaf. But none of this means that a Velvet Revolution is around the corner.

Apart from these four factions, there are two others who are outside the iron-clad circle of Supreme Leader power: the revolutionary left and the secular right. Clerics call them *biganeh* (eccentric), and the denomination may be correct to a point, as both these groups are quite disconnected from the majority of the population, although they also support the nuclear program out of patriotism. The extreme left hates the mullahcracy but has also derided Khatami's moderately progressive agenda. As for the Westernized liberals, which include former supporters of deposed Prime Minister Mossadegh and members of the Freedom Movement of Iran, an opposition party, they are becoming increasingly popular with Tehran students, who are more and more pro-American (if not in foreign policy at least in behavior and cultural preferences).

The regime may be essentially unpopular—because of so much austerity and the virtual absence of social mobility. But for millions it is still bearable. What is actually happening is the slow emergence of a common front—bent on the restoration of the power of the Iranian state through an alliance with Shiism in Iraq, Bahrain and Lebanon. This may be interpreted as a Shiite crescent by alarmist Sunni Arabs, but there's no military, expansionist logic behind it. The common front is also in favor of moving towards a more market economy and a progressive liberalization of morals and public opinion. This is what we hear in Tehran from young people, women, workers in the cultural industry and philosophers—and it is Tehran that always sets the agenda in Iran.

If the regime does not open up, the Iranian economy will never create enough jobs over the next few years to fight unemployment among its overwhelmingly young population. A great deal of the non-oil dependent private sector is controlled by the *bonyads*, whose managers are usually incompetent and corrupt clerics. Any reasonably informed Iranian knows that an economic crisis, high oil prices notwithstanding, will rip the heart out of the lower middle class—the regime's base—and more crucially the industrial working class, which used to be aligned with the Tudeh, Iran's communist party.

They key to "liberate" Iran of most of its problems lies in finding a nuclear compromise with the West—with the E.U. but especially the U.S. For all his vocal, popular support in the provinces, if Ahmadinejad and his Pasdaran hardliners go against this national desire for stability and progress, they are doomed. In June 2006, in an interview to Germany's *Der Spiegel*, Ahmadinejad stressed that "if the Europeans rally to our side, they will act according to their interests and ours. If they oppose us, they will betray themselves...The Europeans risk losing every role in the Middle East and their reputation in other regions of the world, where one will think they are not capable of solving crisis." He also added that "the European countries were ready to allow the Shah's dictatorship the use of nuclear technology, something they refuse to the Islamic Republic."

Demonizing Western parallels of Iran enriching a few grams of uranium to Hitler's march into the Rhineland are positively silly. The uranium enrichment program may be under the operational control of the Pasdaran, but Ahmadinejad does not set Iran's nuclear policy: the Supreme Leader does, his guidelines followed by the Supreme National Security Council, which is led by the Leader's protégé Ali Larijani. The point is not that Ahmadinejad is a suicidal nut bent on confronting the

"Great Satan" by all means available. The point is that he leads just one of four key factions in a do-or-die power play, and he is following an agenda which is not necessarily the Iranian theocratic leadership agenda.

It's as if Ahmadinejad is playing the typical Bonapartist—using a political deadlock to try to go all the way towards dictatorship. Rafsanjani may also be a Bonapartist—but the difference is he's not interested in dictatorship. The ideal outcome of this whole "nuclear crisis" would be an Iran moving to a moderately liberal alliance between eternal pragmatist Rafsanjani—the only one capable of subduing the Pasdaran—and the semi-secular left which still regards Khatami as the least bad of all possible models. It may not be Paradise, but it certainly beats war.

One day before the fifth anniversary of 9/11 Khatami delivered a speech at Harvard; the Iranian proponent of "dialogue of civilizations" addressing the temple where the American proponent of the "clash of civilizations" is a professor might have been the equivalent of Imam Ali giving a speech at the Vatican. Samuel Huntington's belligerent mish mash remains a neocon foreign policy Bible, legitimizing the clash between Western civilization and the Sino-Muslim civilizations. As Edward Said always noted, Huntington based most of his speculation on a 1990 article by famed Orientalist Bernard Lewis; for both Lewis and Huntington, the West is the West and Islam Islam, and no complex internal contradictions apply. Khatami for his part fought belligerence with dialogue. His concept was presented at many global forums, including the U.N., which even declared 2001—of all years...—the Year of Dialogue Among Civilizations.

U.S. corporate media did not even bother to debate what Khatami had to say to Harvard. Now *this* is what dialogue is all about.

It's impossible to deal with Iran without understanding the complex dialectics behind the Iranian religious leadership. In their minds, the concept of nation-state is regarded with deep suspicion, because it detracts from the *umma*—the Muslim community. The nation-state is just a stage on the road to the final triumph of Shiism and pure Islam. But to go beyond this stage it's necessary to reinforce the nation-state and its Shiite sanctuary, which happens to be Iran. When Shiism finally triumphs, the concept of nation-state, a heritage from the West, will disappear anyway, to the benefit of a community according to the will of Prophet Muhammad.

Reality often contradicts this dream. One of the best examples was the 1980s Iran-Iraq war. Saddam Hussein invaded Iran first. Iranians reacted culturally—this was a case of Persians repulsing an Arab invasion. But Tehran at the same time also expected Iraqi Shiites to rebel against Saddam, in the name of Shiism. It did not happen. For the Shiites in southern Iraq, the Arab nationalist impulse was stronger. And still is. This fact in itself destroys the neocon charge that Tehran fuels a guerrilla war in southern Iraq with the intention of breaking the country up. The Ba'athist idea of integration of Iraqi communities under a strong state, in the name of Arab nationalism, persists. Nobody in the Shiite south wants a civil war—or the break up of Iraq. What they want is more autonomy.

Now let's examine Shiitestan at large. Azerbaijan—where 75% of the population is Shiite—could not be included in a Shiite crescent by any stretch of the imagination. Azerbaijan by the way is a former province of the Persian empire which Russia took over in 1828. Azeris speak a Turkish language close to Turkish, but at the same time they are kept at some distance by the Turks because they are in their majority Shiites. Unlike Iran, the basis of modern, secular Turkey is national—not religious—identity. To complicate matters further, Shiism in Azerbaijan had to face the shock of a society secularized by seven decades of Soviet rule. Azeris would not be tempted—to say the least—to build an Iranian-style theocracy at home.

It's true that Azeri mullahs are Iranified. But as Iran and Azerbaijan are contiguous, independent Azerbaijan fears too much Iranization. At the same time, Iran does not push too hard for Shiite influence on Azerbaijan because Azeri nationalism—sharing a common religion on both sides of the border—could embark on a reunification of Azerbaijan to the benefit of Baku, and not of Tehran. And if this was not enough, there's the Nagorno-Karabakh conflict, where Iran supports Armenia for basically two reasons: to reduce Turkish influence in Azerbaijan and to help Russia counteract Turkey—perceived as an American Trojan horse—in the Caucasus. A fair resume of this intractable equation would be that Azerbaijan is too Shiite to be totally pro-Turkish, not Shiite enough to be completely pro-Iranian, but Shiite enough to prevent itself from becoming a satellite of Russia—again.

On Iran's eastern front, we find the Hazaras of Afghanistan, the descendants of Genghis Khan. In the 17th Century the Hazarajat, in central Afghanistan, was occupied by the Persian empire. That's when they converted to Shiism. Hazaras have always suffered the most in Afghanistan—totally marginalized in political, economic, cultural and religious terms. Under the Taliban they were massacred in droves— as the Taliban were surrogates of Saudi Wahhabism: that was a graphic case of rivalry between Iran and Saudi Arabia being played out in the heart of Afghanistan, as much as a case of pro-Pakistan Pashtuns against pro-Iranian Hazaras.

Hazaras comprise a significant 16% of the Afghan population. As far as Tehran is concerned, they are supported as an important political power in post-Taliban Afghanistan. But once again it's not a case of Shiite crescent. Iranian military aid flows to the Shiite party Hezb-e-Wahdat. But there are more important practical issues, like the road linking eastern Iran with Tajikistan that goes through Mazar-e-Sharif and bypasses Hazara territory. And there's the strong Iranian political influence in Herat, in western Afghanistan—the privileged fiefdom of warlord Ishmail Khan. When Khan was jailed by the Taliban in 1997 in Kandahar, he was liberated thanks to Iranian mediation. Khan is now Energy minister in the Hamid Karzai government, but he still controls Herat. The road linking Herat to the Iranian border—previously a nightmare—was rebuilt and paved by Iranian engineers. People in Herat can't get a single TV program from Kabul, but they get 3 Iranian state channels. Western Afghanistan is as much Afghan as Iranian.

Now for Shiism in South Asia. The Moghul empire in India was heavily Persianized. The Moghuls had been speaking Persian since the 14th Century—it was the administrative language of the sultans and the empire's high officials in Delhi, later carried as far away as Malacca and Sumatra. India—as much as Central Asia—was extremely influenced by Persian culture. Today, Shiites concentrate in northern India, in Uttar Pradesh, around Lucknow and also in Rajahstan, Kashmir, Punjab, the western coast around Mumbai and around Karachi in Pakistan. Most are Ismailis—not duodecimal(believing in 12 Imams), like the Iranians. Pakistan may have as many as 35 million Shiites, with a majority of duodecimal. India has around 25 million, divided between duodecimal and Ismailis. The numbers may be huge, but in India Shiites are a minority inside a minority of Muslims, and in Pakistan they are a minority in a Sunni state. This carries with it a huge political problem. Delhi sees the Shiites in Pakistan as a factor of destabilization. That's one more reason for the close relationship between India and Iran.

The Gulf may be a case of Trojan horses. Seventy-five percent of the population of the Persian Gulf—concentrated in the eastern borders of Saudi Arabia and the Emirates—is Shiite, overwhelmingly members of a rural or urban proletariat. Hasa, in Saudi Arabia, stretching from the Kuwaiti border to the Qatar border—and concentrating all the oil—has been populated by Shiites since the 10th Century. 70% of the skilled workforce in the oilfields is Shiite: by all means a time bomb.

Yet one more historical irony rules that the bitter rivalry—geopolitical, national, religious, cultural—between Iran and Saudi Arabia has to be played out in Saudi territory as well. A Shiite minority in the land of hardcore Sunni Wahhabism—and the land that spawned al Qaeda—has to be the ultimate Trojan horse. What to do? Just like in Iraq under Saddam, the Saudi royal family swings between surveillance and repression, with some drops of integration, not as much promoting Shiites in the kingdom's ranks but heavily promoting the immigration of Sunnis to Hasa. Deeper integration has to be the solution, as the access to power of Shiites in Iraq will certainly motivate Saudi Arabian Shiites.

Kuwait lies north of Hasa. 25% of Kuwaitis are Shiite—natives or immigrants, and they provoke the same sort of geopolitical quandary to the Kuwaiti princes as they do to the Saudis. Although they are a religious, social and economic minority as well, Shiites in Kuwait enjoy a measure of political rights. But they are still considered a Trojan Horse. South of Hasa, in Qatar, where also 25% of the population is Shiite, is the exact same thing.

And then there's Bahrain. 65% of Bahrain is Shiite. Basically they are a rural proletariat. It's the same pattern—Sunnis are urban and in power, Shiites are poor and marginalized. For decades, even before the Islamic Revolution, Iran has insisted that the Shiites in Bahrain are Iranians because the Safavid dynasty used to occupy both margins of the Persian Gulf. Tehran still considers Bahrain as an Iranian province. The Shiite majority in Bahrain is prone to turbulence. Repression has been inevitable—and Bahrain is helped in the process by, who else, Saudi Arabia.

But there are some encouraging signs. The small Bahrain archipelago is separated from Saudi Arabia by just a bridge. Every weekend in the Muslim world—Thursday and Friday—Saudis abandon Wahhabi suffocation in droves to relax in the malls of Manama and its neighboring islands. Women in Bahrain are closer to women in Tehran than to Saudi. They wear traditional clothes but not a full black chador; they drive their own SUVs; nobody stops them or questions them; they meet boys and men in restaurants, shops or cinemas. For them, there are no forbidden places or professional activities.

The locals tend to believe this is due to the relative modernity of the Al-Khalifa family in power. Even the South Asians are treated way better than in the neighboring Corporatistan dream Dubai. Bahrain is not particularly wealthy—compared to the other Emirates—and unlike Dubai it does not strive to become an economic powerhouse. There are plenty of schools and a good national University—although most women prefer to study in the U.S. or Lebanon. But all this can be illusory. Shiites in Bahrain won't stop fighting for more political participation. Grand Ayatollah Sistani and Iran's Supreme Leader Ayatollah Khamenei are extremely popular in Bahrain.

There are only 6% of Shiites in the ultra-wealthy United Arab Emirates. But they can compound a problem as acute as in Kuwait or Qatar because of the enormous trade and business Iranian influence in Dubai. The whole equation of Persian Gulf Shiites has to do with a tremendous identity problem. The key argument in favor of them not being an Iranian Trojan Horse is that first and foremost they are Arabs. But the question remains in the air. Are they most of all Arabs who practice a different form of Islam, which the Sunni majority considers heretic? Or are they Shiites bound to pledge allegiance to the motherland of Shiism, Iran? The multilayered answer is not only religious; it involves social and political integration of Shiites in regimes and societies which are basically Sunni. Shiism in the Arab Gulf may be "invisible" to the naked eye. Only for the moment. Sooner or later the sons of Imam Ali will wake up.

Syria, Lebanon and Iraq are the key protagonists in the specter of a Shiite crescent, according to the Saudi royal family, King Abdullah of Jordan and right wing American think tanks. Once again, the facts on the ground are much more complex than a simplistic formula.

Syria, although 86% Muslim, is a multiethnic and multi confessional country. The Sunni majority cohabits with 13% of Alawites (who are Shiites), 3% of Druze and 1% of Ismailis. The Alawites derive from a schism in the 9th Century around the 11th imam, al-Askari, whom they consider the last legitimate descendant of Prophet Muhammad. Sunnis as well as Western scholars consider them Shiites. But many serious Islamic scholars are still in doubt.

Since the early 20th Century Syrian nationalists have never accepted the creation of Lebanon, Jordan and much less Palestine—which became Israel. Alawites—a persecuted minority for centuries—have reached their current enviable position in Syria thanks to the Ba'ath party ideology, which has always been secular and nationalist. Ba'ath ideology exalted Arabism. So Alawites joined en masse both the Ba'ath party and the army. The result was inevitable: at the end of the 1960s they took over power in Syria. The incarnation of this process was strongman Hafez al-Assad. Sunnis in Syria always felt they had been "robbed" of power. But Assad never feared the Sunnis as much as he feared Islamic fundamentalism.

Damascus is, of course, close to Tehran. In Lebanon—to counteract Christian maronite power—Syria has always supported the Shiites. Does that mean that Alawite-controlled Syria is part of the Shiite crescent? Not necessarily. Lebanese Shiism is practically the same as in Iran. But for the Iranian ayatollahs in Qom, Alawites themselves are heretics. During the 1980s, in Damascus, there was plenty of official talk about a Shiite International from the Mediterranean to Pakistan. But Assad—coming from a sect considered heretic by the duodecimal—could never be the head of such an entity.

The point now with Hafez's son Bashar is if he will be able to keep the Alawites in power by modernizing the Syrian state. Not if Washington neocons can have a word on the matter. Regime change in Syria may remain a priority in Washington. But nobody knows how Syrian unity would be affected—the country could become another factionalized Lebanon, or another factionalized Iraq—or what the consequences would be over the stability of Lebanon and the Israeli-Palestinian conflict. Who needs a Lebanonized Syria?

Shiites in Lebanon are predominant in two non-contiguous regions, the south and the northeast near the Syrian border. Lebanese Shiites finally achieved political representation as they became the predominant Lebanese community (around 60%). They woke up from decades of political and social torpor, their political consciousness determined by the fact that they were Shiites. This extraordinary, painful process has served as an example for Shiites in Iraq, and may serve as an example for Shiites in the Persian Gulf.

Lebanese Shiites essentially want to be able to co-direct the country along with Christian maronites—the financial power. This could only happen in a Lebanon free from the current confessional, institutional model, something that is unlikely in the short-term. The only possible solution for Lebanon would be a broad agreement between the maronites (the financial power), the Shiites (the demographic power) and the Sunnis (the link with Saudi financial power, and until recently with Syria as well). With the powerful business Hariri clan—known as Hariri Inc.—stressing the Saudi connection that seems unlikely to happen. The point is that for Lebanese Shiites, Lebanon the motherland is the most important thing, not a Shiite crescent.

Under whoever was in charge—the Ottoman empire, the Hashemites, the British, the Ba'ath party, Saddam Hussein—Shiites in Iraq were always denied political influence. That was the main reason, in the end of the 1950s, for the creation of the Da'wa party—which became the expression of Shiite specificity. In the end History delivered it: the current set up, with Shiite religious parties in power, is what Iran had wanted in Iraq since the Islamic revolution in 1979.

The Ba'ath party and Saddam wanted to create a strong, secular, Arab Iraqi nation. They had everything they needed: a sea of oil, lots of water (unlike any other Arab country) and a significant population. In this ambitious project there was no room for religious or ethnic affirmation. So Kurds as well as Shiites were immolated in the altar of this concept —a modern and secular Iraq. During the 1980s—because of the appeal of Khomeini's Islamic revolution—Saddam Hussein's ultimate nightmare was seeing Iraq break up in three weak statelets: a Kurdistan, a "Shiitestan" and a Sunni center with no oil. That was a key reason for Saddam to launch the Iran-Iraq war. The pretext, according to Saddam himself, was to recover what Iraqis call Arabistan—the Iranian province of Khuzestan where lies most of Iran's oil.

George Bush senior, as is well documented, decided to keep Iraq intact. He knew that the inevitable consequence of an implosion of Iraq would be a Kurdistan and a Shiiteistan near the Gulf. That spelled the death sentence for the Shiite uprising after Saddam's armies were defeated in early 1991. Sunni repression was horrendous: more than 40,000 Iraqi Shiites were killed and hundreds of thousands had to flee to Iran. In 2002, in a Basra still under Saddam, I was convinced that it's Western wishful thinking to believe that Iraqi Shiites will ever forget this betrayal. In the early 1990s the Americans, the "international community," Arab regimes, nobody wanted to see the Iraqi state break up. By another cruel historical irony, Bush junior administration's terrible blunders may produce exactly this outcome.

Iraqi Shiites for their part always suspected that al Qaeda wants civil war. By the summer of 2005 Grand Ayatollah Sistani was saying that even if half of Iraq's Shiites were killed, there would be no civil war. They were determined not to succumb to provocation—because they knew they had the numbers to seal their arrival to power. So this is not about religion—or a Shiite crescent. The Holy Grail is power. The U.S. wants power over the whole Middle East. The Sunnis don't want to lose the power they thought was theirs in Iraq by divine will. Other Sunni Arab regimes in the Middle East obviously tremble at the sight of a Shiite renaissance. The Shiites reached power after centuries of suffering. And al Qaeda in the Land of the Two Rivers wants power as well, in the form of an Islamic Emirate of Iraq, Taliban-style.

There was a time, up to the fall of 2005, that neocons were dreaming of a Washington-Najaf axis. It would fit in a pattern of divide and rule, splitting the Arab world between Sunnis and Shiites perpetually at each other's throats. This would include, of course, Shiites fighting Sunnis in Hasa, in Saudi Arabia. That's a graphic case of neocon thinking encouraging the rise of a Shiite crescent as a means to weaken the Arab world. But it didn't work. The Americans had to leave holy Najaf and security went to the Badr Organization, the paramilitary wing of the Supreme Council for the Islamic Revolution in Iraq (SCIRI), which rules the whole Najaf province. The neocons wanted exactly what al Qaeda wanted: civil war in Iraq leading to mini-civil wars in Saudi Arabia and in Syria, and ultimately regime change, but to the benefit, from al Qaeda's point of view, of Salafi-jihadist regimes.

No Shiite crescent—and no Shiite International—to speak of may exist because the Shiite galaxy, with the exception of Iran, remains fragmented, polymorphous, an archipelago. Even duodecimal Shiism itself can be fragmented in many factions—Iranian or Arab, with or without a powerful clergy. The only thing that unifies Shiite communities everywhere—and that's been the case for almost 1400 years—is opposition to "illegitimate" Sunni Islam, and rejection of other religions.

Of course there is the Iranian Shiite "sanctuary," sophisticated Iranian diplomacy and still a pan-Shiite Iranian dream. But national and theological antagonisms prevail. The best example is the renewed rivalry between Qom and Najaf. Iranian ayatollahs are extremely concerned by Shiite ramifications opposed to the concept of *velayat-e-faqih*, the Khomeini-concocted base of the Islamic Republic's political system.

That's why the renaissance of Najaf—the site of Imam Ali's tomb, the holiest city of Shiite Islam—can be so problematic. Grand Ayatollah Sistani, arguably the most important religious authority in Shiism today, although an Iranian, sits in Najaf. If the center of gravity of Shiism goes back to where it was before—in Iraq—Iran's influence will be tremendously reduced. And Shiism—traditionally apolitical—will be back to where it was before the Islamic revolution. Rumors about an imminent Iranian bomb have been circulating since at least 1995. What would be the meaning of a hypothetical Shiite bomb? Shiism in this case will have not only a political sanctuary but a nuclear sanctuary. With Iran practically invulnerable to an outside attack, would the religious leadership be tempted to again start exporting its vision of pan-Shiism?

Meanwhile the Shiite dream embodied by Iran, or at least the ayatollahs in Qom, keeps burning—the revolutionary power, the aspiration to be the flag-bearers of the misery of the world, a kind of beggars banquet, or the ticket for the beggars to finally accede to a banquet, the last hope for the damned of the earth. No wonder Sunnis fear the power of an incandescent idea that for Shiites rises straight from the bottom of their hearts.

~ 11 ~

CHINDIA

*A revolution is not a dinner party, or writing an essay, or painting a pic-
ture, or doing embroidery; it cannot be so refined, so leisurely and gentle, so
temperate, kind, courteous, restrained and magnanimous. A revolution is an
insurrection, an act of violence by which one class overthrows another.*

—**Mao Zedong**, *1927*

*Although the boundaries between soldiers and non-soldiers have now been
broken down, and the chasm between warfare and non-warfare nearly filled
up, globalization has made all the tough problems interconnected and interlocking, and we must find a key for that. The key should be able to open all the
locks, if these locks are on the front door of war. And this key must be suited
to all the levels and dimensions, from war policy, strategy, and operational
techniques to tactics; and it must also fit the hands of individuals, from politicians and generals to the common soldiers. We can think of no other more
appropriate key than "unrestricted warfare."*

—**Qiao Liang and Wang Xiangsui**, Unrestricted Warfare, 1999

When the dragon kisses the elephant the result is... Chindia: a nice nuclear
couple uniting nearly 40% of the people of Globalistan.

Singapore's stern father and resident Confucius Lee Kuan Yew believes that
Chindia could "destabilize" what's left of the current global balance of industrial
and political power. But the fact is China's Premier Wen Jiabao now refers to an
India-China "strategic partnership for peace and prosperity." The English-language
China Daily was forced to admit that "it is possible for a dragon and an elephant to
get along fine." Indian Premier Manmohan Singh believes that Chindia could
"reshuffle the world order."

One of the key reasons for this Ramayana-meets-Confucius epic had to be oil
and gas. In the—unlikely—event of the U.S. being capable of provoking regime

change in Iran, both China and India, for their own security, would have to over-whelmingly invest in sound alternatives to oil: the Asian Energy Security Grid would be dead. Both China and India can count on standing armies of hyper-educated engineers and scientists. They would certainly pool their intellectual resources. And sooner rather than later they could certainly present the whole world with an unprecedented scientific breakthrough.

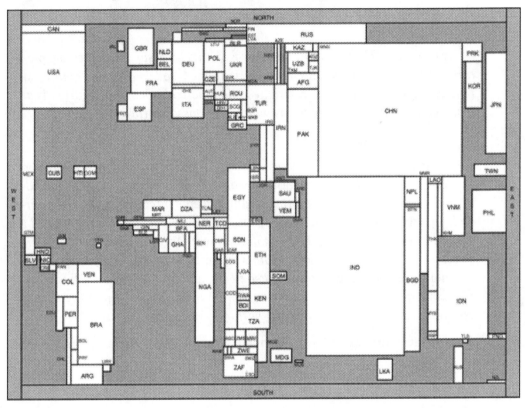

Figure 16. Rectangular cartogram of the world's population (Bettina Speckmann, Technische Universiteit Eindhoven).

It's a long march from the mid-1950s when Nehru and Zhou Enlai would shout in unison *Hindi-Chini bhai-bhai* ("Indian and Chinese are brothers") at the Great Non-Aligned Ball in Bandung, Indonesia. Then there were the 1962 Himalayan wars over Aksai Chin in Kashmir and Arunachal Pradesh in southern Tibet (India lost both). In the Cold War chessboard India was closely linked to the USSR and China courted Pakistan. Post-Mao China boomed, India lagged behind. Then both India and Pakistan went nuclear. And Delhi and Islamabad engaged in a painstaking ballet of détente.

There are still more problems separating Chindia than the number of Shiva's arms. The eternal hot spot Tibet remains critical. Chinese diplomacy cannot swallow that India grants political exile to the Dalai Lama and his followers in Dharamsala. Meanwhile India's military and foreign policy establishments are bitter because China arms India's arch-rival Pakistan. The Indians are also worried onlookers as China arms the ultra-nasty Burmese military junta and in return sets up as many harbors and listening posts as it wants for totally monitoring the Indian Ocean.

Chindia anyway is actually striving to solve their mutual problems in Asia—with no foreign interference. There have been years of endless talks trying to demarcate the 3,500-km mutual Himalayan border. At least some "guiding principles" have emerged—separating economic interest from strategic value. That's unheard of. When Premier Wen Jiabao went to India in 2006—which the Chinese, by decree, predictably turned into the "Year of Friendship" between the two powers—he gave his hosts a map of the Himalayas. The map now shows Sikkim—a former independent kingdom—as part of India, which had annexed it in 1975 (China had always ignored this fact on the ground). India for its part acknowledged that Tibet—under occupation since 1951—is part of China.

India—as much as Japan, Germany and Brazil—wants a permanent seat in the event a new, hypothetical U.N. Security Council comes to light. Nothing will happen if India does not have China's vote. China for its part sees India as a gargantuan new market for cheap Chinese consumer goods and an unlimited business Shangri-La. China also sees investing in a booming India as the ideal counter-strategy towards arch enemy Japan, the third biggest Asian power, not to mention as a way to offset American inroads. Bangalore's privileged IT node is a magnet for Chinese investment.

This being China, a rallying formula had to be coined to excite the masses, so Wen Jiabao's sherpas came up with Chindia as "the two pagodas" of the IT industry—China for hardware, India for software. Thus by working together the "two pagodas" will be in a privileged position to launch the Asian Century—at least in the IT industry. No wonder Chindia is now more than interested in configuring a no-tariff, free trade zone.

This all fits the pattern of China's extreme concentration on securing its own development. China does not need ideology to seduce India or the rest of the world: pragmatism is the name of the game.

In the summer of 2006 Chindia reopened, after 44 years and with great fanfare, the 4400 meter-high pass of Nathu-La, in the legendary Silk Road, strategically located between Tibet and the Indian province of Sikkim. The pass used to connect

Imperial China to India, the Middle East and Europe. Marco Polo came, saw and traversed it. Its geostrategic importance during the 19th Century Great Game between Russia and the British empire was also crucial. Now it's poised to once again become a key communication node of the New Silk Road. A major road and railway are imminent.

Almost simultaneously in Golmud, in the Chinese far west of Qinghai province, at the feet of the Tibetan plateau, a banner in red characters, blaring the inscription "The iron dragon dances in the roof of the world" was kissing the clear blue skies. That's where Chinese President Hu Jintao, also with great fanfare celebrating the "merits of socialism" inaugurated the first Chinese train to Lhasa. Until then Tibet was the only Chinese province not linked to the Middle Kingdom by rail.

For Beijing this is "a great miracle in the world's rail history"—1142 km, 2647 bridges, 11 tunnels blasting though a spectacular mineral moonscape at a median altitude of 4000 meters, to the tune of US$ 3,6 billion and built in only 4 years. For 500 km, all year long, the train will traverse earth perennially covered by ice. There's even environmental protection—in some stretches the railway is elevated so as not to disturb the migration of the legendary Tibetan antelope. The official name of the line is Qing-Zang—Qing for Qinghai province, and Zang for Xizang, which means "Tibet" in Mandarin. Qing-Zang is now the highest railway in the world, having dethroned Lima-Huancayo in Peru, built in the Andes in the 19th Century.

Tibet may remain in the roof of the world—but it has ceased for the first time in its history to be enveloped in splendid isolation. Now with "only" 48 hours from Beijing to Lhasa—for centuries the most mysterious and mythified city in the West—"modernization," which is just another name for Sinification, will be even more relentless. Yet monks from monasteries lost in the plateau will not exactly become train passengers—they will keep setting on their pilgrimages on foot.

The Dalai Lama will also remain in the foreseeable future an outlaw in his own land. Monks will keep journeying to the Norbulingka (the Park of the Jewels), official summer residence of Tibetan religious leaders since the 8th Dalai Lama. In the Norbulingka we find a meditation chamber, a small room adorned with *thang-kas*—Buddhist paintings—and a reception room with a fabulously carved golden throne. It's exactly from this room that the 14th Dalai Lama was forced to flee Lhasa and Mao's communism on March 30, 1959 to his perennial exile. We still find the same Western plumbing, a sink, a bathtub and a radio. The atmosphere of enduring melancholy will be even fiercer now in this palace enveloped by a solitary meditation garden.

The monks in Ganden monastery will keep their supplicant whispers towards visitors for "a picture of the Dalai Lama." Over a half century ago Tibet had six huge monasteries. Sera and Ganden had more than 5000 monks each and Drepung as many as 10,000—the largest monastery in History. Today they are practically empty—with hundreds, not thousands of monks who have to be all Beijing-endorsed. The most brilliant monks are in exile. Samye was the first Tibetan monastery, founded in the 8th Century with help from the flamboyant Indian guru Padmasambhava—who introduced Buddhism to Tibet. Samye looks like a giant mandala. It suffered tremendous devastation under the Cultural Revolution. Today, most of its temples are scattered between houses and stables. In Samye there is an astonishing statue of Avalokiteshvara (Chenresi, in Tibetan), the Buddha of compassion and Tibet's primordial deity, with an eye meticulously painted in each one of its thousand hand palms.

In the Barkhor circuit grand master Tseden Namgyal will keep producing the most extraordinary thangkas of all Tibet. Legend rules that primordial Tibetans were the fruit of the union between an ogre and a monkey—a reencarnation of Chenresi, although etnography tells us that Tibetans descend from nomadic Ch'iang who thousands of years ago roamed from eastern Central Asia towards China's northwest. Lhasa—apart from its Tibetan ghettos—will continue to be the apotheosis of a highly militarized police state. There could not be a sharper contrast to the Disney-trashed Chinese plaza in front of the Potala—a pop celebration to cultural genocide—than the early evening collective prayer inside the Jokhang, the Sistine Chapel and St. Mark's Basilica of Tibetan Buddhism. It will always be impossible to imagine that during the Cultural Revolution the Jokhang was literally turned into a pig sty by Mao's Red Guards. Inside the Jokhang we find the chapel of Jowo Sakyamuni—with a Buddha statue and its sublime, 12-year-old golden face. This is the most venerated statue in Tibet—in arguably the most spiritual place in the whole world.

What Tibetan master could explain us the confluence of 21st Century energy wars and the Long War in terms of accumulated bad karma?

By the mid-2000s China already had to buy at least 5 million barrels of oil a day—roughly 6% of world consumption and 25% of American consumption. Chindia will keep being mired in a madcap Pipelineistan global race where absolutely any strategy—barring nuclear war—fits to secure supplies. The strategies—charm diplomacy, FDI, soft loans, direct aid, technology transfers—also include the perforation of traditional "spheres of influence" assumed by the U.S. and also the E.U.

China has got extremely close to three key OPEC members—Saudi Arabia, Iran and Venezuela—one of which is a certified and the other an unofficial member of the Axis of Evil. When the occasion arises Chindia can be very pragmatic. In Sudan—which is practically China Pipelineistan territory—an Indian firm builds a pipeline while a Chinese firm builds a refinery. In Iran, China controls 50% of a huge oil field while India controls 20%. These Chindia collaborations—in Africa and the Middle East—will increase exponentially as the race goes on.

India: "Full power!"

"Full power!" is the new Indian mantra. Delivered not in Hindi, Pali, Gujarati or Malayalam but in English, with a smile, by the Mumbai taxi driver, the Calicut Brahmin, the IT developer in Cochin. This is the sound of India stepping on the gas to 21st Century great power status—even if the wheels belong to a rickety Ambassador, the good old Indian diesel sedan workhorse. This is the mantra in the cool parts of the Arabian Sea al Qaeda fails to reach.

Outside the Gateway of India—the ultimate vestige of Raj-dom in south India—a plaque reads *Urbs Prima in Indis*. Soon it may be *Urbs Prima in Mundis*—as more people will live in Mumbai than in Sao Paulo or Mexico City; Jakarta, Cairo, Karachi, Shanghai and other developing world beasts have been bypassed long ago. The Portuguese—after sailing from Iberia and arriving near this "gateway" more than three centuries before the British actually built a gate—called it *Bom Bahia*, "good bay." They even called it *Boa Vida*, "good life." Life can hardly be good when 51% of Mumbai's population of at least 15 million—and counting fast—lives in slums or in the streets. For roughly 75% of Mumbai's families, "home" means a single room where five people on average live, cook, eat and sleep. The one-room-fits-all is a given, and not only in sprawling slums like Jogeshwari. In more ways than one Mumbai is *Maximum City*—the title of a remarkable book by Suketu Mehta, whose ancestors come from Gujarat, was born in another maximum city, Kolkatta, but considers Mumbai his spiritual home. But then, in a flash, Maximum Slum gets connected; virtually every young person in these overcrowded rooms seems to be learning computer programming. They believe they are only a click away from one-room-fits-all to an air con office and the chance of perhaps one day buying a condo with an Arabian Sea view. They just have to be among the more than 2.5 million Indian graduates churned out every year by over 300 universities and 15,600 colleges, including 350,000 engineers (twice the U.S. total).

Mumbai is essentially run by a concrete-and-real estate lobby. Exclusion is the name of the game. For the price of a gin and tonic at the palatial Taj, one of the best hotels in India, the masses can buy 36 fabulous fruit juices in one of the Muslim-controlled stands. Ever since India was attacked by the "economic reform" virus, the mainstream press has not failed to devoutly worship the new sacred cows—first a new wave of dot com maharajas and Bollywood stars, then any nouveau riche in sight. The Tata family—former opium concessionaries—continues, according to the eternal running joke, to rule India. But newcomers like the flashy Kingfisher guy, Vijay Mallya, who's on everything from beers to airlines, are sprouting as fast as ayurvedic centers. A cross between a Mafia don and a Bollywood superstar, Mallya greets passengers of Kingfisher Airlines with a smooth rap on how he is now "revolutionizing business and leisure travel."

The ultimate Mumbai experience —extreme sports India-style—has to be riding the mad rush of a local train. From Churchgate station, a ticket to the suburbs costs 6 rupees—roughly 12 cents. You may get in, but you may not be able to get off—and vice versa. If you are to get off at an ultra-crowded station like Dadar, for instance, you must fight for positioning yourself in an extremely precise spot. Platforms rush by on both sides of the train. There are no doors—just two enormous holes on either side. You must jump before the train stops at each station, otherwise the incoming mass of people will overwhelm you. Inside the compartment, with its gorgeous black fans hanging from the ceiling like bats, you don't move; the crowd moves you. The number of passengers carried in a nine-car train during rush hour in Mumbai is approaching 6000. Commuters travel in groups. More than 4000 a year die, hit by electricity poles because they were precariously hanging from the "window." That's the Indian miracle on the go, full power.

Vasco da Gama, the ruthless Portuguese Argonaut who "discovered" India—as if Indian civilization had not existed for millennia—was horrified by the non-Christians of South India. He would flee modern, pagan Goa as the plague—but not after applying his own brand of diplomacy that mixed elements of kidnapping, mutilation and murder. The love affair between the West and Asia was never a love affair in the first place. Vasco opened the sea link between Europe and Asia in 1497-99 with only three puny caravels, and this decades after Chinese Admiral Zheng He's seven expeditions from 1405 to 1433, each featuring up to 300 ships carrying up to 30,000 men. Long before Vasco—not to mention Columbus and Magellan—began their globetrotting, or globesailing, the Ming dynasty had already developed state of-the-art technology in shipbuilding, navigation and astrology—but not in gunpowder. The Chinese never tried to usurp local land or local power; their imperial energies were focused more inwardly. They just wanted a piece of global trade.

So did the Portuguese—at least according to the official story in the West. Hence the Monty Pythonesque exchange between a Portuguese convict-exile—not Vasco, who remained in his caravel—as he stepped into the Indian shores and met "two Moors from Tunis" who spoke Castillean and Genoese (the Portuguese were initially thought to be Muslims from the Maghreb):

Figure 17. The globe centered on Mumbai.

The two Moors: The Devil take you! What brought you here?

The Portuguese discoverer: We came to seek Christians and spices.

Now the West goes to India to seek Che meeting Krishna. Kerala, self-described God's own country, or the country where God is inherent to a lot of small things, may be the ultimate magic realism metaphor of all-inclusive Indian cosmology—complete with communists, salafis, IT freaks, Virgin Marys, women in burqas, conspicuous consumption, portraits of Che Guevara and lost souls driving psychedelic buses with DTS® Dolby®-equipped stereo horns at terrifying speeds through the lush, dense, tropical greenery. For comfort, the thing is to forget all things ayurvedic; nothing beats a *thali*—the stainless steel tray the size of a huge pizza on which small bowls of vegetable curries, curds, deserts and other delectable goods are disposed to endless refills. The long and winding one lane road along the Malabar coast, dotted with green mosques, women in burqas, temptresses advertising cell phones, murals of Jesus Christ and dominated by those terrifying buses, is actually a street linking an agglomeration of villages (India after all is a galaxy of at least half a million villages). As road movies go, it offers an unparalleled glimpse into rural India—usually terra incognita for the bulk of India and global media.

India's hundreds of millions of poor suffered tremendously with the 1990s neo-liberal religious dogma. Prices were globalized while their incomes remained Indianized. According to the U.N. Human Development Index, it's better to be poor in Planet Gaza than in the so-called Indian "tiger economy."

Kerala is something else. In 1957, it became the first state in the world to elect a communist government democratically. It bears the most equitable land distribution in India. A glimpse of village life reveals that poverty is much less acute than in other parts of India. Health and education indicators are also much better. The literacy rate is virtually 100%. And political awareness is also high.

Vasco da Gama actually "discovered" Kerala. His "reckless sailing" (according to the locals) during a monsoon led him and his 170 illiterate sailors to land in Kappad, a small, undeveloped beach 23 km north of Calicut. Vasco, for many Keralans the precursor of globalization and Western imperialism, is celebrated with a small plaque; Keralans actually don't think much about him nowadays, nor did they ever. The real action in the Malabar coast is actually in Kochi, the sprawling Indian city a half-an-hour ferry ride away from Fort Cochin—where one can sample the full spectacle of the Indian middle classes in "full power" mode.

Drivers, carpenters, construction workers, they are all in "full power" mode. Not only in Kerala but all over the Gulf. From Kochi, it's easier to fly to Muscat or Dubai than to Kolkatta. According to the World Bank's Global Economic Prospects 2006 report, expat Indians pumped a staggering US$ 21.7 billion into the Indian economy in 2004. Two million Malayalees—Kerala migrants—are responsible for 34% of this total. And most are working in the Gulf, as well as migrants from Tamil Nadu, Andhra Pradesh and Rajasthan. According to the International Labor Organization, there are 10 million Indian migrants around the world—3.6 million of them in West Asia. There may be up to 100 million ethnic Indians across the globe, totally "full power."

The Indian stock market may have risen by more than 20% in 2005. The country once again may grow by an annual 7% to 8%. But India must not be reduced to a tale of successful outsourcing. The entire IT and office service industry—hyped ad nauseam by global corporate media—employs only 1.3 million people in a country of more than 1 billion. The IT industry is simply not enough to absorb more than 10 million young people every year who start looking for their first job. Narayana Murthy, the CEO of IT giant Infosys, has repeatedly warned that India cannot launch an industrial revolution while carrying the burden of mass illiteracy, appalling basic education standards and sex discrimination.

While the Indian middle class is composed of only 150 million people, 35% of the population (compared with 17% in Pakistan) still lives with less than US$ 1 a day. And a staggering 81% of the population lives on less than US$ 2 a day (compared to 47% in China). No less than 500 million—living in the countryside—are totally excluded from everything (right wing Hindu nationalism, heavily connected to the caste system, would love that the poor simply disappear). 3 in 4 people in India still live off agriculture. Inequality is tremendous: while more than 400 million rural workers represent an annual output for the country of only US$ 375 each, the 1.3 million IT workers represent around US$ 25,000 each. In the state of Uttar Pradesh—where more people live than in Germany and Britain combined—child death rates are worse than in Mali. According to UNICEF at least 57 million children are malnourished countrywide. Every Asian specialist and his neighbor say that India needs a boom in export-oriented manufacturing—so the overwhelming masses may be lifted out of poverty. The boom may eventually come, says a Mumbai businessman, but at an Indian pace.

Catastrophic infrastructure (but the Mumbai local trains miraculously arrive on time) and Byzantine regulations have to be urgently tackled. Kerala for its part does not want blind, neo-liberal "economic reform" per se—or a mushroom forest of Wal-Marts; the social effects would be extremely destabilizing. India gets 11 times less foreign direct investment (FDI) than China—mostly because caps are imposed in many politically sensitive sectors like aviation, insurance, coal mining, media and the retail business. The Manmohan Singh government's priorities are essentially sound: investment in infrastructure, agriculture, health and education. Singh publicly recognized that "bureaucratic mindset and corruption continues to act as a roadblock to enterprise and progress," but he also swore that "Indians are ready to take on the world."

The *Indian Express* ("Journalism of courage") offers a road map: "We have to increase agricultural production." Additionally, "states should set up Special Economic Zones and each zone should specialize in different commodities for exports." The textile industry is considered a thing of the past. "Massive and rapid industrialization is imperative to absorb the semi-skilled and skilled manpower now out of jobs." And FDI has to come from the Indian diaspora. "India should explore and motivate overseas Indians to invest in India."

It will happen—at an Indian pace. But certainly not for those taxi drivers in Mumbai, those demented, horn-honking bus ghosts in the back roads of Kerala, those computer whizzes in the back of a shack, those commuters hanging from a train window and dodging lethal poles. All they've got left is the energy to blast ahead and chase their mini India-as-a-great-power dream—full power.

The long Chinese commuter train is way, way faster. As late as 1820—before being humiliated by the West and then Japan—Qing dynasty China accounted for 30% of the world economy. From the 16th to the 19th Century Asia was awash in bars of silver and Spanish silver coins—a reflection of booming trade between Iberia and China, India and Southeast Asia. Speculators and rogue traders joined the banquet. The Dragon had a fit, introduced capital controls, the British cleverly came up with an Opium War, and China plunged into a long decadence.

Globalization cheerleaders probably ignore that China invented free trade (there are not many things China did *not* invent). It's all in the Tao, courtesy of Lao Tzu. The late Ming dynasty was faithful to the ideal state of *wu wei*, when interference by the wise ruler on social life, following Taoist principles, simply does not exist. French Enlightenment thinker François Quesnay loved the idea so much that he merged it with Vincent de Gournay's free market ideas to solidify the concept of *laissez-faire*. Quesnay was a physiocrat—according to which government should not interfere with the economy but follow *laissez-faire* and thus favor the emergence of *l'ordre naturel* ("the natural order of things"). He was later hailed as "the European Confucius." Adam Smith got such a kick out of Quesnay that he published a follow up, the *Wealth of Nations* free market Bible, in 1776.

The Little Helmsman Deng Xiaoping turned *wu wei* upside down and all around by conceptualizing "socialism with Chinese characteristics," or the "socialist market economy": let's trade like mad again, but with the ruler keeping a good eye on the proceedings. Now for China it's basically a question of "we're back"—with a bang. The ears of the whole planet were shattered. "We" of course is configured as The Benign Dragon, whose path is officially spun as a "peaceful emergence." In fact this is an extremely complex Beijing opera of sapping American influence in Asia while not incurring the wrath of the (spurned, imperial, Western) Gods. Solving the Chindia border problems in this case is essential—part of the emerging Big Picture of China as the great trade partner of all South, North and East Asia.

China consumes twice as much steel as the U.S.—even though its economy is 10 times smaller. No wonder shipbuilders in Shanghai and Guangzhou are ecstatic— their armies of welders gorging a brand new fleet of ships to keep bringing a flood of energy and materials to China, iron ore and natural gas from Australia, minerals from Africa, oil from the Middle East, Africa and South America. Today China has 10 million private cars. By 2020 they will be 120 million.

In their privileged and virtually unassailable position as the factory of the world, China's manufacturers have the matrix for anyone's products, from Nike and Reebok to Max Mara and Muji. They can make a Muji better than Japanese Muji. So the next step is to get rid of the middleman. In the next few years Globalistan may not only buy "made in China" clothes but "designed by China" clothes—with all the profits going back to China.

Workers (flush with cash) unite!

The Industrial Revolution started in Europe with mechanized sewing. Now there's another Industrial Revolution on the march—where the wealthy West imagines and consumes the clothes that China produces. Not much will be left for everybody else. After the end of the Multi-Fiber Arrangement, with all quotas on textile imports lifted by the WTO, China's share of the U.S. textile market may soon hit 50%, and in the E.U. may hit 30%.

Globalistan applied to the textile industry is inevitably perverse —leading, once again, not to a North-South war but to a South-South war. The big losers in the new game were countries in Africa, with their market share shrinking by as much as 70%, or countries that heavily benefited from the WTO quota system, such as Tunisia, the Dominican Republic and Nepal. Triad countries have had enough time to "restructure" their textile industries toward the value-added niche—like deluxe *prêt-a-porter* in Italy and *haute couture* in France. But what's going to happen, for instance, to Madagascar, which imported European, Chinese or Indian textiles, manufactured in sweatshops and then re-exported the finished merchandise to the North?

Hundreds of thousands of jobs in poor countries will be lost. In both the U.S. and the E.U. most garment companies will massively delocalize. Bangladeshi textile merchants in Hong Kong estimate that American and European companies that used to buy from as many as 60 countries will be buying from less than 10 by 2010, and mostly buying from China.

A sign of things to come is what will happen in Shenzhen—the ersatz Hong Kong across the border, a whirlwind of a special economic zone fueled by investment money and cheap sex which now boasts the largest annual GDP per capita in China (US$ 6,510, in 2005 figures). Production costs and land costs constantly rise in Shenzhen. For hundreds of companies, the solution is delocalization—going West to neighboring provinces such as Hunan or going to Far West Xinjiang, as Beijing has been encouraging these companies to do since the early 2000s. Critics in Guangzhou say that many Guangdong province industrial bosses—and many are investors from Hong Kong and Taiwan—use the threat of delocalizing in order to force people to accept 14-hours-a-day, seven-days-a-week, no-overtime-pay work-load.

The name of the game is productivity. An average Chinese worker in the garment industry earns more than double an Indian and four times more than a Bangladeshi textile worker. The Chinese may earn more, but his productivity is also higher. By the mid-2000s he was adding US$ 5,000 a year in value to what he produces, compared with US$ 2,600 by the Indian and US$ 900 by the Bangladeshi. This is because Chinese businesses have invested much more in manufacturing equipment and also in transportation.

By 2015 Guangdong province, China's much-fabled "factory of the world," will achieve "modernization," according to a report by Niu Wenyuan of the Chinese Academy of Sciences. The report defines "modernization" as a level of economic development, social progress, living standards and sustainable development similar to that of a "medium-level developed country." This roughly means that even without the help of a monster E.U.-like structure, Guangdong by 2015 is set to become a Chinese Spain or Ireland.

This is the Beijing view. The Guangdong provincial government is even bolder: it wants modernization as early as 2010 for the Pearl River Delta—the jewel in the crown of the factory of the world. And for the booming city of Shenzhen, modernization should have been achieved by...yesterday.

In 2001, former Guangdong governor Lu Ruihua was already boasting that the province's economy was larger than that of Singapore, South Africa or Greece. Guangdong is indeed a powerhouse compared with the larger ASEAN (Association of Southeast Asian Nations) countries and the four original Asian tigers. In a 2001 table compiled by the *South China Morning Post*, Guangdong's economy was already 53% larger than that of the Philippines and 270% larger than that of Vietnam. The forecast was that it could surpass Thailand, Indonesia and Hong Kong by 2010.

According to Joseph Cheng, professor of political science at the City University of Hong Kong, a specialist in Guangdong and editor of the book *Guangdong: Preparing for the WTO Challenge*, "if the average annual growth rate can be maintained at 10.3% ... and taking population growth into consideration ... per capita gross domestic product in the region will reach US$ 7,000 by 2010." Guangdong's GDP may have reached US$ 240 billion or more by the end of 2006. Everything seems to be on track. Spain and Ireland, watch out.

The myth of China as the world's biggest market disguises the fact that it's really a cluster of small markets. Historically, each Chinese city has always been self-sufficient. The Maoist model, the commune, was not that different. When the model was transplanted to the city, the result was the state-owned enterprise (SOE). Maoist cities were aggregations of industrial communes. In terms of economic production, Maoist cities were like mini-countries. Deng Xiaoping's reforms changed all that. Its consequences—a web of good airports, roads and railways, more efficient production, the rise of Chinese domestic brands—spelled the end of the mini-country syndrome.

The next inevitable step is integration. In July 2003, Guangdong Communist Party secretary Zhang Dejiang proposed the creation of a Pan-Pearl River Delta, or 9+2 plan, expanding and decentralizing trade and investment by linking 9 provinces (Guangdong, Fujian, Jiangxi, Hunan, Guangxi, Hainan, Guizhou, Yunnan and Sichuan) with the 2 special administrative regions (SARs), Hong Kong and Macau. So 9 plus 2, if implemented, will mean no trade or tariff barriers, and totally free movement of labor. In a nutshell, a powerful "mini-China"—20% of the land mass, 450 million people (more or less like the 25-member E.U.) and a GDP of US$ 630 billion by the mid-2000s, representing at least 40% of China's economy.

Can it possibly work? As far as the Communist Party commandments are concerned, the timing could not be better: for the fourth generation under President Hu Jintao and his reformist ally, Premier Wen Jiabao, the number one priority is the development of China's domestic market.

Internal competition will be fierce. Guangdong and the Pearl River Delta are locked in a fierce battle for investment with Shanghai and the Yangtze River Delta, which sells itself as having better access to China's huge domestic market. While exports from the Pearl River Delta are doubling, those from the Yangtze are quadrupling. Shanghai already gets more foreign investment and is leading China in technology and heavy industry. But Guangdong is also moving up. The middle class in a province of almost 90 million numbers more than 20 million. Guangzhou is becoming China's "Japanese Detroit," hosting Honda and Toyota, and is promoting heavy and chemical industry. The Beijing view is that the Pearl River Delta should position itself as the prime processing center for the "factory of the world."

The special economic zones (SEZs) Shenzhen and Zhuhai were also created by a party commandment—in their cases by Deng Xiaoping himself. In the current climate of tremendous competition among Chinese provinces, towns and even local districts, the Communist Party Politburo is certain to convince them of at least not competing too much. As for the Pearl River Delta, the top commandment enunciated by Premier Wen Jiabao is that it should "work closely with Hong Kong in economic, science and technology and cultural areas."

Figure 18. The globe centered on Shanghai.

For the Guangdong Academy of Social Sciences the future of Guangdong is obviously integration—not only with Hong Kong and Macau but also with Taiwan. From Hong Kong's point of view—with its wealth of capital, management and sophisticated financial services—the Pan-Pearl River Delta will be essential for thousands of small and medium Hong Kong producers who cannot export in enormous quantities and thus must concentrate on the Chinese hinterland, with its masses of cheap labor and plenty of natural resources. Yunnan province, for instance, has tin, Guizhou province coal, and Guangxi province has aluminum, tin and manganese.

Hong Kong is the biggest foreign investor in China, followed by the Virgin Islands (because of their fiscal-paradise status), Japan, South Korea, the U.S. and Taiwan. But most of the real investment, as it is widely acknowledged in Hong Kong, comes in fact from Taiwan. Taiwan built China as the second-largest producer of IT hardware in the world, only behind the U.S., as well as the world's biggest exporter to the U.S. More than 60% of these "made in China" exports are in fact made by Taiwanese companies.

Dongguan, with its sea of factories, is practically a mainland extension of Taiwan, and conveniently close to Hong Kong, which means direct flights to Taipei. The investment boom started in the early 1990s, mainly in low-tech industries, and profiting from cheap labor. Now most of it is in high tech but in a worrying trend for Guangdong, moving north towards the competition, the Yangtze River Delta. More than 70,000 Taiwanese companies are established in China—a very potent and perhaps definitive reason to deter any cross-strait turbulence.

Taiwanese investors established in Guangdong and dependent on cheap labor are moving inland or to Vietnam, while no fewer than 300,000 Taiwanese—and counting—live in the Greater Shanghai area, with some tracts replicating Taiwan's high-tech industrial zones. Already more than 30% of China's exports are electronic and IT products. But Taiwanese investors are interested in targeting not only exports but the new, affluent Chinese consumer. An extra incentive is the 2010 free-trade area between China and ASEAN—which will be the largest in the world.

Guangdong's development has been nothing short of exceptional, considering that Mao Zedong relegated the province to the dustbin of history and it was only opened in the early 1980s, finally profiting from its status as China's southern gate, close to Hong Kong and the overseas Chinese. The Pearl River Delta undertook not only a revolution in agriculture but an industrial revolution as well, fueled by joint ventures with "foreign" (Hong Kong and Taiwanese) capital. The poor parts of Guangdong migrated to the Pearl River Delta as well as workers from Hunan, Sichuan, Jiangxi and Guangxi. According to Cheng, the political science professor, "the important question in the coming decades is both the relationship that Guangdong will have to its hinterland ... and the relationship that Guangdong's economic core (the Pearl River Delta including Hong Kong, Macau and the SEZs) will have to the province, and to the world beyond."

By the second half of the 1990s Guangdong realized it had a lot of problems—with then President Jiang Zemin and his "Shanghai mafia" heavily privileging the Yangtze River Delta. In order to upgrade, Guangdong party officials realized that links only to Hong Kong were not enough, so by the end of the 1990s a group of advisers and businessmen started thinking more boldly. Hong Kong and Guang-zhou now agree that Guangdong needs to capture the domestic market and invest all over China. With the strategic support of key officials Li Changchun and Zhan Dejiang in Beijing, "mini-China" may be absolutely unstoppable.

If only the Chinese Far West could also become a mini-China: that may be the Communist Party's ultimate wet dream.

Xinjiang is the richest province in China—with at least 80 billion barrels of oil, not to mention uranium and gas, underneath the Taklamakan desert. The "prob-lem"—from Beijing's point of view—is the indigenous Uighur population, qualified as "splittists" or, worse still, "terrorists."

The Uighur resistance in Xinjiang does not have a Dalai Lama to capture head-lines, but they are not intimidated: bombs have been detonated, attacks have been perpetrated, and the underground remains very active in Istanbul and Germany. The Uighur diaspora in Central Asia—a potential source for financing what is described, hush-hush, as a future "Uighurstan"—numbers at least 400,000. In the early 1990s Kazakhstan allowed two Uighur liberation groups to be based in Almaty. But China under Jiang Zemin developed a turbocharged diplomatic offensive. Kazakhstan and Kyrgyzstan duly obliged: they cracked down on Uighur offices, arrested Uighurs who criticized Beijing and kept the borders open for trade but not for money, weapons or propaganda helping Uighurs inside China.

Urumqi is the capital of the Chinese Far West, the last frontier of civilization from the point of view of Beijing, and in itself quite a surreal spectacle. More than 3000 km away from Beijing, literally in the middle of nowhere—that is, south of the snow-capped Tian Shan Mountains and north of the menacing Taklamakan desert, the name of which in Uighur means "you can get in but you can't get out"—we find a metropolis of more than 1 million: a generic city imported from the Chinese east coast, with 80% of Han Chinese transplanted by force and the remaining volunteers avidly dreaming of getting rich gloriously quick.

Street signs are in both Mandarin and Arabic script. The currency—the Chinese yuan—is totally stable. The main office of the Bank of China is imperially impecca-ble. Urumqi has gone digital, while medieval Kashgar is still in ink-on-paper mode. Colonized-by-force Urumqi is pure modern China: huge department stores selling all manner of cheap knockoffs, skyscrapers sprouting like mushrooms, cranes and chainsaws, hellish pollution coupled with desert winds. Everything runs on—of course—Beijing time: in winter the sun "rises" after 8 A.M.

Uighurs are nowhere to be seen in central Urumqi—except as beggars or tacky felt souvenir dolls. Most have been deported to suburbia at the edge of the desert. But mosques are bursting at the seams. Uighurs—desert nomads—are not particularly religious, but Islam has been a powerful way of expressing their distress. As well as speaking only their own language, Uighurs don't take taxis with Han Chinese drivers and only eat halal food. The young don't listen to ghastly Chinese pop, but to the pungent guitar sounds of Akbar Kahriman. At Erdaoqao market, hundreds of merchants sell the same items that are found in medieval Kashgar. The area around it is a mini-replica of Kashgar. Unfazed, Han Chinese built their own, sanitized version: the "Xinjiang International Grand Bazaar," complete with its own mosque, an array of camel statues (plus one genuine article for tourist snapshots), piped music (Western techno or Chinese pop: no Uighur tunes) and a 5,000-square-meter "Joy Square." There's not a whole lot of joy around, though. Carved in the faces of elder Uighurs, there's a feeling of not so much anger as profound sadness—at the disappearance of their culture and at not even being able to pick up the crumbs from the Great Han Materialist Banquet.

To top it all, Beijing radically cut off aid to the so-called "ethnic minorities": there are 12 in Xinjiang alone, and apart from Uighurs (42% of the population) they include Hui (Chinese Muslims), Manchu, Mongolian, Kazakh, Kyrgyz, Tajik, Uzbek and Tatar. Only Han Chinese could come up with a concept like "minority food street." Beijing is only interested in promoting "mysterious" Xinjiang for tourism purposes: but it has to be a Xinjiang reduced to theme park status.

If you are a Uighur and you happen, by a miracle, to work for a Chinese company, you cannot go to the mosque. Signs on many mosques, in Arabic, say they are forbidden to teenagers—which is a frankly absurd ruling that has nothing to do with Islamic law. All public demonstrations by Uighurs are forbidden. And if you are an Uighur in Urumqi and you talk about independence, you are arrested on the spot, as any trader in Yengisar knives will confirm. In March 2000 Beijing formally adopted an ambitious plan for "the large-scale development of the West." The key point of this massive "Go West" campaign is to resettle millions more Han Chinese in Xinjiang. Beijing would not be too displeased if in the long run this official policy exports many of the 7.5 million Uighur and 1.3 million Kazakh "minorities" toward the more unstable pastures of the former Soviet Central Asian republics.

The Politburo knows very well that Uighurs and other "ethnic minorities" are less than 6% of the total Chinese population of 1.3 billion, but they occupy more than half of Chinese territory. Xinjiang is almost as big as Western Europe. Beijing's nightmare is the remote possibility of new alliances between regional leaders and business elites capable of redrawing China's internal balance of power, as happened so many times in the past. Since the implosion of the USSR and the rise of the new

Central Asian republics a lot of people from Kazakhstan, Uzbekistan and Kyrgyzstan have been to Xinjiang: in fact both parts of historic Turkestan started in a way to unify. That's exactly what Beijing does not want. Beijing wants very well defined—and patrolled—borders. That's one of the main tasks of the Shanghai Cooperation Organization.

Amid mighty Central Asian mountain ranges and deserts it's virtually impossible to talk about defined borders. With more than 25% of the world's population and the most coercive of birth-control policies, China still has not managed to contain its population explosion. Ten percent of Chinese territory, inhabited by two-thirds of the overall population, and producing 70% of the national wealth, is prone to inundation by major rivers. China's economy needs to grow at least 10% every year just to absorb its youth entering the job market.

According to Minister of Labor and Social Security Zheng Silin, in a 2003 report to the National People's Congress, a staggering 150 million Chinese rural workers were unemployed out of a total of 485 million; and of 94 million farmers who had recently migrated to big cities, the majority were still unemployed.

Growth at a median 8% annually—something the West can only dream about—is still not good enough for China. While some sectors of "market socialism" degenerated into gangsterism, and human rights, from Beijing's point of view, means only economic development, hundreds of millions of people remain involved in the largest internal mass migration movement in history. Dozens of millions of unemployed threaten to go on rampage. In the event the Dragon starts to disintegrate, the implosion could begin on the periphery, at the last frontier, in the wilderness that shot from the 14th Century straight into the 21st: Xinjiang.

By contrast, everywhere in developed, urban China—Shanghai, Beijing, Guangzhou—the message is the same. The next "counterrevolutionary rebellion"—as the Communist Party branded the student uprising in Tiananmen in 1989—if it happens, will not come from Xinjiang: it will be a peasant revolution. Now what Mao would have to say about *that?*

I was told by foreign diplomats and Chinese scholars in Beijing and young, urban, internet-connected professionals in Guangzhou in unmistakable terms: nobody from the party's "fourth generation" leadership wants to go back to the Maoist model of economic autarky and foreign-policy isolation. Most of all, however, nobody in the leadership—as well as most influential intellectuals—wants the toppling of the Communist Party by pluralist forces advocating a multi-party democracy: that would amount to, in the words of a Beijing scholar, "an unpredictable, very dangerous destabilization." There's only a slight detail: what 1 billion Chinese peasants will make of all this. Enter Chen Guidi and Wu Chuntao.

Husband and wife Chen Guidi and Wu Chuntao are a very dangerous couple. All because of a book, the notorious *Zhongguo Nongmin Diaocha* or "Chinese Peasant Study," published in January 2004, and banned just before the opening of a new session of the National People's Congress (NPC) two months later by the Communist Party Propaganda Department. It turned into an explosive, underground mega-bestseller—more than 7 million pirated copies sold. By the mid-2000s the 460-page yellow-bound volume with the title in black characters could be easily found under the counter, even in some bookshops, for only 22 yuan (US$ 2.65).

The *Chinese Peasant Study* is gritty, emotion-packed literary reportage depicting economic exploitation, social injustice and political oppression in rural China—as well as some extraordinary tales of resistance. It took three years to write and consumed all of Chen's and Wu's savings. They visited more than 50 towns throughout agricultural Anhui province, talked to scores of senior officials in Beijing and interviewed thousands of peasants to explain how, in its mad urbanization drive, the party not only neglected the lot of 900 million peasants—deprived of decent health care, welfare, education, the right to have more than one or two children—but also treated them harshly, plunging them in a *guaiqian* (vicious cycle) in which nothing has fundamentally changed a social structure that has been systematically exploiting Chinese peasants for centuries.

A constant pattern emerges: if a villager, for instance, accuses a local party boss of corruption, he inevitably goes to jail, accused of "provoking riots." The key issue in the book—and in the whole Chinese modernization process—is corruption. A whole chapter details how local, rural party officials twist their numbers to cheat the party leadership in Beijing out of revenue.

Both Chen, born in 1943 in Anhui province, and Wu, born in 1963 in Hunan province, come from peasant families and spent their childhoods in the countryside before moving to urban China. When they returned to their roots, as they write in the preface, "we observed unimaginable poverty and unthinkable evil, we saw unimaginable suffering and unthinkable helplessness, unimagined resistance with incomprehensible silence, and have been moved beyond imagination by unbelievable tragedy..."

A typical passage reads: "Farmers worked all year long to earn an average annual income of 700 yuan. Many farmers lived in mud-clay houses that were dark, damp, small and shabby. Some even had tree bark roofs because they couldn't afford tiles. Because of poverty, once someone fell ill, he either endured it if it was minor disease, or else just waited to die. There were 620 households in the whole village, of which 514, or 82.9%, were below the poverty line. Even though the village was very poor, the leaders were prone to boasting and exaggeration about their performance, and as a result the government struck it off the list of impoverished villages. So the villagers were burdened with exorbitant taxes and levies."

Chen is no maverick: he is a member of the respected, state-sanctioned Association of Chinese Writers. Chen and Wu definitely are not "splittists"—the unforgivable ideological sin. They are in essence moderate reformists who believe the party is reformable: one of the chapters in the book is a glowing tribute to the fairness of Premier Wen Jiabao, who was just a simple official at the time. Nevertheless, the book had the capacity to scare the fourth-generation leadership because it graphically depicts the workings of a time bomb—the other side of the market-Leninist glitter in Beijing, Shanghai and Guangzhou. It details how the rural masses have gotten next to nothing since Deng Xiaoping's reforms were introduced in the late 1970s. The average annual income in Shanghai in the mid-2000s, 14,800 yuan (US$ 1,790), was seven times as high as in rural Anhui, 2,100 yuan. In a nutshell, the annual income of a farmer in today's China is only one-sixth to one-seventh that of an urban professional—but he pays three times as many taxes, plus a plethora of local taxes of dubious legality. Moreover, untold millions subsist on less than 2 yuan (24 cents) a day.

In practice, China's real "one country, two systems" is represented by the decrepit Maoist *huji zhidu* or household registration system, which ties peasants to their land and was a key instrument to enforce the collectivization of agriculture. The fourth generation is more than aware of the anachronism. Long ago, Luo Gan, the Politburo Standing Committee member in charge of the police and the legal system, proposed a single, nationwide registration system for all Chinese. The State Council approved it, but implementation has been very slow. According to the new system, peasants may migrate to the cities as long as they have been able to find a job. Millions have not found anything, but still they migrate in hopes of finding work.

Inequality in China is much more acute than in India. A recent study by the Chinese Academy of Social Sciences (CAAS) says it is actually the worst on the planet, barring the odd sub-Saharan African country. China's "peasant question" is an economic, social and political crisis of gargantuan proportions. Scholars at CAAS estimate that since the start of Deng's reforms, 270 million Chinese have escaped poverty. That's not enough in a nation of more than 1.3 billion people. The crucial question is how "one system, two countries," where 400 million people advance while 900 million are left behind, can possibly co-exist. One billion peasants—80% of the total population—can never be fully assimilated, no matter the rhythm of the economic miracle.

The impact of Chen's and Wu's book, anyway, was cataclysmic. In the 2004 National People's Congress the fourth generation actually managed to criticize the third generation's obsession with China's GDP growth rate, and is now formally engaged in a new development strategy more respectful of the Chinese people and the Chinese environment. Premier Wen, reformist ally of president and party chief Hu Jintao, coined the indispensable slogan of "The Three Peasant Problems": farmers, villages and agriculture. But the key issue remains corruption—and this strictly concerns Communist Party officials. It's a tremendous contradiction. The party vows to try to solve the "peasant question," but at the same time simply cannot tolerate that 900 million peasants are a de facto underclass, or the idea that the party itself may be responsible for this situation.

Premier Wen, according to diplomats in Beijing, is a passionate proponent of a Singapore-style neo-authoritarian system for China. There's one enormous difference, though: Singapore may have been a one-party state since Lee Kuan Yew's early days in the 1960s, but government corruption is in essence non-existent.

It all comes back to the same point: is the Chinese ultra-authoritarian system reformable? Dialectical contradictions abound. According to a Beijing scholar, the party recognizes that courts should be impartial and trusted by all in a country facing what some believe to be an imminent social volcano. Courts should have a major role in fighting corruption and improving governance. At the same time the party leadership fears that the primacy of the law will spell a clear and present danger to its power monopoly.

Another new slogan dictates that the fourth generation is marching toward the "Comprehensive Well-Off Society" which establishes that China's GDP levels in 2020 should be four times as high as in 2000. The question on anyone's lips is how this development drive will match the lingering communist ideal of a society that by definition has to eliminate poverty, protect the environment, eschew wars and create opportunities for all its citizens.

The West may not know. But in urban China the ultimate threat, the menace, the dangerous Other, the Alien, is not an Arab "terrorist": it's the *mingong*, the Chinese migrant peasant worker.

More than 200 million *mingong* are roaming China. At least 25% don't get paid by their employers, or their lump payment—before the Chinese Lunar New Year—is delayed. According to Zeng Peiyan, a member of China's State Council, by early 2005 the equivalent of more than US$ 13 billion had not yet been paid to *mingong*; in some cases debts are more than 10 years old. 60% of *mingong* have to work more than 10 hours a day. And 97% have no medical benefits whatsoever. Shanghai urban professionals insist that technically, at least for now, no Chinese peasant can dream of having formal employment.

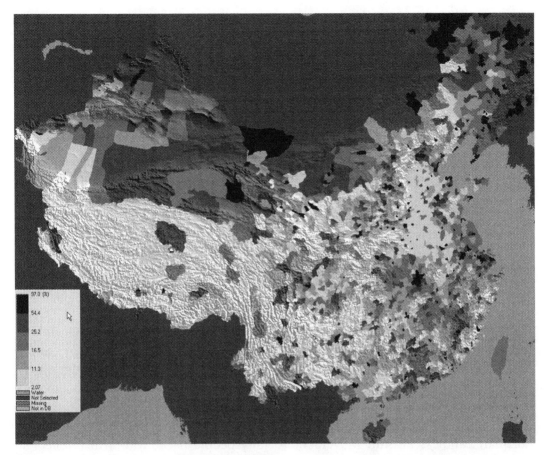

*Figure 19. Data from the 2000 China census showing counties by percentage of
nonagricultural population: darker is more urban, lighter is more agricultural.
Most of China is still predominantly agricultural (China Data Center).*

You can spot a *mingong* from miles away. Their work clothes, blue or brown, are shabby and covered in dust; they are thinner than most Chinese; and they are also shorter, which leads to widespread discrimination because of their height. Whatever their perceived shortcomings, they are the unknown, heroic protagonists of China's spectacular economic miracle. In the big cities there are now more floating *mingong* than urban workers.

Their armies can be seen in countless construction sites in Shanghai and Beijing, living in shelters more crowded than prison cells, the more skilled among them earning 70 yuan a day for a 12-hour workday, with a 30-minute break, the new arrivals making only 30 yuan a day. They must register with the big city government every two months and have practically no health and education rights. There are more than 3 million in Shanghai alone, erecting all those mushrooming steel-and-glass office towers. If all unregistered *mingong* are taken into account, Shanghai's population may be exceeding 20 million by now. In the fierce Beijing winter, late at night, they can be seen working in the streets under freezing temperatures and merciless winds from the Gobi Desert. Sometimes during a lightning-quick break we can spot their shadows gazing longingly at out-of-reach sneakers and mobile phones behind glittering department-store windows.

And there are the girls too, in Guangzhou, Shenzhen, Dongguan, the hordes of manual workers all over the assembly lines in the "factory of the world" churning out global T-shirts, trousers and sneakers; and there are the semi-illiterate girls from desert Gansu province suddenly turned into tour guides in neighboring Tibet.

Every year the army of *mingong* comes back to their home provinces for the Chinese Lunar Year holiday—their one and only holiday—crowding train stations with their notorious striped, oversized red-white-and-blue nylon bags crammed with gifts for their families and precious dirty envelopes stuffed with all their savings (as much as 90% of everything they earn). This annual internal Chinese migration is far bigger than the Hajj.

Meanwhile the countryside is getting angrier by the day: tens of thousands "civic disturbances" involve more than 3 million people every year since 2003. A new protest erupts in China every five minutes or so. Thunderous silence is the official media's norm. It's taken for granted that every city except ultra-policed Beijing has been facing demonstrations or eruptions of spontaneous violence. Media professionals in Shanghai note the glaring absence of a powerful organization like the Brazilian Landless Peasant Movement to rally people nationwide. An intellectual from Henan province is convinced of the absolute necessity of a nationwide rebellion. But in conversations with urban professionals in Guangzhou, the absolute majority admits nothing will happen "because of China's centuries-old feudal system of exploitation."

Anyway, class struggle is alive and thriving in the Chinese countryside, pitting rich farmers against the growing army of landless *mingong*—they may be errant, but always keep close ties to their native villages. Surplus manpower in the countryside may reach a staggering 450 million people, according to the most alarmist predictions, with at least 26 million annually trying their luck in the big cities.

A total of 100 million peasants currently work in the so-called "town and village enterprises." TVEs grew very fast in the early years of Deng's reforms, but lately have succumbed to better-equipped urban-based or foreign-based companies. They have already absorbed all the surplus manpower they could handle.

As a Guangzhou businessman explains it, the army of unemployed has been growing because of two linked factors—China's entry in the WTO coupled with massive layoffs by state-owned enterprises (SOEs): "There are many cities that are forcing peasants back to the countryside, because unemployment is now affecting their own residents." And when and if these millions of peasants go back, they find nothing to rely on, and the same, unchanged pitiful standards of health and education. Chinese economists say the process has been inevitable since collective production has been eroded in order to benefit individual family farming.

What Mao would make of it? China's globalization dirty secret is actually the taming of the Chinese working class. A Chinese peasant earns an average of US$ 30 a month. A factory worker earns an average of US$ 100 a month. There's no evidence their income will substantially grow—and this in an economy growing as much as 10% a year. Compare it to China's new rich—roughly 20,000 people, 90% of which are Communist Party cadres, members of local, regional or national government, or the privileged sons of Party cadres, who are in charge of virtually everything that matters: the country's natural resources, the banking industry, the power generation industry, the transportation industry, the weapons industry and the media. Some Chinese sociologists define this system not as socialism but as high-tech feudalism with Chinese characteristics.

The ultimate, lethal danger for the Chinese Communist Party is the merging of peasant protests with urban demonstrations—peasants, *mingong*, former state employees—all losers in the Globalistan game united. Hence President Hu's frenzied actions to affirm his iron hand.

The party's strategy to counter all these problems, according to Chinese Academy of Social Sciences scholars, is to emphasize domestic consumer demand. This is a remarkable turnaround. Former premier Zhu Rongji and the conservatives based their economic policies on growth fueled by large SOEs. As for the export-led growth model, it was articulated by none other than the late Zhao Ziyang in the late 1980s. Now Premier Wen is in charge of the economy, and he wants a "Third way" (no, not the Tony Blair variety). He wants growth fueled by domestic—not foreign demand. And he wants domestic demand to come from Chinese consumers, not the state.

Intellectuals, speaking anonymously because no one wants to be awakened for forced dead of night sightseeing courtesy of the Public Security Bureau, seem to agree that trying to redistribute a little bit of the pie is the only viable strategy if the party is to regain some popular appeal. Moreover, President Hu, Premier Wen and Luo Gan (Politburo member in charge of the police and the legal system) deeply believe they will be able to "rectify the behavior" of the party's bad apples in order to ensure that the new policies are followed to the letter.

These intellectuals also insist the party will refuse to reassess Tiananmen at all costs—and at its own peril, we might add, because all pre-Tiananmen conditions have again resurfaced: the possibility of massive popular reaction against corruption inside the party, against abuse of power by party officials, and against the unbearable urban-rural abyss. The party will do anything to prevent the emergence of an organized and well-focused opposition. It certainly controls a vast intimidating machinery to do so.

We all know the U.S. is China's top market, and China is the U.S.'s top creditor. But the really crucial point is that as multinational Corporatistan controls 60% of China's exports, the promotion of any color-coded revolution a la Georgia or Ukraine in China is pointless. After all, Corporatistan and the Communist Party are brothers in arms.

Globally, the Beijing collective leadership is already engaged in the promotion of what is defined as China's new historic mission, embodied in the concept of "harmonious world," and based on the Chinese concept of Concord. This is Beijing's answer to unilateralism, the North/South abyss and the global environmental crisis. Internally, if things go wrong the alternative in the horizon is cataclysmic: no less than an asymmetric war to end all asymmetric wars, hundreds of millions of peasants rising to depose the privileged Communist Party Bureaucratastan, once again "an act of violence by which one class overthrows another," just as Mao wrote, in another context, in 1927.

China had the largest economy in the world for almost 9 of the last 10 centuries. In 2015 China may account for 17% of global production. The ultra-ambitious official 2020 goal is for China to have completed the transition towards a US$ 10,000 annual GDP per capita economy in purchasing power parity (PPP) terms—equivalent to Portugal, Argentina and South Korea before the 1997 Asian financial crisis, and able to compete with Japan in technological prowess. Every financial analyst in Hong Kong tells us that for an economy to leave the Third World behind and reach annual US$ 10,000 GDP per capita is not that hard; what's virtually impossible is to go from US$ 10,000 to US$ 20,000 annual—even when you're powered by the mega-creative bamboo internet, the global Chinese diaspora.

The year 2037 should also be taken seriously: it's the date set by Little Helmsman Deng for the official arrival of Western representative democracy in China. By 2049—at the 100th anniversary of the Popular Republic—the Economic Arc of Southern China should boast a GDP equivalent to France. Taiwan should be back to the Motherland (one country, three systems?) Shanghai will be the starting point of the 21st Century New Silk Road to Europe. And China will be largest economy in the world—again.

China's extraordinary culture teaches us to anticipate a next half Century more thrilling than a Jet Li spectacular. And, hopefully, with no Liquid War. But will China be on top already by 2025? Wallerstein sees three huge problems. The first, inevitably, as we have seen it, is internal, "the discontent of about half of the population that has been left behind, and the discontent of the other half about the limits on their internal political freedom." In fact, the "left behind" may account for 70% of the total population.

The second problem "concerns the world economy. The incredible expansion of consumption in China (along with that of India) will take its toll both on the world's ecology and on the possibilities of capital accumulation. Too many consumers and too many producers will have severe repercussions on worldwide profit levels."

The third problem is how China going to manage the neighbors: "Were China to accomplish the reintegration of Taiwan, help arrange the reunification of the Koreas, and come to terms (psychologically and politically) with Japan, there might be an East Asian unified geopolitical structure that could assume a hegemonic position."

It won't be easy, says Wallerstein, but it's doable. That's exactly what they think in Chindia—from Beijing to Delhi, from Guangzhou to Mumbai. Forget Liquid War: we Chinese and we Indians, we're taking over the world. By all means necessary. And if it takes Liquid War, let it be. Take *Unrestricted Warfare,* by Qiao Liang and Wang Xiangsui, published by the People's Liberation Army (PLA) in early 1999 and written by two PLA senior Colonels. The book develops a myriad of tactics by the South—especially China—to be employed in an asymmetric war against the U.S. Anything goes: profiting from the post-modern version of *wu wei* but also digital war and media war. Asian Century, anyone?

~ 12 ~

THE GAZPROM NATION AND ITS "NEAR ABROAD"

Marx reminded us that Russia was addicted to "Asian despotism." That remains the case not only in Russia but all over the "near abroad" in Central Asia. Russia's wealth of natural resources is legendary. Hence former KGB Vladimir Putin could not possibly go wrong by applying a chess/jiu-jitsu move to make the most of these resources using complementary fabulous national resources in science, technology and education. Gorbachev and Yeltsin couldn't do it. "Putinism" now delivers the construction of a Russian Corporatistan. The social oligopoly model and the occasionally raw power economic diplomacy may raise eyebrows in Western dinner parties. But this is Putin's Sinatra-style "my way." And it works. The Gazprom nation is ready to rock 'n roll.

With the U.S.—the E.U.'s number one trading partner and NATO ally—mired in the Iraq quagmire and the E.U. still in open constitutional crisis, the Gazprom nation is exceptionally positioned to have its way in the negotiations leading to the post-2007 "Strategic Partnership Treaty" between the E.U. and Russia. This is one the most crucial dossiers anywhere to define where the world system is going next.

The legal life of the E.U./Russia couple is based on a 1997 agreement lasting 10 years that will be automatically extended beyond 2007. At a summit in Moscow in May 2005 the couple agreed on 4 road maps leading to 4 "common spaces" for deeper integration. These road maps are not legally binding: they are political commitments.

An internal European Commission (EC) paper shows that the couple must seriously get down to business. Take the dream of establishing a Common Economic Space (CES), covering everything from industry, competition and investment to financial services, transport and telecommunications. For an uneasy EC, "Russia considers that the E.U. is ... making unrealistic demands on Russia." The possibility was floated of a free trade agreement (FTA) between the E.U. and Russia. However, "there is no single mention of the words 'free trade' in the road maps." First Russia has to join the WTO. But the Bush administration blocks it.

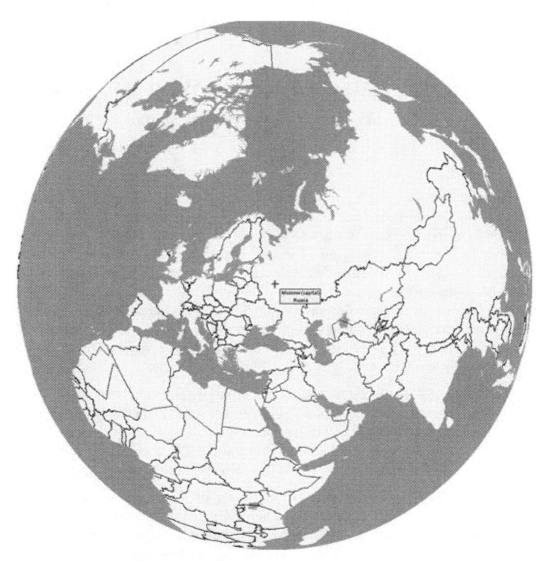

Figure 20. The globe centered on Moscow.

The E.U. knows both sides want a free trade agreement. Russia needs to attract new technology, to diversify its economic base, and to develop high-value and knowledge-intensive goods and services – the basis for Russia to be globally competitive.

The E.U. wants a prosperous neighbor. European and Russian markets are fundamentally complementary. The E.U. is a knowledge-based economy, but it needs to lift its long-term growth prospects. Russia is an emerging economy that needs to internalize a knowledge base and exploit historic strengths in advanced science and technology. But the predominant view in Brussels is that Russia is much less interested in a convergence with the E.U. than a few years ago. Enjoying good macroeconomic indicators, Brussels fears that Russia now wants to exercize a post-perestrojka political revenge on the E.U. – a sort of non-stop Russian Pride parade.

The name of the game is, once again, energy. The EC admits that "by 2030, the E.U. will be dependent for over 70% of its energy needs on Russia." There has been "some progress" but "on many of the more important issues there are still big obstacles"—quite an understatement. An Energy Charter Treaty "contains trade, investment and transit provisions regarding energy products." But the treaty, the EC stresses, "still needs to be ratified by the Russian Duma."

In the security area, "the common commitments to fight international crime, drug trafficking and terrorism have to be materialized in concrete cooperation between Russian security agencies and the growing number of E.U. agencies, such as Europol, Eurojust and the anti-terrorism special representative."

As if this conceptual swamp was not enough, there's got to be more political dialogue, which "has rarely gone beyond the stage of mere consultation." Russia "is still trying to exert some control over the development of an E.U. defense policy by asking to be involved at the various stages of the decision-making." But the E.U. "has rejected such demands and has consistently dismissed Russian calls for an E.U.-Russia Council similar to the Permanent NATO-Russia Council."

Hence "deeper integration" remains a mirage. The EC is forced to admit that "Russia-E.U. relations have been hit by a crisis of confidence and systemic differences." One (crucial) thing is certain: Russia will not apply, and does not want to, become a member of the E.U. The EC is left to complain that "the 'road maps' may have served a useful purpose in masking the vacuum in Russia-E.U. relations, but they have failed to solve the main problems arising from a lack of strategic vision." So it's back to the negotiating table. Everything would be so much easier "if we had a clear strategic vision of where we want our relations with Russia to go, but we do not have that vision."

Switching to the Ministry of Wishful Thinking the EC dreams that "in the long run a lasting strategic partnership with Russia would imply that this country moves towards a model of democracy similar to that of the E.U. As indicated above, this is not the way Russia is going." Hence the EC's astonishing conclusion: "We will continue muddling through." Well, the E.U., now with 27 members, including most of the former (and extremely suspicious) Iron Curtain, may have no idea where it wants to go with Russia. But the Russians certainly know where they're going.

Before the G-8 summit in St. Petersburg in July 2006 Mikhail Gorbachev, in an opinion piece published by the *Rossiyskaya Gazeta* daily, was stressing the E.U.'s huge internal contradiction "between two approaches to economic development, the 'Anglo-Saxon' one, based on unrestricted market freedom and maximization of profits, and the socially-oriented embraced above all by Germany and France... So far a synthesis of the two approaches has been an elusive goal." Meanwhile Russian analyst Sergei Karaganov was warning that energy security is "a powerful catalyst" for replaying the Cold War.

The January 2006 Russian-Ukrainian crisis was the first geopolitical gas war of the 21st Century—Liquid War determined by the intersection of geopolitics and Pipelineistan. The Northern European Gas Pipeline, the Russian-German project under the Baltic sea (bypassing Baltic states and Poland); the pipeline from Siberia to China and then Japan; and the *Gran Gasoduto del Sur* in South America from Venezuela to Argentina via Brazil, may be exempt from conflict. But Liquid War may be inextricably linked to Pipelineistan-in-the-making, as in the Arctic, which pits the U.S. against Canada, in the Barents sea (Russia against Norway) and in Greenland (Denmark against Canada). According to the U.S. Geological Survey, 25% of the world's gas reserves still to be discovered lie in the Artic.

Every diplomat and official in Brussels working on the energy security dossier agrees that the key strategic challenge facing the E.U. is its dependence on Russian gas; for the 10 newest E.U. members it almost reaches 100%. The key to the 153,800 km—and counting—of the Russian pipeline network is in the hands of the Kremlin. The Russian state is thus afforded the luxury of musing on how to reinvest Russian petrodollars when, according to analyst Alexander Blokhin, 95% of the profits beyond US$ 27 a barrel go to the Kremlin. Russia's E.U. ambassador Vladimir Chizhov downplays it all, insisting "much of the tension in the energy sphere is artificial." He may be only partially right.

GUUAM (the acronym for Georgia, Uzbekistan, Ukraine, Azerbaijan and Moldova) was founded in 1997 ostensibly to "favor economic multilateral cooperation" but really as a regional military alliance, under the benign protection of NATO, strategically placed right on the path of the Caspian Sea's energy wealth. In other words, it has always been an anti-Moscow club. Now the alliance is only named GUAM; Uzbekistan, under the unsavory "Saddam of Central Asia" Islam Karimov, decided to leave in 2005—incensed by Western criticism of its internal repression— and reinforced its ties with Moscow.

The Russian daily *Nezavisimaïa Gazeta* denounced GUAM as "a new international organization whose goals are entry into NATO and adherence to European structures"—hardly breaking news material considering that the "GUM" (Georgia,

Ukraine and Moldova) in GUAM openly accuse Russia of supporting separatist movements and are still reeling from Russia imposing commercial restrictions on milk and meat imports from Ukraine, wine from both Georgia and Moldavia, and mineral water from Georgia. Off the record, E.U. diplomats—especially those from Eastern Europe—share an unshakeable consensus: Russia always uses trade as a political weapon against pro-E.U. countries.

In the new scenario, where everyone in the former Soviet sphere seems to be scrambling not only to become a NATO but a E.U. member as well, Kiev has become a de facto "alternative integration center" harboring GUAM's HQ. As the Russian daily *Kommersant* correctly puts it, GUAM is looking for "an alternative to Gazprom." The alternative is even more pressing with the completion in 2007 of another key node of Pipelineistan—the Baku-Tbilisi-Erzurum (BTE) gas pipeline which runs parallel to the oil Baku-Tbilisi-Ceyhan (BTC) pipeline reaching Turkey and the European markets. So the petrodollar-drenched question is whether Azerbaijan will remain part of GUAM. Once again in this respect the E.U.'s—plus the U.S.'s wishes—are pitted against Russia's.

As the undisputed czar of the global gas club—seconded, among others, by Iran's Ahmadinejad, Turkmenistan's Niyazov, Venezuela's Hugo Chávez and Bolivia's Evo Morales—Putin may get away with comparing the U.S. to "Comrade wolf [who] knows whom to eat, eats without listening, and [is] clearly not going to listen to anyone" while Chávez compares the U.S. to "Count Dracula before sucking blood."

With high gas and oil prices, the Kremlin has concluded it does not have to waste time discussing democracy and human rights with the West. What matters are US$ 170 billion in foreign reserves (2006 data)—and rising -, a huge budget surplus and 7% annual GDP growth. According to Arnaud Dubien, Russian specialist at the French Institute of International and Strategic Relations, "this allows the Russian government to finance many programs of very strong social impact, benefiting categories of the Russian population which suffered heavily during the transition." No wonder "Energy Security" became Putin's and the Kremlin's mantra for the world's top gas producer and second-biggest oil producer.

At a "Geopolitics of Energy Security" seminar in Brussels in the spring of 2006, organized by the European Enterprise Institute, Russia was inevitably the star of the show. Russians asked "what does it really mean when the E.U. talks of 'diversification of energy supply'?" The Russians see it basically as a way of putting pressure on Russia, leading to a loss of traditional Russian exports. The Europeans for their part worry about the use of gas as a political weapon, plus the lack of transparency and the "undemocratic processes" in the Russian gas and electric sectors.

Both parties agreed "there needs to be real political and technical dialogue in order to tackle the truly important issues." The Russians agreed that "democracy and human rights are in the Russian constitution"—thus Russia doesn't need to negotiate, but to implement. And they all agreed that Russia and the E.U. "should create a non-discriminatory energy support agreement, including a fair regime for access to the Central Asian energy supply." This agreement, according to European diplomats, could be implemented around 2010.

It's going to be an extremely tricky affair. The E.U. is actively trying to explore deals with Central Asia—with both Kazakhstan and Turkmenistan—and also with Iran, bypassing Russia via the South Caucasus and the Caspian Sea. The key project in this Pipelineistan node is the proposed Transcaspian gasoduct—which would effectively break Russia's monopoly on transit of Central Asian gas. In the New Great Game between Russia, China and the U.S. in Central Asia, Washington privileges close allies Azerbaijan and Kazakhstan—which are also courted by the E.U. But as we've seen in the Pipelineistan chapter, Russia all but killed the Transcaspian with a charm offensive towards Turkmenistan.

The Europeans stress crucial points for the complex E.U.-Russia relationship to work. The E.U. must consider nuclear energy as an alternative. E.U. experts stress that according to E.U. forecasts and figures from the *Russian Energy Strategy*, the incremental offer from Russia can only cover 25% of the E.U.'s energy needs, so it is absolutely imperative to diversify.

Meanwhile, the E.U. has to deal with a trillion-dollar baby.

By April 2006 Gazprom had knocked back Microsoft as the world's third-largest company by market value after shares; Microsoft was valued at about US$ 246 billion, less than Gazprom's US$ 270 billion with Valery Yazov, head of the State Duma's Energy Committee, suggesting that the true market capitalization of Gazprom should be as much as $600 billion. Gazprom had also displaced BP as the world's second-biggest energy company by market value. Already the world's biggest natural gas company by output and reserves (16% of the total), and with its shares more than tripling from 2005 to 2006, Gazprom will inevitably knock back Irving, Texas-based Exxon Mobil as the world's biggest company, valued at US$ 381 billion in 2006.

Gazprom employs 330,000 people and supplies more than 8% of Russia's GDP. It is currently controlled at 51% by the Russian state. Since 2001 Gazprom's executive director is Alexei Miller, who is extremely close to Putin. Gazprom had a gas output of 547.2 billion cubic meters in 2005. This is equivalent to 9.42 million barrels of oil a day, or the daily extraction of Saudi Arabia in 2006. Gazprom's market value may soon reach as much as US$ 1 trillion, according to its Deputy Chief Executive Dmitri Medvedev, who also happens to be very close to the Kremlin.

Putin's gas chess is a joy to watch. The Russian President may occasionally threaten the E.U. that the Russians will go find some other, less demanding customers in case the E.U. decides to look for other less assertive suppliers. But simultaneously he reassures the E.U.—via German chancellor Angela Merkel—that a Ukrainian scenario such as January 2006 will never repeat itself. Eighty percent of Russia's exports to Europe transit via the Ukraine. Since the 1960s Russia is a trusted European supplier—responsible for 50% of the E.U.'s gas imports and 25% of the consumption (for oil, Russia supplies 30% and assures 26% of the E.U.'s consumption, as well as more than 30% of the uranium for Europe's nuclear plants).

Gazprom has launched a no-holds-barred investment offensive in Western distributors and wants to become a global gas giant under vertical integration selling gas to everyone and his neighbor. What Gazprom wants is to control the whole chain—from production to the final consumer in Europe. What the E.U. wants is for Gazprom to bring gas to the E.U.'s external borders, where the gas will be bought by E.U. partners who will then distribute it inside Europe. But this would mean the end of long-term Gazprom contracts with European energy giants—an absolute no-no for the Kremlin.

Igor Chubalov, one of Putin's trusted sherpas, is fond of stressing the difference between the strategy of an independent corporation and state policies—even if the Europeans cannot manage to spot the difference. Basically what Chubalov says is "we invest in distribution, you invest in production." Word in every Brussels corridor is that this scheme was former German chancellor Gerhard Schroeder's idea.

Herr Schroeder is the head of the supervisory board of the consortium building the US$ 4.8 billion Northern European Gas Pipeline, the Russian-German gas conduit under the Baltic Sea. He's being paid 250,000 euros a year for the privilege. Other members of the board include Gazprom's big boss Miller (51% of shares) and officials from Germany's energy giants E.ON and BASF (24.5% each).

So what we have is Moscow and Berlin creating a de facto energy alliance between E.ON and BASF and Gazprom. The inevitable result was that eyebrows were raised all across the E.U.—because the 27-member (since January 2007) union *still* does not have a common energy policy. Poland was bypassed by the gas pipeline. So for Polish diplomats the whole thing was equivalent to "political blackmail." When Gazprom's boss Miller hints in public every once in a while that E.U. trouble will mean more Russian exports to China, Eastern European diplomats always cry in unison "Political Blackmail!!!"

See-saw games apart, it all boils down to Gazprom itching to buy more and more gas pipelines and distribution companies in Europe, like British Centrica. And once again the real fascinating question regards the double standards employed by the North. Essentially, the Kremlin has always been complaining that when European companies go to Russia, it's a matter of investment and globalization; but when it happens the other way around, it's a question of Russian companies' "hostile" expansion into Europe.

In the summer of 2006 Russia introduced the convertible ruble—so it may use its own currency in oil and gas transactions; and shifted some of its wealth of reserves away from the dollar and to buying gold (US$ 247 billion both in gold and dollars as of summer of 2006).

Russia's state-owned natural gas transport company, Transneft, is a major player in Pipelineistan—and now the one and only exporter of Russian gas. With Russia and Iran controlling the largest gas reserves in the world and Iran about to become a full member of the Shanghai Cooperation Organization (SCO)—the Asian response to NATO—what we have is the prospect of the SCO controlling a lot of gas, a lot of oil and overlooking the security of the ultra-strategic Strait of Hormuz, through which an armada of Gulf oil tankers supply the West and Japan. This is the ultimate stuff of Pentagon nightmares.

Problems in the European front? No problem. The Gazprom nation can diversify all the way and Go East. And the Europeans know it. The Gazprom nation is a key node of virtually every strategic Pipelineistan deal across Asia. The more the Asian Energy Security Grid slouches towards full fruition, the more OPEC loses influence (Russia is not an OPEC member). W. Joseph Stroupe, editor of *Global Events Magazine* online, has been one among a few fine analysts sufficiently aware that this decade is witnessing the rise of a New Energy Order—with Russia and Iran as major players.

Russia may be investing in a strategic energy partnership with the E.U. But the Gazprom nation clearly recognizes its priorities: the future of global development is in Asia (call it another way of describing The Asian Century). The Kremlin fully approves of the fact that both China and India are developing alternative strategies to the neo-liberal American model. The Gazprom nation could not be facing a more auspicious confluence of factors: its own fabulous energy reserves; energy dependence from Europe; and larger-than-life Asian interest for these reserves.

The Gazprom nation tough has to be very careful of its strong-arm tactics in Central Asia. There's a key piece still missing for the birth of a kind of Central Asian gas OPEC, a strategic Russian goal: gas republic Turkmenistan—where the flamboyant Turkmenbashi Saparmurad Niyazov remains ultra-independent (and also interested in doing more deals with China). But Russia thinks to have nailed it with the 2006 deal between Niyazov and Gazprom.

Russia is actually in search of Euro-Asian equilibrium. As Natalia Narotchnitskaia, vice-President of the Duma's Commission of Foreign Affairs sees it, Russia now boasts "energy independence; military power; high level of education; a complete cycle of scientific research; no overpopulation; a huge territory; and a modest level of consumption." She is adamant: "The only country in the world to meet all these criteria is Russia."

On practical terms, for Narotchnitskaia, this should revert into a lot more investment to explore eastern Siberia and the Russian Far East. And, crucially, no dreams of integration either with the E.U. or with NATO. She's in favor of a true "independent historical project." Energy security, according to her, means "a geoeconomy which would lift us from demographic decline, reinforce the country and seduce our neighbors, especially those in Central Asia." In other words: a real national project.

For the moment, facts on the ground are telling the story. Gazprom will be associated with the *Gasoduto del Sur*, the hugely ambitious Hugo Chávez project to integrate South America via Venezuelan gas delivered to Argentina via Brazil and with extensions to Bolivia, Paraguay and Uruguay. Gazprom is also investing US$ 3 billion in joint exploration and production in Bolivia. Venezuela, Bolivia and Cuba are united in ALBA (the acronym in Spanish for Bolivarian Alliance of the Americas), a counterpunch to the U.S.-backed Free Trade Area of the Americas (FTAA, whose acronym in Spanish is ALCA). More stuff of Pentagon nightmares.

The Gazprom nation offensive knows no bounds—from the Maghreb to the Middle East, including Israel, which is practically U.S. territory. Russia and Algeria are the two largest gas suppliers to the E.U. Now they work very closely. Gazprom and Sonatrach will be part of the supplying of France. Putin's gas chess once again came up with a fabulous profit. He cancelled Algeria's US$ 4.7 billion debt to Russia but Algeria instead will buy US$ 7.5 billion in fighter jets and weapons.

Gazprom will also supply gas to Israel, via a pipeline from Turkey—the gas diverted from the not-exactly-busy Bluestream (Russia-Turkey) pipeline which for Russia was basically a geopolitical tool to increase its profile in Turkey.

Gazprom bought Baltic refineries. Gazprom bought majority stakes on distribution companies in Georgia and Belarus. Gerhard Schroeder presides the board of the Russian-German gas pipeline under the Baltic Sea, controlled at 51% by Gazprom. Putin managed to convince Russians nostalgic for empires past that Putinism is the best nationalism. All this while the Gazprom nation is shaping up as the new, larger, secular Saudi Arabia; indispensable to the West, but certainly not integrated with it.

After the invasion and occupation of Iraq in 2003, I saw for myself how Russia still looms large over Central Asia and the Caucasus. Twenty-three centuries ago, in his Oriental campaign, Alexander the Great got married in Balkh (northern Afghanistan) and died in Babylon. In our times, after the Afghanistan and Iraq wars, it was possible to see another significant power shift in action: Russia on its way to re-forming a "liberal empire" in the Caucasus and Central Asia.

The concept of a liberal empire is the perfect ideological tool for the Kremlin to exercise more power in what is defined in Moscow as "the near abroad"—without ruffling too many feathers in the E.U.: strategic competitor America is another matter. But the question always remains whether democracy is compatible with any form of post-modern imperialism.

Russia's poster boy—poster executive director, rather—for the concept of liberal empire in these last few years has been Anatoly Chubais, the former privatization czar and then chairman of the energy conglomerate Unified Energy Systems (UES), 52% state-owned. He routinely denounces Putin's authoritarian methods. A paradox? Not really.

In 2003 Chubais published a piece in the Russian daily *Nezavisimaya Gazeta* stating that Russia's top 21st Century priority is to develop "liberal capitalism" and to build up a "liberal empire." In the words of his manifesto, "liberal imperialism should become Russia's ideology and building up liberal empire Russia's mission." This meant in practice a foreign policy driven by hardcore market economics mixed with military muscle. In his drive to paint New Russia as a liberal power Chubais simply erased the czarist and Soviet heritage. His model of liberal empire was none other than the U.S. He believed Russia could become another model. A delighted Kremlin seemed to be applying the concept to the letter—well, sort of.

Chubais demonstrated in practice how liberal empire should work in the Caucasus and in Central Asia. In Kyrgyzstan, Russia combined the opening of a military base in Kant with massive investment by Russian companies. And through a series of deals UES effectively took control of Georgia's power market.

Chubais' offensive meant that Eurasianism was back in Russia. As Boris Rumer of the Davis Center at Harvard University explains in his book *Central Asia—A Gathering Storm*, Eurasianism was a very popular concept in the early 20th Century, after the October Revolution. It is, as James Joyce would put it, a portmanteau word with myriad geographic and geopolitical connotations. Most of all, it implies that peoples living in Eurasia were already integrated into the Russian and Soviet empires, thus legitimizing a new Slavic-Turkic reintegration between Russia and Central Asia. Crucially, instead of a silly neocon clash of civilizations, Eurasianists like scholar Nikita Moiseev talk of a synthesis between two civilizations, Russia and Islam.

But other Eurasianists like Aleksandr Panarin go straight for naked power: "The key question concerns the conditions under which the Muslim people of Eurasia would like to become part of a unified Russian state." Panarin's interpretation of the clash of civilizations is very enlightening. He is sure that one of America's strategic goals is to provoke trouble between Russia and Islam: and the Trojan Horse in this scheme is Turkey, used by America to "gain a foothold in the Muslim regions of the former USSR" with the goal of "weakening Russia."

Figure 21. The Gazprom nation looks east.

I was assured by Central Asian diplomats that not only those addicted to Soviet nostalgia but crucially the cream of Russia's intellectual elite are enthusiastic Eurasianists. But what about the Kremlin itself? One of Putin's most famous quotes is "Russia always felt itself an Eurasian country." The most important factor, according to the diplomats, was that the cream of the FSB—the successor of the KGB—had also thrown their weight behind the concept.

Eurasianism is a powerful concept capable of oiling the Kremlin machine for ages. It appeals to educated nationalists, and most of all it appeals to the excluded, the vast majority of them Putin voters who want nothing but law and order, security, some prosperity and the sense of belonging to a great world power (all favorite Putin themes). Eurasianism appeals because it is not xenophobic: it is inclusive. It is not anti-Islamic. It is not anti-Semitic. And coming from a culture that was instrumental in the defeat of Hitler, it is definitely anti-fascist.

Putin was always clever enough not to set himself as poster boy of Eurasianism—and be accused of naked imperialism by people like ultra-sensitive Uzbek leader Islam Karimov. The Putin circle actively started incorporating the Eurasianist worldview to his platform. Then something really big happened. Central Asian diplomats became convinced that Eurasianism was fast becoming the ideology of the Russian ruling class. The ultimate objective is clear: the Russian empire should be reintegrated around Moscow.

A "Eurasia Confederation" is unlikely. In the case of the Baltic republics, it's out of the question: they are practically integrated into NATO. In the case of Georgia and Azerbaijan, it's fair to talk about economic leverage, but not of integration; both are under the U.S.'s influence. In the case of Belarus, Moldova and Armenia the perspectives are much better. And in the case of Central Asia, Kazakhstan, Kyrgyzstan and Tajikistan are certainly potential members. Kazakh president Nazarbayev is a big fan of the idea of a "Eurasian Union." Kyrgyzstan, the "Switzerland of Central Asia," small and with no oil, needs Russia badly. And Tajikistan is a de facto Russian satellite. Uzbekistan—ruled by ultra-independentist Karimov—and Turkmenistan—ruled by ultra-isolationist Niyazov—seemed to be totally out of the equation. Until Karimov, incensed with Western criticism of his flagrant human right's abuses, decided to kiss the Big Bear.

A Eurasia Confederation does not make a lot of economic sense. Russia matters to these countries basically because it is equated with Mother Subsidy. Russian exports to the "near abroad" cost nothing compared to exports to the E.U. The "near abroad" owes fortunes to Moscow. According to analyst Yuri Shishkov, this is "payment to preserve Russia's political influence, to avoid the breakup of the post-

Soviet military-strategic space, and to use the installations of its infrastructure." Most of all, Russia's bear hug is applied via weapons sales at unbeatable prices.

Eurasianists maintain that nation-states are doomed one way or another: they will inevitably be victims of a takeover—by a global empire (American-led) or by regional empires. So the Eurasianist proposal is a benign Eurasian Union, where the "near abroad" may live under the splendid label of "collective imperial sovereignty." The missing crucial point is what Washington will do about it. Realist Eurasianists know that according to Washington's National Security Strategy, there are no holds barred when it comes to preventing the emergence of any rival power in Eurasia.

For the moment Eurasianists are more than glad that Putin's foreign policy enshrined two central goals: to restore Russian supremacy in the "near abroad"; and to balance international relations by an Eurasian perspective, following the prescription by renowned old diplomatic fox and former Prime Minister Yevgeny Primakov, much admired by Putin. This means close relations with China, India and Iran, and a more incisive Russian presence in the Middle East.

For all practical purposes it is the Gazprom nation out in full force re- conquering to Moscow the role of provider to the whole periphery of the empire. The Kremlin's relations with the "near abroad" could be summarized in one word: Pipelineistan. Lenin used to say that "Communism is the Soviets plus electricity." Putinism kept the electricity—plus the pipelines. UES got involved in Kyrgyzstan and Tajikistan. It controls 80% of the Armenian power market. Chubais' master plan was to create nothing less than a "unified energy system" in Transcaucasia—Georgia, Armenia and Azerbaijan.

At the center of the "liberal empire" things may not be so liberal for years to come. Already in 2003 political scientist Dimitri Furman was positively alarmed: "We have entered a spiral leading to a logic of power without alternative"—meaning a replay of Soviet times. And this logic is inbuilt in Putinesque concepts as "dictatorship of the Law," "verticality of power" and "controlled democracy." Russian democrats for years have been referring to a new form of "Russian fascism" duly accepted by an apathetic society. Gazprom's health is not necessarily matched by the average Russian's. Demographically, Russia faces a time bomb. The population is growing simultaneously older, smaller and much more prone to illness. The birth rate of the Muslim population grows while for ethnic Russians it declines.

Putin installed FSB agents and military officers in all the key nodes of the state bureaucracy: the FSB—the former KGB—are his former colleagues, and the military are behind the Second Chechen War which in fact elected Putin in March 2000. A 2003 sociological study determined that what Russians call "structures of force" now represent 25% of the managerial elite, compared to only 4% under Gorbachev.

Putin always tried to strike a balance between competing Russian power groups: the *siloviki* (security services people); the oligarchs close to the Yeltsin family; the privatization czars like Chubais; and a cluster of powerful regional governors. The Yukos affair was the turning point. By going after billionaire oil oligarch Mikhail Khodorkovsky, Putin signaled that the *siloviki* are really in control. Their tough guy approach answers to the widespread, popular Russian call for "order" after the 1990s Wild West and the anger felt by millions of decrepit poor Russians at the enormous fortunes amassed by the oligarchs. In Russia, for generations people were conditioned to see the means of production in the hands of the State; and the State, at least in theory, was supposed to defend popular good. So no wonder the dispossessed masses saw the new oligarchs as a bunch of gangsters stealing public property.

There is no evidence that either oligarchs or reformers will have a shot at power in Russia anytime soon. The nationalist, heavy-handed *siloviki* rule. The industrial-military complex was reinforced. The Gazprom nation is a leading exporter of weapons. The economic bonanza predominantly benefits the industrial-military complex. The Russian Duma was turned into a little more than a rubber-stamp parliament for Putin. The nomad elites of global liquid modernity in Moscow and St. Petersburg don't give a damn to politics and only think about conspicuous, ostentatious consumption and traveling to Southeast Asia five-star resorts, a pattern replicated by the Central Asian elites in Tashkent or Almaty. The abyss between Moscow and the provinces is so big—as well as between Tashkent or Almaty and the Uzbek or Kazakh periphery – that soon "they won't be speaking the same language," a common Russian joke. The press is not exactly free. The Judiciary is under severe constraints. If *siloviki* and the Army rule there's not exactly much space for democracy. For the sociologist Olga Krystanovskaia, Russia today is a "militocracy."

After the Iraq invasion I was keen to examine how this militocracy, the heart of a possible, new "liberal empire" would fare in Central Asia when compared to the "original" (in a classic political theory sense) liberal empire, the U.S. Traveling around Central Asia and talking to the local people, urban and rural, Sunni and Shiite, educated and illiterate, civil servants and private entrepreneurs, familiar or unfamiliar with Western lifestyle and institutions, and giving few credence to the official propaganda in these ultra-censored countries, an informal inquiry produced some unshakeable trends.

- Virtually everybody followed what was happening in Iraq, even though internet access in some countries like Turkmenistan is very problematic, and is invariably slow everywhere else. When they surf the net for information, they get it in Russian. Everybody watches TV—and the bulk of the coverage is on Russian channels, RTR, ORT, NTV. Practically nobody watches CNN or the BBC.

- There's an overwhelming perception that Washington's "war on terror"—rebranded The Long War—is a war against Islam. And we are not talking only about conservative Ferghana valley clerics and madrassa students, but Westernized students and teachers at the American University in Bishkek, the KIMEP in Almaty or the Economics Faculty in Samarkand.

- Most people equated the conditions —and the possible outcome—of the American invasion of Iraq with the Soviet invasion of Afghanistan. And they expected America to get really burned in both Afghanistan and Iraq, and to be out of Central Asia sooner rather than later.

- There was severe, widespread criticism of the arrogance, belligerence and cultural ignorance of the Bush administration; hence the fear that Central Asia could sooner or later be attacked on some flimsy pretext. University students in Almaty, Bishkek, Tashkent and Samarkand invariably thought that the Iraqi occupation would lead to more wars, more terrorism and more problems in Central Asia. The future educated elites invariably criticized American support of corrupt regimes completely divorced from the plight of their own populations. In Uzbekistan and Turkmenistan, if such complaints are even barely articulated in public, they may lead to summary execution.

- Most kids may wear baggy jeans and fake, Chinese-made Reeboks, eat burgers in ersatz McDonald's, listen to Snoopy Dogg and spend most of their free time on Sony Playstation booths. But they make a sharp distinction when it comes to American militarism. And especially in rural areas they make sure they may like the trappings, but they don't want to live an American lifestyle.

- Most people, especially above 30, still considered the collapse of the USSR as a monumental disaster. And virtually everybody blamed the U.S. for it. Putin officially described the collapse of the USSR as "the greatest geopolitical catastrophe of the 20th Century." People in Central Asia said they had freedom of movement over 25% of the Earth's surface, and they had a standard of living much, much higher than in the subsequent emerging—or submerging—republics. Any gypsy cab driver—that means virtually anybody with a car—in his battered Volga or Lada, said that the Americans destroyed his way of life and now are after the natural resources, especially oil, gas and minerals. The thirty-something generation had just finished University and started out in a good job when the USSR began to crumble. Most of these young men and women with a family to support now have to juggle with three or even four jobs and also drive their cars as taxis to make ends meet. At least sometimes they can vent their anger—unlike the silent armies of elderly people begging in the streets of every Central Asian capital.

- Americans were not welcomed even when they paid for prostitution. There were strip bars in Bishkek and Tashkent—American soldiers were regular visitors. The hostess of a bar in Bishkek, owned by a Han Chinese, said that the dancers, most of them classical dancers or teachers, were appalled, but there was no other way to make money fast. Freelance sirens in five-star hotels in Almaty, Tashkent or Ashgabat preferred to deal with Europeans or the loaded Russian mafia.

- Central Asia's secret love story was—and remains—definitely with Europe. When a foreign visitor mentions he's from Europe, he's always more than welcomed. People instinctively attribute to Europe a non-belligerent status and the capacity to treat local people with respect. France and Italy especially enjoy a very positive image—synonymous with fashion, good food, high aesthetic standards and, last but not least, glamorous soccer teams like AC Milan, Barcelona and Manchester United. A great deal of the Uzbek elite studied in Germany. For most people, the ideal of a good life is "European."

- Russia is in the hearts and minds of virtually everybody. Every Central Asian capital has been dealing for decades with their Russian residents. The new Central Asian generations have been educated in Russian, and a great deal finished their studies in Russia itself. Moreover, Putin has been a chess master in dealing with Central Asian governments, in both his pronouncements and official visits.

Russia is also not inert militarily. There's a new Russian military doctrine in place, adopted by the Kremlin in October 2003, according to which all post-Soviet airspace may be subjected to "preventive" attack by Russia, as Russian Defense Minister Sergei Ivanov made very clear in a meeting with NATO in Brussels. Putin reserves himself "the right to the use of force in a preventive manner if the interests of Russia or its allies are threatened and all other means are revealed to be ineffectual."

As Russia advances the new Eurasian game of recolonization—economic and cultural—of the whole former socialist space, from the former Yugoslavia to western China, Central Asian diplomats fear the clash with Washington will be inevitable, according to the recipe of "Grand Chessboard" master Zbigniew Brzezinski. Washington will keep considering Central Asia and Transcaucasia (the southern Caucasus), including the Caspian basin, as zones of "strategic interest." If we add Ukraine, this means all the southern half of the former USSR, or Moscow's current "near abroad." The American strategy relies on Pipelineistan, coupled with a cultural blitzkrieg via a myriad of "foundations," in the media, academia, through historic revisionism, TV reality shows, private radios, Hollywood, videos, DVDs, in fact any tool that may be manipulated as cultural colonization. This is all the more remarkable when we know there is no direct connection between Jerry Bruckheimer and the Ford Foundation, although there is a solid Bruckheimer-Pentagon axis.

But even with all this firepower the U.S. seems to be losing the battle for hearts and minds in Central Asia, while Eurasianists may revel that at least at the level of the general population, hearts and minds in the "near abroad" remain fine-tuned in Russian.

A renewed U.S. onslaught would be inevitable. The strategy is called "Great Central Asia": a "cooperative partnership for development"—focused on energy, transportation and building infrastructure —with the five "stans" plus Afghanistan, and with South Asia (India and Pakistan) as associate members. The "Tulip Revolution" in Kyrgyzstan and the uprising in Andijan, in the Uzbek part of the ultra-volatile Ferghana valley, may have been embarrassing flops, but Washington will never give up. The key allies in this new scheme are Kabul and Delhi—as India entertains the notion of becoming a key power in Central Asia. The U.S. thus wants to counterpunch Russia, China and the SCO. A key "stan" now extensively courted by the U.S. is de facto Russian satellite Tajikistan. So the plan is obvious: "divide and rule" the SCO—as well as, crucially, the Asian Energy Security Grid.

Moscow and Beijing would claim in unison: wishful thinking. Central Asia and South Asia are practically two separate galaxies. Half of Afghanistan is now Taliban country: Hamid Karzai rules over his own palace chair in Kabul, and that's it. Someone has to tell the Taliban that Afghanistan is the crucial "bridge" in the American project—crisscrossed by two-lane highways and Pipelinestan: it's unlikely the Taliban will abandon their jihad for a piece of the action. Those Pashtuns literally *kill* for a good fight.

Moreover Russia controls all the key distribution channels for Central Asian oil and gas. *Krasnaya Zvezda*, the influential daily newspaper of the Russian Armed Forces, has laid down the law: the U.S. may deploy what it wants, but Russia will do anything to prevent any more U.S. bases built in Central Asia. Meanwhile in China scholars like Liu Jianfei from the International Strategic Research Center at the Central Communist Party School are on 24/7 mode analyzing the new configuration

of Liquid War chess: it's Asian Energy Security Grid against "Great Central Asia."
The Gazprom nation does not even consider the possibility of ending up checkmated.

~ 13 ~

FORTRESS EUROPEISTAN

(Jarring Chord)

(The door flies open and Cardinal Ximinez of Spain [Michael Palin] enters, flanked by two junior cardinals. Cardinal Biggles [Terry Jones] has goggles pushed over his forehead. Cardinal Fang [Terry Gilliam] is just Cardinal Fang)

Cardinal Ximinez: NOBODY expects the Spanish Inquisition! Our chief weapon is surprise...surprise and fear...fear and surprise.... Our two weapons are fear and surprise... and ruthless efficiency.... Our three weapons are fear, surprise, and ruthless efficiency... and an almost fanatical devotion to the Pope.... Our four... no... Amongst our weapons... Amongst our weaponry... are such elements as fear, surprise... I'll come in again.

(Exit)

—**Monty Python's** *Spanish Inquisition sketch*

For a long time I have been interested in the decadence of the Roman Empire, whose desperate, complete, shameful end is a model for all civilizations. And if at present I'm so interested by the West, the contemporary West, it's because it evokes the sunset of great past civilizations.

—**E. M. Cioran,** *1983*

Who can define the meaning of Europe? Who's actually part of Europe? If there is a European project, what is it aiming for? Where does Europe end? What's this thing all about?

The armies of Eurocrat suits moving like a larger than life Magritte painting in and around Brussels—the capital of Europe Inc., and surrealism —couldn't ask for a more succulent full course menu to fill their sleepless nights.

I always felt that the ideal of Europe might be contained in the stunning fresco *Effects of Good Government,* painted by Ambrogio Lorenzetti in 1337-1340 and immaculately preserved at the Palazzo Pubblico in Siena, Tuscany. It's the ideal city in motion—and much earlier than the Renaissance when humanism, via Andrea Mantegna or Piero della Francesca unveiled the city as a harmonic symbol of civil and political virtue. Already in Lorenzetti the city was an apotheosis of civic virtue: Wisdom, Courage, Justice and Tolerance. Siena in the mid-14th Century is of course the image of this ideal city—with its *botteghe artigiane* (artisan's shops), merchants selling on retail and peasants with their animals detailing the economic system of a medieval urban center. The dancers on the lower part of the fresco symbolize Concord—an indispensable virtue for peaceful coexistence.

Figure 22. Lorenzetti's Effects of Good Government.

This harmony (heaven on Earth?) certainly is imprinted in every European's DNA (except for the unfortunate European Neandertals who did not long survive the advent of European Cro-Magnons). But what happened after the civic flowering of the Renaissance, and how did Europe lose her way?

Peter Sloterdijk, author of the seminal *Critique of Cynical Reason* and widely respected as one the greatest contemporary philosophers, may be as good a guide in our quest as anyone. In a precious little volume on Europe originally published in Germany in 1994, Sloterdijk with just a few brushstrokes paints the Ascension, Decline, Fall and possible Rebirth of this small part of Eurasia as the geopolitical and ideopolitical focus of the globe.

Referring to German scholarly studies, Sloterdijk observes how European cartography and European globe makers "fulfilled the need of an almost divine panoramic vision, which lately has been transferred to observation satellites." For almost half a millennium "the world was, we might say, an experiment of curious Europeans." Europe, in the decisive phase of her History, was "a Middle Kingdom—but unlike traditional China, a static and defensive center, it was rather the general headquarters of a movement of appropriation which transformed in sources of raw materials and zones of influence everything it laid its hands on."

Yet from a white man's burden pedestal Europe was dragged into what Sloterdijk characterizes as "a devastating geopolitical lesson." After two World Wars, "Europe, former heart of the idea of the Crusades, became in the 20th Century the object herself of a crusade,"—the story told in Eisenhower's *Crusade in Europe*—thus suffering "a monumental and maybe irreversible blow in her geopolitical narcissism." Europe—who arguably "civilized" the whole world—lost her pretension to a civilizing mission.

Then came the long lethargy from 1945 to 1989. Europe—"marked by the omnipresent atmosphere of unreality of these fifty years"—took all this time to basically leave hospital. Sloterdijk dubs it "a transition from existentialism to consumerism"—Sartre meets the package holiday. In between, starting in the 1980s, a new *zeitgeist* was conformed: "the lack of seriousness as lifestyle and the deconcretization of the world as theorem." From freedom to frivolity: Europeans gorged themselves on "the world as a menu." Of course the feast also had tremendous resonance in the U.S.—from Manhattan to Berkeley—and in South America—from Rio to Caracas.

Then Europe saw the (new) writing on the (Berlin) Wall. The Cold War vanished. And after 1990 Europeans had to learn a new script in the world stage.

The Franco-German builders of this new Europe started to believe again that yes, Europe actually extended from San Francisco to Vladivostok (even though historian Norman Davies had always insisted it is difficult to decide where does Europe start and where does it end). Both the U.S. and Russia might be regarded as European ramifications, or historical labs, which refined Europe to new, unpredictable levels. Yet at the same time European intellectuals tended to agree that Europe, in Sloterdijk's formulation, "is an insoluble jigsaw puzzle—indefinable and ultracomplex, a total work of art made only of fragments." As a *coup de grace*, an array of European historians finally decided to give up establishing the criteria of Europeanness.

Sloterdijk defines the quintessential formative function of Europe as "a mechanism of imperial transmission," reenacting and reinventing the previous empire, that is, the Roman. French sociologist Edgar Morin has been careful to remind us that

"Roman conquests were among the most barbarian in all Antiquity"; but at least they were conducive to a great civilization.

In Sloterdijk's formulation "Europe is a theater of imperial metamorphosis"; its essence "an imperialist *commedia dell'arte* extended to millennia." If we accept this definition the ever-expanding E.U. would be nothing but "a minimal empire characterized by free trade and unbridled consumption," a playground for Bauman's nomad elites of global liquid modernity, peppered with fabulous, Michelin Guide 3-star restaurants. In this case what could possibly be the future of Europe? Just resigned to being "a colony of its own utopia," in the succinct formula of multi=disciplinarian French intellectual Jacques Attali?

The E.U. boom since the fall of the USSR built the massive economic base necessary for the euro to be launched, successfully, in 1999 and soon start challenging the U.S. dollar as a global reserve currency. By any standards this in itself is a monumental achievement. But the E.U. idea, in a sense, also made the rest of the world dream—by demonstrating how a cluster of perpetually warring principalities-turned-into-nation-states can solve their basic differences, merge, smash borders, harmonize industries and services and try to engage in further economic and political integration. The E.U. project suddenly became the talk of the town in South America, the Middle East, Africa and Asia. By the early 2000s the E.U. had become, in a sense, the premier superpower, if not militarily certainly in median quality of life, caring about the welfare of citizens and defending a truly humanistic conception of human rights.

The welfare state—taxes are very high—may be a burden on business. But success stories are legion. The E.U. competes equally with the U.S. in an array of high-tech and financial niches. The E.U. also has more successful small businesses than the U.S. Compared to E.U. children, U.S. children would rank 9th in the E.U. in reading, 9th in scientific literacy, and 13th in math. 22% of U.S. children grow up poor; that would place the U.S. in 22nd place out of 23 industrialized nations. Few in France, for instance, would be tempted by the folly of trading a 35-hour work week, 6 weeks of holiday a year and free medical care in some of the best hospitals in the world for a hire-and-fire capitalism roulette.

This success took at least four decades to be achieved. But at what price? A case can be made of Brussels—the former Habsburg city—as the capital par excellence of a power vacuum, a sort of Belgian black void with its mix of degraded elegance and misleading mildness (after all it's the European capital of all sorts of trafficking and smuggling).

Les Bruxellois still prefer to sweep under a silk Persian the direct relation between their pompous architecture and the appalling rape of Congo by King Leopold

II. The choice of Brussels may have been a clinical approach, as Sloterdijk argues that Europe after the Fall needed more a rehab center than a true capital. Hence Rue de la Loi, the HQ of nearly 10,000 Eurocrats, or "eurotherapists; a good deal of the continent was transformed by them into a medical clinic," essential for managing all those decades of lethargy.

Figure 23. E.U. members and candidates are shaded (European Union).

Sarajevo sort of woke Europe up. Between "indifference and impotent indignation" Europeans were confronted with "the obscene consequences of their own political lethargy," that is, once more the U.S. stepping in, via NATO, to advance its geopolitical interests this time in the Balkans.

By the early 2000s Sloterdijk would propose that Europe's 9/11 was August 1914. Since 1945 "primitivisms conditioned to war" were no longer admissible for Europeans. Sloterdijk is convinced that "typologically, the gunshots in Sarajevo and the towers crumbling in New York are related," as our Western culture as a whole remains obsessed with "victory cults in the Greco-Roman style." The difference is that Europe's "syndrome of Roman warriors" is finished. While Europe has been peppered with soldiers' cemeteries and monuments to victims of war, and there are no triumphal altars to be found the U.S., says Sloterdijk, "is nothing more, nothing less than a network of podiums for the celebration of triumph.." For their part many American public intellectuals would argue that without this "victory culture" a Stalinist USSR would be stretching from the Urals to the Atlantic.

French sociologist Jean Baudrillard, the eminent deconstructor of simulation, for many in Europe—and in selected American universities—one of the greatest intellectuals alive, did agree at the time that the crumbling towers on 9/11 were a metaphor of our, well, moral decay: in the "rubble of global power" we could "only, despairingly, find our own image." In *L'Esprit du Terrorisme*, Baudrillard writes that "it was the system itself which created the objective conditions of this brutal response. By monopolizing all the cards in the game, it forces The Other to change the rules of the game." 9/11's ne plus ultra in the symbolic sphere was "the violence of the real in a universe supposedly virtual. 'Stop with this virtual thing—this is real!" That was one up on the 1960s when Michelangelo Antonioni, in *Zabriskie Point,* films his main character, a hippie chick, mentalizing the explosion of the ideal bourgeois home and all its consumer society symbols to the sound of Pink Floyd.

The superstars of European intelligentsia overwhelmingly did not see 9/11 as a clash of civilizations or religions. In Baudrillard's words, "through the specter of America (which is maybe the epicenter, but not at all the incarnation of globalization only by itself) and through the specter of Islam (which also is not the incarnation of terrorism)" 9/11 represented "triumphant globalization clashing with itself." For Baudrillard we are already facing World War IV—as many a strident neocon would rave about—but for completely different reasons: "It's the only true world war because what's at stake is globalization itself. We are left with "fractal war of all the cells, of all singularities which revolt in the form of antibodies." In sum, for Baudrillard, "it's the world itself which resists globalization."

War and globalization. Globalization at war. Once again, Liquid War.

How does Europe respond? By expanding like a bubble. With the entry of both Romania and Bulgaria in 2007 the E.U. becomes a 27-member behemoth. Territorial continuity has already been achieved—even though no one still can pin down the project as geographic, democratic, religious, political, economic, or all of the above.

Figure 24. The globe viewed from Brussels. Africa, the Middle East, and South Asia are all in relatively close proximity to the E.U.

To the north only the Arctic can stop Europe. To the west only the Atlantic. To the south only—maybe?—the straits of Gibraltar; Morocco wanted to become a candidate in 1992 and was barred because not part of the "European" continent. But the Balkans is allowed because geographically they are located in Europe. From the point of view of Paris or Berlin, the Balkans is in a *Blade Runner*-like "off world."

But from the point of view of Rome or Athens, they are neighbors. Italy badly wants the Balkans in the E.U. because that would translate into less immigration. Greece invests more in the Balkans than in the E.U. itself. Slovenia was admitted to the E.U. in 2004—that was the first step. Slovenia's southern border with Croatia— which was just a formality during Yugoslavia—now is an E.U. border. Croatia trades heavily with the E.U. and badly wants to join the club.

To the east: does Europe stop at the Urals, where Asia begins? Anyway Russia, the Gazprom nation—which is predominantly in Asia—has no intention of being absorbed by the E.U. If it did, now *that* would be a real Eurasian Union —from Lisbon to Vladivostok. Ukraine, Belarus and Moldova are legitimized by geography. Geographically, everything from the Atlantic to the Urals can be E.U.—including Switzerland, Norway and Iceland, which all said thanks but no thanks.

Turkey includes just a little bit of Europe—3%, in Oriental Thrace and Istanbul. But Turkey yearns to be admitted before 2015 (it's been lobbying for admission since 1987). The capital, Ankara, is in Asia, in the Anatolian plains. Turkey would be the most populous E.U. country already by 2010—with 97% of Muslims. But Turkey is secular since Ataturk in 1923, and the E.U. does not give importance to religion (at least nominally: on dinner parties it's another story). The E.U. is a secular project. Turkey in the E.U. would discredit for good the already discredited clash of civiliza- tions fallacy—which Sloterdijk hilariously describes as "that incredible Huntington [selling] the good, old European war against the Turks under a new package, without the Americans noticing it."

The certified way to start a fight in any European dinner table is to serve the "Turkish problem" after cheese, desert and coffee (espresso, not Turkish). You can't erase History with the stroke of a Brussels pen. As much as millions of Arabs distrust Turkey as the former Ottoman colonial power, millions of Europeans myopically do not see a secular State with a moderate Islamic government, but the specter of hordes of Muslims invading Judeo-Christian Europe (with Turkey, Albania and the current resident population put together, 15% of Europe would be Muslim).

Other millions, on the other hand, see E.U. admission as the right reward for Turkey defending the West for more than half a century during the Cold War against the Red Menace (for NATO purposes Turkey remains a kind of U.S. battle carrier in the Eastern Mediterranean). Turkey itself, to get into the E.U., will have to solve its "Kurdish problem" and atone for the Armenian genocide—not to mention pedestrian problems like overwhelming corruption, high inflation and a US$ 120 billion external debt.

The E.U./Turkey question poses a stark choice. Admission signals the marriage of Islam and democracy in Globalistan. Refusal means a triumph of Islamophobia, perhaps the ultimate graphic proof that the West prefers to keep the Muslim world at bay. It may be even more cynical: Brussels may tell Turkey thanks for defending us (as part of NATO) but no thanks, you're not part of the European family.

As Monty Python immortally inscribed, NOBODY expects the Spanish Inquisition. Well, nobody expected what amounted to an Inquisition by Pope Benedict XVI, a subtle theologian (in fact a lot of people did: Joseph Ratzinger is the head of the Congregation for the Doctrine of the Faith, the ministry at the Vatican that used to organize the Inquisition itself; before he was crowned Pope Ratzinger was known as "God's Rottweiler").

The Bavarian Pope knew exactly what he was saying while delivering a treatise in Bavaria in early September 2006 that left the German press, well, speechless. The Pope didn't exactly command a Crusade, like some of his illustrious predecessors, but considering the ultra-sensitive, Islamophobic times—and with two Muslim countries, Afghanistan and Iraq, occupied by Western Christian armies—it was very, very close: he defined Christianity as a synthesis of "Biblical faith" and "Greek philosophical questioning" (in other words, reason) while essentially implying that Islam had nothing new to offer apart from the concept of jihad.

The incandescent passage was when Benedict XVI quoted an erudite debate that took place in 1391—one century after the last major crusade—between Byzantine Emperor Manuel II Paleologus and a Persian sage: "Show me just what Mohammed brought that was new, and there you will find things only evil and inhuman, such as his command to spread by the sword the faith he preached." Subsequently the Byzantine Emperor—hardly an Enlightenment icon—demonstrates why spreading faith by violence is counter-productive. The Pope used the quote to stress what *separates*, and not unites, Christianity and Islam: "For Muslims," said the Pope, "God is absolutely transcendent. Its will is not linked to any of our categories, even reason." As if Christianity had not martyred reason enough during its history (crusades, persecution of Jews, Spanish Inquisition, colonial slavery in Africa). As if the Byzantine Empire had been a "dialogue of civilizations" model.

The Pope at best omitted a great, significant part of Western history. Christianity in fact launched an offensive jihad against Greek reason. As Edgar Morin reminds us, "once Christianity was recognized as the sole State religion, it closed down the School of Athens and finished off with any autonomous philosophy." The School of Athens was closed by Emperor Justinian in 529 A.D. Before that the fabulous Library of Alexandria had been burned down by Christianity Inc., in 391 A.D. We can put them all in the same sack: Christians burning books in the 4th Century; the Mongol Hulagu burning refined Baghdad in the 13th Century (impregnated with Greek thought); the Taliban bombing the Bamiyan Buddhas in 2001. No faith has the monopoly of intolerance. Christianity's jihad against luminous Greek rationality gave us the Middle Ages. For Vatican Inc., for centuries, the earth was flat. And Darwin is considered a dangerous subversive. Were it not for Islam—and Oriental Christians—institutional Christianity would have buried Greek rationality six feet under. The source of European humanism is Ancient Greek thought—celebrating the autonomy of the human spirit—plus Jesus' message of fraternity, not Christianity Inc.

Edgar Morin also crucially reminds us "one of the weapons of Christian barbarity has been the utilization of Satan. Under this figure, one must see the separator, the rebel, the nihilist, the mortal enemy of God and Men. Those who do not agree [with the established order] and do not want to renounce their difference must necessarily be possessed by Satan. It's with this delirious argumentative machine that Christianity has exercised its barbarity." Cue to star-studded "evil" casting of Fidel, Brezhnev, Khadafi, Arafat, Khomeini, Saddam, Osama et al.

The Pope, according to the *Frankfurter Allgemeine Zeitung*, asked "who is the God of Prophet Muhammad. No less." It's naive to believe that fine theologian Benedict XVI had not taken into account the inevitably explosive repercussions. He may have wanted to question nihilist, Salafi-jihadists. But all over the Muslim world, from Turkey to Lebanon and from Egypt to Pakistan the overwhelming impression was, once again, of the West—sustained by its twin pillars of rational Greek mind and the Church—attacking Islam's irrationality. And even if the Vatican was subsequently forced to issue an unmistakable, public "I'm so sorry" on behalf of the Pope, plus explanations in Arabic at the *L'Osservatore Romano* website, the volatile impression of a Vatican allied to the U.S. neocons and the Islamophobic armies also remained. That was exactly the interpretation of Iranian Supreme Leader Ayatollah Khamenei, for whom these were "the latest link in the chain of a crusade against Islam started by America's Bush."

Worse. The Pope's verbal missile gave a pretext from heaven for al Qaeda copycats to strike Rome. And it goes without saying that Benedict XVI is against Turkey's admission to the E.U.

Religion doesn't cut it. Arguably the best criteria to define the E.U. is History. The E.U. was born out of war—or the desire to end war. Europe can be depicted as a grim geography of cemeteries. The E.U. gained traction against European History, also against the USSR, all the time formulating institutional responses to geopolitical challenges. The problem is that it could not come up with anything beyond expansion as foreign policy. And still the crucial border issue has not been solved. The E.U. is getting old, there's no demographic dynamism. That implies accepting a huge wave of migration from the South: it's economic imperative versus political resistance.

Take the case of Spain. The Catalan daily *La Vanguardia* had to admit on its front page that "the Spanish economy grows only because of immigrants." Immigrants have been "saving" the Spanish economy from recession since 1995. According to a report by the Caixa bank, without immigrant work Spanish GDP per capita would have fell 0.6% a year every year during this period, when Spain received 3.3 million foreigners out an E.U. total of 11,9 million.

Anyone can create a free market zone. But simultaneously assuring a high standard of living, democracy and guaranteed rights for individuals—like the E.U. does—and even more importantly peace and stability, is not that obvious. The E.U. may have fabricated a political project. But it's not a magic formula. It's not an Eurasia free market zone; and it does not provide a ready-made State to Everyman. At a minimum the E.U. may be a new geopolitical model that gives people—and States—some tools to think about the idea of nation and what sovereignty is all about.

The British Labour Party may eventually come up with a creative solution. According to David Goodhart, author of *Progressive Nationalism: Citizenship and the Left*, the party has been juggling like crazy trying to simultaneously satisfy the left, cosmopolitan middle classes and the former working class, in search of an equilibrium between individual rights and national security. Goodhart tries to go beyond the tension between immigration and the welfare State; and most of all against the terrifying prospect of a Balkanized society, "where people vote and identify themselves along race and religion lines instead of economic and social interests."

Sloterdijk is one among a plethora of European intellectuals worried by "the code of heroic behavior" forcefully imposed by Washington, which has led to even further U.S. isolation from the absolute majority of the rest of the world, Europe included. In Western Europe virtually nobody—apart from former Italian Premier Silvio Berlusconi and his cronies—took seriously the strident Axis of Evil-derived rhetoric, while China at the same time kept going, going, going like a monster Duracell bunny. Sloterdijk derives the inevitable conclusion: "We can guess from these reactions the scenario for the civilization conflicts of tomorrow."

How should Europe position itself? Jacques Attali has been a committed Europeanist. In his book *Europe(s)*, published in France in 1994, he argues that Europe should not be "a Christian club, but like a region without limits, from Ireland to Turkey, from Portugal to Russia, from Albania to Sweden: it should culturally privilege nomads in relation to the sedentary...tolerance in relation to identity...multi affiliation in relation to exclusion."

So the builders of the new Europe have concluded that it's not gonna be a supremacist Leviathan. But it's not gonna be just a mega market either. For all his acid proposals Sloterdijk somehow trusts his confused European co-religionists: "Europeans nowadays already live in a post-heroic and post-imperial way, although they still have grandeur in their sights." Thus he sees the fundamental 21st Century question—at least in the Western sphere—as how "Big Ideas over global political and economic questions are compatible with a post-heroic global management." Europe's answer seems to be, up to now, "intelligent fragility," as he dubs it. It's certainly not enough to counter-act a disoriented U.S. that still has not found a politico-spiritual response to 9/11.

"Intelligent fragility" has not been very effective as well to deal, for instance, with what the E.U. really means—symbolized by its proposed 256-page (in English) E.U. Constitution. Apparently this was a progressive tour de force—setting every human rights standard such as outlawing the death penalty, promoting universal health care and child care, guaranteeing paid annual leave and housing for the poor as well as equal treatment for gays and lesbians.

But then the people said no. Brussels immersed in a deep, existential funk. Everyone started wondering "how to deliver Europe back to its citizens" over their steak *au poivre* after E.U. founding fathers France and the Netherlands rejected the European constitution in 2005 for completely different reasons. Blame it on the bubble. As a Dutch diplomat put it at the time: "We used to like Europe when we were only 6—not 25." France had voted largely against the Anglo-Saxon model of unbridled neo-liberalism; but not the Dutch, who hyper-pragmatically profited from globalization (exports account for 54% of GNP).

However, much as in France, refusing the constitution for the Dutch accommodated a vast array of different "nos": against too much capitalism (the extreme left); against the loss of national identity (the orthodox protestants); against Turkey and immigration (assorted populists); against the euro pushing prices up; against the Dutch guilder being devalued in relation to the euro; against unemployment;

against "the bubble" (Brussels costs the Dutch 180 euros per capita annually, the highest cut in the E.U.); and most of all against the political establishment. Talk about an information deficit.

The E.U. constitution was rejected by both sides of the spectrum—from federalists to Atlanticists. The monumental crisis would spell catharsis or catastrophe. Europe's disaster movie at least generated an all-out hyperinflation of European debate—from Englishmen praising people power, E.U.-style, to Turks and Portuguese blaming a bunch of over privileged fops afraid of the future, from Spaniards perplexed by France's flirtation with nihilism to hopeful Swedes proposing a new start to get a new text, from the Swiss deriding "status quo revolutionaries" to Polish right-wingers screaming that Polish identity as well may be lost. Even in Buenos Aires the Argentine daily *Clarin* worried that the "no" would have serious consequences for other regional integrations, including Mercosur, South America's smaller E.U.-like cousin.

E.U. officials breathlessly fired emails to the rest of the world complaining that "the neo-liberal turning of the screws will be terrible" or lamenting that a more "social" Europe seemed doomed: "This is when we will see to which extent we shot ourselves in the foot. Social Europe is even more affected than any other policy. The dynamic of national egos is back in place."

Neocons in the U.S. of course loved it: disunion at the heart of the E.U. is always as tasty as Texas T-bone. Unlike the so-called *neo cons sur Seine* in Paris, who blamed the disaster on the Left. Amid all the gloom and doom, the E.U. will survive before trying again: some sort of institutional collage to keep the machine running; an inter-government conference in 2007; and maybe arrive at a new constitution by 2010, where, according to an E.U. cynic drenched in Petrus, "we will be re-served the worst while the best, the values of the union and the social charter, will be left in the background."

Committed Europeans circulated a text in Brussels evoking the best Civilization had to offer: "courage"; "humanism"; the capacity to look beyond nationalist cultures; "fraternity"; the European adventure of a "unique community, a model in many aspects to other continents." But could it be that the double French-Dutch "no" will lead to people finally being consulted about their dream of Europe—in the cleansing ritual of a pan-European debate? Or maybe the truth was much simpler, and infinitely more brutal: the dream of a politically united Europe—a salutary counter power to the U.S. superpower—had been lost because there are no more visionaries to sell it to their own citizens. Baudrillard—once again—let it rip: European citizens, never consulted on the inner workings of the ever-expanding

E.U. "bubble," had become "hostage-citizens, taken captive by the ruling powers"; in other words, that was "a democratic form of state terror."

The doom and gloom didn't last long—as Europe is blessed with astonishing geopolitical biodiversity. Everybody got back to work,   integrating Europe through its array of mini-Europes.

The five, very pragmatic Nordic nations function almost as a State in itself—with the same culture and the same conception of a welfare state open to Globalistan. But there are many nuances inside this mini-universe. Finland, ultra-integrationist, adopted the euro because it fears being absorbed by Russia, while Denmark rejected the euro because it fears being absorbed by Germany. Sweden, on top of it, rejects NATO because this would compromise its neutrality. Both Norway and Iceland didn't even bother to enter the E.U.

On the other side there's the Euro-Mediterranean—a sort of perpetual dolce vita that still has the power to make the rest of the world dream.   Not only a strategic, progressive union between Spain, Portugal and Italy is being configured but it is being extended to the south Atlantic, especially to Brazil and Argentina, along cultural and economic lines.

At the center we find the crucial European node—France, Germany, Austria and Benelux (Belgium, Netherlands, Luxembourg). The key question is whether the Franco-German couple will remain a *primus inter pares* or conform as just one more mini-Europe among the others. The business/political elite knows the Bundestag/Marianne couple must achieve total economic, industrial and research and development synergy. The optimal end result of these parallel processes anyway seems to point to an E.U. as the sum of small, dynamic and ambitious regions.

But there's the other side of the coin (not as flattering as the Italian 1 euro coin, which has a Leonardo da Vinci design). The Eastern Europe new arrivals have become the post-modern euro-slaves of liquid modernity while at the same time protecting the sensitive Eastern borders, as the Mediterranean protect the sensitive Southern borders. It's an ugly E.U. self-portrait. Worse: the configuration, for vast masses of the South, is of a rich Citadel trying to defend its privileged way of life from a hostile, insidious, treacherous, perfidious and very angry world—especially for globe-trotting Western tourists and traders. The masses of the South have much to be angry about when the median subsidy to each European cow equals the US$ 2 a day poverty level of almost 3 billion people. In a sinister way, as Bauman noted, the world in fact increasingly looks like a battlefield getting ready for that abominable nonsense, the "clash of civilizations." But it's always a clash of the haves and have-nots.

Assuming these are all fragments of a "model" of integration—closely scrutinized by all other regions in the world—the E.U. still has to discover where to go in social and economic policies, and how to position itself with an independent foreign policy. Still no one seems to agree on what an E.U. "market social economy" really is. Be it neo-liberal or social democrat, the South is also keeping it clear the E.U. may not necessarily represent an alternative to U.S. hegemony. It's not that U.S. hardcore capitalism would be replaced by "civilized" European capitalism. What we have in competition remain two ruling classes—American and European—with not such a different hegemonic agenda. The South will not easily forget colonialism, fascism, nazism and two World Wars. The E.U. has not formalized how Globalistan affects Europe and how Europe should deal with it. Or what the European project now has to offer in practical terms to the indigent masses of the world.

Would Europe have something really significant to offer apart from Airbuses, Nokia mobiles, Armani suits, vintage Bordeaux and Barcelona against Chelsea at the Champions League? Germany—the premier economic and demographic power in Europe—may be willing to become the engine of New Europe. Berlin may be the great European lab of the future.

But can Germany pull it off? The top of the bill Wagnerian drama is how to pay for an unparalleled system of social protection while questioning an opulent consumer society. Demographically, Europe is getting older while the world is getting younger: the cake is getting smaller while increasingly there are more people at the table. The fight is on inside Germany. West Germany has seen it all. East Germany has not enjoyed any of the banquet. The welfare state will have to be curtailed. Germany actually has to write the book on "social market economy." Set the stage. Find the equilibrium. Find the German way to Globalistan. No wonder the most important dossier in Europe at the moment centers on the E.U.-Russia strategic pact—which will condition any future alignment.

Globally, Europe yearns to become a Lamborghini Diablo, hitting sixth gear with all the engine components roaring in unison. As this is still a pedestrian Fiat, the road ahead couldn't be more tortuous. European romantics, who dream of the day when the E.U. will forge a common foreign policy, will keep getting a reality check. NATO is being reshaped from a defensive alliance for Europe against the USSR to an offensive proxy war machine for the U.S. The split in Brussels is cataclysmic. The U.K. and the Eastern Europeans (former Iron Curtain hostages) are quite enthusiastic. France and Germany, plus Italy and Spain under progressive governments, notoriously less so.

So instead of playing a European final like Barcelona, the E.U. has humbly accepted to do a Juventus relegated to Serie B. In fact, the E.U.'s new role fell on its lap just in time for redemption after the constitutional debacle. The test match is in Lebanon—after the summer of 2006 Israel-Hezbollah war. It started with Germany vetoing a NATO deployment: that would amount, as Jacques Chirac correctly identified, to sending "the armed wing of the West" to a Muslim country (NATO is in Afghanistan, where it will reap blowback to Kingdom Come). Military commanders and politicians may spin that "NATO will not fight a war against Islam"—but that's exactly what the majority of the Arab and Islamic world sees with NATO battling Pashtun tribals in Afghanistan.

In Lebanon, both Italy and France—under the U.N. banner—took the plunge. That meant a mini E.U. revival in the frontlines of the key conflict of the times. Renzo Guolo, a specialist on Islam, writing for *La Reppublica,* dreamed of Italy as a bridge between the E.U. and the Middle East: "Our country is at the crossroads of ancient and new conflicts, fundamentalisms, mass migrations and the possible proliferation of nuclear weapons." This was no less than the E.U. claiming center stage.

The E.U. had to be there by all means because the Arab world after all is the E.U.'s strategic southern neighbor—12,000 km of borders from Mauritania to Latakia, in Syria, via the Strait of Gibraltar. The E.U. may even have the chance now to start elaborating a serious, ambitious Trans-Mediterranean policy, with the Latin countries acting as a bridge between Islam and the West. In 2025 France, Italy, Spain and Portugal will have 170 million people. The southern Mediterranean will have almost 400 million. Might as well start seriously integrating now.

Bauman hopes that "Europe is prepared, if not to *lead,* then certainly to *show* the way from the Hobbesian planet to the 'universal unification of the human species' according to the vision of Kant." If this is the somewhat biblical road to be followed it starts, for Europe, on foot, in the treacherous Arab-Israeli divide in southern Lebanon.

Ulrich Beck places us facing a stark option between two rival, world order models: *Pax Americana* and an alternative model which he has defined as "global cosmopolis," essentially "a planetary, federal system of States, governed not by the 'sun' of a world State, but alliances of regional-continental States in a kind of cooperative (Europe, South America, Asia, Africa, North America), forming 'points of crystallization' that regulate the centralization of power." Call it a true multipolar world. It's fair to say the E.U. as a whole totally subscribes to this idea.

Some may not be convinced that the E.U. has become a decisive interlocutor in the Middle East. Some may deplore that what is left for the E.U. is just the mopping up in the wake of U.S. political decisions and military disasters. Some may hail the E.U. is back from the dead (while others may mock the return of the living dead).

Some may dance to the new—political—sounds spinning in the Middle East without an American accent. Some may cheer the E.U. reinforcing the U.N. in true multilateral fashion. Some may dream that there may be no political solution to the intractable, wider Middle East conflict without a moderating E.U. And some may fear that it's exactly two superpowers of the hegemonic West—or two-thirds of the good old Triad—which will keep fueling the logic of Liquid War.

~ 14 ~

(SOUTH) AMERICA THE BEAUTIFUL

Do you recognize our right to create literature?

Then recognize our right to create our History.

*—**Gabriel Garcia Márquez**, winning The Nobel Prize of Literature in* 1982

The history of the past four centuries is a history of barely recorded holocausts. For the peoples and nations under assault, those belittled wars were always "systemic" and often total wars that had profound historical consequences.

***Eqbal Ahmad**, The Cold War from the stand point of its victims, 1991*

There was a time, as the great Uruguayan writer Eduardo Galeano acidly observed in his seminal *Open Veins of Latin America*, first published in 1971, when "we even lost the right to call ourselves Americans, although Haitians and Cubans had already landed in History, as new peoples, one century before the Mayflower pilgrims establishing themselves in the coast of Plymouth. Now America is, for the rest of the world, nothing more than the United States: we live, at best, in sub-America, a second-class America, of nebulous identification."

By the mid-2000s "sub-America" was gone; a Renaissance was on everyone's map; and for the overwhelming majority of the global South the America that really fired people's imagination was, well, in the South. It was not only because of ever forceful literary masters, Brazilian soccer stars forming a truly global diaspora of joy, the new Argentine cinema, the Buena Vista Social Club, Peruvian fusion cuisine or the non-stop sonic orgy from electronic tango to neo-cumbia and Rio's funk do morro. It was, for the first time ever, because of politics. Perhaps South America was finally heeding Garcia Márquez's call—and had started building its own History after more than 4 centuries of plunder.

Carefully chosen words, in Portuguese, were already telling the full story of Latin America's second half of the 20th Century, with the launch in August 2006 in Brazil of *Latinoamericana*, an ambitious, 938-entry, 123 contributing authors, 1500-pages long encyclopedia to be published also in Spanish and later on in English charting territories a Google search simply cannot reach.

Now South America has—literally—stepped on the gas. The *Gran Gasoduto del Sur* (the Great Gas Pipeline of the South), the South American entry into Pipelineistan, alongside networks from Siberia to Europe and Asia as well as the Caspian-to-Turkey BTC, can be regarded as the ultimate metaphor of continental integration. It will happen thanks to formidable political will applied by the new Mercosur power axis, Caracas-Brasília-Buenos Aires, and following "strategic lines of cooperation, integration and South American unity," in the words of Venezuelan President Hugo Chávez.

The pipeline—with a daily capacity of 150 billion cubic meters—will snake from Puerto Ordaz in eastern Venezuela to Buenos Aires in Argentina. The main trunk line is estimated to be 6603 km long—and the total length may peak at 9283 km. The estimated cost is a staggering US\$ 23 billion. The first phase—to Manaus, in the Brazilian Amazon rain forest—should be ready by 2010. The last phase should be completed by 2017.

Chávez is more than aware that "a global energy crisis is approaching. We in South America, what are we going to do? We can't have nuclear power, otherwise they [a reference to the U.S.] will bomb us." Chávez has always praised Brazil's biodiesel—green fuel—efforts. But the best integration strategy, in his view, is gas; the formation of a South American Energy Security Grid—much as Iran, India, China and Russia are working for the emergence of an Asian Energy Security Grid. "Our energy equilibrium is here. We're not going to be vulnerable anymore."

For the king-of-polemicists Venezuelan President, the *Gasoduto* is much more than a pipeline; it means "hope for people" (possibly generating more than one million jobs) and a crucial tool in "the fight against poverty and exclusion." Chávez always bills ambitious projects like the mega pipeline as "the only way towards our independence." It's the same approach regarding the bilingual, pan-South American TV network Telesur (financed by the governments of Venezuela, Argentina, Uruguay and Cuba); the proposed Petrosur (a pan-South American oil company); and the proposed common South American Bank, evidently divorced from IMF/World Bank policies enshrined by the dreaded Washington consensus.

Cristina Marcano and Alberto Barrera Tyszka have provided a unique insight into Chávez's mind in a biography first published in the Spanish-speaking world in 2004, tracking his trajectory from humble village boy raised by his grandmother in a straw hut to Army colonel and then supreme Washington puzzle (Is he a neo-liberal in disguise? A communist? A revolutionary? A pragmatic neo-populist? A nutcase?) One of the President's advisers swears Chávez never entertained the idea of a Fidel-style revolution in Venezuela. Marcano and Barrera stress that Chávez's power lies not much in his military discipline as "in the affective and religious ties he establishes with the popular masses." It's as if he were a cross between a mobile military fortress and a mystic.

No mysticism for Donald Rumsfeld, who has described Chávez as "a Hitler" (wasn't that supposed to be Iran's Ahmadinejad? Or that favorite Arab scarecrow, Saddam Hussein?) Spy czar John Negroponte—who after a counterinsurgency-drenched stint in Baghdad is once again well positioned to set up covert operations in Central/South America—described Chávez as "the biggest challenge to the security in the hemisphere," a key member of the Southern Axis of Evil, the "Western Hemisphere Version."

Notorious neocons and bearers of Iran-Contra shame like Otto Reich and Roger Noriega, Assistants Secretary of State for Western Hemisphere Affairs respectively in the first and second Bush administrations, as well as the editorial page of the *Wall Street Journal*, will inevitably keep disgorging bucket loads of bile towards Fidel Castro's "evil genius," the "leftist-populist alliance engulfing most of South America" (Reich) or the multiple geostrategic implications of Chávez's plethora of moves—business, oil, technical assistance and weapons deals with France, India, China, Russia and Iran and of course "subversive" policies like selling Venezuelan oil for very low prices to Cuba in exchange of thousands of well-qualified Cuban doctors and teachers badly needed in Venezuela's countryside and slums. Conservative think tanks like the American Enterprise Institute will continue to demonize Chávez as a regional populist or the last incarnation of Peron—an authoritarian by popular will. After Osama bin Laden, Saddam Hussein, Mahmoud Ahmadinejad and countless others before them—starting with Fidel—Chávez has been voted by Paranoia Inc. as the new star of (anti)*American Idol*.

Chávez is a master at playing a nimble New Great Game. He attracted billions of dollars of China and India investment and trade. He is extremely close to Russia—buying everything from kalashnikovs to heavy weapons—and even closer to fellow OPEC member Iran (the Bolivarian Revolution and the Islamic Revolution, according to Chávez, are "sisters"). He was the architect of what he dubbed "OPEC's Renaissance." He got Venezuela into Mercosur. He perfected his connection to Spain's Prime Minister José Zapatero, offering oil and gas to solidify E.U.-Mercosur partnership. He even made a Pipelineistan deal with his right wing neighbor, Colombian President Alvaro Uribe, which will open the Pacific to Venezuela: that is, a shorter, cheaper trading route to China. He moved cheap oil to poor U.S. neighborhoods in New England and Chicago—brilliantly bypassing Washington and directly striking a fraternal relationship with local governments.

And the most crucial point of them all: Chávez is painstakingly building up Venezuela as the unavoidable strategic node connecting the Andes, the Caribbean and southern South America to Spain and the wider E.U., Russia, the Middle East, India and China.

Figure 25. The globe centered on Caracas. Venezuela is well positioned to connect South America to the rest of the world; but it is also, inescapably, in close proximity to the U.S.

When Chávez went to Beijing in August 2006 he hailed nothing less than a new strategic alliance, a "Great Wall" against U.S. hegemony. China will be importing 1 million barrels of oil a day from Venezuela by 2012 (by 2006 China was importing 3,6 million barrels a day globally, and Venezuela was exporting 1,9 million barrels a day, mostly to the U.S.). China promised to back Venezuela for a seat in the U.N. Security Council (after an acrimonious battle between Venezuela and Guatemala, the seat ended up with a consensus candidate, Panama). Petroleos de Venezuela (PDVSA), the state-owned oil and gas giant, announced that China will build 13 oil drilling platforms, supply 18 oil tankers and be part of a joint venture to explore a new heavy oil field in the Orinoco—arguably the largest oil reserves in the world. China will also build popular houses for 20,000 people and a fiber optic network, besides updating a goldmine, railways and farm irrigation.

For ballistic neocons Chávez is a portrait of evil for a basket of reasons. He's a good pal of Fidel (it's practically a father-son relationship; in fact he's Fidel's heir). He buys too many guns in a "non-transparent" way (Rumsfeld). He's destabilizing the Andes (Rumsfeld again). He supports the Colombian FARC guerrillas (no hard evidence was ever uncovered). He's building overlapping Axes of Evil with Iran, China and Russia. He uses oil as a geopolitical weapon. And he's a dictator. In a (somewhat) lighter side of the spectrum Corporatistan cheerleaders like the insufferable *Lexus and Olive Tree* bore, totally ignorant of Venezuelan socio-politics, whine about a "buffoon" who uses "oil riches" to "sway democratic elections" and promote "economic populism" that will lead Venezuela "into a ditch." Somebody give him a ticket to Caracas.

Chávez can go on *Nightline* with Ted Koppel, right after Hurricane Katrina, and say that "we've donated millions of dollars to the governorship of Louisiana, to the New Orleans Red Cross...and now we're going to supply gasoline, freely in some cases, and with discounts in other cases, to the poorest of communities, starting with New Orleans and its surroundings." He can go to the U.N. and say that Venezuela "will, in a few days, be declared an illiteracy-free territory... 17 million Venezuelans, almost 70% of the population, are receiving, and for the first time, universal healthcare, including medicine, and in a few years, all Venezuelans will have free access to an excellent healthcare service..." He can go on al Jazeera and be watched by 25 million Arab-speaking viewers who instantly start cheering him as Chávez of Arabia. No wonder: as a democratically elected President and a committed anti-imperialist socialist, there's no ruler remotely similar to Chávez in the whole Arab world.

And then came that astonishing speech at the U.N. General Assembly on September 20, 2006. Jon Stewart aptly defined it as "ballsilicious." All over South America the talk of the town was of the *par de pelotas* ("he's got balls") kind. It takes a lot of guts to climb the U.N. podium, watched by all Globalistan, and deliver, in Everyman's language, a howl stuck in the throats of hundreds of millions. Chávez took the fight to Bush's own court—and he won by a knockout in the first round, a la Muhammad Ali. The U.N. floor gave him a 5-minute standing ovation (blacked out by all TV networks). U.S. Corporatistan media was conceptually tear-gassed—no one actually *listened,* or the ones who did didn't get it or scrambled to spin it in Bush's favor. The liberal bourgeoisie everywhere was also stunned (confirming once more that they love to talk about "progressive" change, but are not exactly fond of seeing it live; as their slice of the plutocratic cake seems to be in danger, it's safer to defend the status quo.)

Chávez's presentation was subversive in a way that Nikita Khrushchev banging his Cold War shoe on the table couldn't dream of. Not because of Bush-bashing, although the theatric antics were priceless. It's a classic Chávez grand entrance: he starts by displaying, book-reviewing and recommending to the world's cameras Chomsky's 2004 best-seller *Hegemony or Survival: America's Quest for Global Dominance* (sales immediately shot to the roof on amazon.com; from 160,772[nd] place to Number One in less than 48 hours. Is this pop power or what?)

Then comes the punch line: "Yesterday the devil came here. Right here." [he crosses himself] "And it smells of sulfur still today." The only thing missing was Robert Johnson singing *Me and the Devil Blues* in the U.N. soundtrack. The young translators at the U.N. booths were having a ball with the "evildoers" rhetorical chickens coming home to roost. Chávez was of course talking about "the president of the United States, the gentleman to whom I refer as the devil... talking as if he owned the world. Truly. As the owner of the world." Then he turned Bush into a movie star: "An Alfred Hitchcock movie could use it as a scenario. I would even propose a title: *The Devil's Recipe.*" Or perhaps a Bush-starring remake of *Funeral Plot*?

Chávez's Oscar-winning performance was effective because he totally unmasked the Bush administration by posing Everyman's questions in non-Bureaucratese: "What type of democracy do you impose with marines and bombs?" And why everyone who expresses dissent is an extremist—"Evo Morales, the worthy president of Bolivia, looks like an extremist to him [Bush]." Then, once again, it takes the leader of a South American nation to defend the rights of Palestinians, Lebanese and Iranians: added shame on cowardly Egypt, Jordan and Saudi Arabia. He stressed the obvious: "The U.N. system, born after the Second World War, collapsed. It's worthless... We, the assembly, have been turned into a merely deliberative organ. We have no power, no power to make any impact on the terrible situation in the world." And he proposed solutions: a Security Council reform, suppression of veto power, "effective methods to address and resolve world conflicts, transparent decisions." He hailed the "momentum to the Nonaligned Movement for the birth of the new era."

But the whole point is that the times they are-a-changin'. The whole point is the Global Rebel Yell: "The era is giving birth to a heart. There are alternative ways of thinking. There are young people who think differently. And this has already been seen within the space of a mere decade. It was shown that the end of history was a totally false assumption, and the same was shown about *Pax Americana* and the establishment of the capitalist neo-liberal world. It has been shown, this system, to generate mere poverty. Who believes in it now?"

Washington's awesome power does not intimidate Chávez. Since 2005 he has admitted on the record that yes, he will deploy oil as a geopolitical weapon as part of an "asymmetric counter-offensive" in case he's harassed by the U.S. or Venezuelan proxies, following a strategy detailed by one of his key advisers, German-born Marxist economist Bernard Momer. But business is business. Untouchable. Venezuela remains the U.S.'s fourth largest oil supplier, after Canada, Saudi Arabia and Mexico. As Marcano and Barrera have noted, "a great deal of the exploring of Delta Platform, a gigantic project with five gas fields 250 km away from the Orinoco delta, is held by Chevron Texaco. And Ali Moshiri, president of the company for Latin America, has this clearly in mind."

The Orinoco River basin roughly contains 235 billion barrels of heavy crude: added to the 77.2 billion barrels in official reserves, the total (more than 300 billion barrels) catapults Venezuela to Number One oil nation in the world. The problem for Venezuela is the cost of extraction: profits only flow when oil is at least US$ 40 a barrel. This particular problem seems to have been removed. Now Chávez has gone on a worldwide offensive to attract at least US$ 70 billion in foreign capital to maximize the Orinoco's potential. Ideally he would need around US$ 200 billion. He sees no reason not to get it—think China and India: "Venezuela has the largest oil reserves in the world. In the future, Venezuela won't have any more oil -- but that's in the 22nd Century."

Meet Hugo Boss

Virtually no politician alive can match Hugo Chávez in front of a media pack. Compared to enduring the soporific spin of American, European, Asian and U.N. Bureaucratastan, it's like being whirled about by a (political) hurricane. Take the axis of gas summit meeting in the spring of 2006 in Sao Paulo between Chávez, Brazil's Lula and Argentina's Kirchner. Every few minutes, presidential communicators vocally build up the frenzy. He's almost two hours late, the room is absolutely packed, people are dying for a latte, unruly TV crews threaten to leave. When the expectation level at the sweltering room is at fever pitch, suddenly Chávez's backing vocals—ministers, security, military attaches —take to the stage. He surges into the room by a discreet side lift. The President of the Bolivarian Republic of Venezuela is in the house, but he might as well be James Brown. Arguably the hardest-working man in (political) show business, Hugo Boss can be as hypnotic as The Godfather of Soul.

Chávez in action might have come straight from a Garcia Márquez novel, weaving reminiscence and future dreams, relentlessly crunching data, addressing his team for any additional information, showering people present and absent with praise and attacking imperialism in all its forms so relentlessly we fear he may be arrested after he leaves the building. He has a formidable capacity of assimilation, in a Clintonian way. His vision is continental; in the same breath he reminisces about a dinner with Bush father, the devastation of Nicaragua and a liberation figure in Guatemala. He embarks on a rap on Simon Bolívar—the great South American liberator—just to blend in a condemnation of macho culture and praise for women from all over the continent. He considers each question carefully, may stray away for minutes but always goes back to the point. He doesn't lecture; he talks like he's downing a few beers with friends in a bar, displaying his storyteller's flair. He does not refrain from cracking jokes and deploys a very healthy degree of self-deprecation—unusual for a leading politician in the global arena.

Garcia Márquez himself, in 2000, qualified him as "a natural narrator. A legitimate product of Venezuelan popular culture, which is creative and riotous. He has a great sense of time manipulation and a kind of supernatural memory." And the best part is that the whole Chávez show may be the fruit of cold calculation. According to Venezuelan vice-President José Vicente Rangel, "everything he does results from planning." Thus his discursive ferocity follows, according to Marcano and Barrera, a "military strategy based on provocation, a permanent clash." Trotsky would love this permanent discursive revolution.

Officially, Venezuela by the mid-2000s held gas reserves of 151 trillion cubic feet (compare to the U.S.'s 189 trillion cubic feet); that means almost 50% of the reserves of the whole continent, 80% of South America's reserves and, the President stresses, "5% of the reserves of the whole world." The gas will be sold in South America "very cheaply," as Chávez confirms that PDVSA is part of the pipeline project (later joined by the Gazprom nation). "If Venezuela was only moved by an economic-financial interest, I would be in Washington." He delights in quoting Venezuela's monstrous oil reserves—"313 billion barrels"—to add that the days when the country "was an American oil colony" are over. Deriding the Bush administration's desire of curbing U.S. dependence on oil, Chávez mentions how the U.S. "consumes 20 million barrels of oil a day" while producing only 8 million. "The U.S. will never be able to become independent from foreign oil. And as a producer of both oil and gas, we for our part cannot maintain an unsustainable model like the American."

Venezuela, Chávez unveils, is "currently producing 3 billion cubic feet of gas a day." But it is not exporting anything, at least not yet. "The first exports will be to South America," then to China and India. Chávez confirms that as much as China is a preferential client of Venezuela's oil, the same will apply for gas. Clutching a color map of South America and pointing to the most probable pipeline routes, he says that "we are going to build a network going to Colombia, Ecuador and Chile, and a commission will inform Chile, Uruguay, Paraguay, Peru, Surinam and even France"—an ironic reference to French Guyana. Bolivia—with the second largest gas reserves in South America—will also be on board; in this case, "the project will be sustainable till the end of this century." The gas may be even sold in the end to the U.S., but for a much higher price. All of this "does not mean that we have a conflict with the American people. Our conflict is with *El Jefe* ["The Boss," a reference to George W. Bush], who wants to take over the riches of all the world."

The *Gran Gasoduto del Sur* is gaining traction amid an extremely complex political context in South America pitting two opposing trade and integration models.

In the summer of 2006 Venezuela officially entered Mercosur, the South American trade bloc led by Brazil and Argentina. This move implied Venezuela's exit from the Andean Community. Chávez explains that after the thunderous failure of the U.S.-led Free Trade Area of the Americas (FTAA) summit in late 2005 in Mar del Plata, Argentina, "the U.S. started to strike mini-FTAAs in Central America or the Caribbean." As far as he's concerned, an Andean community does not exist. He sees Venezuela's exit "as a divorce. The two (Mercosur and the Andean Community) are incompatible. If a country in the Mercosur strikes a free trade agreement with the U.S., it has to leave. They are like water and oil."

MERCOSUR

Figure 26. A new star has joined Mercosur, but in 2006 the change had not yet been reflected in the organization's logo.

The President is adamant. "If anything has the power of a nuclear missile against our economies in South America, these are free trade agreements with the U.S." Chávez is right. When Colombia signs a FTA with the U.S., Bolivia is the loser, as 60% of Bolivia's main export, soybeans, used to go to Colombia. Not anymore, with a flood of subsidized U.S. grains. When Peru signs a FTA with the U.S. the loser once again is Bolivia. Colombia, according to Chávez, "is opening its doors for the subsidized overproduction of the U.S., in products like rice and chicken." Venezuela, on the other hand, wants to protect itself: "We want to abandon the oil monoculture, boost our agriculture and our small and medium enterprises." The whole complex game is defused with a joke. "Chávez is blamed for the end of the Andean community. Chávez is blamed for the end of Mercosur. When they start blaming me for everything, I tell them that if they become pregnant, they will also say it's Chávez's fault."

Empire, of course, is ever present on Chávez's mind. "They gave a honeymoon to Fidel Castro. But when they noticed what he wanted to do, two years and three months later, they came up with the Bay of Pigs. In Venezuela, I also had a honeymoon. I visited the White House, I visited the IMF, I had dinner with Henry Kissinger and Bush father. Aznar [former Spanish Prime Minister] used to call me every week. But when they realized that we wanted a revolution with a national character, they did another Bay of Pigs, in April 2002. Now they are already trying to do the same with Evo [Morales, the Bolivian President]."

The "dinner with Bush" was in fact a power breakfast in Houston; "the devil," a.k.a. George W., was there as well. The CIA was key in the failed coup against Chávez in April 2002. Significantly, only Washington—via then White House spokesman Ari Fleischer—Spain (under right wing Aznar) and the Vatican hailed the "success" of the short-lived coup: Washington was obviously dreaming of an Operation Condor revival. The IMF, showing its true colors, immediately offered to "advise" the new regime, after not lifting a single finger to halt Argentina's 2001/2002 financial bleeding.

Washington keeps financing all things anti-Chávez with a vengeance, via usual suspects like the National Endowment for Democracy (NED) and the Agency for International Development. A new special CIA mission was created in August 2006 to spy on Venezuela and Cuba—officially promoting Venezuela to the Axis of Evil. For the CIA since early 2005 Venezuela is one of the "Top 5 Unstable Countries" in Latin America. Unstable for who? Not only Chávez's is the most popular elected government in the whole of Latin America; he is also thunderously popular all across the global South. For instance, the reason why Chávez is a superstar in the Arab street is because he did what no Arab ruler has dared: as a true nationalist he has been a ferocious critic of Venezuelan elites—as corrupt, rapacious, inept, arrogant and exploitative as in the Middle East; and at the same time he has been a ferocious critic of the U.S. who supports and profits from these elites.

Venezuelan intelligence does not take anything for granted, surveying a myriad of fronts of possible destabilization of the Bolivarian revolution: low-intensity war (which includes Washington-sponsored subversion); the action of "corporate predators" (which includes industrial sabotage); the volatile relation with U.S. ally Colombia; and multiple plots to assassinate Chávez, which considering the gloomy record of the U.S. vis-à-vis "undesirable" foreign leaders from Mossadegh and Patrice Lumumba to Allende and Fidel, remain a real possibility. Chávez has constantly referred to "warnings from within the White House" that the Bush administration is plotting to kill him or topple his elected government before Bush leaves office in early 2009.

For all his dream projects, Chávez admits "the new Latin America is not mature yet. It is still being born. I am the premature child; we were born before the right time to fight the Empire." He's worried that "the Fourth World War has already started. The U.S. is after oil. They know they are already in crisis and wander around like Count Dracula before he's able to suck some blood. So goes the Empire." Three days after the *Gasoduto* summit Chávez met with Fidel in Havana to deliver another blow against "the Empire." The U.S. wants a FTAA? The FTAA acronym in Spanish means "ALCA." To counter ALCA, Chávez founded ALBA— *Alternativa Bolivariana* (Bolivarian Alternative), which also means "dawn" in Spanish, a pact promising a socialist version of regional trade and cooperation. Another end of the spectrum would bill it as the neocons' worst nightmares come true: Fidel, Hugo and Evo denouncing the FTAA as the U.S. trying to "annex" Latin America.

In the extraordinary *Fidel Castro: biografía a dos voces*, published in the Spanish-speaking world in 2006—with 600 pages of frank dialogue between Fidel and the director of *Le Monde Diplomatique* Ignacio Ramonet—the octogenarian *El Comandante*, who remains an iconic figure all over Latin America and vast swathes of the South, apart from giving his version of the Bay of Pigs impasse (praising President Kennedy), the fall of the USSR, the way the Vietnamese were inspired by the Cuban revolution, and how Cuba has managed to survive the U.S. blockade, also provides illuminating insight into the North/South economic abyss.

Fidel recalls how, "after the triumph of the Revolution, I went in May 1959 to Buenos Aires for a OAS [Organization of American States] meeting, and then proposed a Marshall Plan for Latin America ...and I calculated an investment of US$ 20 billion... Do you know how much Latin America owed at the time? ... Five billion dollars." He adds, correctly, that the plan, if adopted, "would have prevented many tragedies in this continent."

Today, referring to what is behind the U.S. push for free trade, Fidel stresses "they want to obtain from us three things: raw materials, cheap workforce and clients, markets. FTAA would be an enormous disaster for our countries. A new form of pitiless colonization." And he comes back to the heart of the matter—debt service: "Hunger in Latin America cannot be eliminated as long as governments have to dedicate one-fourth of their export revenues to paying a debt they already paid twice and is now almost double of what it was ten years ago" (by the mid-2000s accumulated Latin American debt had reached a staggering US$ 850 billion).

FTAA is a neo-liberal wet dream, the perfect framework for U.S.-based Corporatistan. But by 2006 it was overwhelmingly clear across most of South America that Mercosur was a more sensible way out towards true, solidary integration. South American Bureucratastan even tried hard to add a human face to a process that must imperatively touch civil society—thus the increased participation of social, ecological and human rights movements, peasants, Indians, students, artists, culture industry workers and owners of small and medium enterprises in Mercosur discussions. At the 2006 Mercosur summit welcoming Venezuela as a member, Brazil's Lula stressed that "we changed the political profile of our America and we are changing the social profile of our America"; and Chávez stressed that the Venezuelan decision over oil and gas becoming an engine of development not only for his country but for the whole region would turn Latin America into "a world power."

For Argentinian economist Aldo Ferrer, "Mercosur is the backbone of South America's integration from the Caribbean to Patagonia—the real mechanism. It is not against the U.S. or the E.U. We live in the same continent of the hyperpower. But neo-liberalism did not work. So we know that the mechanism for our success cannot be the FTAA imposed by the U.S."

Brazilian sociologist Emir Sader, one of the coordinators of the extraordinary intellectual adventure of the *Latinoamericana*, also forcefully points out that "social forces which led neo-liberalism, as they are so restrictive, based on financial capital, could never create a support base." The overwhelming majority of the populations of Brazil, Argentina and Venezuela—the three major South American powers — subscribe to the death of the Washington consensus. After all, most had to personally suffer its failure.

Figure 27. Mercosur membership 2006 (Mercosur).

9/11 *South*

History shows that since the early 1980s virtually every country that followed neo-liberalism has faced a Hurricane Katrina-style economic cataclysm. The much-vaunted World Bank-coined "East Asian Miracle" happened because the Asian tigers did not ingest the neo-liberal prescription. In South America, post-Allende Chile in the 1970s was the first big experience in Corporatistan—a Brave New (Neo-liberal) World. Well, at least on paper. Even Chile did not exactly behave as a totally deregulated free market economy; its biggest exporter is the state-owned copper conglomerate nationalized in Allende's time.

To understand the failure of neo-liberalism in South America we must replay a very painful drama: South America's 9/11.

Scene 1: Washington, the Oval office, September 1970. Dr. Salvador Allende, a man of culture, *grand bourgeois* and charismatic founder of the Socialist Party, has just won the Presidential election in Chile fair and square, with 36.22% of the votes. President Nixon and his National Security Adviser Henry Kissinger receive CIA director Richard Helms. Nixon tells Helms, according to Kissinger, thathe wants "a major effort to see what could be done to prevent Allende's accession to power. If there were one chance in ten of getting rid of Allende we should try it."

Scene 2: Santiago, La Moneda palace, September 11 of the year 1973, 8 A.M. Dr. Salvador Allende, the democratically elected President of Chile, is worried about a general called Pinochet. Radio stations are mute. The Navy has taken over Valparaiso—where the President was born. But he worries about his new Army Commander, chosen less than 3 weeks ago: "Poor Pinochet, he must have been arrested..." General Pinochet was far from arrested: he was conducting a coup d'État.

Troops march over Santiago. At 8:30 A.M. a solemn military declaration makes treason official. Tanks roll into the city center. At noon, four Stuka planes destroy Allende's private residence on Tomas Moro street and bomb La Moneda palace. The President chooses resistance, fighting the troops surrounding the palace and spurning offers of a plane for himself and his family to leave the country. When his capture is imminent, Salvador Allende presses his chin against the AK-47 that Fidel Castro gave him, and fires. At 2 P.M. the military junta takes power. Systematic arrests, torture and executions start almost immediately.

Between these two scenes is the story of a coup d'État that unfolded in slow motion for virtually three years. The U.S. was still embroiled in Vietnam. Nixon's policy for the whole of Latin America was one word short of "war on terror": "to prevent another Cuba." Nixon simply could not tolerate "that bastard Allende" (in his own words). Chile had the largest copper reserves in the world. Allende was about to nationalize Chilean copper—thus sabotaging the monstrous U.S. corporate profits of Anaconda Copper Mining Co. and Kennecott Copper Co., who had been hemorrhaging the country for decades.

The Chilean destabilization strategy was presided in minute detail by Kissinger. The CIA tried to stage a coup even before Allende's inauguration. It didn't work. Allende played then the role Hugo Chávez is playing now. He wanted to develop "a peaceful Chilean way towards socialism." He was elected by workers, peasants and the marginalized, urban lower classes. Educated urban youth celebrated the "socialism of red wine and *empanadas*." Washington's "counterinsurgency" was to devastate the Chilean economy, deploying mass bribing, spying and blackmail.

Allende in fact was a moderate compared to popular movements further to the left that occupied factories, lands or just property (1278 occupations only in the year

1971). Then strikes started to spread out (3200 only in the year 1972). Industrialists sabotaged production. No one could explain how Chilean credit was suddenly cut off in international markets. Loans were suspended. The CIA, apart from non-stop sabotage, financed strategic strikes—doctors, bank clerks, a very long truck drivers' strike. Conservative newspapers conducted a non-stop, vicious disinformation campaign. There were coup rehearsals. And political chaos compounded economic chaos: the Christian Democrats—the centrists—ended up joining the right and the extreme-right against Allende.

Nixon got exactly what he wanted. On 9/11, 1973 U.S. Navy ships monitored all Chilean military bases to warn the plotters about who might be supporting Allende. Pinochet took over and entered History as the definitive, sinister Latin American dictator from central casting. And crucially, bloody dictatorship in Chile coincided with the ascension of neo-liberalism (which in the 1990s would be remixed as "globalization").

Chileans with scholarships had been a fixture of the University of Chicago for years. The charter of neo-liberalism—and Pinochet's Holy Economic Grail—was written by two of them, Sergio de Castro and Arturo Fontaine. Afterwards it was classic division of labor: the Armed Forces killed while the "Chicago boys" applied neo-liberal economic policies. Military repression assured economic "freedom." Latin America in the 1970s graphically demonstrated how, for mobile global capital, hardcore dictatorships are absolutely irresistible: repressed labor movements plus comprador, dependent ruling classes guarantee fabulous rates of return on investment (after all there's no wealth distribution).

Some other U.S.-backed dictators were in place in South America before Pinochet, more were to follow. By the mid-1970s six U.S.-backed South American dictatorships—Chile, Argentina, Brazil, Bolivia, Uruguay and Paraguay—were united in deep secret under the infamous, transnational Operation Condor, a Latino war *OF* terror eliminating everyone who was or might become a political adversary. Condor was ruthless: leftist intellectuals or party leaders were simply assassinated.

Condor had two key players: Pinochet in Chile (who kept Condor's centralized computers) and Stroessner in Paraguay (he died in 2006 in Brazil, at 93). Stroessner protected Nazis like Joseph Mengele and sponsored the genocide of the Guayaki Indians. The Pinochet regime kept a small lab for the fabrication of botulism soup and nerve gas—certified weapons of mass destruction (WMDs); the chemist responsible later escaped to Uruguay and was assassinated. Orlando Letelier, Chile's Ambassador to Washington under Allende in 1970-72, was assassinated under Condor. Who cared? Military fascism was Washington's daily special, every single day.

Pinochet and Condor, in Chile, were responsible for as many victims as 9/11: around 3000, including 1198 "disappeared." In Argentina there were officially at least 10,000 dead: but for human rights organizations there were in fact more than 30,000 between dead and "disappeared," mostly under the sinister, U.S.-backed Videla military dictatorship. In Paraguay there were at least 2000 dead; in Bolivia at least 350 between dead and "disappeared," in Brazil almost 300, in Uruguay almost 200. Families of the "disappeared" are absolutely convinced Kissinger knew about everything. He will take his secrets to the grave, as will model dictator Pinochet—who still refuses to die: after all it's hard to part with the 1000 gold bars, valued at US$ 160 million, he has stashed in a Hong Kong bank.

The rest of the South—from Islamic countries to Asia—paid a lot of attention to the hardball played out in South America. Pakistani Eqbal Ahmad, who Edward Said appropriately described as "perhaps the shrewdest and most original anti-imperialist analyst of the post-war world," nailed it in a landmark 1981 text included in his *Selected Writings*: the real war fought by the U.S. power elite has always been against nationalism as expressed all over the South, from Mossadegh in Iran to Goulart in Brazil and Allende in Chile. Ahmad observed how "nationalization of natural resources is the primary economic expression of nationalism. It appears to threaten American corporations, which exercise a near monopoly of influence over United States foreign policy and which continue to have a stake in a policy characterized by militarization at home and interventions on behalf of right-wing oligarchies abroad. Similarly, an independent foreign policy and rejection of foreign military ties are expected of radical-nationalist governments; this displeases the American national security establishment, whose growing power is based on the accumulation and expansion of military power and political leverage over other nations."

The South American military dictatorships may be gone. But the aversion of the U.S. plutocracy/Corporatistan node for nationalism in the South remains. Chávez, Evo, Ahmadinejad are the modern counterparts of "evil communists" Mossadegh, Goulart and Allende. They're just being demonized with different tools. And shall we never forget nationalist Supreme Evil Fidel, of course, who has outlasted no less than ten American presidents.

The crisis of neo-liberalism was inevitable in all three major Latin American "model" countries: in Mexico in 1994, in Brazil in 1999 and in Argentina in 2001. By the early 21st Century in South America the bleak picture was of undisguised social war between neo-liberal regimes on one side, and "invisible" rural/Indian movements and the vast nebula of the urban unemployed on the other. Public companies in Brazil, Argentina and elsewhere, at a total value of up to US$ 350 billion, ended up being sold in a Russia wild west-style privatization wave to U.S. and E.U. multinationals for next to nothing. In the end, virtually three decades of systematic plunder—from 1975 to 2005—netted a profit of almost US$ 1 trillion to Corporatistan and banks based on the Triad. The result at street level was a monster socio-economic crisis. From this continent-wide Waste Land came a political "we're mad as hell and we're not gonna take it anymore."

The most tragic case was Argentina—golden child and faithful disciple of neo-liberal IMF prescriptions. The reward: the worst economic disaster in Argentina's history. Straight after the New Afghan War I found myself in the streets of Buenos Aires in early 2002, side by side with the most well-educated and sophisticated middle class in South America, all of them impoverished to near abjection, banging their cooking pans and singing "Throw them all away!" at the top of their lungs. It took a little over 3 years, and the Kirchner government, to find the way out.

Argentina spurned the IMF's catechism. Kirchner offered 30 cents on every dollar—paid in long-term, low-interest bonds—on Argentina's U$ 100 billion foreign debt. He could do it for a number of reasons: Asia had started to invest heavily in Argentina; the economy was on the way up; and Chávez's Venezuela bought at least US$ 3 billion of Argentina's debt. Knight Ridder Business News described it as "the biggest sovereign debt restructuring in history, with international creditors accepting unprecedented losses." What was good for the average Argentine could not be good for "international creditors." But this time there was nothing the IMF—a branch of the U.S. Treasury Dept.—or those "international investors" could do about it.

State power and social power were back in South America with the emergence of the Left nouvelle vague. 16 years after the end of the murderous Pinochet dictatorship, Chile's center-left Michelle Bachelet—a pediatrician and former Trotskyst militant—promised to lead "a new style of politics, more participative," just as Bolivia's Evo Morales—an Indian and former union leader. They were preceded by Chávez in Venezuela, Nestor Kirchner in Argentina, Tabaré Vázquez in Uruguay and Lula in Brazil.

In a nutshell, U.S. neocons, armed with their proverbial Manichean finesse, now see a sharp divide in South America between "democratic leftists" like Brazil's' Lula and "evil, radical populists" like Bolivia's Evo Morales. Even Kirchner—who has smashed military impunity for the Videla dictatorship's killing spree—may be accused of populism.

This binary reductionism even spills over to an arc of moderate right wingers and the center-left in two poles of the Triad, the U.S. and the E.U., who praise, for instance, Lula's moderation—"respecting the rules of market economy" and guaranteeing "the trust of international investors"—while depicting both Chávez and

Morales as bogeymen. Former Brazilian President Fernando Henrique Cardoso does not see Latin America turning left—unless Chile or Uruguay was setting the example. What he sees "in some countries" is "anti-Americanism with a gradual comeback of populism, and in others, a lot of hesitation on the paths to follow." Cardoso, a former sociologist and one of the stars of the "dependence theory" in the 1960s, has always taken enormous pride that "we had conceived the economic and political integration of South America in the 1990s based on the principles of political democracy and market economy."

Cardoso's ideal may be social democracy—but social democracy has never mounted an ideological attack on the logic of capital. Social democracy has essentially agreed—much like the ultra-neo-liberal Iron Lady Margaret Thatcher—on TINA (there is no alternative).

Bachelet, Kirchner, Lula or Vázquez are certainly not anti-neo-liberalism, although they also do not believe in TINA. What they really want is to negotiate the rules of the game. Historically, democratic transition in South America has been an affair of pacts among the elites. When the military dictatorships negotiated their "back to the barracks," they always went to bed with traditional, conservative political parties. But the new breed—from Chávez to Bachelet and Kirchner—are outsiders. Their merit is to have listened—the times they-are-changin'-style—to which way the (historical) winds were blowing, from the emergence of the Zapatistas in Mexico in 1994 to the Argentine crisis of 2001; they listened and they learned something, from Indians, the excluded poor, the pauperized middle classes.

Bachelet understands very well that Mercosur may be an essential tool to develop better social policies all over South America—but she also wants to profit from the fact that Mercosur mechanics is essentially aligned with neo-liberalism. Kirchner in Argentina is investing in a sort of mixed national-foreign capitalist alliance with the E.U., the U.S. and China. The Non-Aligned Movement (NAM) in Africa and Asia, as well as big players China, Russia, Iran and the Arab petro-monarchies are all on deal-making mode with Mercosur.

But with Uruguay's Vázquez ready to reach an FTA with the U.S. (he backed out in late September 2006) fatal blows to Mercosur are also part of the game. The exceptionally useful website www.bilaterals.org—which tracks virtually every single bilateral agreement on the planet—has defined the "dialectical nature" of FTAs with the U.S.: "You and me, we open our economies and our markets, but as mine are infinitely bigger than yours, guess who wins. If you win, you get a ticket to Disneyworld, all expenses paid." Thus, "diplomacy by the U.S. and a huge corporate complex of transnational companies are behind Brazil when the country opposes the just, nationalizing policy of Evo Morales in Bolivia; they are behind Chile when

266

its government says loudly that the priority are FTAs and not Mercosur, which encompasses its geographical and cultural scope; and they are behind Peru when Alan Garcia, aligned with Washington, leads a campaign of provocation against Hugo Chávez's government in Venezuela."

The struggle between Washington's bilaterals and Mercosur will define whether Latin America in the long run will lean towards more of the same—neo-liberalism—or will integrate with a view that "another world is possible."

Meanwhile, Uncle Marx will be smiling in his corner of heaven; class struggle—in Venezuela, Colombia, Mexico, Bolivia, Paraguay, Brazil—is still the name of the game. Take Venezuela, an extremely complex case, where the working class and the urban poor are pitted against local elites—Americanophile landowners, business tycoons and the local media elite captained by multimillionaire Gustavo Cisneros, a fishing pal of Bush father and business pal of Otto Reich in dodgy tobacco, rum and weapons deals. The split is replicated in the midst of the vast masses who support Chávez—pitting wealthy managers of State companies, elite bureaucrats, national-ist businessmen and National Guard Generals against landless farmers, trade unions, the urban slum ghosts and the underemployed or unemployed workers of the "informal sector." In Morales' Bolivia, the conflict is exacerbated by his orthodox macro-economic policies and the ridiculous raise to the already meager salaries of workers in Education, Health and other public services.

The Lula government in Brazil—which by 2003 was the Great Hope of the in-ternational Left to deliver the Third Way Tony Blair had thrown in the dustbin of History—had promised more national control of Brazil's wealth, more funds for the State, and thus more "redistribution of the cake." The balance of his first mandate is mixed at best; good on the economy, health issues, social work and the environ-ment, very good on foreign trade, and mediocre in labor issues, security, agricul-ture, infrastructure building and the fight against corruption: Lula's own Workers' Party (PT), an emerging bourgeoisie mesmerized by power, got entangled in a non-stop series of monstrous corruption scandals. The balance could have been worse. Historically, the 50% poorest Brazilians were left with no more than 12.5% of the national wealth; now it's 14.1%. In four years, Lula created more jobs than Cardoso in eight. Public debt was reduced to 50% of GNP, inflation is under control, there's a healthy trade surplus and Brazil honored all its debts. But progressive social movements were hugely disappointed: there was no agrarian reform. (Official) unemployment is at 10.6%. Half of the Brazilian workforce is in the informal sector.

Lula's regime is pure neo-liberalism disguised as Left nouvelle vague—no head-aches for Big Banking, Big agro-business and Corporatistan. No wonder no one in Wall Street ever cast him in the Axis of Evil horror movie. Lula came to power decided to spread Mercosur to the whole of South America as a real common market. David Harvey, in his book *The New Imperialism*, prefers to stress Lula's international role: "Although he may be a disappointment for his domestic supporters Lula, as he signed with India an important bilateral agreement in the name of Mercosur, said that India, Brazil, Russia and China, together, could redesign the world's economic geography in the 21st Century following more equal lines. This may doubtless indicate the coming of an anti-neo-liberal power bloc in the world." But the so-called BRIC countries are emerging following completely different paths. China is a ruthless export machine. India needs a manufacturing revolution to become more competitive. Russia is Gazprom nation. And Brazil needs to invest in education and infrastructure to become more productive. They are still far from forming an anti-neo-liberal power bloc.

Why Lula is acceptable while "populists" like Chávez and Morales remain so dangerous to "our civilization"? Because they have boldly embarked on a full experiment of decolonization, applied to the State and to the economy at the same time. Not radically—but in stages. As the vice-president of Bolivia, the extremely articulate Alvaro Garcia Linera, puts it, "it is not necessary for small producers and entrepreneurs to subordinate themselves to financial capital. There are other forms of interdependence, other forms of globalization, other ways to generate regional exchanges of products, ideas, and necessities."

It's very enlightening to learn that private property, foreign ownership of assets, profit repatriation to the Triad and attraction of foreign investment (from all regions of the world) remain very much on the cards in both Venezuela and Bolivia. Those sprawling heavy oil fields in the Orinoco, in Venezuela—the richest oil reserves on the planet—essentially remain the property of foreign capital. What Chávez and Morales did was to fight for tax and royalty increases, from less than 15% to up to 50% —and that is still much less than Big Oil pays in the Middle East, Western Africa or in Canada. Triad governments and multinationals had to be angry—perhaps they thought the barely disguised plunder would last forever.

Yet even some sectors of Big Oil admitted the new reality. The president of Royal Dutch Shell, Jeroen van der Veer, told the *Financial Times* in the spring of 2006 "in Venezuela we were one of the first to renegotiate. Under the circumstances we are quite satisfied we can work our future there. We have harmony with the government, which is very important. In Bolivia, I assume we will come to a solution." This "new reality" also applies to mining in Bolivia. Essentially Bolivia is saying: if you want to make a killing exploiting our strategic raw materials, you have to pay higher taxes, higher royalties, accept joint ventures, use local management for distribution and export sales, have us represented in the board of directors, accept a more equal distribution of shares and accept a legal revision of contracts.

It's not a Reform or Revolution scenario. It's reform—actually very mild, because the social contract with capitalist globalization remains intact.

Evo was forced to act in Bolivia for two main reasons: to satisfy his electorate—peasant, trade union and indigenous Bolivian movements; and to counteract the FTAs virtually imposed by Washington on Colombia and Peru that simply destroy Bolivian exports across the Andes. The whole project of Evo's socio-economic reforms depend on getting more money; and if the money does not come from exports, it has to come from a more equitable tax regime on oil and gas Corporatistan. And to make matters worse Evo still has to deal with the horror story he inherited—an IMF-style "austerity program."

Bolivia's acute poverty problems could be solved with a mere US$ 1 billion or so. The crucial point—contrary to Corporatistan's interests—is that if Evo manages to do it, he will set a sterling example that will be celebrated and emulated all over the South. It's very easy to forget that Bolivia is the poorest country in a continent where half of the population is poor. Almost a million people live in hilly El Alto, overlooking Bolivia's capital La Paz. The story of El Alto might qualify as a video clip of South America's history: it was a hill practically coated in silver and exploited by slave labor to the sole benefit, for 3 centuries, of the Spanish crown. Today it's a mega-slum, largely populated by Indians, which in Bolivia were, until Evo, the invisible majority. Former President Sánchez de Lozada, a corrupt multimillionaire locally known as *El Gringo* (he spoke better English than Spanish) was the one who, supported by the IMF, sold off Bolivia's gas and water for next to nothing to Brazilian and Triad Corporatistan.

Evo's fatal mistake was to assume that the Left nouvelle vague in Brazil, Argentina and Spain would accept more tax over their multinationals and a modest increase on gas prices. Globalized Corporatistan trumps any ideology. One fact is enough to confirm that exploiting the poor is a universal sport. The U.S. usually pays US$ 6 for each thousand cubic feet of gas it buys. But the Lula, Kirchner and Spain's Zapatero's governments screamed in anger when Evo proposed to raise Bolivia's asking price to US$ 5 for each thousand cubic feet. In the early fall of 2006 Evo finally got more or less what he needed. Multinational Corporatistan agreed to Bolivia's new conditions – similar to what already applies in Angola, Nigeria or Lybia. By the mid-2010s Boliva will be getting around US$ 4 billion a year from is gas, compared to US$ 200 million in the mid-2000s. The surplus will be largely invested in social projects.

Corporatistan also continues to make a lot of money in Venezuela. Big Oil has been reaping record profits since the early 2000s, and no one in the Triad—despite bureaucratic bile—is talking about abandoning Venezuela. What freaks out Triad power brokers is that Chávez is also leading by example: he is setting up a mixed economy, and he raised taxes on big capital. This represents the kiss of death on neo-liberalism—and a remarkable turnaround on everything that happened in Latin America since Pinochet took over. Enough of "deregulation." Enough of Wild West-style privatization. Enough of frantic denationalization. In fact Iraqis are now the ones starting to pay the price for these "policies."

In South America there's no viable counter-argument against democratically elected nationalist leaders who want a mixed economy to finance social welfare. Chávez's mantra of integration privileges indigenous integration and self-determination—not subservience to the Triad. Cardoso and other more strident critics may deride it as "populism," but if populism means a more equitable society able to manage the sometimes devastating processes unleashed by big capital-fueled globalization, the masses not only in South America but in the Arab world, Africa, Russia and Asia are ready to side with Chávez.

Yet Chávez wants even more. He wants a "social economy," not following the logic of capital, whose principles are enshrined by the Bolivarian Constitution of Venezuela. On a parallel track French sociologist Alain Touraine remembers how sections of the educated urban youth in 1960s South America hailed the role of the *foco*, that is, the revolutionary vanguard supporting peasant struggle, but without recognizing the role of the Indians. Guerrilla failure in 1960s South America, says Touraine, didn't take into consideration local realities, like Che's foray into Bolivia, "rejecting all contacts with Bolivian parties and unions and entering a peasant zone of Guarani language where an agrarian reform had taken place." Compare it now to Sub-commander Marcos in Chiapas who, "aware of the motives of this failure," wanted to link "the defense of the Mayan communities to a program of democratization in Mexico, and wanted to create a great social and political movement." That's the way to go, says Touraine: "The defense of communities and a political transformation of the national State."

The crucial struggle of the Zapatistas, a true "people's army" (composed of peasants hailing from the poorest state in Mexico) has been analyzed in a powerful book by the Midnight Notes collective, *Auroras of the Zapatistas*. The book highlights how "the Zapatistas have had to remind us [that] the land is the source of tremendous revolutionary power and those who wield the sickle are often the instigators of revolutionary change -- even in the stratosphere of high-tech production—because they have the power to subsist without capitalist mediation..." Tell it to the collective leadership in Beijing, which is busy trying to prevent by all means that the next revolution in China be a peasant revolution. For the Zapatistas we are already at World War IV—but not exactly the neocon version.

This war played out inside Mexico itself during the summer of 2006 Presidential elections—which were, just like in the U.S. in 2000, a fraud. No less than 50% of Mexicans live below the poverty line. Andrés Manuel Lopez Obrador, who lost the election, had a sound platform: pensions for the elderly; health care for the poor; massive job creation (via badly needed infrastructure projects); a renegotiation of NAFTA as subsidized U.S. grains (once again) were blowing Mexican peasants out of the market; and a massive fight against entrenched corruption (which in Mexico means a crooked duopoly of business and official Bureucratastan).

The balance of 6 years of neo-liberal Vicente Fox translated into social disaster—except for a tiny white minority that became even wealthier. With virtually no job creation—except in *maquiladoras*—and the countryside turning into a wasteland more than 4 million Mexicans had to choose exodus for *El Norte* by any means available. NAFTA has had the negative social impact of several, successive Hurricane Katrinas. The U.S. has refused to negotiate NAFTA's agricultural clause, which includes total "liberalization" of the corn and beans market by 2008 (this will translate into a death sentence for no less than 3 million farmers). Lopez Obrador is not against NAFTA per se: what he wants is a more equitable treaty. He may have lost a fraudulent election but what he stands for remains. There will be a parallel government. Grassroots social movements are mushrooming. A "popular insurrection" developed in Oaxaca. The new presidency is doomed. An authentic democratic transition, over time, is inevitable. The mass refusal of (corrupt) neo-liberalism is already a fact. In sum, a revolution is already goin' on in Mexico.

According to the Bolivarian Constitution of Venezuela, to develop a "social economy" means "to transform informal workers into small managers," that is, "to create an emergent managerial class." In other words: empowering people. This has always been at the heart of Chávez's policies. Among them: the re-nationalization of PDVSA (the state now owns 51% of all oil production and Big Oil will have to shell out to improve drilling and refining); *Misión Robinson* (a plan to fight illiteracy); *Misión Mercal* (distribution of subsidized food to the poor via a network of popular markets); *Misión Miranda* (benefits to everyone who has been engaged in the Armed Forces); *Misión Vuelvan Caras* ("face-turning")—teaching of self-management and how to set up cooperatives; the creation of *Empresas de Producción Social* (EPS); and Chávez's drive to build up a new communal system of production and consumption based on communal councils (from 200 to 400 families in urban areas, around 20 in rural areas, and 10 among Indians).

Communal councils are a creative alternative to the bureaucracy/corruption plague. And of course an alternative to a paternalist State. Soon there will be 50,000 councils all over Venezuela—constituting a de facto basic government structure of a "new State," the face of this "21st Century socialism." Chávez's model has absolutely nothing to do with state capitalism; he may define it as "a new type of socialism, humanist, putting humans and not machines or the state ahead of everything." But better than any label, it's a system based on solidarity network.

Who benefits from this system? The urban and rural poor, and women of all classes—Chávez's political base (*Misión Cristo* aims to end with poverty by 2021). Who doesn't? Venezuela's big capital, a Triad-connected oligarchy in industry, unproductive landowners, banking and mainstream media. But it's the next step in the construction of a "social economy" that is the most difficult: there's got to be some serious political strategy to promote an all-inclusive pact between unionized workers, people in the cooperatives, peasants, liberal professionals and the vast "informal sector" (something like 50% of the workforce; but at least they have access to free social services, like in the North). And then the social economy will have to forcefully redistribute the wealth of the country internally.

Noam Chomsky has noted how "the U.S. in the past has had two fundamental mechanisms for controlling Latin America: one is violence, the other is economic strangulation. They're both weakening... And so, the U.S. is preparing for more use of violence... In fact, for the first time ever, there are now more U.S. military personnel in Latin America than personnel for the major federal aid organizations. That never happened during the Cold War. Also military training for Latin American officers, and you know what that means."

Ciudad del Este, at the Triple Border Brazil/Argentina/Paraguay, is the epitome of savage Globalistan—at least 20,000 shops, stalls, tin shacks and mini-malls crammed into 15 blocks selling everything under the (tropical) sun. Little Asia is definitely doing business —thousands of Taiwanese, mainland Chinese and Koreans. But above all there are some 20,000 Arabs of Syrian and mostly Lebanese descent (another 12,000 live in the Brazilian resort of Foz do Iguaçu, across the Friendship Bridge). Ciudad del Este, pop. 200,000, is a free trade cesspit and WTO wet dream, realm of *sacoleiros* (bag carriers) crossing the bridge every day and dreaming of the ultimate knockoff, but mostly realm of money changers, prehistoric armored cars, gun-and-coke dealers, dodgy pharmacists and stolen Mercedes with tinted windows.

The border is virtually non-existent, as Paraguay is a Mercosur member. Air space is free—virtually no radars. Cocaine comes by plane or truck from the Bolivian Andes. Brazilian weapons are everywhere—not to mention real and fake kalashnikovs and an orgy of RPGs. Tons of laundered money whirl in free flow. The whole thing is a dizzying black void of billions of dollars in contraband, narcotrafficking, weapons smuggling, money laundering, car theft, piracy and corruption of public officials.

And it gets worse: it's crammed with terrorists. At least if we follow the head of the U.S. Southcom, the vociferous General Brantz Craddock, who is absolutely convinced the Triple Border is the abode of "the transnational terrorist, the narco-terrorist, the Islamic radical fundraiser and recruiter, the illicit trafficker, the money launderer, the kidnapper and the gang member." The emphasis is on "terrorist" and "Islamic." Miami-based Southcom—whose budget is larger than the Depts. of State, Treasury, Commerce and Agriculture combined—is the eyes and ears of the Pentagon over Latin America.

Essentially, this is how it works. Armchair gurus in Washington and New York theorize on the so-called five wars of globalization—terrorism, trafficking, money laundering, piracy and migration—and the Pentagon sends the Special Forces posing as cleaners to make it all proper for the "free" world. The underlying assumption is that Hezbollah, Hamas, al Qaeda—in sum, "terror"—is profiting like mad from the so-called five wars.

The "new threats of the 21st Century recognize no borders," according to the Pentagon. Ergo, everyone may be a terrorist, at least a potential one. Not accidentally General Craddock hates "anti-globalization and anti-free trade demagogues." Sunni or Shiite, Marxist or anarchist, ruralist or existentialist, the Russian mafia, the Hong Kong triads, the Nigerian mafia, the Ukrainian mafia—they are all in cahoots. And as far as the Pentagon is concerned Hezbollah will keep selling pirate DVDs of *Desperate Housewives* to finance more Katyusha rockets.

In the real Triple Border though, everyone may be a spy, or a would-be spy, because absolutely everyone is cruising around: the Russian mafia, the Mossad, the Nigerian mafia, the CIA, the Hong Kong triads. A rule of gold in the underworld is that Brazil is neutral territory and not subjected to turf wars; everyone is entitled to join the fun (technically Ciudad del Este is in Paraguay, but it does business as a Brazilian annex via the Friendship Bridge). There's no chance of catching one of Ayman al-Zawahiri's lieutenants slipping US$ 100 bills into the G-string of dancer Harlem Roux at the Casino Paraná. He—and his al Qaeda affiliation—would be spotted in minutes.

General Craddock had to grudgingly admit that the Pentagon has "not detected Islamic terrorist cells" in the Triple Border, nor anywhere else in South America for that matter. But he'll keep trying (as will his replacement, Navy Admiral James Stavridis, a former senior Donald Rumsfeld aide). If he dropped by Ciudad del Este's mean streets, Craddock would hear a lot of Mandarin—but not Arabic. He would see every cheap plasma in every audio video shop tuned to Lebanese TV—or al Jazeera, hardly a terror ID. In his search for preemptive strikes, he could try the Condominio Mesquita—which, as the name attests, is a condo in the shape of a gold-painted mosque (they would love it in Peshawar). But he would see no Hezbollahs in fake Nikes chowing an *empanada* and sipping mate with Jet Li look-alikes.

Anyway annual State Dept. terrorism reports will keep explicitly regarding the Triple Border as a main source of financing for both Hamas and Hezbollah, although admitting "there's no confirmed information" either Hamas or Hezbollah have "an operational presence" on the ground. Irrespective of the facts on the ground, as far as the Pentagon is concerned the Triple Border will remain a nest of subversive activity to be preempted along with Syria and Iran.

Take what happened in 2005 when the Foz do Iguaçu municipality ran a full-page ad in leading newspapers with an Osama bin Laden photo. The caption read: "When he's not busy blowing up the world, bin Laden spends his time relaxing at Iguaçu." Craddock may have taken it literally—and blown the place apart.

Meanwhile civil society—in the form of social, political, cultural, environmental, student, religious and human rights organizations—will continue to discuss what really matters: a controversial military agreement between the U.S. and Paraguay, and the preservation of the Guarani Aquifer. "Yankee troops" have been holding "training exercises" in Paraguay. And the World Bank is developing a program towards mapping the Guarani Aquifer—which is the first step towards commercial exploration of its precious waters. The Guarani Aquifer is arguably the biggest reservoir of fresh, potable water in the world—right under Triple Border soil. The majority (71%) of its 1.2 million square km—more than Texas and California put together—lie in Brazil. According to the U.N., in 2025 worldwide demand for potable water will be 56% higher than what will be on offer.

In this context, what to make of George W. Bush's spectacularly dodgy land grab in Paraguay? In the fall of 2006 Bush sent none other than his daughter Jenna to buy a humongous—even by Texas standards—98,840-acre ranch in Paso de Patria, in the Chaco region, close to the Triple Border, close to enormous Bolivian gas reserves, close to the precious Guarani aquifer and especially very close to the Mariscal Estigarribia U.S. military base.

When you combine a huge Arab community plus lots of non-commercialized water in a Pentagon-defined "lawless area," no wonder bells start ringing. I heard the best local version of the "war on terror"/Long War from a Lebanese-Brazilian businessman: "In Iraq they said there were WMDs. They wanted the oil. Here they say that we are terrorists. But what they want is our water."

What is actually happening in South America—and what makes it so enticing for the whole South—is a second decolonization process. South American countries—and their democratically elected governments—want to be the real masters of their natural wealth and of their economy. This process is non-negotiable. China and Russia have both noticed it, applauded it, and are busy making huge deals over it. Asia has entered South America with a bang—with China investing on oil, gas, iron ore, copper, soybeans. South-South integration is growing: Brazil, South Africa, India and China are ever more connected. The E.U. is starting to wake up to the fact that a truly equitable, strategic relationship with South America works for its best interests. If only the E.U. would drop those monster agricultural subsidies... Especially as the E.U. knows that multilateral South America is much closer ideologically to Europe than to the U.S.

The overwhelming majority of the ultra-rapacious South American elites has never been responsible for the welfare of their countries, and have always profited from parasitical deals. Compared to emerging East Asia, South America has absolutely appalling inequality, health, education and social welfare indicators. At least now this is (slowly) changing. When the dynamic, vital democracy on show in South America is denounced as "populism," this means only one thing: rapacious elites now feel threatened in substance, not only in style. True, there is still a long way towards a common foreign policy. But the Argentina-Brazil-Venezuela axis is consolidated. The only missing leg is Mexico, which may eventually constitute by the 2010s a new Latin American "chair" able to occupy a leading position in the world.

This is largely due to the role of the Bolivarian Nation. Chávez, an avid reader, has digested everything about Bolívar. He "is," in a sense, the new Bolívar, dreaming of integration by any means necessary. Chávez's wake up call unleashed an awareness chain reaction in Bolivia, Ecuador and Paraguay, countries where the perverse structure of colonial domination was still intact, including a de facto apartheid against Indians and *mestizos*. There's a new, continent-wide articulation of social movements, away from traditional party politics, from the beggars in the neo-liberal banquet to the impoverished middle classes, who will go for nothing less than a Fourth Way: they want to leave behind the classical paradigm of liberal-representative democracy as the only form to institutionally organize popular will. This is not "socialism" as we've seen it in past *realpolitik*: this is what true democracy is all about. It's still in its formative years: a completely new political theory— let's say one step ahead of Tocqueville and Locke—still has to be forged. Everything has to be remixed—Rousseau, Marx, Bolívar. In Caracas they auspiciously call it *gobierno de la calle*, government of the streets. So what if, right here, right now, a better, more equitable future for Globalistan slouches towards America to be born?

~ 15 ~

AFRICASTAN

Until lions have their own historians, stories of hunting will always glorify the hunter.

—*Central Africa proverb*

Africa was home to 850 million people in 2005. They will be almost 2 billion by 2050. Today, more than 400 million barely subsist with less than US$ 1 a day. Life expectancy used to be 50 years in 1982. Today is 49—and falling.

Bayaye is the Ugandan term for street children. Hundreds of millions, in Africa, are *bayaye*. Not every *bayaye* is illiterate. I have seen *bayayes* who disguised in rags could speak English, Italian, Portuguese, Sierra Leone dialect and could read and discuss Dumas, Dante and Balzac. Yet by 2015 Africa will have 57 million children with no access to school. One third of the children who today go to school go in fact to a shade under a mango tree—that is, a school without even a blackboard. But 1 in every 3 children does not even go to school; and two-thirds of these 40 million non-schooled are girls.

African governments spend an average of less than 1% of GDP on basic education. The priority is for war gaming. For each US$ 1 billion Africa receives in aid from the North it buys US$ 1.8 billion in weapons from the North. Debt servicing in Africa absorbs the funds which would be directed to education. Because of the IMF's "structural adjustment" gangsterism practiced since the 1990s dozens of African countries slashed their education budget.

The key for Africa is investment in universal basic education. The World Bank wanted to advance the chariot in front of the ox, promoting the installation of computers in villages with no electricity. But UNICEF data in the early 2000s proved that an African project of universal basic education would cost pennies to the "international community": just US$ 3.6 billion a year for 10 years. That is less than two days of global military spending.

Women suffer the most. According to UNDP data, African women work an average of 10 hours a day. Their literacy rate is only 53.2%, compared to the overall population. Life expectancy is 46 years old, against roughly 80 in Western Europe. There are 920 deaths in childbirth a year (per 100,000 people), compared to a little more than 10 in Western Europe, and 29,800 deaths by abortion a year (compared to less than 10 in Western Europe). Only 15% of women use contraceptives. And a staggering 13,200,00 women are HIV-positive.

Asia has shown the way to break this infernal circle: education.

Numbers cannot possibly tell the wrenching African story. Can Africa be saved? Yes, but it has to be saved by Africans, not by gormless, Jeffrey Sachs-advised Bono. In 2001 four African Presidents—Abdelaziz Bouteflika (Algeria), Olusegun Obasanjo (Nigeria), Abdulaye Wade (Senegal) and Thabo Mbeki (South Africa) started promoting NEPAD—a New Partnership for Africa's Development not inspired by the IMF or the World Bank and their dreaded "structural adjustments." NEPAD is a true Pan-African project, pro-democratic and establishing clear rules for public and private administration. Drawing on the success of the Asian Tigers in the 1970s, its priority had to be education as the key tool for poverty eradication.

Kids all over rural Africa are traditionally encouraged to help their fathers in the fields or to take care of their animal stock, while at the same time there's virtually no interest in the education of girls. So in Africa the school must absolutely reach the kids—not vice-versa. Internet yes, it's wonderful—as the World Bank suddenly started cheerleading in the late 1990s. But first of all people need electricity. This means more African networks in synergy.

Africa needs everything. So no wonder NEPAD has extremely ambitious—but sound—plans. Among them: a US$ 6 billion electrical grid from Cairo to Kinshasa—5300 km via Khartoum and Kisangani. Pipelineistan from Lybia to Tunisia. Pipelineistan from Algeria to Port Harcourt (so Nigerian gas can be sold to Europe). Pipelineistan from Lagos to Ghana with an extension to Dakar. A North-South trans-coastal road between Tripoli and Lagos. An East-West trans-Sahel road from Dakar to N'Djamena. A Western Africa railway—from Ouagadougou to Dakar, then along the coast to Lagos. A proposed train from N'Djamena to Cape Town. Modernization and integration of container ports in Tanger, Conakry, San Pedro and Mombassa.

It's still unclear who will pay for all these infrastructure programs and which benign private investors will finance education projects. NEPAD at least has everything going for it—demanding transparence, public governance and democratic alternation of power. It's an authentic, autonomous African vision, based on close cooperation between states and generations. It may be "the last chance" for Africa to facilitate the exchange of its wealth of commodities, create an attractive internal market, and at least try to prevent the non-stop, heartbreaking exodus trespassed by personal horror stories by people from all African countries rushing towards the Spanish border, Calais and the U.K.

That, of course, is the dream. The (white?) devil is in the details.

The OECD sees Africa advancing on two different gears. Countries blessed with oil and minerals contrast sharply with those plain exporters of agricultural products. Illegality is bound to prevail—especially in the Great Lakes region, of which turbulent Eastern Congo is part. And the fruits of Africa's natural wealth are not bound in large part to benefit local populations.

Burkina Faso's GNP per capita is a little over US$ 1000. The country is a case history of the ravages of post-colonialism. Since the mid-1950s two million Burkinabés emigrated to join the economic miracle of the Ivory Coast. But then since 2001 a civil war in the Elephant Nation forced hundreds of thousands back—creating an immense refugee problem for Burkina.

This is an agricultural country: 50% of exports depend on cotton, feeding 20% of the population. The cotton business is subject to delicate climate variations, price variations and hardcore Globalistan competition (for instance, by U.S. subsidies to the Cotton Belt). On top of it Burkina is being plagued by desertification. Corruption is rife. There's no political alternation. More than 60 ethnic groups coexist. Three religions also coexist; the North is mostly Muslim (almost 40% of the total population). Christians, mostly Catholics, make 15%, and 30% are animists. The only good news may be that there is no inter-ethnic or inter-religious tension.

Senegal is a democracy—a country 60% agricultural basically exporting products and raw materials with little added value. 30% of Senegalese Muslims are affiliated with the powerful Mourid Brotherhood, founded in the 19th Century. The countryside is organized in small agricultural communities, religion-based, everyone working under the patronage of the *marabout*—the community chief. Teaching, in Koranic schools, is in Arabic. Alcohol, tobacco and trousers for women are forbidden.

National integration is a nightmare because railways date from colonialism; riding the famous Bamako-Dakar train is a Western African form of Chinese torture, and still today it takes at least 48 hours. Dakar port will be modernized, thanks to a loan from the Western Africa Development Bank. But there are border problems with Mauritania. And in the south Gambia almost cuts Senegal in two; no wonder during the 1980s separatism in a region south of Gambia, Casamance, emerged with a vengeance.

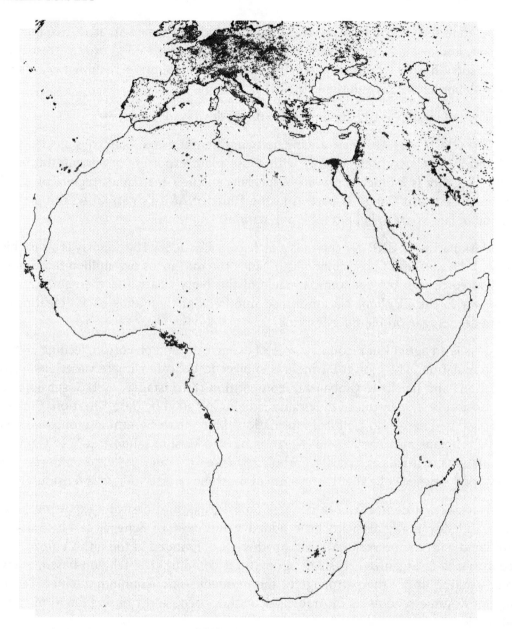

Figure 28. In this inverted map, black dots represent "night lights" visible from space. The densely populated and highly developed areas of northwestern Europe are packed with lights. Most of Africa is dark at night.

The Ivory Coast is the former stability model for Western Africa. During its economic miracle, from 1950 to 1980, GNP increased ten times; this was the third economic power in the continent behind South Africa and Nigeria. But in the 1980s cacao and coffee prices tumbled down, with the inevitable consequences of economic crisis, foreign debt and the dreaded IMF structural adjustment.

There's a huge imbalance between north and south (where 70% of the population lives). Roughly, the north is Islamicized and the south is animist and Christian. The tension between the natives and the 30% of immigrants (from Burkina, Mali, Senegal, Guinea and even Lebanon) has reached boiling point. There are 60 ethnic groups. No wonder the new religion became Ivoryness—all the country's problems blamed on the 30% of foreigners. The Ivory Coast is bound to remain divided between north and south, with a simmering anti-government rebellion. It all boils down to a question of power.

Africa currently represents 7.3% of global known oil reserves, and 10.2% of production. This will rise fast. Equatorial Guinea, Gabon, Angola and OPEC members Nigeria, Algeria and Lybia are all Pipelineistan insiders. The Gulf of Guinea will become one of the biggest hits in Pipelineistan—with the added bonus for Big Oil of much higher political stability compared to the Middle East. Cepsa and Spanish Gulf Oil are very active in Equatorial Guinea, as much as Gulf Oil and Royal Dutch Shell in Gabon.

Mauritania, Madagascar and Chad are the new players. 75,000 barrels a day of high quality light crude started flowing from offshore Mauritania in early 2006; another huge nearby field will be producing an extra 100,000 barrels a day, plus natural gas. 7500 km to the east Exxon Mobil is ready to attack the high seas near Madagascar, which may enter Pipelineistan with a bang by 2010. And there's more expected to come from Senegal, Gambia, Ivory Coast, Sierra Leone, Liberia and Guinea.

The relationship between Big Oil and Africa is fraught with potential disasters. Take what happened in Chad. Idriss Deby, the President of Chad announced in the summer of 2006 a "revolution" against Corporatistan exploiting the country's oil. Deby in effect threw Chevron and Malaysia's Petronas out of the country because they had not paid US$ 488 million in corporate taxes. And then he did a Bolivia, or a Venezuela, announcing partial nationalization, with Chad entering production "at a reasonable level of 60%." The other 40% happen to be controlled by Exxon Mobil, which is also a producer and built a US$ 4.2 billion, 170,000 barrels a day pipeline in Chad running through Cameroon to the Atlantic—the largest private investment in sub-Saharan Africa ever. The deal was brokered by the World Bank, who pressed for a "revenue management" scheme forcing the Chad government to spend 72% of their royalties on poverty reduction. Nobody knows how this is actually working out in hyper-corrupt Chad as people remain mired in deep poverty. And to top all these problems, according to PFC Energy consultancy, Chad in fact got a very bad deal from Big Oil: it is getting 28% off its oil, less than half than Equatorial Guinea. Angola, Congo, Cameroon and Gabon get more than 60%. And Nigeria gets 80%.

In Sudan, it's the south that is rich in oil: Pipelineistan is already active from Bentiu, north of the oil-rich Wau region, to Port Sudan in the northeast. As we will see, Sudan is China country. But the key drama in Sudan concerns civilians—who in effect suffer as triple hostages.

They are hostages of the Arab government in power in Khartoum, obsessed with its own arm wrestling with humanitarian operations and linking the distribution of humanitarian help to Islamization. They are hostages of the Popular Army for the Liberation of Sudan—at war with Khartoum; humanitarian aid is frequently kidnapped by the Popular Army for the benefit of their warriors, or else they impose taxes on the humanitarians. Finally, Sudanese civilians are hostages of the humanitarians themselves—some of whose hidden agenda goes to uncharted territory, tying the Evangelization process with political interest of the West. The U.S. once again is at the center of the drama as Washington may profit from fighting the Islamist, "rogue state" Khartoum regime without firing a gun, that is, having to arm or finance a guerrilla. A civilian Sudanese minority who manages to flee the country finds refuge in Cairo, in Dickensian conditions, despised by the Arabs.

The E.U. has also been itching to intervene in Africa. By the mid-2000s there was a flurry of NATO communiqués on the lines of "advancing peace and international security." Then the European Commission went on overdrive, affirming the E.U.'s will to be "a political and commercial partner," in fact a "strategic partner."

This resulted, in the sensitive case of Congo, in some sort of military intervention program named Eufor-RDCongo—with a HQ in Potsdam, Germany. Theoretically these 2000-strong forces would only intervene locally as a fourth layer if Congolese police and Army and the U.N.'s 17,500 blue helmets deployed on site would not be able to take care of a particular problem. Civil and regional war has left Congo with a staggering 3 million dead from 1997 to 2003. The Bundestag was immersed in heated debate to approve the deployment of Eufor-RDCongo. That was until the key winning argument, not by accident, was provided by German Defense Minister Franz-Joseph Jung: "The stability in this region rich in raw materials would be very profitable to German industry."

Of course: Congo has the world's largest reserves of cobalt—not to mention gold, diamonds, coltan (essential for manufacturing cell phones), niobium, copper, manganese, tin, lead, zinc... Already during the civil war Congo's fabulous mineral wealth was the object of global pillage, a demented free for all where "all" meant a plethora of mafias: to secure the loot one just needed to pay one of the warlords wielding real power in three giant provinces "managed" by militias.

The South African mining industry regards Central Africa as the next Holy Grail. It plans on conquering it allied to Western Corporatistan. A report by the Dutch Institute for Austral Africa (NIZA), available on www.niza.nl details the previous pillaging. Now Globalistan takes over —with the World Bank forcing the adoption of a new, ultra-liberal mineral code privileging a Corporatistan only encumbered by minimum obligations and taxes.

André Linard of the InfoSud agency in Brussels asks a crucial question: when democracy is absent, which is the case in most African countries, must the push to improve the welfare of local populations come from the West, for instance by preventing oligarchies from monopolizing precious resources? Or is sovereignty the rule, with the danger that this may lead to an even higher concentration of wealth?

If you are an oil-rich country you can always do like Mauritania, which had a certain margin of negotiation when it had to discuss a fishing deal with the E.U. But then Nigeria derives more than 95% of its export income from oil. In the local market prices are always going up, and there are shortages; so the locals will keep being squeezed because the absolute majority of the 2,5 million barrels of oil a day is exported to the U.S.

Inevitably the Pentagon's Long—or Infinite—War would have to have the whole of Africa in its sights. In what is dubbed in military circles as a "significant strategic shift" an African Command is already on—a lean, mean fighting machine which will broaden the mandate of the born-in-2002 Combined Joint Task Force-Horn of Africa, previously locked in "war on terror" mode in Kenya, Somalia, Ethiopia, Sudan, Eritrea, Djibouti and Yemen.

Bets could be made on how many Pentagon analysts understand what's actually going on in the black void of the Horn of Africa. It's basically a vicious war of all against all—which in a sinister tragicomedy of errors happened to have been fueled by the Pentagon itself.

There's only one ethnic group and a single, unified language in Muslim Somalia. Like all over the Arab world, this is a clannish society. When dictator Siad Barre was deposed in 1991, the inevitable result was clannish-based civil war. Every American knows of *Black Hawk Down* on October 1993 in Mogadishu—not least because of Ridley Scott's swooping Panavision moves. And of course there's Hawa Elmi, a.k.a. the *Black Hawk Down* lady, a former nomad from the Somali desert who lives in the mega-crowded Tokyo slum and charges US$ 3 admission to anyone who wants to contemplate a piece of the Pentagon-versus-Slumistan war in the form of a battered Black Hawk nose. The U.S. left Somalia in 1992. The U.N. left in 1995. What was left behind was beyond *Mad Max*—or the Taliban heyday: an absolutely failed state infested with "technicals"—pickups with mounted machine guns and anti-aircraft cannons roaming around a deserted wasteland filled with demented, drugged adrenaline junkies, the *mooryaan*, shooting, raping and pillaging at random.

Then came 9/11. For Washington this black void—an extreme-sports-violent, government-deprived Islamic wasteland—simply could not be tolerated. The U.S. tried to set up some sort of government. A U.N.-sanctioned, inevitably unpopular warlord, Abdulahi Yusuf, was rushed to power. But he was the wrong warlord—according to the three others who actually controlled Mogadishu, profiting from piracy, cell phone smuggling and *qat* (an euphoric plant) trafficking. Yusuf would "rule" only his own backyard in Baidoa (echoes of Hamid Karzai).

Mogadishu then developed into the realm of Islamic Courts—the local, practical, business sector solution of using *Sharia* (Islamic law) to regulate society. The courts are of course clannish. But in 2004 they finally congregated under the banner of the Union of Islamic Courts (UIC). Washington inevitably freaked out, big time—and responded the "war on terror" way. The CIA, always acting reflexively, showered Gun and Gold on those three unsavory warlords—sort of a remix of Afghanistan 2001. The warlords even formed their replica of the Northern Alliance: this one was called Alliance for the Restoration of Peace and Counter-Terrorism (a CIA suggestion, perhaps?) In theory, this alliance goes after al Qaeda. In practice, it fights the UIC.

Thus Papa got a brand new war—the Alliance against the Courts.

Once again this kind of scheme went—if anybody had any doubt—spectacularly wrong. The Courts were able to regiment support from all over southern Somalia. The warlords were expelled from Mogadishu. And the Courts took over the whole city. For all Western cries of Talibanization, this was not a Taliban state, far from it. Finally the capital was under law and order. The Courts—although financed by private, wealthy Saudi Arabian and Gulf individuals—will not necessarily evolve into anything resembling Taliban Afghanistan. The chairman, Sharif Sheikh Ahmed, wants good relations with the U.N., the U.S. and the E.U. He strongly denies ties to al Qaeda. The majority of Somalia is moderate. Normally the Somalis would elect a moderate Islamic government with a huge popular mandate.

Over neocon Washington's dead body, of course. With essential U.S. clearance neighboring Ethiopia, five times more populated than Somalia, decided to muddle through, sending troops to protect the innocuous, unelected "interim government" of warlord Yusuf. Ethiopia is predominantly Christian, with a huge and very impatient Islamic minority; no wonder Ethiopia's President, Meles Zenawi, is freaking out with the nightmare of Islamists in Somalia encouraging their Ethiopian brothers to rise. The Islamists in Mogadishu were clear: the Ethiopians face a jihad. And more players are bound to join: Eritrea, which may go to war with Ethiopia again, of course is helping the Islamists in Mogadishu.

The whole Ubuesque spectacle spells the possibility of non-stop disaster in the Horn of Africa for years to come. Egypt and Yemen are also helping Yusuf. The Pentagon's African Command will have no problems justifying its budget. After all, from Liberia to Sierra Leone, from Sudan to Casamance in Senegal, from Somalia to Congo, the stenographers of clash of civilizations and the pawns of Infinite War are just betting that hunger and ethnic conflicts will coalesce into anti-Western and anti-U.S. feeling and be the perfect conduit for the spread of radical Islam. The U.S. reaction to the Islamic Courts in Mogadishu reveal the fallacy of this scenario: if only people would be left alone to take care of their lives as they wish.

While the U.S. remains petrified by the Long War, China accumulates hits in Pipelineistan. When the Council on Foreign Relations forcefully asked the U.S. to "act on its rising national interests on the continent," not surprisingly these interlinked "interests" were defined as oil and gas and the inextricable competition with China.

Pipelineistan in Sudan is responsible for 7% of all China's oil imports. The Darfur drama simply does not register in Beijing. China supports the Arab Sudanese government in Khartoum, which for its part backs rebels in Chad who almost did a regime change and got rid of the U.S. and France-supported Idriss Deby. Sudan prefers China—and not Western Big Oil—to exploit its oil fields. U.S. Big Oil is basically out of this game because the U.S. imposed sanctions on Sudan in 1997. If there is indeed regime change in Chad the Exxon Mobil-built pipeline from Chad to Cameroon may run into big trouble. And China would kill for the chance to develop Chad's oil fields as well.

China-Africa trade was US$ 40 billion in 2005, when China had distributed US$ 5.5 billion in aid. The China-Africa Forum was created in 2000. Since then China eliminated tariffs on 190 imported products from 28 LDCs (least developed countries) and cancelled US$ 1.2 billion in debt of 31 LDCs. An array of African leaders regard China as a development model—so Chinese influence has only one way to go: up. China is now the solution for scores of African countries trying to get rid of the IMF stranglehold.

For instance China's export-import bank advanced a US$ 2 billion soft loan to Angola to be spent in badly needed infrastructure. In return China got a stake to explore oil off the coast of Angola. The Chinese are modernizing roads and railways, schools and hospitals, installing fiber-optic networks, building housing developments and will help in the construction of a new airport—where of course one will be able to fly Luanda-Beijing direct.

For China there are no U.S. or Western (oil) spheres of interest. In Nigeria—which exports 95% of its oil to the U.S.—China will invest US$ 4 billion in infrastructure, building railways and power stations in exchange of four drilling licenses. China got a controlling stake on the Kaduna oil refinery (110,000 barrels a day) and a 45% stake to develop a huge offshore oil and gas field. When President Hu Jintao visited the Nigerian Parliament and propped up "new Sino-African strategic relations," the next day Nigerian media was celebrating the emergence of Africa's China. The Middle Kingdom is applying the same seduction strategy in Gabon, Ivory Coast, Liberia and Equatorial Guinea. Africa is already China's number 2 source of oil after the Middle East—ahead of neighboring Central Asia. The West is reduced to cries of "Chinese neocolonialism." It may be a case of "soft" neocolonialism as Beijing always proclaims its altruistic principles towards its African brothers, and always refrain from interfering in internal politics.

In the summer of 2006 the IMF "reformed" by increasing the voting power of China, South Korea, Mexico and Turkey. But the basics remain the same. The IMF is run by the original G-7—U.S., Japan, Germany, Britain, France, Italy and Canada—before it became a G-8 with Russia. It may be the most blatant case of the rich North deciding life and death of the poor South like in a Roman amphitheater.

Each IMF thumbs up requires 85% of votes. The U.S.—with 17%—can vote out anything it wants. The E.U.-3 plus Japan have 22%. The U.S., the E.U., Canada and Japan—the Triad, roughly—have 63% of the votes. The 80 poorest countries in the world are left with a meager 10%. Although they cannot decide even on a new pencil for the head office in Washington, they come up with the cash: a great deal of the IMF's funds comes from loan repayments by poor countries. George Monbiot correctly argued in *The Guardian* that "the internal political process looks as if it was contrived in North Korea, not Washington." After it lost any influence over the economic policies of the G-7 the IMF became, in Monbiot's formulation, "the rich world's viceroy."

Everyone remembers how the IMF blew its customary kiss of death after the 1997 Asian financial crisis—to the benefit of voracious U.S.-based hedge funds and investment firms. Asia will never fall into this trap again. But Africa is bound to remain captive of what any African would describe, as I often heard in Burkina, Mali or Senegal, as a white supremacist band of bloodsuckers.

With the current rules of the game Africa cannot possibly win—ever. When the WTO Doha cycle collapsed the biggest loser was once again Africa. African countries will keep being condemned to sign bilateral treaties under nearly Mafiosi terms. There are at least 250 bilaterals in place, and dozens are on the pipeline. These 250 already account for more than half of world trade.

The U.S. for instance will keep imposing intellectual property laws protecting American software, cinema and music—but this has nothing to do with the WTO. The U.S. forbids controls on capital flow.

In agriculture the E.U. will definitely not suppress its subventions before 2013. And the U.S. will not be forced to reduce their US$ 15 billion subvention package—it may even increase it. Subsidized U.S. cotton will keep blowing African cotton out of the market.

This means the Great African Exodus will become increasingly intractable—to Malta, the Canary Islands in Spain or the island of Lampedusa in Italy, and deeper into the E.U. The news cycle does not even bother anymore to list in detail the grim procession of these precarious fishing boats filled with desperate sub-Saharan Africans, with no food or water for days, disappearing into the high seas or suddenly disturbing the jet-skiing ennui of hordes of package mass tourists: an amorphous bunch of desperate, famished black people unleashed on shore not carrying gin and tonics on a tray certainly is not how the travel agency back home pocketed all those euros.

The gate crashers will keep coming—from the shores of Mauritania, from Senegal, from Gambia, paying at least US$ 1500 a head to buy those fishing boats and embark on the unbelievably perilous journey (it's 800 km in the high seas from Nouadhibou, in Mauritania, to the Canary Islands). Once in a while the Spanish and Italian governments will eventually legalize the status of hundreds of thousands of illegal aliens in the E.U. who were lucky enough to find a menial job. But border repression will also increase exponentially—like in the Spanish enclaves of Melila and Ceuta, for instance, the only terrestrial border between Fortress E.U. and Africa.

To counter all this gloom, the Africanist Thabo Mbeki, South Africa's President, has a vision: the African Renaissance—a cultural and economic project based on an extraordinary History forgotten and denied during colonialism, when the rape and pillage of Africa was parallel to the refusal to honor and respect it. African leaders who studied in the U.S.—like the first Nigerian President, Benjamin Azikiwe—were also heavily influenced by the African Renaissance. There's a deep humanist tradition in South Africa—expressed in sayings and proverbs. In Zulu, we usually hear the expression *umuntu ngumentu ngabantu*: it means "each person's humanity is defined by its sociability." Mbeki's vision of the African Renaissance is based on the respect of the idea of culture as an integration between the individual and the community. That is Africa trying to preserve its humanity when confronted to internal struggle and external exploitation. But will that Zulu spirit be enough to tame the tsunami of resource-hungry Corporatistan?

~ 16 ~

NUCLEARISTAN

GRIM REAPER: You are all dead. I am Death.

HOST: Well, that's cast rather a gloom over the evening, hasn't it?

HOWARD: I don't see it that way, Geoff. [sniff] Let me tell you what I think we're dealing with here: a potentially positive learning experience to get an--

GRIM REAPER: Shut up! Shut up, you American.   You always talk, you Americans. You talk and you talk and say 'let me tell you something' and 'I just wanna say this'. Well, you're dead now, so shut up!

—**Monty Python's** The Meaning Of Life

Dear Leader Kim Jong-il definitely has a macabre sense of humor. Or maybe—as a certified film buff—he loves playing Dr. Evil. The Dear Leader chose the 4th of July of 2006 to test six North Korean missiles, including a Taepodong-2 with a theoretical range of 6000 km and capable of carrying a nuclear warhead. True, the Taepodong-2 stayed a mere 40 seconds on air before crashing in the Sea of Japan. The *Asahi Shimbun*, with spectacular understatement, dubbed it "a failure." Well, in Kim Jong-ilistan thinking, not exactly. When it goes really ballistic, a Taepodong-2 will be able to hit Los Angeles. The result will not be exactly of the Dr. Evil vs. Austin Powers kind.

It may take time, but in a typically infuriating, inscrutable Kim Jong-ilistan way, Axis of Evil superstar North Korea seems to be getting there. Taepodong-1—with a range of 1400 km—was tested in 1998. It successfully overflew Japan. Then, total radio silence. But since 2003—not surpisingly after having been inducted in the Axis of Evil Hall of Fame—North Korea started to accumulate the necessary plutonium to build up to eleven nuclear devices. The Russians said the North Koreans in essence were building notoriously erratic SCUD missiles equipped with extra fuel tanks. But North Korea also obtained new technology from Pakistan, courtesy of radioactive black marketer A. Q Khan. President Musharraf admitted in October 2006 that Khan only contributed to North Korea's uranium enrichment: nothing about bomb-making, triggering mechanisms or missiles. It's a no holds barred guessing game. Some experts say Pyongyang may be far from mastering ICBM technology. Some say it's already there.

Whenever in doubt, which is all the time, all that's left for the "international community" is to switch to Greek Chorus mode urging the multilateral brigades to act. But the six-party negotiations—the two Koreas plus the U.S., China, Japan and Russia—had been deep-sixed. Kim Jong-ilistan had formally announced in early 2006 that it was a proud nuclear weapons power—without once again providing the evidence. Then in early October 2006 came the Big rhetorical Bang that sent shivers from Tokyo and Seoul to Washington and the U.N. in New York: we're going to test a nuclear bomb at a "secret" date. And they did. Globalistan was stunned: this was King Jong-ilistan's October Surprise, rocking Asia to the core.

South Korea may have offered security guarantees. Unification Minister Chung Dong-Young may have personally delivered a South Korean proposal to Kim Jong-il including a South-North line to transfer much-needed electricity. The other participants in the perpetually collapsing six-party talks might offer massive economic aid. But all this presupposed Pyongyang renouncing nuclear power. And that, of course, was wishful thinking.

There was only one way out—and that would be for both South Korea and China to cut off financial aid to the North. After the Korean War China was left with 420,000 killed, 500,000 wounded, 25,000 victims of war-related accidents and illness, and 29,000 MIAs: that's more casualties than suffered by the U.S. during World War II. Mao's own son, Mao Anying, was killed in Korea. North Korea suffered 215,000 killed, 310,000 wounded and 110,000 MIAs. Without China, there would be no Kim Jong-ilistan today—and he knows it.

But now China and North Korea might not be as "close as lips and teeth" anymore—as the famous Jiang Zemin formula ruled. The U.S.—in a wily deployment of money-laundering reasons—imposed a blockade on North Korea's overseas bank accounts. It worked—to the point that in the summer of 2006 the notoriously travel-adverse Kim Jong-il took one of his secret train trips to complain in person to the Beijing collective leadership. While the U.S. and its protectorate Japan favored pressure, China and Russia favored compromise, with Beijing the only player that could possibly solve the impossible equation: the collective leadership in Beijing knew that a North Korean bomb would make a Japanese bomb all but inevitable.

But even before the October 2006 nuclear test foreign relations expert Shen Dingli, of Fudan University in Shanghai, admitted in a newspaper of the China Youth League that North Korea now "considers its national interests to be greater than its relations with China."

So what does Kim Jong-ilistan really want?

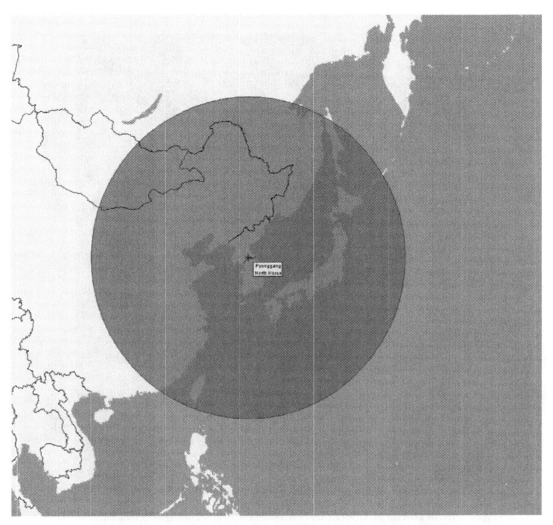

Figure 29. Large portions of China and the entirety of South Korea and Japan are within 2000 km Nodong-2 range of Pyongyang.

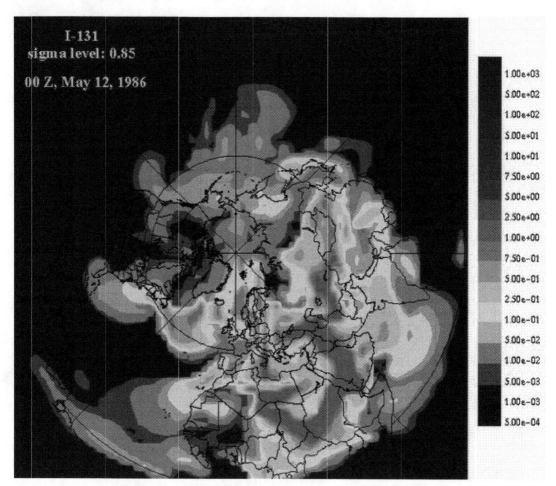

Figure 30. The accident at Chernobyl caused worldwide panic as radiation spread across the globe. The dispersion plume is seen here in a view looking down from above the North Pole. A U.S. nuclear attack using tactical nuclear "bunker busters" on North Korea or Iran might cause more or less radioactive material to be released, but the resulting panic would inevitably be much greater.

The whole strategy boils down to carefully orchestrated provocation as a means to obtain a better negotiating hand. At the center of the storm lies North Korea's Second Economic Commission—directly linked to Kim Jong-il's personally controlled Defense Commission. This Commission controls the production, distribution and export of all North Korean weapons—including the bombs and missiles, of course. For the South Korean National Intelligence Service, in a summer of 2006 Parliament session, "it's possible that the missiles have been tested to consolidate the regime and secure their export market." This tied directly to the huge problem of Kim Jong-ilistan's dwindling cash after the imposition of economic sanctions.

Shock and Awe over Saddam Hussein was the textbook demonstration that to actually possess WMDs is Kim Jong-ilistan's iron guarantee there won't be regime change in North Korea. Kim Jong-il's supreme objective is direct negotiations with the U.S. To provoke negotiations by means of a nuclear test may be a "diplomacy of the abyss"—but that's Kim Jong-ilistan script to the letter. And if Kim Jong-ilistan allowed itself this move it's because the Nuclear Non-Proliferation Treaty (NPT) is in fact dead.

This death certificate also explains why the Iranian nuclear dossier is so intractable. It's as if Pyongyang and Tehran were examining each other's every move on how to deal with the "Great Satan." Their strategy differs. Iran prefers stalling. Kim Jong-ilistan—in a mix of desperation, gall and "diplomacy of the abyss"—prefers provocation, willing to affirm itself as a nuclear power equipped with ballistic missiles. As for Iran the stated mission is to develop a civilian nuclear program—something perfectly in accordance with the NPT.

Panmunjon can only be described as a historic anachronism. A village right on the 1953 ceasefire line of the Korean War, 56 km north of Seoul, Panmunjon is just a dot in the DMZ separating both Koreas—a strip 4 km-wide and 248 km-long peppered with tanks and electrified barbed wire, sealed to everything that moves except migratory birds.

Panmunjon is the Cold War as amusement park. The military on both sides even behave as if they were security agents in Disneyworld —or vice-versa. Good and Evil are face to face like they were ritualized by Kurosawa. On "our" side is Freedom Village; relative freedom actually, with a curfew at 11 P.M. On "their" side is what the U.S. calls "Propaganda Village." The only difference to the capitalist counterpart is that it is a ghost village—like a set in a Sergio Leone spaghetti-western. A huge mast exhibits a giant North Korean flag, and strategic loudspeakers blast slogans 18h a day.

Roughly 37,000 U.S. troops protect South Korea. Not sure about the tunnels though. Tunnels had been part of the late Kim Il-sung's strategy since 1971. For the Eternal Leader, a tunnel was more effective to breach the DMZ than 10 atomic bombs. But his son Kim Jong-il grew fonder of the seas and the skies: he prefers submarines and missiles.

The contrast between the Koreas is like a photograph of Globalistan. The South—48.5 million people crammed in less than 100,000 square km, less than half of the North's area—is firmly in the global Top 12. By 2005 data, with a GDP of US$ 787 billion (605 times bigger than in 1953), South Korea was ahead of Russia, just behind Brazil and almost as wealthy as the ASEAN 10 put together. 90% of the South is urban, which means around 44 million people (20 million in Greater Seoul) crammed into a little over 13,000 square km: virtually a city-state like Hong Kong or Singapore, but way, way bigger, as University of Leeds North Korea specialist Aidan Forster-Carter noted on *Asia Times*. Compared to the North, it's a case, says Forster-Carter, of "one country, two planets." But united, they would be a powerhouse, with more than 70 million people and sooner rather than later catching up and perhaps surpassing Japan.

Kim Il-sung, the founding father of the Democratic People's Republic of Korea (DPRK) was a Korean nationalist. Communism came later—a classic ideological itinerary followed by most Third World leaders fighting imperialism. Kim Il-sung was one among many who have followed Lenin to the letter: if imperialism is an advanced stage of capitalism, you must use communist tactics to fight it. At first, as a Korean nationalist, Kim Il-sung fought Japanese imperialism trying to subdue the rest of Asia. Japanese designs of course had grown out of Japan's Westernization after the Meiji Restoration. After World War II Kim Il-sung confronted what he regarded as the new imperialism—America's.

To deescalate his nuclear program Kim Jong-ilistan first demanded money. Then he demanded 1 million tons in grains. Then he demanded nothing; after all both sides, the U.S. and North Korea, are still technically at war, as there has not been a formal peace treaty. Kim Jong-ilistan assumes the U.S. knows the basic demands: no more American troops in South Korea, and a peace treaty signed with the U.S., not South Korea.

The roadmap to peace should travel through the economy—the South providing the North with raw materials for the manufacture of clothes, shoes and soap; and the North would provide the South with a wealth of natural resources, from zinc to coal. On paper, it looks terrific—resources and labor complementing technology. It didn't work.

In 1999, on the margins of the—then—groundbreaking North-South summit in Pyongyang, I had a very instructive talk in Seoul with Prof. Rhee Tong-chin, research director of the Kim Dae-jung Peace Foundation. Prof. Ree said that basically both the U.S. and Japan wanted the status quo unchanged. Japan—out of its ferocious, 2000-year old rivalry with Korea—would not even consider the emergence of a unified Korea. Japan wanted Korea as a buffer state between Japan and China—thus the necessity of U.S. troops in both Japan and South Korea. On top of that Japan was "very worried" with the rise of Chinese influence in both Koreas.

Prof. Rhee himself was very worried with the bigger picture—worried enough to identify with remarkable precision what would happen next: "U.S. unilateralism, in spite of the excess of self-confidence and even the substance of American power, has generated, in silence, many counter-answers; and these counter-answers will expand and change global geopolitics. The continuation of present U.S. unilateralism will place it in a collision course with virtually every nation; and the degree and intensity of this reaction must determine the basic nature and the speed of emergence of a new world order."

Kim Myong-chol, writing for *Asia Times* in the summer of 2006 explained in detail why Pyongyang is going nuclear. He is the executive director of the Center for Korean-American Peace, is a PhD from the Democratic People's Republic of Korea's Academy of Social Sciences and is also widely regarded as an "unofficial" Kim Jong-il spokesman. The way he framed the whole question is very revealing: "The time is coming fast to decide who is the winner and who is the loser in the long-standing conflict between the Korean people, with a history of 5,000 years—proud descendants of *Dankun* and *Paedal Korea* and *Koguryo*—and the United States, with a history of a mere 200 years. The Korean people have many scores to settle with the U.S." That's not exactly the kind of air brushed discourse the "international community" is used to.

Kim Myong-chol is convinced that "the Korean People's Army (KPA) is capable of repelling invading physically superior U.S. forces." He singles out three critical factors that will assure victory: "The first is mental, the spirit of martyrdom and discipline; the second intellectual, the art of war; and the third physical, weapons. The third is ineffective in the absence of the first two."

Quite a few *ulema* would interpret Kim Jong-il's masterplan as a form of defensive jihad. Kim Myong-chol explains it with the relevant terminology: "Kim Jong-il has embraced the *tamul*-inspired (*tamul* is an ancient *Koguryo* term meaning standing up to a big power, developing newer weapons and restoring the lost land to settle long-standing scores with the enemy) army-first policy, upholding the banner of the *samjoku* (three-legged black bird symbolizing three gods—heaven, man and the good earth; it also symbolizes the sun, life, harmony and people). He has successfully equipped the KPA with nuclear weapons, including hydrogen bombs, and their intercontinental means of delivery, after transforming the whole land into a national underground fortress."

This "national underground fortress," according to him, is "now capable of detonating hydrogen bombs far above the metropolises of the U.S. in case of war." Warnings are predictably apocalyptic: "U.S. attacks on missile sites and nuclear facilities in the country would all too naturally shower massive lethal radioactive fallout on the Japanese archipelago in a quantity produced by 150 hydrogen bombs."

Against a "national underground fortress" Axis of Evil bluster simply does not cut it. "Unlike the other so-called 'axis of evil' states, North Korea is a nuclear-weapons state and has the will and capability to torch urban U.S. With history as the guide, the North Koreans are great at badly mauling big enemies. They routed Sui China and Tang China. They routed the Toyotomi invasion forces out of Korea. They were the first to drive fear into U.S. troops... North Korea controlled ground warfare in the last Korean War with Korean pilots downing many U.S. warplanes. They helped Egypt win the fourth Mideast war with Israel and the Vietnamese win the liberation war with the U.S."

Bewildered Washington may have to come to grips to how, according to Kim Myong-chol, it was the U.S. itself that facilitated North Korea's membership into the nuclear club. After that "Kim has lost any appetite for talks with the U.S. His interest is in how to settle the long-standing scores of the Korean people with the U.S."

If only Iran had deployed 10% of this ICBM-laden rhetoric. As much as hawks in the Republican Guards might love it Iran could never afford to choose this kind of confrontation because it actually develops a peaceful nuclear research program—as the IAEA has conclusively established. An array of scientific studies have proved that even if Iran was developing a nuclear weapon it could not be able to produce one before at least 2015. Should that happen, with Iranian territory sanctuarized, it would be goodbye to all neocon dreams of privatizing Iranian oil and gas, blocking off China and the Asian Energy Security Grid to the benefit of the U.S.

As it stands there is absolutely no IAEA evidence of a bunch of Iranian scientists buried deep underground in the Dasht-e Kavir desert concocting a bomb. There may have been secret contacts with Kim Jong-ilistan. But this proves nothing. The tragedy is that for the Bush administration any hypothesis is enough to warrant a preemptive attack using tactical nuclear weapons like the B61-11 NEP thermonuclear bomb against a nonexistent nuclear weapons program. Iran in this case would fall in the category of a "rogue enemy" who is "developing" WMDs, according to the *Doctrine for Joint Nuclear Operations* (DNJO). Samir Amin has stressed that U.S. threats against Iraq, North Korea and Iran regarding WMDs are nothing "compared to the effective use of these weapons by the U.S. (the bombs on Hiroshima and Nagasaki, the use of chemical weapons in Vietnam, the threat of using nuclear weapons in future conflicts)."

It's enlightening to compare Iran's program with Brazil's. In May 2006 Brazil launched a uranium enrichment center for its power plants. The rationale: it will "save Brazil millions of dollars it now spends to enrich fuel at Urenco, the European enrichment consortium," according to Brazilian Science and Technology Minister Sergio Rezende. The point is Brazil's energy self-sufficiency. Nobody in Washington thought that Brazil would start building a tropical bomb.

Brazil is already one of Globalistan's leaders in alternative energy with its groundbreaking ethanol programme—a successful, commercially viable alternative to gasoline. In 2006, according to the Brazilian government, energy exports for the first time balanced imports. The success is due to ethanol, produced out of sugar-cane. The first "conversible" Brazilian cars rolling on either ethanol or gasoline were introduced in 2003, first by Volkswagen and then by others such as GM and Ford (they will try the same in the U.S. And some American states may even import Brazilian ethanol). Most gas stations in Brazil sell gasoline, Super and ethanol. By 2006, a litre of ethanol cost only 53 cents, compared to 99 cents for gas. According to the Cambridge Energy Research Associates (CERA), ethanol has replaced 40% of the country's consumption of gasoline. And the only way is up.

For the future, Brazil bets on a mix between biofuels and nuclear power. It is already self-sufficient in oil. It wants to be self-sufficient, period: the name of the game for Brazil is independence (while the name of the game for globalization is interdependence). Tehran may rightfully ask: If Brazil can pursue its civilian nuclear program, why not us? Their civilian nuclear programs are both on the same stage. How could a U.S. preemptive nuclear strike against Iran be possibly justified under these circumstances?

Iran may also argue its nuclear program was in fact set off by the U.S.-supported Shah in 1973. At the time Western Corporatistan was rubbing its hands with the mega-lucrative prospect of selling him enrichment technology and nuclear reactors. The Bushehr reactor—now supervised by the Russians—was started by Siemens. Washington in the 1970s never freaked out when the Shah proclaimed Iran's right to possess nuclear weapons. It was Ayatollah Khomeini, the leader of the Islamic Revolution, who closed down Iran's nuclear program. But then Saddam Hussein, supported by the U.S. when he was one of the West's pet dictators, started using banned chemical weapons in the ghastly 1980-1988 Iran-Iraq war. So from an Iranian defensive point of view Bushehr had to be reopened.

Iran can also be puzzled at the way India is now receiving privileged treatment. India, unlike Iran, has not signed the NPT. But the country is treated as an exceptional case. India in effect has been granted—by Washington—its right to enrich uranium and thus develop a civilian nuclear program with no hassles. There's only one condition: the IAEA, up to 2014, must have access to 65% of the country's nuclear installations to verify that dual technology is not being diverted to military use. Eight out of twenty-two nuclear reactors will remain under exclusive control of India. India could not possibly get a better deal. It keeps its privileged relations with both Iran and Russia and even its strategic relation—at least on paper—with China. And under the Project Seabird naval construction programme, India in fact will become the policeman of the Indian Ocean, instead of the U.S.

U.S. nuclear policy boils down to essentially forcing or bribing any nation out of access to nuclear weapons—via a mix of treaties, threats of sanctions and, during the Cold War, the de facto nuclear umbrella provided by one of the two superpowers. The underlying logic is plain and simple double standards. The U.S. may have "contained" South Africa, Brazil, Argentina and Libya. It may have "persuaded" Iraq—through a war and then years of draconian sanctions—to give up what in fact did not exist anymore: Saddam Hussein's regime destroyed its nuclear weapons program way back in 1995, 8 years before Shock and Awe.

But the U.S. has not been able to restrain India and Pakistan from going nuclear. In fact the U.S. tremendously facilitated the Pakistani nuclear program under General Zia during the 1980s. Every year the White House told Congress there was no Pakistani nuclear weapons program. Washington knew China sold missiles to Pakistan. Funds were never a problem; both China and India developed their nuclear weapons when their economies were relatively weak. The U.S. embargo on the Indian Space Research Organization barely registered in Delhi.

Now Ukraine, Belarus and Kazakhstan also have nuclear capacity. The U.S. may strive—in principle—for every nation to respect the NPT. But they reserve themselves their—and Israel's—right to always break any rules and limitations. Israel has never signed the NPT and has never officially announced it is a nuclear power holding up to 600 nuclear weapons.

And when the five Central Asia "stans"—Kazakhstan, Kyrgyzstan, Tajikistan, Uzbekistan and Turkmenistan—announce the creation of a nuclear weapons-free zone, as they did in Almaty in late summer 2006, the Bush administration is against it, warning that "other international treaties could take precedence over the provisions of this treaty, and thus obviate the central objective of creating a zone free of nuclear weapons."

This is a groundbreaking treaty, as it sets up the first nuclear-weapons free zone in the North. Most of the South—from Latin America to Africa and Southeast Asia—is already a nuclear-weapons free zone. Daryl Kimball of the independent Arms Control Association succinctly nailed to OneWorld the real U.S. motives: "This is a very strategic region. The U.S. is reticent to give up the option of deploying nuclear weapons in this region in the future." The U.S. has a key, sprawling military base in Manas airport, in Kyrgyzstan, very close to the capital Bishkek (only a 20 minute-drive away from the Russian base in Kant). The U.S. base is close enough to be monitoring Afghanistan, as it's been doing since 2001; and crucially close enough to be monitoring Russia, China and the energy wealth of the Caspian Sea.

Meanwhile the furore over North Korea and Iran—alleged parallel poles of the *Monty Python*ish "Axis of Evil"—has already spawned a new arms race, this time in Japan, who remains, as Prof. Rhee saw it already in 1999, very "worried" about rising China. Officially, Japan has always denied it wants to be part of Nuclearistan. But Japan has already mastered the nuclear cycle. Iran wants to do the exact same thing for sound economic reasons—so it would not have to rely so much on oil for its industrial development. But Tehran would also relish the possibility (although no one in the theocratic nationalist leadership will ever admit it publicly), under extreme U.S. pressure, to go one step further and, backed up and not backing down, assemble a bomb as a deterrence mechanism.

Immanuel Wallerstein holds a benign judgment, considering that the NPT is condemned to failure "not only in the long run but also in the medium term. The best the U.S. can do in the next 25 years is to somehow contain this process." With unilateral teeth on show this is unlikely. The U.S. wants to inspect Kim Jong-ilistan; but it would never allow the IAEA to inspect the U.S. Wallerstein: "The U.S. trusts it will know how to use such armament wisely and in defense of freedom; a concept seemingly identical to American national interests." Jimmy Carter has routinely denounced U.S. threats to attack non-nuclear states with nuclear weapons. The *Washington Post* has editorialized that "America traverses History like a sleepwalker, armed with its nuclear arsenal."

Pakistan for its part now traverses History wide awake, carrying a miniature Ghauri. In virtually every Pakistani village there's a kitschy statue of a missile against a cavernous background—the Chagai Hills, near the border of southwest Afghanistan, where Pakistan carried its first nuclear tests. The missile is the Ghauri—a copy of the made-in -Kim Jong-ilistan Nodong. Pakistan got the technology by offering North Korea essential info on production and tests of nuclear explosives.

The new nuclear age was actually born in the Rajasthan desert in 1998—with the Hindu nationalist nuclear essay replicated two weeks later by Islamic Pakistan. In this nuclear-laden narrative framed by religious populism, top billing was configured by Western media as the almighty clash of the Hindu bomb versus the Islamic bomb: hopefully, since the fall of 2005, India and Pakistan have installed a "red line" to prevent a nuclear accident.

This bomb clash was in fact globalization giving birth to Nuclearistan. With Globalistan configured as a technophile menu, "nuclear" was just one more technology on offer—like internet porn. Hence the ensuing think tank blues. The North Korea bomb would lead to the Japan, South Korea and Taiwan bomb. The Iran bomb would lead to the Turkey, Saudi Arabia and Egypt bomb. And the whole epic drama played out among ancient, traditional, proud Asian cultures impenetrable to Western linear thinking. How to figure out Kim Jong-ilistan's ways—selling weapons to any bidder to finance its nuclear effort? How to figure out the post-USSR nuclear black market?

The NPT is like a villain in a gory B-movie, always reluctant to meet its maker. Before killing the NPT *again* in the Iranian case, the Bush administration had already killed it with Shock and Awe on Iraq. For the Bush administration the NPT is in fact useless. The point has never been the WMDs themselves; it's always the "rogue," "evil" regimes that may possess them. So fundamentally this is a regime change issue. Washington at the same time does not want to abide to any treaty precluding its divine right to develop mini-nukes, Star Wars, or employ its preemptive nukes in any given zone (especially juicy Central Asia).

As Kim Jong-ilistan proliferates, Taiwan may inevitably proliferate, and Japan may inevitably proliferate; but in parallel the U.S. actually wants both Taiwan and Japan as participating co-actors in Star Wars. "Good guys" in the end may get away with everything. From a U.S.-as- unrivalled-superpower point of view, the ideal situation in North Asia is the current status quo: a divided China and a divided Korea. As Henry K. Liu noted on *Asia Times* in a series about U.S.-China relations, Taiwan and Korea are the relics of "two unfinished civil wars in Asia into which the U.S. interjected itself at the beginning of the Cold War and linked as key elements in its policy of global containment of communist expansion. The Taiwan issue was created by the U.S. in response to an escalation of the Korean civil war. It is not surprising, therefore, that the recurring crises over Chinese military warnings on escalating Taiwanese maneuvers toward independence are also linked to a mounting crisis over the North Korean nuclear weapons program."

Liu's assessment is realistic: "If History is any guide, there is little reason for optimism that the current crisis over the Korean nuclear/missiles issue can be defused or that the Taiwan issue can be resolved peacefully without fundamental changes in U.S. policy."

As far as "evil" states are concerned, a booming global market for dual-use technology spells virtually impossible proliferation containment. Economic sanctions are counter-productive: under Globalistan logic you may end up punishing delocalized operations of U.S. multinationals as well. Regime change is meaningless: as a nuclear power you cannot expect to impose non-proliferation rules to be duly followed by the non-nuclear world. Moreover the problem of National Defense has not been tackled by the avowed nuclear powers. Is it a sovereign right for all nations? If it is, everyone has the right to go nuclear. If it's not, who's going to guarantee these nations that sooner or later they will not be shocked and awed with a preemptive, possibly nuclear, attack?

Once again it took "unofficial spokesman" Kim Myong-chol to outline the "far-reaching implications" of Kim Jong-ilistan's nuclear test. Writing for *Asia Times,* he praised "the process of achieving the long-elusive goal of neutralizing the American intervention in Korean affairs and bringing together North and South Korea under the umbrella of a confederated state." He also stressed "the sole reason for the development of nuclear weapons is more than 50 years of direct exposure to naked nuclear threats and sanctions from the U.S. The Kim administration seeks to commit nuclear weapons to actual use against the U.S. in case of war, never to use them as a tool of negotiations."

Kim Myong-chol was adamant: "Nuclear-armed North Korea will be a major boon to China and Russia," who are both "friendless in case of war with the U.S." China should welcome it because "the nuclear deterrence of North Korea is a major factor in reducing U.S. military pressure on China on the question of the independence of Taiwan."

And it doesn't matter what Japan thinks or does: "The main enemy to North Korea is the U.S... Acquisition of hundreds of nuclear weapons by Japan and South Korea will not have any serious impact on the total balance of nuclear power. Japan and South Korea have too much to lose in a nuclear war with North Korea, while North Korea has little."

The final point had to be the death (again!) of the NPT: "Had the Americans been steadfast in upholding the nuclear Non-proliferation Treaty by reducing their nuclear weapons and respecting the sovereignty and independence of the non-nuclear states, North Korea would not have felt any need to defend itself with nuclear weapons."

So Kim Jong-ilistan's logic tell us that were it not for almost 6 years of non-stop threats, sanctions and apocalyptic rhetoric by the Bush administration, North Korea would have never been driven to build a bomb and the delivery systems capable of transporting radioactive hell to Seattle or L.A. And Bush better not try a pre-emptive strike: North Korea will retaliate with nuclear war.

Kim Jong-ilistan had finally made its point: if this Bang does not force the U.S. to listen, nothing will. The press in Asia was bewildered. In South Korea, the *Chosun Ilbo* worried this was "a very different world," where the "survival strategy" of South Korea was at stake. The *Joong-a Ilbo* lamented that the Korean peninsula was "pungled into extreme chaos." In Hong Kong, the *South China Morning Post* lamented China's "diplomatic failure." In Beijing, the *China Daily* pleaded for the return to the negotiating table. For the *Yomiuri Shimbun* in Tokyo, this might be the chance for China and Japan to start talking seriously.

From Liquid War to Fissile War. Dear Leader Kim Jong-il did know how to open Pandora's box. And because the legality is so fuzzy, and pre-emptive attacks can now be launched by the Holy Ghost (no justification necessary), many nodes of the non-nuclear world, out of pure self-defense instinct or out of fear, are bound to seriously start considering their accession to Nuclearistan. Call Kim Jong-ilistan a trendsetter.

~ 17 ~

PETROEUROSTAN?

The souls of emperors and shoemakers are forged in the same mould.

—**Montaigne**

The relentless demonization of Iran may be explained in the larger context of petrodollar warfare, a key branch of Liquid—and Viscous—War.

Since mid-2005 selected corridors of the energy wars flux have been transfixed by a silent soap opera whose outcome has the potential to incur the Wrath of the Gods: the birth pangs of the Iranian Oil Bourse. Once again the Islamic Republic of Iran was at the center of the plot—with its desire to directly compete against London's International Petroleum Exchange (IPE) as well as the New York Mercantile Exchange (NYMEX), both owned by American corporations (IPE was bought in 2001 by a consortium including BP, Goldman Sachs and Morgan Stanley). What Iran was about to do was absolute anathema in the Anglo-American world: to directly challenge Anglo-American, banking-energy Corporatistan's domination of the international oil trade.

It makes sense that OPEC member countries try to set up an alternative to both NYMEX and the IPE, which exercise a de facto monopoly of the oil and gas market, are comfortable to exploit volatility and are able to wreak havoc against the interests of producer countries. An avalanche of contracts related to Iranian or Saudi oil, for instance, are indexed to the price of the U.K.'s North Sea Brent oil, whose production is terminally declining.

The plot thickened considerably by the spring of 2006. Russian sources leaked that the Iranian Bourse had been registered in early May 2006—but still no one knew who was in it. Then on May 10, 2006 Vladimir Putin announced that from July 1st the ruble would be convertible. The inevitable consequence would be the creation of a Russian Bourse to sell its oil and gas: Russia exports 15.2% of the world's oil (compared to Iran's 5.8%) and 25.8% of the world's gas.

The first-ever oil, gas and petrochemical exchange in the Islamic Republic—also the first in the Middle East and the first within OPEC—has been welcomed by scores of oil-producing as well as oil-consuming countries. The immediate consequence of the opening of the Iranian International Petroleum Exchange (IIPE), commonly referred to as the Kish bourse, registered in the free zone (declared by the Shah) of Kish island, in early 2005, would be a new Persian Gulf blend-denominated contract appearing in the global oil market. Kish, the Iranian Saint-Tropez in the Persian Gulf, is the perfect sort of *laissez faire* place for the Bourse: no Khomeini mega-portraits, an apotheosis of duty free malls, hordes of young honeymooners shopping for made-in-Europe appliances.

In the summer of 2005 I was received at the Petroleum Ministry in central Tehran by Mohammad Javad Asemipour, the executive in charge of the Kish bourse since its inception. Asemipour, a former deputy Oil Minister, had already established Iran's metal exchange. At the time, the soap opera was still in the initial chapters. The bourse, he said, should start operating "in March 2006, dealing at first with petrochemical products" and then with what everybody wants—light-sulfur Caspian Sea crude (as this book went to press the Bourse was still not on). Although this was a project started during the Khatami presidency, the Ahmadinejad government was fully behind it. This was not going to be an Iranian-style exchange, but "an international exchange, fully integrated in the world economy."

Asemipour led a technical committee on long, extensive rounds of consultation including contacts with both the IPE and NYMEX, as well as in Singapore, Hong Kong and Shanghai—"contacts with 180 stock markets, institutes and universities all over the world," before the decision to open the bourse. Chris Cook, a former IPE director, was associated with the project from the beginning, in 2001. Writing in *Asia Times* in January 2006 Cook explained how, in a letter to the then governor of the Iranian Central Bank, he "pointed out that the structure of global oil markets massively favors intermediary traders and particularly investment banks, and that both consumers and producers such as Iran are adversely affected by this. I recommended that Iran consider as a matter of urgency the creation of a Middle Eastern energy exchange, and particularly a new Persian Gulf benchmark oil price."

Based on his extensive conversations in Iran—including with former President Khatami—Cook also became convinced over the years that the Iranian nuclear program is civilian, legal and for the Iranian authorities vital for assuring the country's economic independence.

The Kish Bourse shareholders are the National Iranian Oil Co. (20%); National Petrochemical Co. (25%); National Iranian Oil Refining and Distribution Co. (20%); Iran Oil Industry Pension and Deposit Fund (5%); Tehran Stock Exchange (10%);

Kish Free Zone Organization (10%); and the Mostazafan Foundation (10%). The financial, economic and legal consortium in charge of the bourse includes the Tehran Stock Exchange, ICT of Tehran and South Korean companies. A building was purchased in Kish island and hardware and software were bought—the same as in the Tehran stock market, integrated with Europe.

Asemipour said "IPE and NYMEX wanted to implement their conceptual model, but we decided to have our own system." An extraordinary fact is that "the bourse employs a group of former IPE managers in London as our advisers. They are all Westerners." Thus, it was not a conspiracy; these people designed and integrated different models to come up with the unique Iranian mix.

The secret of the success of both IPE and NYMEX is the abundance of both sellers and buyers. So Asemipour went to London rallying commodity traders to join the Kish bourse, and he hoped both NYMEX and the IPE would cooperate with Kish. He was very precise in asserting that the Kish bourse is a national, independent bourse with its own system, based on NYMEX, IPE, the London Metal Exchange and the Singapore and Vienna bourses. "It's not a stock market." Kish will do "paper and physical transactions and will deal in petrochemical products, gas products, oil and its products and downstream petrochemical products such as hydrocarbons and polymers."

As far as Iran's Petroleum Ministry is concerned, the absolute priorities for the country are to attract much needed foreign investment in the energy sector and to expand its address book of oil buyers. In this context, the Kish bourse could not possibly fail—with Iran exporting at least 2.7 millions barrels of oil a day by the mid-2000s and producing 13 million tons of petrochemicals a year.

The whole point, for Iran, is to eliminate the middlemen. "Especially in crude oil, there's no Iranian company in the oil market at the moment," said Asemipour. Oil trading firms—most of which trade in other commodities and even invest into upstream oil—include Glencore, Arcadia, Vitol, Philip Brothers (owned by Citicorp), Cargill, Koch and Taurus. Enron—until its debacle—used to be one of the most profitable. Big Banking is heavy into it—from Citicorp to Deutsche Bank, Goldman Sachs, Morgan Stanley and Mitsui from Japan. Some oil companies like TotalFinaElf and Exxon Mobil trade under their own names. The Russians use trade subsidiaries.

It's an open secret in the oil business that high oil prices are not due to the ghost of Osama bin Laden, the odd hurricane in the Gulf of Mexico or OPEC shortages. The main profiteers are middlemen—"traders" to put it nicely, "speculators" to put it bluntly. Refiners usually have buy options on oil supplies—so they won't be subjected to shortages. They almost never buy directly from producers.

They buy on the open market, which means the NYMEX or the IPE. Up to the year 2000 IPE was a closed shop monopolized by roughly 35 traders—most of them Corporatistan. After a lot of grumbling regarding price manipulations, IPE was forced to open its auction room to outsiders. But the big players remain the Big Oil firms. A producer—for example, Iran—knows for how much he sells oil to the trader. But he never knows for how much the trader will sell the oil to a manufacturer. That's how mountains of petrodollar profits are made.

Asemipour said that "in Iran, we are deprived of revenues from future and optional deals. Most are carried out in the IPE and in NYMEX, or even in SIMEX in Singapore. For us, an oil bourse is a national necessity." The point, he emphasized, is "to manage the risk price, and thus increase Iran's income, and at the same time bring prices down on an international level. We will be selling to everybody in the bourse. Transactions will be transparent, and we will be able to prevent monopolies. We will not only announce prices but manage prices."

The US$ 60 billion question has been inescapable: will the Kish bourse trade in petroeuros instead of petrodollars? Asemipour's answer in 2005 could not have been more diplomatic: "You let the market make the decisions. The exchange rate between the euro and the dollar is already a factor. The players in the exchange will decide the prices and the currency." It could be even a basket of currencies, including the dollar, the euro, the yen and the yuan.

The consequences of a successful Kish bourse may be unprecedented.

Any oil-buying country needs dollars—the global standard. This means keeping dollars in their Central Banks. But with Iran—followed by other oil-producing countries—accepting euros, the more people choose to buy in the Kish bourse paying in euros or even in a basket of currencies including the euro, the more trade volumes at both the dollar-dependent NYMEX and IPE will fall. Moreover, other OPEC members as well as oil producers from the Caspian will inevitably be seduced by the advantages of selling at Kish—with no middlemen.

For middle-income countries and lower income countries all over the South this will be a more fair and more evenly distributed system than the current one which is only beneficial to the U.S. And once Iran's civilian nuclear program is on (barring U.S. bombing) there will be more Iranian oil and gas on the market. So prices inevitably will fall, and the winner once again will be the oil-importing South.

William R. Clark, manager of performance improvement at Johns Hopkins University School of Medicine, has argued in his book *Petrodollar Warfare* that the invasion and occupation in Iraq was as much about controlling oil fields as controlling global oil trade.

Clark has been one among scores of fine oil geopolitics analysts who pointed to Saddam Hussein's key November 2000 move of switching all his reserves from dollars to euros and trading Iraqi oil only in euros.

Washington had to make OPEC understand that any move towards the petroeuro would incur the Wrath of the Gods. Like clockwork, in June 2003, two months into the occupation, "liberated" Iraq reverted to petrodollars.

Kish will inevitably provoke the emergence of an oil marker in euros—although in the first stage it may be in a basket of currencies. The three current oil markers—all in dollars—are West Texas Intermediate crude (WTI), Norway Brent crude, and UAE Dubai crude. Iran had been accepting euros from E.U. and Asian buyers since the spring of 2003. Russia, Hugo Chávez's Venezuela and even Saudi Arabia have been tempted to diversify from the petrodollar. Since 2003-2004 Russia and China have both increased their Central Bank reserves in euros. For both China and Japan the diversification into euros is ideal as protection against dollar depreciation.

As the Bourse opens Central Banks around the world would inevitably diversify their reserves into more euros. For the E.U. is a logical move, as it buys 70% of Iran's oil. For Russia is also a logical move, as it sells two-thirds of its oil to E.U., but still not in euros. Russia is also getting rid of depreciating dollars: it prefers to hold reserves in gold.

Arab OPEC members—who trade heavily with the E.U.—would also prefer the euro as an antidote to dollar depreciation. The single best reason for why Britain did not adopt the euro has to do with the IPE. If Britain dropped the pound, the IPE would have to trade in petroeuros.

So in a nutshell the emergence of a fourth oil marker in euros may lead the way to the petroeuro global oil trade. It makes sense as the E.U. imports much more oil from OPEC than the U.S., and 45% of Middle East imports also come from the E.U. For most major players—the E.U., China, Russia, Japan and the Arab world—the petroeuro seems a much better deal than the petrodollar.

Iran is carefully orchestrating its moves. Kish may not only challenge the hegemony of IPE and NYMEX—and thus of the Anglo-American compound London-New York; it has the potential to establish the Middle East as a Mecca of global trade. "With changes in the geography of demand—India and China—and integrated with Singapore, Hong Kong and Shanghai," Asemipour defined Kish as "our gate for Iran to lead in trading. We cannot build a Chinese wall around Iran."

Up to 70% of the world's exports, around 60% of global currency reserves, 80% of all currency transactions and 70% of all bank credits are still dollar-denominated. There may be around US$ 100 trillion around the globe circulating as a universal currency. The euro for the moment does not even reach 10% of this gargantuan figure.

There's always the possibility the petroeuro might one day defeat the petrodollar. But it may not be the case of the Kish Oil Bourse—defined by some as the real Iranian weapon of mass destruction—being the messenger of doom. Of course this has not prevented wild speculation on Washington's designs to "neutralize" the Kish Bourse —including infiltration of a computer virus, a *coup d'état* and even the dreaded unilateral, pre-emptive nuclear strike.

Igor Tomberg, a researcher at the Center for Energy Studies at the Institute of World Economy and International Relations, Russian Academy of Sciences, argued by the summer of 2006 that IPE and NYMEX quotes for Russian Urals oil "are so far removed from the real cost of oil, and are influenced by so many speculations and other factors, that it is simply ridiculous to view them as a real indicator of price." But he was careful to add "the idea that Iran's switch to euros will ruin the dollar is preposterous because oil prices may be quoted in one currency while payments may be made in another."

Tomberg clarified that "what really influences the dollar's value, and the choice of reserve currency, is a massive switch to payments in a different currency by real buyers and sellers. The start of a euro-denominated exchange will not by itself affect the dollar."

Tomberg quoted the former head of the Russian Central Bank Viktor Gerashchenko, now chairing the Yukos Board of Directors: "If you trade in oil, stick to the dollar. I believe that in the next ten years nobody will quote oil in euros, rubles, yuan, or anything else. The price is going to be set in dollars no matter what, especially considering the size of the U.S. economy. Only China may catch up."

What Gerashchenko had not taken into account are two crucial developments: the Russia-E.U. negotiations leading towards a far-reaching 2007 strategic agreement; and Russia making the ruble convertible while at the same time progressively decreasing its transactions in petrodollars. As Russia downsizes its dollar holdings, the same may happen in the long run with China. The real WMD would be the day that Russia turns to euros *en masse*. Meanwhile, with a weak dollar and high oil prices, petrodollars—especially for huge importer China—don't make much sense.

F. William Engdahl in his seminal *A Century of War* detailed *"a new phase of U.S. global hegemony in which the petrodollar export earnings of OPEC oil lands would be recycled into the hands of the major New York and London banks and re-lent in the form of U.S. dollar loans to oil-deficit countries such as Brazil and Argentina, creating what soon came to be known as the Latin American debt crisis."*

The point, argued Engdahl writing in *Asia Times*, "was not that the U.S. dollar became a 'petro' currency. The point was that the reserve status of the dollar, now a paper currency, was bolstered by the 400% increase in world demand for dollars to buy oil."

Engdahl stresses "the status of the dollar as reserve currency depends on the status of the United States as the world's unchallenged military superpower. In a sense, since August 1971 the dollar is no longer backed by gold. Instead, it is backed by F-16s and Abrams battle tanks, operating in some 130 U.S. bases around the world, defending liberty and the dollar." For the moment, argues Engdahl, "there are no signs of Japanese, E.U. or other dollar holders engaging in dollar-asset liquidation. Even China, unhappy as it is with Washington's bully politics, seems reluctant to rouse the American dragon to fury." That would be a de facto declaration of war on the Full Spectrum Dominance—real or imagined—of the U.S. The only—still far-fetched—counterpunch would be an iron clad union of Eurasian interests grouping the E.U., Russia, China and Japan.

Or change can come via disaster—Liquid War.

For the moment, in the world economy, what we have is a dizzying speed virtual circus orchestrated by Bauman's nomad elites of global liquid modernity—a circus providing unheard of mega-profits for those able to speculate in highly leveraged, mega-risky derivatives. Derivatives were estimated to be worth an astonishing US$ 180 trillion by 2006—17 times the U.S. GDP. Warren Buffet described them as "instruments of mass destruction."

After such frenzy the Fall may be as inevitable as in a Poe horror story. Samir Amin has detailed how the "substance of the U.S. deficit is covered by capital inversions from Europe and Japan, and from the South (rich oil countries and comprador classes from all the Third World countries, including the poorest), to which one must add the bleeding applied under the label of debt service imposed to almost the totality of the countries in the periphery of the world system."

Immanuel Wallerstein is extremely skeptical of a "superpower proclaiming its superiority over the world by the affirmation of military capacity"; this means all power to the industrial-military complex, which is a parallel economy, to the detriment of "investing the same money to create more productive enterprises in the long run."

Wallerstein sees only two possibilities for the U.S. in the next ten years: either to follow the hawkish way, or to be sensible. He sees no way of preventing the country from further sliding "into decadence as the determining force in world affairs during the next ten years." So "the real dilemma is not whether the U.S. is in decadence as an hegemonic power, but whether it will be able to find a way to fall with grace, with the least harm for the world and itself."

As Gore Vidal—America's Tacitus - wrote in the London *Independent*, "celebrating" the five years of 9/11, "busy republics tend to turn themselves into empires. Certainly, the French intellectual godfather to the American republic, Montesquieu, warned that republics which took the empire route would cease to be republics altogether while Vico, in his cyclic view of human societies, saw imperial republics evolving into dictatorships, chaos, barbarism. In the last five years American behavior in the Middle East has been barbarous and will not soon be forgiven."

The lessons of History are iron-clad. An Empire has only two reasons to go to war—in self-defense or to increase its wealth. Professor Paul Kennedy of Yale, in the seminal *The Rise and Fall of the Great Powers* has conclusively demonstrated that empires collapse by military overstretch. That's exactly the case with the U.S. in the first decade of the 21st Century.

All empires—Akkad, Sumeria, Babylonia, Assyria, Persia, Macedonia, Greece, Carthage, Rome, Mali, the Mongols, Tokugawa, Gupta, Khmer, the Habsburgs, the Incas, the Aztec, the Mayas, Spanish, Dutch, Ottoman, French, British, Soviet— inevitably fall. Neo-Luddite Kirkpatrick Sale, a keen student of Empires, has determined four reasons that explain their fall with almost 100% accuracy.

1) Environmental degradation. Even Pentagon studies have predicted "abrupt climate changes" within a decade, leading to "catastrophic" shortages of water and energy, warfare that "would define human life."

2) Economic meltdown. "I foresee that in just a few years the dollar will be so battered that the oil states will no longer want to operate in that currency and will turn to the euro instead, and China will let the yuan float against the dollar, effectively making this nation bankrupt and powerless, unable to control economic life within its borders much less abroad."

3) Military overstretch. "The American empire, which began its worldwide reach well before Bush II, now has some 446,000 active troops at more than 725 acknowledged (and any number secret) bases in at least 38 countries around the world, plus

a formal "military presence" in no less than 153 countries, and nearly a dozen fully armed courier fleets on all the oceans. Talk about overstretch: the U.S. is less than 5% of the world's population... And as anti-American sentiment continues to spread and darken—in all the Muslim countries, in much of Europe, in much of Asia—and as more countries refuse the 'structural adjustments' that our IMF-led globalization requires, it is quite likely that the periphery of our empire will begin resisting our dominance, militarily if necessary."

4) Domestic dissent and upheaval. "Traditional empires end up collapsing from within as well as often being attacked from without, and so far the level of dissent within the U.S. has not reached the point of rebellion or secession—thanks both to the increasing repression of dissent and escalation of fear in the name of 'homeland security' and to the success of our modern version of bread and circuses, a unique combination of entertainment, sports, television, internet sex and games, consumption, drugs, liquor and religion that effectively deadens the general public into stupor."

Sale thinks a combination of all these causes may bring the fall of the American Empire before 2020.

To compound matters we find the extreme social tensions caused by inequality. There are 400 Americans worth way more than US$ 1 billion. The top 1% of the U.S. elite is worth an average of US$ 15 million net. Middle class holdings are worth an average of US$ 81,000 (which is considered an immense fortune all over the South). But 30% of U.S. households are worth less than US$ 10,000. And 17% of the households are in the negative.

As Billmon, one of the most lucid voices in U.S. Blogistan put it, also "celebrating" the 5th anniversary of 9/11: "The physical symptoms—a lost war, a derelict city, a Potemkin memorial hastily erected in a vacant lot—aren't nearly as alarming as the moral and intellectual paralysis that seems to have taken hold of the system. The old feedback mechanisms are broken or in deep disrepair, leaving America with an opposition party that doesn't know how (or what) to oppose, a military run by uniformed yes men, intelligence czars who couldn't find their way through a garden gate with a GPS locator, TV networks that don't even pretend to cover the news unless there's a missing white woman or a suspected child rapist involved, and talk radio hosts who think nuking Mecca is the solution to all our problems in the Middle East. We've got think tanks that can't think, security agencies that can't secure and accounting firms that can't count (except when their clients ask them to make 2+2=5). Our churches are either annexes to shopping malls, halfway homes for pederasts, or GOP precinct headquarters in disguise. Our economy is based on asset bubbles, defense contracts and an open-ended line of credit from the People's

Bank of China, and we still can't push the poverty rate down or the median wage up."

The trend in the mid-to-long term would be Euro Up in global trading. The U.S. economy and lifestyle would still depend on cheap oil. Yet the U.S. may not be able to control more oil fields as oil production declines, with the project of controlling the remaining oil in the Gulf through hardcore threats or invasion actually floundering in Iraq. Under this scenario, what's left? Liquid War.

Iraq going wrong legitimizes grabbing Iran. The "Greater Middle East" is the only Bush/Cheney system legacy: but in true "Empire of Chaos" fashion, instead of legating "only" two wars to their succession they may legate *three*: Afghanistan, Iraq and Iran. In Dick Cheney's—and, perhaps reluctantly, U.S. Big Oil's—Globalistan the Holy Grail is physical control of oil fields: that's how you guarantee the American way of life, you profit from high oil prices, and you deliver a blow to emerging strategic competitors.

Of the myriad of papers dedicated to the U.S.-Iran showdown one of the most precise is *The End of the 'Summer of Diplomacy': assessing military options in Iran*, by retired USAF Col. Sam Gardiner, available at the Century Foundation website (www.tcf.org) Col. Gardiner has conducted war gaming on Iran, knows how a war would be a disaster, and clearly identified how the Bush administration's discourse and actions boxed itself in nowhere to go except Liquid War.

Col. Gardiner lists all the major war "reasons": massive U.S. intelligence gaps on Iran's nuclear program producing "further pressure to attack"; the convergence of "red lines" ("Israel's red line is enrichment. Now the "red line has drifted closer to Israel's. Bush has repeatedly said that the United States could not allow Iran to have the knowledge to make a weapon"); the portrayal of Iran as "the Central Banker of Terrorism"; the supreme goal of regime change; and messianic Bush himself, convinced he's on another *Blues Brothers*-style Mission from God.

U.S. commandos have been inserting themselves in Iran since 2004. They are extremely active in Iranian Baluchistan. Gardiner's information ties exactly with what I learned in Iran in the spring of 2006. Gardiner tells the story of his meeting with the Iranian ambassador to the IAEA, Ali Asghar Soltanieh: "I told him I had read that the Iranians were accusing the United States of supporting elements in Baluchistan. I asked him how they knew that. Without any hesitation, Soltanieh told me that they have captured militants who confessed that they were working with the Americans."

After going through a detailed military analysis, Gardiner concludes "the United States can and will conduct the operation by itself. There may be low-visibility support from Israel and the U.K., and France may be consulted. But it will be an American operation." Sensibly, and unlike the civilizationist-clash brigades, Gardiner knows "air strikes are unlikely either to eliminate the nuclear program or to bring about the overthrow of the Islamic regime in Iran." The cataclysmic consequences are well known, from Pipelineistan sabotage to Muqtada al-Sadr raising hell in Iraq, from Iran blocking Gulf oil flow in the Strait of Hormuz to Syria being pushed into the war. Oil may hit US$ 130 a barrel—that's the minimum figure taken for granted in Western Europe. A global recession will be inevitable. Hugo Chávez and Vladimir Putin, non-Middle East oil producers, will be swimming (even more) in petrodollars—and arguably paving their way to petroeuros.

Gardiner, ever the military man, never mentions the crucial, Cheney Big Prize element: we need those oil fields. For this to happen regime change is an absolute must. But whatever the military outcome, Iran will not abandon its nuclear program. And there will not be a velvet revolution plus regime change. All this death and destruction will amount to nothing. The whole, sad docudrama could be titled (but for different reasons) *The Sorrows of Empire*, like the splendid, homonymous Chalmers Johnson book.

Wim Dierckxsens, author of *The Limits of Capitalism: An Approach to Globalization without Neo-liberalism*, has extensively proposed a better way of regulating capitalism—for instance by taxing speculative capital, eliminating tax havens and replacing pension funds with more retirement protection. He has also argued that the Russians may actually be jealous of the Kish Bourse—and that's why they also want to set up their own. Or perhaps the Russians are dying for the Bush/Cheney system to embark on one more cataclysmic strategic blunder and unilaterally bomb Iran—chaos exponentially increased by Liquid War.

Dierckxsens points out that "the division of the world market via war historically has led to the opposite: the fractioning of the capitalist system. The First World War led to the Bolshevik Revolution and the appearance of the Soviet Union. The Second World War significantly increased the process of disconnection of the capitalist system with the appearance of the Chinese and Vietnamese revolutions, North Korea and the expansion of the Soviet Union to the east and west. An eventual global war implies a strong deregulation of international trade, which would cause a mortal crisis for transnational companies depending on such trade. Massive disconnection is a logical consequence. This would force a massive and generalized substitution of imports in peripheral countries. These facts would stimulate a probable generalized disconnection which would probably imply a mortal crisis in the capitalist system."

NIMBLE BOOKS LLC

We should expect in this case "the worst global depression in the history of capitalism," which would signal in effect the end of the capitalist system as we know it. We're not there yet. But that notorious geopolitician of our hearts and minds, Bob Dylan, might say we're fast approaching it, "90 miles an hour on a dead end street."

~ 18 ~

CONDOFORNIA VERSUS SLUMISTAN

When you got nothing

You got nothing to lose

You're invisible now

You got no secrets to conceal

—**Bob Dylan**, Like a Rolling Stone

The Man controls the day

While WE!

Control the night

—**Urban Takeover**, Bad Ass

*Nomads invented a war machine against the State. History has never un-
derstood nomadism, the book has never understood what's outside. Throughout a long history, the State was the model of the book and of thought: the
logos, the philosopher- King, the transcendence of Idea, the interiority of concept, the Republic of spirit, the tribunal of reason, the officials of thinking,
Man as a legislator. What pretention of the state to be the interiorized image
of a world order, and to root Man.*

⁻**Gilles Deleuze and Félix Guattari**, Mille Plateaux, *1980*

This may be the ultimate 21st Century time bomb. More than half of the world's
population is now urban. One out of every three global urban citizens lives in
slums. By 2020, according to the U.N., global poverty may reach no less than half of
the world's urban population. By 2030 there will be more urban citizens in Africa
than in the whole of Europe; and there may be 2 billion people barely surviving in

slums all over the world. How will they find work? How will they get access to health and education? What if they start rioting *en masse*—as free market social Darwinism erases any possibility of social cohesion? Prospects are extremely grim. After two decades of "development"—which then turned, via the Washington Consensus, into "globalization"—the U.N. found out that no less than 2.8 billion people, almost half of the world population, are poorer than they were in the early 1980s.

First there was the City-State. Then the Nation-State. Now geopolitics is some-how doomed: dissolving states are drifting towards globalization-induced *metropo-litics*, fueled by "aero-orbital deterritorialization," as configured by architect and cross-cultural deconstructionist Paul Virilio. In our new world Ministries of De-fense, crammed with decomposing weapons to which hyperterrorism is oblivious, are being replaced by an omni-present Ministry of Fear. Virilio, in his 2004 book *Ville Panique* ("Panic City") observes "in recent conflicts, losses are at 80% from the side of civilians while in traditional war it was exactly the opposite." So now "every self-respecting war is a bit of a WAR AGAINST THE CIVILIANS!" (Iraq during the 12 years of U.N. sanctions plus post-Shock and Awe; southern Lebanon in 2006; Palestine for the last four decades). The next total war—which is in fact ongoing Liquid War—is nothing but a global civil war. Virilio: "The metastasis does not concern nations and their institutions anymore, but their populations offered in holocaust to chaos."

In this context, rationality is over: "rogue state" after all is not even a political concept, much less "axis of Evil," which smashes any rationality in the concert of nations. The name of the game is hysterical hyper-communication: as Virilio puts it, "a trans-political emotion on the scale of so-called global civilization." Political intelligence is gone, as political "re-presentation" disappears to the benefit of "presentation" (somebody call Karl neo-Macchiavelli Rove). Even psy ops spin doctors are becoming redundant: hysteria is oblivious to reflection and contextuali-zation. In an infowar global environment, information is above all militarized: when the mirror of reality is smashed, there is no more perception of what is right or wrong, true or false, just and unjust. Virilio refers as an example of this logic to the Pentagon's armies allowing the looting in April 2003 of the Archeological Museum and the Baghdad library—the treasures of Sumer, the memory of Mesopotamia. Martin Amis later wrote about Donald Rumsfeld's reaction at the time, "looking like he had sniffed a mountain of coke." Rumsfeld said: "Stuff happens." Amis noted this was "the remark of someone not just corrupt but floridly vulgarized by power."

My own reaction was equivalent to what Virilio would later conceptualize, "in-fowar affirming itself for what it is, a conflict against History." No wonder after allowing cultural looting the U.S. war logic subsequently destroyed public services, the police, the Iraqi Army, in effect the whole Iraqi State.

Infowar destroying History and the new pillage of Babylon, this reminds me all the time of Hussein Sahab, a frail, gentle man in his late 50s, married, two sons and two daughters, who by 2003 had held the same job for 27 years. His salary: 24,000 Iraqi dinars a month (less than US$ 8). Sahab was one of the caretakers of Babylon, the mythical *Bab Ilou* ("God's gate"), founded in the 24ᵗʰ Century B.C. by the Amorite king Sumu-Abum.

Nothing could be more enlightening than to roam around Babylon guided by this quintessential Mesopotamian. That's what I did in one of those dark, end-of-the-world days after the "fall" of Baghdad. Hussein talked of how Babylon started to make History after the fall of Ur in 2003 B.C. He talked about the great king Hammurabi, a skilled diplomat who turned Babylon into the center of an empire settled in a territory comparable to contemporary Iraq. He showed me around the Babylon of king Nebuchadnezzar in the 6ᵗʰ Century B.C.—as reconstructed by Saddam Hussein. At the time of Nebuchadnezzar, the prophet Jeremiah described Babylon as "a cup of gold in the hands of the Lord which inebriates the whole of the earth." He took me to some of the visible ruins of Hammurabi's Babylon (most are 40 m underground). He showed me the exact corner where Alexander the Great died of malaria in June 323 B.C. He talked about sexy Semiramis, the legendary founding queen of Babylon—who chose her lovers amongst her most handsome soldiers and executed them when she was satiated.

According to legend Babylon was built in 365 days by 2 million workers. At the outset of the 1980-1988 Iran-Iraq war, Saddam Hussein set out to rebuild Babylon. The Summer Palace, the temples of Ishtar, Nabu and Ninmah, the ramparts, the Greek amphitheatre were all restored. Using our imagination, we could listen to the prophecies of Daniel and the echo of the chanting of pilgrims escalating the *Etemenanki*, the "House of Foundation of Heaven and Earth"—the ziggurat the whole world knows under the Biblical name Tower of Babel. "It's over there," said Hussein Sahab, pointing to the top of a hill less than 800 m away from Nebuchadnezzar's palace walls.

Hussein Sahab figured out Saddam was gone when he noticed the surrealist Minister of Information Muhamad Saeed al-Sahaf did not show up on Iraqi TV on April 9, 2003. At the time, he said "we are not satisfied with the Americans, but we are satisfied because they destroyed Saddam's family." What he did not expect was the orgy of destruction that would take place afterwards—an orgy that did not spare Babylon.

Babylon's museum was pillaged and torched. Although most of what was discovered on site since the end of the 19th Century is in European museums, it held some priceless objects recently excavated by Iraqi archeologists. The arsonists, Hussein said, were "not people living in the area." The tribune in the Greek amphitheater where Saddam's family used to watch concerts was vandalized. The restored, sprawling Nebuchadnezzar's palace at least was not bulldozed: originally it had more than 200 rooms and courtyards linked by corridors, with royal apartments, administrative buildings, courtesan quarters and shops whose ruins were long mistaken for vestiges of the famous Hanging Gardens.

What happened in Babylon was only a tiny fraction of what happened in Baghdad. The transformation of the siege of Baghdad into the pillage of Baghdad was considered by Iraqis and concerned foreigners alike as a crime against humanity, a crime against civilization and a crime against Islam. In Mesopotamia, the "land between the rivers," the home of the Garden of Eden (which is 74 km north of Basra in the direction of Baghdad, in a place where the two rivers meet), the human race invented agriculture, alphabets, codes of law, mathematics, astronomy, poetry, epic literature and organized religion. Without Mesopotamia, we would still be living literally in darkness.

Before meeting Hussein in Babylon I had been to the thoroughly looted Iraqi Museum in Baghdad, housing more than 170,000 priceless sculptures, bass reliefs, ceramics and ancient texts, chronicling Stone Age settlements of half a million years ago, the rise and fall of the great civilizations of Uruk, Sumeria, Babylon, Assyria and Persia, and the spread of Islam. Among the irreparable losses were the tablets containing Hammurabi's Code—the first code of Law in History—and the 4600-year old Ram in the Thicket from Ur. The 4300-year old bust of an Akkadian king was smashed. Baghdadis referred to the "stuff happens" Americans as the new Mongols: they said that what was not destroyed by the Mongols when Hulagu, Genghis Khan's grandson, invaded and looted Baghdad in 1248, was allowed to be destroyed by Tommy Franks's armies in April 2003.

Iraqi curators were all adamant: one Abrams tank and a couple of armed marines would have been more than enough to prevent the looting. I heard from Dr. Doni George, director of general research and studies at the State Board of Antiquities, that "the whole administrative compound was completely destroyed and looted. The first point is that there were people who knew what they wanted. They've taken the precious vase of Uruk, an Akkadian bronze statue from 3200 B.C., Abbassid wooden doors. Before they started looting, there were American armored cars outside, and people inside. They asked for the American troops to intervene, but they did not. The chairman of the State Board of Antiquities went to the

American HQ and explained the situation. But they sent no help. This shows they wanted the Iraqi Museum to be destroyed."

At the time, the curators were too traumatized to discuss what was lost, and how. In the following days, they started collecting extremely disturbing evidence that this was a very well organized operation. Archaeological files and computer disks simply disappeared. Glass-cutting tools were found on the museum's floor. Replicas were still there, but many genuine artworks were stolen. The museum's vaults had been opened with special keys: an armed guard at the museum told me American soldiers had not taken anything, but they had opened the doors for "people from other nationalities" to loot: "The way they opened the locks, no Iraqi could do it." UNESCO specialists, in their HQ in Paris, were convinced this was a concerted operation organized outside of Iraq. Not all the oil in the world—which as a matter of fact will not benefit Iraqis anyway, but will serve to pay foreigners for Iraq's destruction—would be enough to compensate the Iraqi population, the whole Arab nation, and the whole civilized world for what was lost in the orgy of looting.

Meanwhile, in a deserted Babylon tormented by sandy winds, Hussein Sahab just wanted to keep his job. He showed me how the Lion of Babylon was still standing: it had not been stolen or vandalized. The Lion of Babylon—supposedly a trophy from Hitite times, middle of the 2nd millenium B.C.—is an enigmatic basalt statue representing a man who is about to be killed by a lion. But in fact the man is resisting: with one hand he tries to shove the lion's mouth away, and with another he fights one of the lion's menacing paws. Legend rules that as long as the statue is there, Babylon will never be conquered. As for Hussein Sahab, he could have stolen anything on Babylon, and sell the loot for millions. Cultural resistance, historical memory and plain, old integrity urged him not to.

Babylon revisited

What happened in Sao Paulo, South America's premier hypercity in May 2006 must have sent Pentagon planners into ballistic overdrive; as urban warfare goes, and a sign of things to come, it was more illuminating than Planet Gaza in quagmire Baghdad. The leaders of the PCC (the Portuguese acronym for First Command of the Capital), a prison super-gang involved in drug and arms trafficking, bank robberies, extortion and controlling most of Sao Paulo's overcrowded and notoriously corrupt prisons declared war against Brazil's wealthiest state. From inside their prison cells, using US$150 mobile phones, they ordered motorbiked "bin Ladens"—warriors indebted to the organization, heavily armed with guns, shotguns, hand grenades, machine guns and Molotov cocktails—to conduct an orgy of riddling police cars with bullets, hurling grenades at police stations, attacking officers in their homes and after hours hangouts, torching dozens of buses (after passengers had been ordered off) and robbing banks. Almost 100 people were killed in three days. The PCC managed single-handedly to virtually paralyze Sao Paulo, the third largest of the world's hypercities (19 million people, and counting).

This was reaction—not action: PCC leaders were basically demanding better jail conditions. That remains their key demand. The system was not listening. Police admitted they were dazed and confused. Former Brazilian President Fernando Henrique Cardoso predicted the beginning of urban guerrilla war in Sao Paulo. Cardoso was at least a decade late.

Brazilian political scientist André Moisés Gaio is involved in an ongoing research highlighting the notion of "delinquent State"—and not "organized crime" or "Mafia organization"—to explain this new crime pattern. It all started with the 1960s military dictatorships in Latin America, which stimulated an organized crime boom by creating the institutional framework for criminal freedom. Under Cold War logic, the priority for the dictatorships was internal repression. "Micro-criminality," as Gaio puts it, was irrelevant. The results of what, for certain regimes, amounted to two decades of negligence were catastrophic. Police were left with no investigative capacity. And "the Judiciary was politicized if not suppressed by the Generals."

Social anarchy, unstable governments and high concentration of wealth were the hallmarks of the neo-liberal, post-dictatorship era. Crime flourished in Brazil, Argentina, Uruguay, Paraguay, Chile and Peru, with Colombia setting up powerful, regional Mafia organizations, defined by Gaio as those where "the nexus between politics and crime are well established." Mafia organizations "practice *intimidazione* (intimidation), *assoggettamento* (solid hierarchy) and *omertá* (the law of silence)"; the terminology, of course, had to be Italian. On a global level, novelist and essayist Leonardo Sciascia had already noted that what we're really facing is not Balkanization, but Sicilianization: the collapse of laws and common values (examples range from Colombia to Sierra Leone). Or worse: anomie, the loss of any criteria of differentiation.

Gaio establishes the Italian *Mani Puliti* (Clean Hands) operation as the paradigm in the repression/contention of Mafia activities in the context of a democracy. In Brazil the story, as usual, was more complicated. The military dictatorship ended in 1984; that was the same year when "snow" heavily started falling in sensuous, tropical Rio—that is, Brazilian/Colombian narcotraffickers unloading pure cocaine at ridiculous prices into an incipient consumer market. The explosion of demand led to the consolidation of a group called Red Command, extremely powerful in the Rio *favelas* and associated with Colombian and Paraguayan *narcotraficantes*. Then in the 1990s Globalistan remixed it all with special effects—courtesy of the Italian and Russian mafias, which for their part diversified into kidnappings, weapons trafficking and buying into the Wild West Brazilian State companies' privatization campaign.

Globalization inevitably accelerated fragmentation and social disintegration (jobs crisis, less investment in social welfare). A key consequence was the "informal economy" Big Bang. No social protection and a powerful feeling of alienation led, for many, to crime. Still today almost 50% of the Brazilian workforce is "informal." In Rio, drug trafficking employs almost 200,000 people.

In Colombia, the fragmentation of drug cartels led to a proliferation of smaller groups, much harder to detect. In Brazil the process was the same. PCC is one of these groups, but much more sophisticated, with arguably 100,000 "warriors" and hundreds of thousands of supporters. Gaio correctly does not qualify PCC as organized crime (at least not yet) or Mafia association. This is a brand new mutating virus.

PCC was born in a prison in Sao Paulo state in the aftermath of the bloody 1993 Carandiru prison massacre, when 111 inmates were exterminated point blank by state police. The government at first even denied the existence of PCC. The foundation myth of this monolithic Brotherhood is the stuff of legend; but actually things happened almost by accident, according to public prosecutor Marcio Christino.

PCC was the name of a soccer team in a Sao Paulo state maximum security prison known as "Big Piranha" (the regime, directed by one "Joseph Mengele," was so hardcore that inmates would attack anyone like piranhas). It was after a literally murderous soccer match that a group of 4 inmates—seeing the repression on the wall—decided to create a self-protection code to fight the common enemy: the indiscriminate violence of the penal system itself. One of PCC's founders has cerebral damage courtesy of torture with iron bars. For the same reason another PCC founder, already dead, carried a dislocated shoulder. The PCC motto from the inception was "Peace, Justice and Freedom," copied from Rio's Red Command. The symbology referred to Yin and Yang, just like in the South Korean flag.

A 1995 letter from one of PCC's founders is key to understand where they're coming from: "We are neither a criminal organization nor a faction, we are not a utopia but a transformation and a new philosophy: Peace, Justice and Freedom." The letter frames their struggle as "a strong arm fighting for all the oppressed massacred by a coward, capitalist and corrupt system." PCC charges "the system itself created the Party [of Crime]." And their overall ambition is already clear: "The revolution started in the prison system but the objective is bigger, to revolutionize the governmental system, to finish with this capitalist regime in which the rich grows and survives by massacring the needy." Thus PCC members do not see themselves as "criminals by option, but subversives and idealists," who "hope that our war cry will spread all over the country."

The nexus between crime and politics in Brazil, analyzes Gaio, incorporates police, the Judiciary, the Executive, the Legislative, private enterprise and criminals in the same schemes—for instance winning bids with no competition, plundering public patrimony, profiting from narcotrafficking. That's what Gaio calls "the Brazilian delinquent State." That's what many would call the global wave of the future.

A mid-2000s Parliamentary inquiry on narcotrafficking in Brazil indicted no less than 567 people, including 143 officials—mayors, senators, Congressmen, judges, civilian police, district attorneys. They were invariably scheme ringleaders. And they made much more serious money than, for instance, the *favela*-based Red Command drug ring.

PCC's war is justified "as a direct reflex of what the government itself planted inside the State Penitentiary System." They frame their struggle as a human rights problem, their "families and lawyers treated as prisoners." With a delinquent State run amok, they have a point.

In its official charter PCC states "we have consolidated at the state level and in medium to long term we will consolidate at a national level. In tandem with the Red Command we will revolutionize the country inside its jails and our armed wing will be the terror of powerful oppressors."

Brazilian public prosecutors admit PCC's formidable power emanates from behind bars—and they also admit PCC's enormous recruiting appeal feeds on the power vacuum left by the State. They agree that the State does not even follow the norms it created to re-socialize inmates. The system is contaminated by a repression logic, very much like in the U.S.; the only P.R. is to extol the construction of more security prisons in far-flung corners of Sao Paulo state. Even the former top official in Sao Paulo's prison system, Japanese-Brazilian Nagashi Furukawa, had to admit that the greedy local elites were partially responsible for the tremendous social inequality in Brazil, as well as being foolish enough to believe that by living in gated condos they would be protected. He also condemned "the American model of inducing security by jailing more people all the time." He compared the number of inmates in Sao Paulo's jails—330 for each 100,000 citizens—to the U.S. (800 for each 100,000). He'd rather follow the E.U. model: France and England have a maximum of 70 inmates for each 100,000 citizens.

To guarantee its services—which include a lot of social work—PCC demands monthly contributions. "Brothers" in jail pay up to US$ 25. Those "well structured" outside prison pay up to US$ 350. Those who don't pay are sentenced to death. PCC money is pulverized into hundreds of bank accounts. Management involves close to a 1000 people. According to a former PCC member, the bulk of the funds come from street crime, heavily organized bank robbing and kidnapping, control of front businesses like car dealerships and alternative transportation by vans to the vast proletarian masses. PCC tries to sell itself to these masses as true revolutionary guerrillas, post-modern Che Guevaras: PCC is indeed structured as non-networked guerrilla cells which can be set in motion by a simple mobile call from inside prison. But according to a non-PCC bank robber with a contract on his head, although the commands are issued behind bars PCC growth is now fueled outside, amidst the dirty dealings of a delinquent State: civilian and military police, prison system top officials, Judicial authorities and politicians.

Public prosecutor Christino sees PCC as a mutating virus obsessed by the confluence of coke, sex, money and death. For the new, unified leadership, extremely efficient, what matters are loads of cash flow and smooth trafficking. PCC controls all trafficking points in Sao Paulo and dominates 90% of the slums. How PCC may influence society is now much more important for the organization than what's happening behind bars. PCC has retreated into the shadows. This has to do with the ascension of who Sao Paulo police and top investigative bodies swear is PCC's current leader: Marco Willians Herbas Camacho, a.k.a. Marcola, born of a Bolivian father and a Brazilian mother in the iconic, revolutionary year of 1968 and a bank robber purging a 39-year sentence. He has already spent 19 years of his life in more than a dozen different jails, and at least 4 in solitary confinement, with no radio or TV, with 2 hours of sunshine a day and closely monitored weekly visits.

Marcola read Dante and Machiavelli and is a sterling expert on Sun FkTzu's *The Art of War*. Behind bars, he became rich with Cocaine Corporatistan and could always conduct conference calls between jails. But he always denied he was part of PCC and was never caught on a mobile conference call. He is against spectacular, eye-catching operations—because they expose PCC to State repression; the May 2006 riots were an exception. Under his watch PCC grew into a formidable machine—bribing State power and substituting for the State behind bars by offering security. Jails became faculties of crime. Marcola was there at the Big Piranha when PCC was born. He was tortured with iron bars. He's been to hell. He survived. Now it's his time to apply Sun Tzu by fighting his own brand of the Long War.

Marcola could say "we're already another species, different from you." Or he could say that "post-misery generates a new assassin culture, helped by technology, satellites, mobile phones, the internet, modern weapons. Shit with chips." He could also say "the proletarians and the exploited are no more. There's a third thing growing up out there, cultivated in mud, educated in absolute illiteracy, getting a diploma in prison, like an *Alien* hidden in the cracks of the big city. My commandos are a mutant social species." These quotes are all from a fake Marcola interview widely circulated on the net. The point is they accurately reflect what PCC is all about.

PCC admits the "reflex of armed action are negative for all and hurt the innocent." But they promise they will increase their attacks to "unprecedented proportions" in case their grievances are not investigated, taking "to the ultimate consequences" their war for justice. A measure of their power is what happened in August 2006. They kidnapped a TV reporter from Globo—the fourth largest TV network in the world after CBS, ABC and NBC—and forced the network to interrupt their schedule and broadcast a 4-minute PCC video. The inevitable ski-masked spokesman hit the screen against a white background sprayed with the "Peace, Justice and Freedom" motto, quoting almost verbatim a human rights report on the dreadful situation of Rio's prisons for the young: "The Brazilian penal system is in truth a true human deposit where human beings are thrown as if they were animals. All we want is not to be massacred and oppressed. We want measures to be taken, since we are not prepared to remain with our arms crossed."

And then the ski-masked character did a full bin Laden. The message—substituting destitute inmates for oppressed Muslims—was clear: "Our fight is with the governors and the police. Don't mess with our families and we won't mess with yours."

Brazilian historian Paulo Alves de Lima defines PCC as "the emerging bourgeoisie of crime, the kings of the lumpen proletariat in miserable   capitalism. Some sectors of this proletariat are engaged in open war against the State. The penitentiary population is the equivalent of modern slaves. Marcola is Spartacus." The big question next is whether the vast masses of dispossessed will be attracted to the PCC struggle. PCC is already an extremely valued criminal brand. Sooner or later they will have to catapult themselves to the next strategic level. They already set fire to bank offices. But they still don't have political conscience.

Yet this is just the beginning. After all PCC ambitiously claims a vanguard role in a "revolution of the poor." According to NGO human rights lawyer José de Jesus, "they want to launch their own candidates to the Legislative." Considering PCC numbers, they could be elected. Prisoners don't vote in Brazil, but provisional prisoners do. According to Jesus these are "30% of the prison population. The idea is to get at least some Congressmen linked to the PCC."

As that 1995 letter advanced sooner or later PCC demonstrations of force will inevitably be coordinated with the drug-dealing beehive of Rio's slums. Brazil's twin megacities are used to urban civil war; unofficially it's on since at least the early 1980s. "Gaza is here," "Afghanistan is here" or "Baghdad is here" have always been branded as self-deprecating mantras. The comparison is chilling. During the 2006 Israel-Hezbollah war in southern Lebanon, around 1,000 Lebanese civilians were killed in 34 days. In Baghdad, a little over 3,000 are being killed per month. In Afghanistan, roughly 500 Taliban, according to NATO, were killed during a late 2006 summer offensive. In Sao Paulo, during the May 2006 PCC attacks, no less than 492 people were killed—by both sides—in little more than one week.

When I saw PCC in action against the police in Sao Paulo I was immediately reminded of Mike Davis' *City of Quartz*, published in 1990—I was living in L.A. at the time. Helicopters circling over the ghetto. Police harassing young black kids. The rich stuffing themselves with every form of armed response. Hardcore repression. The privatization and militarization of public space. The politics of fear.

In the early 2000s Ulrich Beck was one of the first European public intellectuals to alert to "the Brazilianization of the West." Mike Davis, arguably America's premier urban theorist and analyst of urban hell, should have been watching Sao Paulo's civil war first hand; this was everything the future predicted in his *Planet of Slums* is all about—the slums of the world's megacities rebelling against the State.

Davis warns we're heading towards a Globalistan where "cities will account for virtually all future world population growth, which is expected to peak at about 10 billion in 2050." Already the combined population of China, India and Brazil roughly equals that of Western Europe and North America. By 2025, Asia will have at least ten hypercities, including Jakarta (24.9 million people), Dhaka (25 million), Karachi (26.5 million), Shanghai (27 million) and Mumbai (with a staggering 33 million). Davis had to refer to the coming leviathan of the Rio/Sao Paulo Extended Metropolitan Region (RSPER), a 450 km-long axis between the two Brazilian megacities already encompassing 37 million people and bigger than the Tokyo-Yokohama axis. And then, in China, there's the expansion of the Pearl River delta (Hong Kong-Guangzhou), the Beijing-Tianjin corridor, and the Yangtze river delta, which includes Shanghai: China's model of urban development at breakneck speed is none other than Tokyo-Yokohama's.

Davis sees the future as a realist, not as an apocalyptic visionary: "This great dragon-like sprawl of cities will constitute the physical and demographic culmination of millennia of urban evolution. The ascendancy of coastal East Asia, in turn, will surely promote a Tokyo-Shanghai "world city" dipole to equal the New York-London axis in the control of global flows of capital and information." Most of all the dire consequences of the hypercity explosion will be inevitable: appalling inequality within and between cities. China is going through the largest Industrial Revolution—and the largest internal migration—in History. Hence the unmitigated terror gripping Chinese urban experts—in the form of growing, unbridgeable gap between small inland cities and East coast hypercities. Nobody yet has examined in full the implications of China ceasing to be the predominantly rural society it has been for millennia.

What we already have in the early 21st Century, in rich as well as poor countries, is a new paradigm coined by the German architect and urban theorist Thomas Sieverts: the *Zwischenstadt* (the "in-between city"). Referring to Indonesia, Davis points out the advanced rural/urban hybridization of Jabotabek, the greater Jakarta region; "researchers call these novel land use patterns *desakotas* ("city villages") and argue whether they are transitional landscapes or a dramatic new species of urbanism." They are a new species: Jakarta is not a city but an agglomeration of *kampungs* (villages) crowned with a high-tech Japanese-American CBD (Central Business District).

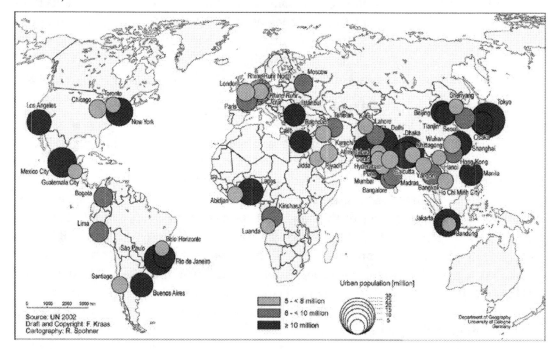

Figure 31. Megacities in 2015 (Kraas).

As Davis points out with glee, "80% of Marx's industrial proletariat now lives in China or somewhere outside of Western Europe and the U.S." A great deal of this industrial proletariat—as in Sao Paulo—is ready to explode. This staggering accumulation of the wretched has been enhanced by "policies of agricultural deregulation and financial discipline enforced by the IMF and World Bank" which increased "an exodus of surplus rural labor to urban slums even as cities ceased to be job machines." So this "overurbanization" was driven "by the reproduction of poverty, not by the supply of jobs. This is one of the unexpected tracks down which a neo-liberal world order is shunting the future."

Davis proves his point by quoting an array of U.N. data, from the 16.4% annual growth rate of Sao Paulo *favelas* in the 1990s to the 200,000 floaters (unregistered rural workers) which arrive annually in Beijing or the 500,000 who migrate annually to Delhi (of these, 80% end up in slums). Davis dedicates a whole chapter in his book—SAPing the Third World—to examine the dire consequences of the dreaded, one-size-fits-all, IMF-imposed "structural adjustment programs" (SAPs). But as much as he can't stand the IMF-World Bank "development" crowd, Davis' post-modern neo-realism also has no time for "portentous post-Marxist speculations" like Toni Negri's "multitudes" acting in "rhizomatic spaces."

Abandon all hope those who dream about the glamour high-tech cities of the future. They will be largely constructed of "crude brick, straw, recycled plastic, cement blocks and scrap wood. Instead of cities of light soaring toward heaven, much of the urban twenty-first Century squats in squalor, surrounded by pollution, excrement, and decay." To see it live, right now, we just have to drive by Kolkatta, Mumbai, Karachi, Manila, Jakarta, Cairo, Chongqing or Sao Paulo. According to U.N.-HABITAT figures, most places with the world's largest percentage of slum-dwellers are in Asia: war-torn Afghanistan (98.5%) and Nepal (92%). Mumbai holds de dubious record of slum capital of the world—as many as 12 million squatters, followed by Mexico City and Dhaka and then Lagos, Cairo, Karachi, Kinshasa-Brazzaville, Sao Paulo, Shanghai and Delhi (where there are even secondary slums in the periphery of the city). Twenty-five percent of the population of Bangkok lives in slums. Mumbai, Delhi, Kolkatta, Karachi and Dakha account for 15,000 slums altogether.

The U.N.-HABITAT report *The challenge of the slums: global report on human settlements 2003* has provided the basis for Davis' research: that was in fact the first, serious, wide-ranging global study on urban poverty. Its great merit was to kick out proverbial U.N. bureaucratese and ram it on neo-liberalism and the IMF's "structural adjustments" as key vectors in the worldwide Slumistan explosion.

Exclusion, of course, is the norm. Mumbai is a classic case, already mentioned in this book, where the rich own 90% of the land while the poor are overcrowded in the remaining 10%. Davis argues "these polarized patterns of land use and population density recapitulate older logics of imperial control and racial dominance.

Throughout the Third World, postcolonial cities have inherited and greedily reproduced the physical foot prints of segregated colonial cities... despite rhetorics of national liberation and social justice."

As far as exclusion is concerned, Davis could not but refer to the most Orwellian "urban beautification" program in Asia—the build up for Visit Myanmar Year 1996 coordinated by the Burmese junta. "One and a half million residents—an incredible 16% of the total urban population—were removed from their homes...and shipped out to hastily constructed bamboo-and-thatch huts in the urban periphery, now creepily renamed the New Fields," thus leading to Rangoon being transformed into "a nightmare combination of a Buddhist tourist wonderland, a giant barracks and a graveyard."

Another crucial process—the criminalization of the slum, as it happened, among other examples, in Rio and Jakarta—runs parallel to the explosive multiplication of Condofornias, those "exclusive," gated suburbs usually on the greenish peripheries of the South's megacities. Chinese urban designer Pu Miao dubs it "the most significant development in recent urban planning and design." The postmodern city of the future had been conceptualized as early as 1972 by a group led by superstar Dutch architect Rem Koolhaas. And yes: it was conceived as a self-sufficient fortress in the first place.

Gated community heaven—be it in Beijing or Sao Paulo, Bangkok or Manila, Bangalore or Cairo —is an "off world," and Davis is happy to borrow the terminology from Ridley Scott's *Blade Runner*. These replica Southern Californias are also the epitome of the "architecture of fear," as Nigerian researcher Tunde Agbola, quoted by Davis, defines fortified lifestyle in Lagos. Davis correctly points out that its most extreme forms are "in large urban societies with the greatest socio-economic inequalities: South Africa, Brazil, Venezuela and the U.S." It is indeed a "culture of the absurd"—as every upper middle class condo in Sao Paulo comes with armed guards, banks of CCTV cameras, electrified wiring connected with emergency alarms and sometimes connected to "armed response" security companies. Rich and poor, in this environment, rarely intersect. And there's also a language barrier—even if people, in theory, speak the same language. It's what some Brazilian writers call "the return to the medieval city." Or what a go-getter real estate developer in Dubai would define as the way of the future: a selective filter on residential areas clustered in archipelagos of islands along axis of communication (that's as good a definition of Dubai—which could be in Nevada—as any).

Take Sahyadri Hills, a greenish Shangri-La planted in the dusty and booming Indian state of Maharashtra. The Singapore-style Hills will "protect" 35,000 happy few from India's overwhelming poverty raging outside. This includes 11,000 acres of forest being converted into a fortress city, Aamby Valley, crisscrossed by hiking trails, the inevitable 18-hole golf course, 5-star restaurants, even an airport for the mini-jets of India's new rich, the whole thing built by India Corporatistan.

Bauman tells us about "extraterritorial, isolated and fenced residential areas, equipped with intricate inter-communication systems, ubiquitous video cameras for vigilance and heavily-armed guards on 24h a day patrol" bearing "a notable semblance with the ethnic poor's ghettos. But they differ in an important aspect: they were freely chosen as a privilege for which a high price must be paid." And of course the guards on salary carry their weapons legally.

Gated community heaven, as reached by the upwardly mobile in the developing world, plunges them, in Davis' words, in "fortified, fantasy-themed enclaves and edge cities, disembedded from their own social landscapes but integrated into globalization's cyber-California floating in the digital ether." The whole thing also means the death of civil society as we know it.

To understand what the rest of the world dreams of we must always keep in mind the epitome of urban civilization as we know it. Let's assume that when we're cruising the Pacific Coast Highway (PCH) in a convertible, top down, a warm breeze blowing, listening to the Beach Boys on 95.5 KLOS ("the legendary"), we may have waves of reasons to believe the California Dream will never die.

L.A. is still the key node of the sixth-largest economy in the world—only behind Triad members U.S., Japan, Germany, Britain and France. If L.A. County (with a population of 10 million) were a country, it would be the sixteenth-largest economy in the world, ahead of the Gazprom nation Russia. It's not only the exuberance of intellectual capital available that is overwhelming—constantly creating software extravaganzas or the latest in biotech to nanotech. It's the explosive, ostentatious wealth, the anacondas of red and white lights on the freeways, millions of perfectly toned bodies which can afford to go holistic instead of ballistic. Compared to the real world of Planet Gaza—in Fallujah, Kandahar, Chechnya, Mogadishu, southern Lebanon—this is outer space. Yet the grid is not so remote from the succession of "cops and cars, topless bars" immortalized by The Doors. The avalanche of cool, trash, junk and gore occults the fact that in the world's most unequal industrialized economy California is one of its most unequal states—Condofornia meets Slumistan redux. In this L.A. collection of ghettos in search of a city, driving at night from ultra-affluent Santa Monica, via the quintessential Sunset Boulevard, towards downtown L.A. we swing from the California Dream to a post-*Terminator* no man's land peppered with mini-Asias (Chinatown, Japantown, Koreatown, Thai town).

California may not have an explosive race problem—even though some WASPs may fear Mexifornia (in 2040 the population is expected to be 48% Latino and 31%

WASP). But it definitely has an education problem, not to mention an energy problem and a transportation problem. Forty-five percent of students in California's public schools are Latino (a staggering 70% in Los Angeles). They may be learning English, but not necessarily the skills to squeeze something out of life other than mere day-labor jobs. WASP students go to private schools or schools in safe, small suburban districts. There are not enough public schools in California to educate a majority of Latino kids—although L.A., for instance, always finds torrents of dollars when it comes to building the spectacular Frank Gehry-designed Disney Concert Hall or the Staples Center. California ranks as the 30th American state in terms of per capita spending on education—a positively sub-Saharan ranking.

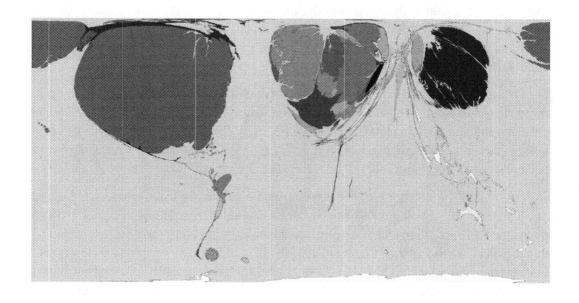

Figure 32. Only 18 countries are net exporters of royalty and license fees, which play a key role in California's great wealth (IMF via WorldMapper).

California's comparative economic advantage has everything to do with speed—networks, crucial nodes, enterprising spirit. L.A. business is not only the Glimmer Twins, Hollywood and aerospace: it's also jewelry, furniture, carpets, toys and of course porn (in San Fernando Valley). The whole Japanese auto Corporatistan has its creative HQs in Southern California. If Southern California is the Empire of Suburbia, the Inland Empire—the suburban sprawl in Riverside and San Bernardino counties—is one of its new key nodes. 660,000 of these 3.6 million Inlanders (and counting) have arrived during the 1990s—and 550,000 are Latino (talk about integration). Here, the California dream explodes in all its glory —the detached suburban home with attached flotilla of SUVs. Nine out of ten Californians want to live in a single-family detached home. In Victorville—sort of heart of Inland Empire—they are (still) affordable. In Orange County they're not. According to Inland Empire experts, the first imperial rule of attraction is "multimodality." We're talking about an integrated circuit, where if you're willing to spend most of your life on the freeway you're able to move anywhere. This is supposedly what freedom is all about. And this is what they're selling in Shanghai, Sao Paulo, Manila, Jakarta, Bangkok. In this Condofornia mall rat paradise Yuppiestan rarely intersects with Gangstastan. When it does, and it increasingly will, we should expect true fireworks, PCC-style.

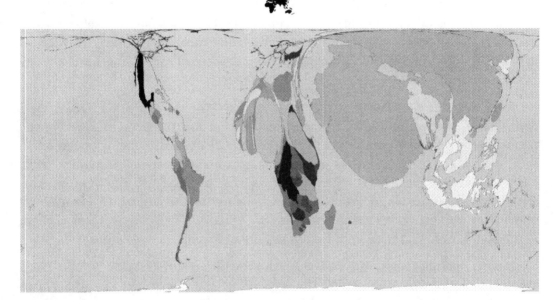

Figure 33. Absolute poverty, less than $2/day (WorldMapper).

All over the world, almost 1 billion people barely survive by juggling within the "informal sector" (but this does not necessarily mean they live in slums): it's the fastest-growing social class anywhere, by any measure. The concept of "informal sector" was coined by anthropologist Keith Hart in 1973, when he was working in Ghana. Informal workers already represent two-fifths of the economically active actors in the developing world. U.N.-HABITAT showed that by the early 2000s informal workers already accounted for up to 40% of urban employment in Asia, 60% in Africa and up to 75% in Central America. The informal sector explosion is a direct by-product of neo-liberalism. Brazilian sociologists call the process "passive proletarization."

Across Latin America, the informal economy already supplies four out of five "new jobs." Davis cannot but mock development aid bureaucrats and their air-con utopian vision of slums as Strategic Low-Income Urban Management Systems (SLUMS). There's nothing romantic about Varanasi, the "world capital of enslaved and exploited children" or the 200,000-plus rickshaw wallahs of Dhaka—"the unsung Lance Armstrongs of the Third World" earning about one dollar for pedaling at least 60 km everyday.

The Philippines has over 8 million migrant workers scattered all over the world, from doctors and nurses to the musicians who weave the soundtrack of Asian and Middle Eastern nights, all of them supporting what by any definition is an official remittance economy. While the not-wretched-of-the-world find solace listening to Filipino versions of "Hotel California" Islamists—preaching solidarity, self-help and fraternity—comfort the masses in the Maghreb and Evangelicals console the masses in South America and sub-Saharan Africa. Ten percent of Latin America is already Evangelical.

In *Planet of Slums* Davis saves the best for last—the chapter titled "Down Vietnam Street." Reflecting reality in the streets of the world's hypercities, where the permanently redundant masses will never stand a chance of being included in socio-economic terms, he writes that "the late capitalist triage of humanity, then, has already taken place." The enterprising CIA has also reached the same conclusion, he notes, as a 2002 report stressed that already by the late 1990s "a staggering one billion workers representing one-third of the world's labor force, most of them in the South, were either unemployed or underemployed."

Davis remembers how the Kennedy administration "officially diagnosed Third World revolutions as 'diseases of modernization' and prescribed—in addition to Green Berets and B-52s—ambitious land reforms and housing programs." Everyone living in Latin America in the 1960s remembers the dreaded Alliance for Progress—advertised American-style as a sort of Marshall Plan which would "lift pan-American living standards to southern European, if not *gringo*, levels." The results were disastrous, just as the ultra-spun U.N. Millennium Development Goals (MDGs), which will not be met. Davis quotes the U.N.'s Human Development Report 2004, which warns that measuring by recent "progress," sub-Saharan Africa will not reach most of these goals "until well into the twenty-second Century."

So we're left with massive repression—the definitive neo-liberal paradigm, a literal Great Wall of high-tech border "containment" trying to suppress migration to the North as in the U.S. vis-à-vis Mexico and Central America and the E.U. vis-à-vis the Maghreb. Meanwhile slum populations, according to U.N.-HABITAT, will keep growing at least by 25 million people a year all over the world; that's Globalistan as an assembly line of Slumistan.

Squattable land is rapidly eroding everywhere on earth. So welcome to "the radical new face of inequality," as Davis put it, "a grim human world largely cut off from the subsistence solidarities of the countryside as well as disconnected from the cultural and political life of the traditional city." This is the edge of the abyss, the new Babylon; and their inhabitants more than ever will include the young, dispossessed neo-jihadis who attacked Casablanca in May 2003 as well as the motorbiked "bin Ladens" attacking Sao Paulo police.

That's an apocalyptic urban background that virtually no politicians, Corporatistan or think tank "experts" ever visit—but that's what real, gritty, polluted, precarious, non-digital life us all about. Conventional State power and Bureaucratastan are simply too overwhelmed by the turbulent implications of megacities crammed with angry, jobless masses. Thus the French elite perplexity with the Paris *banlieues* on fire in late 2005, the American perplexity with the dispossessed becoming Salafi-jihadists in the outskirts of Istanbul, Cairo, Karachi and Casablanca, the Brazilian authorities' impotence facing street gangs and *narcotraficantes*. For the powers that be, the easiest way out is to demonize. Thus the "war on terror," the "war on drugs" and the obliteration of serious and honest debate about the unspeakable daily violence of perpetual economic exclusion—fed by Globalistan.

"Do you know who I am? I'm the Anti-Christ. You got me in a vendetta kind of mood. You tell the angels in heaven you never seen evil so singularly personified." Delivered in inimitable Christopher Walken drawl in Tony Scott's *True Romance*, the line epitomizes the secretions produced by the system. When the State is absent, Gangstastan and militia hell take over (think Baghdad; or Mogadishu before the Islamic Courts). The whole concept of "rights" is thrown in the dustbin. It's an Ouroboros logic—the snake eating its own tail: the no-holds-barred criminalization of Slumistan generating a Long—Infinite—War on street level while virtually nobody in positions of political power has the guts to address the terrifying social and geopolitical implications of a planet of slums.

So it's back to the standing order—I repress, therefore I am. Davis has conducted a succinct analysis of the Pentagon's Long—Infinite—War on global urban poverty. He inevitably had to refer to MOUT—Military Operations on Urbanized Terrain. As the journal of the Army War College declared, Davis quotes, "the future of warfare lies in the streets, sewers, high rise buildings and sprawl of houses that form the broken cities of the world." We can read this as the Pentagon declaring war on virtually *two billion people*.

Santa Monica-based Rand Corporation—which helped to set strategy for the Vietnam War in the 1960s—added a little more concept to MOUT. Rand concluded that the urbanization of world poverty has produced "the urbanization of insurgency"; insurgents are "following their followers into the cities, setting up "liberated zones" in urban shantytowns." The Rand experts were obviously talking about Baghdad's Sadr City—with 2.5 million people one of the world's largest slums—where the young and the wretched joined Muqtada al-Sadr's Madhi Army to make life hell for the American occupier (no wonder Sadr City's squalid main boulevard is called Vietnam Street). But the Rand crowd could also be talking about the drug-infested slums of Sao Paulo, where "faculties" are prisons dominated by the PCC, monthly contributions by members—ranging from US$ 25 to US$ 350—finance drug trafficking, prison exchange and attacks and "bin Ladens" have either to fulfill their mission and pay their debt to the organization, scoring merit points, or they become traitors of the "Party of Crime."

The Great Helmsman Mao was fundamentally right when he theorized the ultimate global contemporary clash as the City against the Village. How further on down the highway to hell have we gone in the last two decades. When cross-cultural deconstructionist Paul Virilio first published his *L'Horizon Négatif* ("Negative Horizon") in France in 1984, there were only "two solitary citadels, Moscow and Washington" in our Cold War world. But Virilio was already perceiving the Slumistan nebula as "the sketch of a future project: immense abandoned zones, left to the illusion of self-management of an increasing poverty." And immune to it all we would find "transit capitals...transfer cities...destined to provide the perpetual movement of political, economic and culture delocalization," the prelude to "global biopolitics." Virilio already knew there would be no nuclear Third World War; we would all plunge into a global, intestinal war. We were already on our way to "a universal purgatory for exploding populations," trespassed by "supra-natural delinquency," with "feudality restored" paving all roads towards "transpolitical anarchy" and the *definitive supremacy of the mode of destruction over different modes of production.*" Virilio's "Pure War" of 1984 is our 21st Century Liquid War.

In *L'Homme Nomade*, published almost two decades after Virilio's analysis, Jacques Attali was able to assert that humanity is now divided into three categories: *infra-nomads*; the *sedentary*; and *voluntary nomads*. In these Dantesque circles of hell in perpetual flux, homeless, immigrant workers, political refugees and economic deportees are pitted against peasants, merchants, artisans, liberal professionals and pensioners who are pitted against the hyper-nomads of the financial sector and the cultural/pop industry. Hordes of sedentary, under pitiless Globalistan logic, are plunged into infra-nomadism and become nomads of the void (unemployment, poverty, homelessness, asylum, street life, perpetual begging). Hordes of infra-nomads are transposed from rural misery to urban misery, and progressively take over immense zones deserted by state power, as in Rio, Lagos, Kinshasa, Jakarta, Manila. Chinese and Indian infra-nomads dream of taking over Central Asia and the Russian Far East. Infinite legions of sub-Saharan Africa infra-nomads dream of getting a job in Fortress Europe.

Meanwhile, in "hyper-world"—a world of masks—everyone is in flux as a virtual immigrant, or a virtual sedentary; this is the privileged world of time zone residents, topological beings, a world without a past, with English as a lingua franca, our Orwellian-lite world of malls, hospitals, airports all looking like prisons under hyper-surveillance. By 2020 Muslims will represent almost 25% of the global population; hence Islamophobia in the West may proliferate like an avalanche of cluster bombs. The centurion of hyper-world, Rome-over-the-Potomac, just like Rome in the last three centuries of Empire will keep focusing on fighting and taming the exterior infra-nomads: that's another way of stating the Long War's mission.

Lord have mercy against the New Barbarian Invasion. Already in 1993 German cultural critic Hans Magnus Enzensberger was alerting to the global effort to "strengthen the *limes*, that must serve as protection against the barbarians." *Limes*, as we know, were the border fortifications built by the Roman Empire against the barbarians. Hence the new, 1200 km-long Rome-over-the-Potomac Wall to protect the U.S. southwest from Latino barbarians; the Israeli Wall of Shame to protect it against Palestinian barbarians; and the proposed 900 km-long Saudi Arabian Wall to protect it from Iraqi "terrorist" barbarians, part of a US$ 12 billion package and to be completed by 2012 (the fact that the majority of these "terrorists" are Saudis themselves is of course a minor detail).

The temptation—for those hooked on Jack D. Ripper Long War logic—will always be there to nuke 'em all. But as mass genocide—at least for the moment—remains taboo (mini-genocides are allowed), it's hard to see how Rome-over-the-Potomac may simultaneously subdue all the state-collapsing nodes in the infra-nomad periphery (Afghanistan and Iraq are of course included). It doesn't matter that Gabriel Kolko, the great historian of war, has been telling us, over and over again, how the U.S. "cannot recognize the limits of its ultra sophisticated military technology. The result has been folly and hatred, which is a recipe for disasters."

Although still obsessed by its aero-orbital strategy, the Pentagon has in fact realized it needs to build what Virilio defines as a futuristic "anti-chaos Army." Hyper-terrorism, anonymous and deterritorialized, as well as nationalism-with-balls don't give a damn to air power and laser targeting. Hence the Pentagon's ambitious, global, hyper-police program, a de facto state of siege applied on a global scale. We will all watch it live on YouTube, via helmet cams, the images of our world dissolving. Fire in the hole!

Attali may sound like a post-modern Gibbon as he sees Rome-over-the-Potomac "directed by elites from ancient vassal peoples, attacked on all sides, financing its presence on all continents and its security expenses by massive foreign loans." Such an arrangement is doomed to collapse by overextension, as Gibbon and Professor Paul Kennedy have already taught us. But unlike Wallerstein, Attali sees the simultaneous fall, before the end of this century, not of one but of two Triad members—the U.S. Empire and its European allies, paving the way for the birth of a new, hybrid civilization.

We may be slouching towards Omnipolis, a monster ghost city, a giant meta-city, limitless and lawless, the capital of our spectral world, the omni-center of nowhere, as Virilio would see it. But we're not there yet. On the contrary: 9/11, when rebel nomads used nomad means (Boeings turned into missiles) to assault proud sedentary towers, was just the beginning. So this is the way neocolonial liquid modernity ends: not with a whimper, but with replayed bang after bang, the "homeland," frightened cities of a dissolving world encroached in their defense against infra-nomad "forces of darkness," or "axes of Evil," or "terrorists," Islamic and otherwise, who threaten the Citadel, also known as "freedom." But nomads know how to wait: and they have infinite patience. Swarms of hornet-like Apaches—real and metaphorical—will be fighting swarms of iPod-detonating suicide bombers—real and metaphorical—to Kingdom Come. It's happening right now, in the mean streets of Baghdad, in the vast, messy hypercity of Sao Paulo, real time reality video live from the (overcrowded) dome of Hell. Call it Globalistan's theory of "pacification": let's build a planet full of Palestinians. By bye Globalistan: welcome Planet Gaza.

CODA: BEYOND HUBRIS

America when will you be angelic?

When will you take off your clothes?

When will you look at yourself through the grave?

—*Allen Ginsberg*, America, 1956

We know they have weapons of mass destruction!

—*Donald Rumsfeld*, September 22, 2002

Globalistan, the book, is a work in progress. Ideally it should be a Joycean "river-run", the world non-stop writing itself. Which brings us, "by a commodius vicus of recirculation," back to 11/7, 2006. The (digital) manuscript was already finished and being revised when the Blue Wave, as Tom Engelhardt so lovely put it, "crashed on our shores, soaking our imperial masters." For millions of American voters—and for the overwhelming majority of global public opinion—gloom gave way to the euphoria of surfing History as Iraq won a decisive election in Americastan.

Iraq did it ("It's the war, stupid!") but most of all American voters did it. It was like the Borges fable where vanquished peoples are condemned by the Empire to be imprisoned behind mirrors and can only reflect the image of their victors. But then the resemblance starts to fade until, in a silent rebellion, they break on through to the other side of the mirror and invade the Empire. To be free, one must break the mirror of representation. For six years – the timeline in which most of this book takes place— these millions of Americans had been living behind mirrors.

My first instinctive reaction on 11/7 was a flashback to Baghdad and the Sunni belt's sprawling Red Zone. Apparently the whole Bush/Cheney system, with its warmongering PNAC agenda, at least as we knew it, was over—and only 44 months after Shock and Awe. True, the agenda had been previously shattered by a few thousand *keffiah*-masked Sunni Arab guerrillas with kalashnikovs, hand grenades and IEDs. But even after Guantanamo, Shock and Awe, Abu Ghraib, Fallujah, Katrina, the smashing of civil liberties, the abolition of habeas corpus, the overlapping corruption scandals, still some American states voted by 60% for the Republican Party. The temptation was irresistible to evoke the dispute between the Silly Party and the Sensible Party in Monty Python's Flying Circus Election Night Special sketch when one of the talking heads says "there's a big swing to the Silly Party but as big a swing I'm not gonna tell you."

But anyway, in the U.S. and around Globalistan, it was party time. After all the per-ceived Death of the Ugly American also carried its sterling metaphor: the axing of Donald "leaner and meaner" Rumsfeld, the face of the "war on terror" rebranded Long War. The temptation was irresistible to reach for The Doors— "the end...of all elaborate plans...the end." After a quick check on known unknowns, Rumsfeld had to flee center stage the minute the Bush/Cheney system knew a subservient, Republican-dominated Congress always able to cover for the secretary's murderous incompetence was no more. More than 655,000 Iraqis, according to the *Lancet* study, died because of his hubris. Globalistan could sing "I'll never look into your eyes... again" (unless it was in a war crimes tribunal) – as the politics of fear, permanent war and a suicide-bombing Islamo-fascist lurking in every corner seemed to be on its way to extinction.

Not so fast. After all de facto foreign policy chief Dick Cheney—not exactly a spring fountain of nuance— had already laid down the law: "it doesn't matter" if the war in Iraq was terribly unpopular; the administration would proceed "full speed ahead." It was naïve to believe the Bush/Cheney system, like in one of those fabulous mid-18th century Tiepolo frescoes in Venice, would be suddenly struck from on high by Virtue. The logic, and raison d'être of the Bush/Cheney system is, and will continue to be, Liquid War.

Hollywood couldn't have scripted it better - the cliffhanger before 11/7. We had the contrite, homophobic evangelical buying crystal meth from a gay hooker. We had The Revolt of the Generals – asking on military papers for the head of Rumsfeld on an Iraqi bronze tray (they got it). We had the leaking of classified plans for making a nuclear bomb—in Arabic—on the "internets", for full jihadi regalia. We had Daniel "Sandinista!" Ortega back at the helm in Nicaragua (with Reaganite backing vocals singing "Will he try to invade us—again?") And for the killer plot twist we had the indispensable Roman empire/courtroom drama: former "Hitler" Saddam Hussein sentenced to hang by an American stage-managed tribunal—victor's revenge (not justice) at the 11th hour. The E.U. and the Vatican may abhor the death penalty. But for the Empire and its decon-structed Iraqi satrapy, it's still bread and (bloody) circus.

11/7 ended up being a referendum on "the little emperor", as Gore Vidal describes him. That the Bush/Cheney system had to resort to quoting Osama bin Laden in the campaign trail and go for an extra-time neck breaker on Saddam speaks volumes worth of Tacitus. But neither Osama—in full, illegal alien, cross-border mode between Chitral in Pakistan and Kunar in Afghanistan—or Saddam were able to deliver for the Bush/Cheney system. Collective amnesia in U.S. corporate media ensured no one pointing out that the "crimes against humanity" for which Saddam was condemned (specifically against Shiites in Dujail) happened no less than 15 months before Reagan messenger boy Rumsfeld himself landed in Baghdad in December 1983 to shake his hand and seal an iron clad Washington-Baghdad axis of anti-Shiites.

Flash-forward to the Bush/Cheney system-imposed kangaroo court in occupied Iraq. Were it to be in The Hague, Rumsfeld and Reagan and Bush senior administration officials-Saddam's accomplices-would be subjected to very embarrassing questions.

This is entitled, by all means, to receive Top Drama award in Globalistan. The U.S. hyperpower simply cannot afford to be defeated by a bunch of armed tribals/infra-nomads in Iraq – as it was defeated by a popular army in Vietnam: a replay would be perceived as the end of American global hegemony – for good.

Anyway we look at it both— illegal —Bush/Cheney system wars, in Afghanistan and in Iraq are, for all purposes, already lost. How the Democrats reclaim the U.S. Constitution will at least allow Americans - and world public opinion - to see some accountability for the labyrinth of lies that led to the invasion, the condoning of torture, the "extraordinary renditions," the secret offshore concentration camps, the orgy of dodgy contracts.

The players who really decide the Iraq endgame are not American. They are fierce Shiite nationalist Muqtada al-Sadr and his Mahdi Army, and the new Unified Political Command of the Sunni Arab Iraqi resistance, established in October 2006. The command groups the Ba'ath Party, previous Iraqi Army commanders, assorted nationalists, communists, Nasserists, the powerful Association of Muslim Scholars (AMS) and three hardcore military brigades—the Islamic Army, the 1920 Brigades and the Al-Rashidin army. They did not exactly rejoice with Saddam's kangaroo trial and are prepared to raise guerrilla hell to even more demented levels.

And then there are "the terrorists"—which the Bush/Cheney system itself imported into "the central front in the war on terror". By November 2006 al Qaeda in Iraq could count on no less then 12,000 jihadis in Iraq alone. For all purposes Anbar province was already configured as an Islamic Emirate of Iraq.

Some misguided Democrats elected on 11/7 subscribe to good ol' Divide and Rule - breaking up Iraq into three provinces under a helpless, under siege federal government in Baghdad: now *that* is a recipe for Sunni Arab guerrilla hell for generations. The next U.S. President will be faced with tremendous popular pressure to leave Iraq. Meanwhile the Bush/Cheney system, dodging subpoenas and wasting time, still has a blank sheet— the last two lame duck years—to imprint its historical legacy. With or without gridlock, and cornered like wild animals, as it may seem to many, the Bush/Cheney system may unleash even more ferocity.

For the Bush/Cheney system, the only thing that really matters is the energy war front. The agenda spells PSAs (production sharing agreements) in Iraq and/or regime change in Iran. "Leaving the oil to the jihadis"—as it would be spun to death in the U.S.—is simply not an option. Furthermore, the U.S. establishment/industrial-military Corporatistan axis would never be willing to abandon those sprawling, precious, costly military bases in Iraq and rely on just a few compounds in Gulf sheikhdoms for an imperial presence in Arab lands.

The supreme strategic objectives of the Iraq invasion and occupation have always been to control Iraq's oil reserves; to control oil production (ensuring a barrel priced at less than US$ 30); to sabotage OPEC's power (remember the neo con boasting of "we are the new OPEC"?); and to guarantee no flirting anywhere with a petroeuro.

Saddam converted into a Sunni Arab martyr and Iraq's natural wealth looted by four Anglo-American Big Oil corporations: once again this will ensure any Shiite-majority government barricaded in the Green Zone the prospect of a truly apocalyptic Sunni Arab unified guerrilla making the current savagery look like Disneyworld.

Inside the U.S., de-Cheneyization, were it to happen, would take years. From the Ugly American to the Quiet American: certified Cold Warrior, intelligence manipulator (in favor of Saddam's Iraq during the 1980s), Daddy Bush's career CIA guy and Iran-Contra un-indicted co-conspirator Robert Gates won't make much difference at the Pentagon. The Long War may even be rebranded once again—as "global counterinsurgency"—according to what is suggested by the Princeton project. But certainly the Long War won't be razed from the map. On the contrary: Gates is a practitioner of the "overwhelming force" doctrine. Anti-Rumsfeld, retired U.S. Generals even want to go after Muqtada al-Sadr and launch the much-dreaded Battle of Sadr City—which would, like the bombing of Fallujah, accomplish absolutely nothing.

Way beyond the Blue Wave, all around Globalistan the perception lingers of U.S. "blue" Democratic neo-liberals essentially agreeing with "red" Republican religious conservatives and neocons: we want a fully deregulated global market for our multinationals, secured by a benign, hegemonic U.S. "Differences" in this project are a matter of minor detail. Especially in the global South, but even across Western Europe, the perception remains that the American power elites—with minimal ideological, internal differences—will never truly acknowledge "the horror... the horror" unilaterally unleashed on Iraq.

The odd golden nugget may be dug up in U.S. Congressional committees, illustrating the Bush/Cheney system's perversity. But it's unlikely Guantanamo will be closed any time soon. It's very unlikely the global archipelago of American military bases will be dismantled. And it's extremely unlikely George W. Bush will be subjected to impeachment proceedings.

Italian philosopher Domenico Losurdo, a professor at the University of Urbino and author of a much-discussed book in Europe on Nietzsche as an aristocratic rebel, preparing a new book about the Language of Empire has identified six basic categories by which the U.S. establishment always smothers any serious criticism. So if one criticizes the U.S. one favors terrorism; one favors fundamentalism; or one has succumbed to anti-Americanism. If one criticizes Washington and Israel, one is anti-Semite. If one criticizes Israel, one is anti-Zionist, or guilty of ignoring the Islamic peril. Finally, if one criticizes Washington's war policies, one is accused of hating the West. These categories, according to Losurdo, are always "used to expel from the West each and every critic of American policy."

Some things never change. Once again, in November 2006, the U.N. General Assembly passed a resolution—183 votes against 4—condemning the ruthless 1966 U.S.-imposed blockade against Cuba. Virtually nobody in the U.S—Democratic or Republican—seemed to be listening. Trends in Globalistan will not change. The Gazprom nation will keep ruling over Central Asia. China will keep seducing Africa with billions of dollars in deals in exchange of oil and gas. South America will become ever more independent. The state of Israel will keep decimating Palestine (with human victims dismissed as "technical errors"). And Iran will not relinquish its nuclear program.

The Bush/Cheney system's pressure on Iran will remain on steroids. The system's strategy is to use all its power to go over the U.N. and present Iran with a unilateral ultimatum—which the Democratic Congress would be hard-pressed to fight for fear of being relentlessly depicted as soft on a nuclear threat by a "rogue" regime. 2007 and 2008 may be two more versions of *The Year of Living Dangerously*—but this time with everyone waiting for the Bush/Cheney system's ideal pretext for a nuclear strike on Iran. On a parallel track, the system may "ignore" the evidence before a terrorist attack against the U.S.—a la pre-9/11; it may "encourage" a terrorist attack; or it may even fabricate an attack via a false flag operation. Then it's back to the war on Terra/Long War script full speed ahead all over again, with full Democratic-controlled House support.

"Riverrun" Globalistan... Chindia will keep blasting full power, the center of the world economy will keep drifting towards Asia, Pipelineistan will get even more frantic, Islam— moderate or jihadi—will increasingly offer solace to dispossessed masses, the abyss between wired nomads and sedentary/infra-nomads will keep expanding. We might be tempted to quote disgraced Rumsfeld, that Kierkegaard of the times (well, every sorry epoch has the philosophers it deserves): "There are things we don't know we don't know." But we should rather keep on hoping for one, two, a thousand mirror-smashing silent rebellions.

Nimble Books LLC

SELECTED BIBLIOGRAPHY

Afrique 2025. Quels Futures Possibles pour L'Afrique au Sud du Sahara? Futurs Africains/Karthala, Paris, 2003.

Ahmad, Eqbal. Selected Writings, Columbia University Press, New York, 2006.

Akbar, M.J. The Shade of Swords, Routledge, London, 2002.

Ali, Mohammed, The Afghans, Kabul University, 1969.

Amin, Samir. Estados Unidos: El Control Militar del Planeta, La Jornada, Mexico, May 5, 2003.

Anonymous [Mike Scheuer]. Imperial Hubris: Why the West is Losing the War on Terror, Brassey's, Washington D.C., 2004.

As-Sadr, Mohammed Baqr. An Inquiry About Al-Mahdi, Ansariyan Publications, Qom, 1999.

Attali, Jacques. L'Homme Nomade, Fayard, Paris, 2003.

Baudrillard, Jean. L'Esprit du Terrorisme, Galilée, Paris, 2002.

Bauman, Zygmunt. Europa (uma aventura inacabada), Jorge Zahar, Rio de Janeiro, 2006

Bauman, Zygmunt. La Sociedad Sitiada, Fondo de Cultura Económica, Buenos Aires, 2004

Bauman, Zygmunt. Modernidade Líquida, Jorge Zahar, Rio de Janeiro, 2001.

Beck, Ulrich. La Mirada Cosmopolita o La Guerra es la Paz, Paidós, Barcelona, 2005.

Beck, Ulrich. Poder y Contra-Poder en la Era Global, Paidós, Barcelona, 2004.

Beck, Ulrich.What is Globalization? Polity Press, New York, 2000.

Bentham, Jeremy. El Panoptico, including El Ojo del Poder by Michel Foucault, Ediciones de la Piqueta, Madrid, 1978.

Bishara, Marwan. Palestine, Israel: la paix ou l'apartheid? La Découverte, Paris, 2005.

Braudel, Fernand. Grammaire des Civilisations, Flammarion, Paris, 1993.

Brzezinski, Zbigniew. A Geostrategy for Eurasia, Foreign Affairs, September-October 1997.

Caros Amigos. PCC edição extra, Sao Paulo, 2006.

Chaliand, Gérard. Anthologie Mondiale de la Stratégie, Robert Laffont, Paris, 1990.

Cheng, Joseph. Guangdong: Preparing for the WTO Challenge, Chinese University Press, Hong Kong, 2003.

Chossudovsky, Michel. Guerre et Mondialisation—À qui profite le 11 Septembre, Le Serpent à Plumes, Paris, 2002.

Clark, William R. Petrodollar Warfare: Oil, Iraq and the Future of the Dollar, New Society Publishers, 2005.

Davis, Mike. Planet of Slums, Verso, London, 2006.

Deleuze, Gilles. Guattari, Félix. Mille Plateaux, Les Éditions de Minuit, Paris, 1980.

Dickens, P. Social Darwinism, Open University Press, Buckingham, 2000.

Dierckxsens, Wim. Los Límites de un Capitalismo sin Ciudadanía, Ed. DEI, San José de Costa Rica, 1997.

Dunn, Ross E. The Adventures of Ibn Battuta, University of California Press, Berkeley, 1989.

Easterly, William. The Effect of IMF and World Bank Programs on Poverty Economies, Oxford University Press, 2001.

Engdahl, F. William. A Century of War: Anglo-American Oil Politics and the New World Order, Pluto Press, London, 2004.

Everest, Larry. Oil. Power and Empire, Common Courage Press, 2003.

Fiori, José Luis. Sistema Mundial e América Latina: Mudanças e Perspectivas, 2006 paper

Gabel, Medard. Global Inc.—An Atlas of the Multinational Corporation, The New Press, New York, 2003

Gaio, André Moisés. O Estado Delinquente: Uma Nova Modalidade de Crime? 2006 paper

Galeano, Eduardo. Las Venas Abiertas de América Latina, Pehuén, Santiago, 2003.

Giap, Vo Nguyen. Selected Writings, Gioi Editions, Hanoi, 1992.

Gibbon, Edward. Histoire du Déclin et de la Chute de l'Empire Romain, Laffont, Paris, 1983.

Giddens, Anthony. La Tercera Vía y sus Críticos, Taurus, Madrid, 2001.

Goodhart, David. Progressive Nationalism: Citizenship and the Left, Demos, London, 2006.

Grousset, René. *L'Empire des Steppes: Attila, Gengis Khan, Tamerlan, Payot, Paris, 1996.*

Harvey, David. *O Novo Imperialismo, Loyola, Sao Paulo, 2004.*

Hobbes, Thomas. *Leviatán, Alianza, Madrid, 2002.*

Ibn Khaldun. *The Muqaddimah, Bollingen Series, Princeton University Press, 1967.*

Joxe, Alain. *L'Empire du Chaos, La Découverte, Paris, 2002.*

Juhasz, Antonia. *The Bush Agenda, Regan Books, New York, 2006.*

Kepel, Gilles. *Fitna: Guerre au Coeur de l'Islam, Gallimard, Paris, 2004.*

Khosrokhavar, Farhad. *Les Nouveaux Martyrs d'Allah, Flammarion, Paris, 2002.*

Kolko, Gabriel. *The Age of War, Lynne Rienner, Boulder, 2006.*

Kurnitzky, Horst. *Una Civilización Incivilizada—El Imperio de la Violencia en el Mundo Civilizado, Editorial Oceano de México, México, D.F., 2002.*

Lacoste, Yves. *Dictionnaire de Géopolitique, Flammarion, Paris, 1993.*

Le Monde Diplomatique. *Crisis energética: un mundo sin petróleo?, Editorial Aun Creemos en los sueños, Santiago, 2005.*

Le Monde Diplomatique, Edición Española. *Geopolítica del Caos, edited by Antonio Albiñana, Random House Mondadori, Barcelona, 2003.*

Lévi-Strauss, Claude. *Anthropologie Structurale, Plon, Paris, 1974.*

Liang, Qiao, Xiangsui, Wang. *Unrestricted Warfare, PLA Literature and Arts Publishing House, Beijing, 1999.*

Maalouf, Amin. *The Crusades through Arab eyes, Al Saqi Books, London, 1984.*

Marcano, Cristina, Barrera Tyszka, Alberto. *Hugo Chávez sem Uniforme—Uma História Pessoal, Gryphus, Rio de Janeiro, 2006.*

Midnight Notes collective. *Auroras of the Zapatistas: Local and Global Struggles of the Fourth World War, Autonomedia, New York, 2001.*

Morin, Edgar. *Breve Historia de la Barbarie en Occidente, Paidós, Buenos Aires, 2006.*

Negri, Antonio. Hardt, Michael. *Multitude: War and Democracy in the Age of Empire, Penguin Press, New York, 2004.*

Nyazov, Saparmurad. *Rukhnama, State Publishing Service, Ashgabat, 2003.*

OECD. *OECD Economic Outlook, OECD, Paris, 2002, 2003, 2004, 2005.*

Petras, James, Veltmeyer, Henry. *Social Movements and the State: Brazil, Ecuador, Bolivia and Argentina*, Pluto Press, London, 2005.

Politkovskaia, Anna. *La Russie selon Poutine*, Buchet-Chastel, Paris, 2003.

Qutb, Sayyid. *Milestones*, American Trust Publications, 1991.

Ramonet, Ignacio. *Fidel Castro—Biografia a Duas Vozes*, Boitempo, Sao Paulo, 2006.

Rifkin, Jeremy. *L'Âge de l'Accès: La Révolution de la Nouvelle Économie*, La Découverte, Paris, 2000.

Roux, Jean-Paul. *L'Asie Centrale, Histoire et Civilisations*, Fayard, Paris, 1997.

Sassen, Saskia. *Cities in a World Economy*, Pine Forge/Sage Press, California, 1994.

Shell Global Scenarios to 2025. *Shell International Limited*, 2005.

Simmons, Matthew R. *Twilight in the Desert: The Coming Saudi Oil Shock and the World Economy*, Wiley, London, 2005.

Roy, Olivier. *Globalized Islam: The Search for a New Ummah*, Columbia University Press, New York, 2004.

Rumer, Boris, ed. *Central Asia—A Gathering Storm?*, M.E.Sharpe, Armonk, New York, 2002.

Sader, Emir; Jinkings, Ivana;, Nobile, Rodrigo;, Martins, Carlos Eduardo. *Latinoamericana—Enciclopédia Contemporânea da América Latina e do Caribe*, Boitempo, Sao Paulo, 2006.

Sloterdijk, Peter. *Se a Europa Despertar*, Estação Liberdade, Sao Paulo, 2002.

Thesiger, Wilfred. *Les Arabes des Déserts*, Plon, Paris, 1959.

Thual, François. *Géopolitique Du Chiisme*, Arléa, Paris, 1995.

Touraine, Alain. *Um Novo Paradigma*, Ed. Vozes, 2006

UNCTAD, *World Investment Report*, United Nations, New York and Geneva, 2001, 2002, 2003, 2004, 2005.

U.N.-HABITAT. *The Challenge of Slums: Global Report on Human Settlements*, London, 2003.

Van Creveld, Martin. *The Transformation of War*, The Free Press, New York, 1991.

Victor, Jean-Christophe; Raisson, Virginie; Tétart, Frank. *Le Dessous des Cartes—Atlas Géopolitique*, Éditions Tallandier/ARTE Éditions, Paris, 2006.

Virilio, Paul. *L'Horizon Négatif*, Galilée, Paris, 1984.

Virilio, Paul. Ville Panique, Galilée, Paris, 2004.

Wallerstein, Immanuel. La decadencia del poder estadounidense, LOM Edicciones, Santiago, 2005.

Wallerstein, Immanuel. The Modern World-System: Capitalism Agriculture and the Origins of European World-Economy in the Sixteenth Century, Academic Press, New York, 1974.

Wallerstein, Immanuel. Un mundo incierto, Libros del Zorzal, Buenos Aires, 2005.

Woodward, Bob. Plan of Attack, Simon and Schuster, New York, 2004.

SOURCES FOR THE FIGURES

China Data Center, University of Michigan, Ann Arbor, Michigan. The Completed Collection of National and Provincial Population Census Data Assembly (Electronic Version). http://chinadatacenter.org/newcdc/census2000prov.htm

CIA World Factbook [on-line]. https://www.cia.gov/cia/publications/factbook/index.html

Consortium for International Earth Science Information Network (CIESIN). Atlas of Poverty. www.ciesin.org/povmap/atlas.html

Kraas, F. (2003): Megacities as Global Risk Areas. In: Petermanns. Geographische Mitteilungen 147 (4): 6-15.

Pudykiewicz, J., 1988 : Numerical Simulation Of The Transport Of Radioactive Cloud From The Chernobyl Nuclear Accident. Tellus, 40B, 241-259.

Worldmapper: The World As You've Never Seen It Before, http://www.worldmapper.org.

Uncredited maps were prepared by Nimble Books LLC.

GREATER BLOGISTAN

Asia Times—www.atimes.com

Albasrah.net—www.albasrah.net

AMERICAblog—http://americablog.blogspot.com

Antiwar.com—www.antiwar.com

ASPO—the Association for the Study of Peak Oil and Gas—www.peakoil.net

Bilaterals.org—www.bilaterals.org

Billmon—www.billmon.org

Buzzflash—www.buzzflash.com

Centre for Research on Globalization—www.globalresearch.ca

China Digital News—http://journalism.berkeley.edu/projects/chinadn/en

Counterpunch—www.counterpunch.org

Courrier International—www.courrierinternational.com

Daily Kos—www.dailykos.com

Dar Al Hayat—http://english.daralhayat.com

Dawn—www.dawn.com

Defense Tech—www.defensetech.org

EastSouthWestNorth—www.zonaeuropa.com/weblog.htm

Economist.com—www.economist.com

Empire Notes—www.empirenotes.org

EUobserver—www.euobserver.com

Europe 2020—www.europe2020.org

EU-RussiaCentre—www.eu-russiacentre.org

Fernand Braudel Center, Binghamton University—www.binghamton.edu/fbc

Foreign Policy in Focus—www.fpif.org

F W Engdahl—www.engdahl.oilgeopolitics.net

Guardian Unlimited—www.guardian.co.uk

Guerrilla News Network—www.gnn.tv

Horizons et Débats—www.horizons-et-debats.ch

Ifri—www.ifri.org

Independent—www.independent.co.uk

Information Clearing House— www.informationclearinghouse.info

Informed Comment—www.juancole.com

Institute for War and Peace Reporting—www.iwpr.net

Iran Daily—www.iran-daily.com

Iraqi Body Count—www.iraqbodycount.org

IraqWar—www.iraqwar.mirror-world.ru

Jihad Unspun—www.jihadunspun.com

Kommersant—www.kommersant.com

La Jornada—www.jornada.unam.mx

La Repubblica—www.repubblica.it

Le Monde Diplomatique—www.monde-diplomatique.fr

New Left Review—www.newleftreview.net

Nueva Mayoria—www.nuevamayoria.com/ES

Open Democracy—www.opendemocracy.net

Página 12—www.pagina12.com.ar

People's Daily Online—http://english.people.com.cn

PIN—www.petroenergyinfo.net

PLATFORM Crude Designs—www.carbonweb.org/crudedesigns.htm

Rebelión—www.rebelion.org

Russia Intelligence—www.russia-intelligence.fr

Salon—www.salon.com

Spiegel online—http://service.spiegel.de/cache/international

Talking Points Memo—www.talkingpointsmemo.com

The Angry Arab News Service—http://angryarab.blogspot.com

The Brussells Tribunal—www.brussellstribunal.org

The Cutting Edge—www.nafeez.blogspot.com

The Institute for Policy Studies—www.ips-dc.org

The Lancet—www.thelancet.com

The Moscow Times—www.moscowtimes.ru

The Nation—www.thenation.com

The Oil Drum—www.theoildrum.com

The Raw Story—www.rawstory.com

The Senlis Council—www.senliscouncil.net

TomDispatch—www.tomdispatch.com

Truthdig—www.truthdig.com

What Really Happened.Com—www.whatreallyhappened.com

Wonkette—www.wonkette.com

Ximphora— http://xymphora.blogspot.com

Xinhua—www.chinaview.cn

Znet—www.zmag.org/weluser.htm

INDEX, GLOSSARY &
FREE PDF UPDATES

Good news! If you liked this book, you can get free PDF updates direct from Nimble Books by joining the discussion list

GLOBALISTAN-readers@googlegroups.com

Just go to http://groups-beta.google.com/group/globalistan-readers and join the group (you'll need a Google Account). You can also send email to Globalistan-readers-subscribe@googlegroups.com. All we ask in return is that **if you liked the book, post a review on Amazon explaining why!**

The *Globalistan* page on Amazon.com is:

http://www.amazon.com/exec/obidos/ASIN/0978813820

As an added bonus (and to keep the price of the book down), a complete index to the text of this book and a glossary of "Pepeisms" are available in the "Files" section of the Google Groups web page for GLOBALISTAN-readers:

http://groups-beta.google.com/group/globalistan-readers/files

ORDERING IN A BOOKSTORE

If you want your bookstore to buy a copy of *Globalistan,* simply ask them to place a special order through Ingram. The ISBN number is 0-9788138-2-0.

DIRECT SALES POLICY

Nimble Books will be happy to ship copies of *Globalistan* directly to you, but we do not accept purchase orders; advance payment is required. We offer a 35% discount for orders of two or more copies.

US AND INTERNATIONAL RIGHTS

US and international rights are available to interested publishers; please send email to rights@nimblebooks.com.

PUBLISHING WITH NIMBLE BOOKS

Nimble Books LLC is an innovative publisher of timely material on topics ranging from Harry Potter and Dan Brown to politics, business, science, and medicine. We use electronic publishing technology to reach markets that are moving too fast for the large publishing conglomerates to address. Because our marketing strategy is tightly focused on the Internet, we look for titles that respond well to keyword searching in on-line markets, or on-line promotion via blogging.

We publish twelve titles per year and we are selective. We are looking for books that are substantially ahead of the curve in that they address emerging trends that are readily connected with large, literate on-line communities.

Please send proposal and sample chapters to submissions@nimblebooks.com.

ABOUT NIMBLE BOOKS LLC

Our trusty Merriam-Webster Collegiate Dictionary defines "nimble" as follows:

1: quick and light in motion: AGILE *nimble fingers*

2 a: marked by quick, alert, clever conception, comprehension, or resourcefulness *a nimble mind* b: RESPONSIVE, SENSITIVE *a nimble listener*

And traces the etymology to the 14th Century:

Middle English nimel, from Old English numol holding much, from niman to take; akin to Old High German neman to take, Greek nemein to distribute, manage, nomos pasture, nomos usage, custom, law

The etymology is reminiscent of the old Biblical adage, "to whom much is given, much is expected" (Luke 12:48). Nimble Books seeks to honor that Christian principle by combining the spirit of nimbleness with the Biblical concept of abundance: we deliver what you need to know about a subject in a quick, resourceful, and sensitive manner.

COLOPHON

This book was produced using Microsoft Word 2007 B2R and Adobe Acrobat 8.0. The cover was produced using The Gimp 2.0.2 with Ghostscript. All fonts are Constantia, chosen because it is a nimble-looking font that is new enough to be fresh on the eyes.

Webster's Revised Unabridged, copyright 1996, 1998, MICRA, Inc. defines col·o·phon as follows:

> \Col"o*phon\ (k[o^]l"[-o]*f[o^]n), n. [L. colophon finishing stroke, Gr. ko-lofw`n; cf. L. culmen top, collis hill. Cf. Holm.] An inscription, monogram, or cipher, containing the place and date of publication, printer's name, etc., formerly placed on the last page of a book.

Along the same lines, American Heritage® Dictionary of the English Language, Fourth Edition, copyright © 2000 by Houghton Mifflin Company

> An ancient Greek city of Asia Minor northwest of Ephesus. It was famous for its cavalry.

Thus the publishing term "colophon" has two interesting connotations: that finishing a book is like reaching a summit, and that finishing a book is like the "finishing stroke" of a sabre-wielding cavalry charge.

It's also interesting to learn from *Encylopedia Brittanica* that Colophon the city was noted for being ruled by "a timocracy (a government based on wealth)" and that some accounts identify Colophon as the birthplace of Homer.

With Pepe Escobar climbing to the summit of Wallerstein's "world system" to give its readers a global vista, then making an Odyssean journey through the Circean marvels and dangers of the "stans," *Globalistan* might fairly be called a Homeric description of the current timocracy whose technocratic cavalry seeks to deliver the "finishing stroke" to a grounded, humane civil society. I am proud to publish this outstanding book.

Fred Zimmerman, Nimble Books LLC
Ann Arbor, Michigan, USA
November 2006

CPSIA information can be obtained
at www.ICGtesting.com
Printed in the USA
BVHW051601080920
588354BV00005B/84